The Interpretive Process
in Clinical Practice

The Interpretive Process
in Clinical Practice:

PROGRESSIVE UNDERSTANDING AND
COMMUNICATION OF LATENT MEANINGS

Philip F. D. Rubovits-Seitz

JASON ARONSON, INC.
Northvale, New Jersey
London

This book was set in 11 pt. Centaur by Alpha Graphics of Pittsfield, New Hampshire and printed and bound by Book-Mart Press, Inc. of North Bergen, NJ.

Library of Congress Cataloging-in-Publication Data

Rubovits-Seitz, Philip F. D., 1921–
      Interpretation in clinical practice : progressively communicating latent meanings/ by Philip F. D. Rubovits-Seitz.
          p.   cm.
      Includes bibliographical references and index.
      ISBN 0–7657–0351–3
      1. Psychoanalytic interpretation.   I. Title.
      RC489.I57 R83 2001
      616.86'17—dc21   2001046080

Printed in the United States of America on acid-free paper. For information and catalog, write to Jason Aronson Inc., 230 Livingston Street, Northvale, NJ 07647-1726, or visit our website: www.aronson.com

To Chuck, Diane, and Franz

Contents

Part II
The Interpretive Process through an Entire Treatment

Part III
Summary and Conclusions

Preface

$\mathcal{R}$OLAND DALBIEZ, a French philosopher of science and relatively friendly critic of psychoanalysis, wrote more than half a century ago: "It is strange indeed that so little emphasis has been laid on the absolutely primal role of methodology in psychoanalysis" for "methodology is the very essence of psychoanalysis" (1941, p. x). Methodology is important because we can only know what our methods enable us to know. Methods largely determine both the empirical findings and basic conceptions of scientific fields. Even slight changes in method can produce major alterations in one's findings.

This book illustrates the process of interpretive inquiry, and the methodologic concepts on which clinical interpretations rest. As such, this volume represents a continuation and expansion of my previous publication, *Depth-Psychological Understanding: The Methodologic Grounding of Clinical Interpretations* (1998). While the previous volume dealt with the methodologic *grounding* of clinical interpretations, the present volume focuses on and illustrates the sequential clinical *process* of interpretive inquiry: that is, construing, justifying, progressively modifying, and communicating latent meanings and determinants in depth-psychological therapies.

Methodologic writings can be descriptive, prescriptive, or both; the present volume combines the two. Whenever clinical experience and methodologic rationale appear to favor a particular strategy or procedure, I call attention to its advantages. I also point out the disadvantages of some commonly used methods whose rationale and results appear to be questionable.

To make this relatively unfamiliar subject as accessible, useful, and interesting as possible, clinical illustrations are used throughout the book to demonstrate interpretive inquiry, process, problems, and methodology. Following each clinical illustration I present my interpretation and methodologic commentary, so that readers can compare their own constructions and interpretive reasoning with an alternative, partially justified interpretation (see below for the methods I employ in attempting to justify interpretations).

Like the previous volume, however, the present work is not a "how to" book. Since there is no single or certain method of interpreting latent mental states and processes, any book claiming to provide completely reliable information on how to carry out clinical interpretations would merit only our skepticism. Both this and the previous volume come closer to representing "how *not* to" employ interpretive inquiry, process, and methodology; for both volumes stress the difficulties, fallibilities, and pitfalls of interpretive work.

The present volume attempts to supplement and complement the previous work by providing clinical illustrations of common clinical situations and interpretive problems, with associated methodologic analyses of the clinical and epistemologic issues involved in them. The illustrations do not indicate or imply that this is *the* way to interpret the reported clinical data. Rather, the illustrations are intended to provide clinical examples that can be considered and used as exercises in clinical interpretations and the methodologic concepts underlying them, thereby encouraging readers to reflect on, analyze, and compare their own interpretive methods and practices.

I have attempted to protect patients' rights to privacy in the clinical illustrations of this book by a combination of strategies, which are described and discussed in some detail by Glen Gabbard (2000). The strategies include (1) thick disguise (2) patient consent (3) the process approach, and (4) the use of composites. My approach to this problem agrees with Gabbard's statement that, rather than a uniform approach, all of these methods have a place, and combinations of the options are possible.

CLINICAL INTERPRETATION AS
A FORM OF INQUIRY

Clinicians tend to think of interpretation mainly in terms of therapeutic interventions, that is, communicating depth-psychological information to patients; but the interpretive process is first and foremost an attempt to *gain* depth-psychological information and understanding. During therapy sessions, for example, the therapist's mind is engaged in a process of continual interpretive inquiry, attempting to recognize and understand clues to unconscious meanings and determinants (in both patient and therapist). The therapist's job is thus primarily to learn, not to teach (Schwaber 1990b). Communicating such information to patients is an important but only sporadic feature of the interpretive process.

A further misconception concerning interpretation has developed in recent years, namely, that focus on relational aspects of the therapeutic process makes interpetation relatively unimportant or even passé. This view may be based in part on the previously mentioned tendency of clinicians to consider interpretation primarily as an intervention rather than a form of inquiry. The goal of interpretive inquiry is to *understand* the patient in depth; and it is difficult to imagine how any of the newer psychoanalytic schools—object relational, intersubjective, self psychological, or others—could carry out their therapeutic methods and goals effectively without a basic grounding in depth-psychological understanding of the patient, therapist, and therapeutic dyad. In a searching analysis of this question, Meissner (1991) concludes:

> While the last decade has seen a shift in the emphasis given to various factors, the role of interpretation and the development of insight still retains a preeminent position. This approach rides on a commitment to the principle that knowledge and truth have healing power, especially the truth of the unconscious (Michels 1986). [p. 179]

THE PROCESS OF INTERPRETIVE INQUIRY

Dictionaries define a process as a series of progressive and interdependent steps by which some end is attained. By that definition, clinical interpretation is a process, for even though depth-psychological understanding sometimes seems to occur as a sudden flash of insight, close study reveals that the unexpected intuition is a culmination of less noticeable but necessary preceding steps that led to an understanding of latent meanings and determinants.

Characteristically, clinical inquiry and understanding evolve gradually and progressively, starting with the use of specialized procedures for generating extensive amounts and varieties of clinical data in both patient and therapist—data that contain subtle clues to underlying mental states and processes in both participants. The therapist (and eventually also the patient) employ specialized methods of observing the data, in the course of which clues to possible latent mental states are noted. As the suggestive clues accumulate, the therapist (and in time also the patient) apply special methods of assessing, imaginatively rearranging, and transforming the clues, in an attempt to discover or construct plausible explanations of the clues in terms of underlying disturbances in the patient's (and/or the therapist's) mind. Various plausible latent disturbances are tested by comparing which of the posited explanations accounts for the clues most comprehensively and coherently.

If and when a "best explanation" is determined, further decisions must be made, namely, whether, what, how much, when, and how to convey the posited depth-psychological information to the patient. If the question of whether to communicate is decided affirmatively, the hypothesis must be transformed further into a verbal form that the patient can understand, and also into a contextual form that will be maximally useful to the patient while at the same time only optimally anxiety provoking. Once the interpretation is communicated, the patient's immediate and longer-term reactions to it comprise still further important phases of the interpretive inquiry, process, and methodology. As further depth-psychological information and understanding accrue throughout the course of the ongoing therapeutic process, the interpretive hypotheses undergo a process of gradual progressive modification.

ORGANIZATION OF THE BOOK

Part I illustrates and discusses the major sequential phases of interpretive inquiry, process, and methodology. Chapter I focuses on both the fundamental concepts and the fallibilities of clinical interpretations, illustrating the latter by an example of the consensus problem—that is, the difficulties clinicians have in agreeing on the interpretation of the same case material. Chapter 2 illustrates a group of general methodologic strategies that apply to the interpretive process and inquiry as a whole. Chapters 3 through 9 deal with the principal methodologic features and functional phases of the interpretive process: empirical strategies, that is, clinical data, methods of observation, and records; data processing; construction and reconstruction; justification; verbal reformulation and communication of interpretations; progressive modification of interpretations; and the development of self-interpretive competence. Each of these overlapping stages of the interpretive process is illustrated and discussed (see Diamond [1983] for some controversies concerning the various substages of the clinical interpretive process).

Part II presents an entire, continuous treatment of a patient similar to Freud's (1919) "A Child Is Being Beaten," which provides further illustrations of interpretive inquiry, process, and methodology. Specific interpretive problems are selected from various periods of a three-year therapeutic process, and are reviewed, along with summaries of intervening case material. Interpretations of the selected therapy sessions are evaluated methodologically, and alternative strategies for dealing with specific interpretive problems are discussed.

Part III consists of a single chapter, a summarizing review that integrates interpretive inquiry, process, and methodology.

THE "RECURRENT CYCLES" METHOD AND THE JUSTIFICATION OF INTERPRETATIONS

Most of the clinical illustrations in this book are from completed cases in which I was the therapist. Completed cases offer the special advantages of hindsight. Freud (1911) maintained, for example, that definitive interpretation of any fragment must await the completion of the whole analysis. In keeping with that concept, I attempt to justify interpretations by studying the occurrence and recurrence of specific dynamic constellations throughout the entire therapeutic process of each case.

I employ multiple justifying methods as part of a methodology called the "recurrent cycles" (RC) approach—the latter being an adaptation of Thomas M. French's (1952, 1954, 1958a,b) method of investigating the therapeutic process. French discovered that the therapeutic process follows repetitive dynamic cycles that become steadily shorter as the treatment progresses. After an analysis or dynamic psychotherapy has been completed, I carry out a form of content analysis on the treatment record, starting at the end of the treatment where conflict-defense patterns are less disguised and the recurrent dynamic cycles are much shorter, making them easier to identify. Freud (1918) wrote about his analysis of the Wolf Man, for example, that all of the information that made it possible to understand the patient's neurosis "was derived from the last period of the work, during which resistance temporarily disappeared and the patient gave an impression of lucidity which is usually attainable only in hypnosis" (p. 11).

Recurrent dynamic cycles are formulated for the entire therapeutic process, and are used as part of the evidential base for assessing the plausibility of the treating therapist's interpretive reasoning and the probity of his interpretive hypotheses. Thus if a latent meaning or determinant interpreted during the treatment was accurate, it should be consonant with the specific phase of the patient's recurrent dynamic cycles at that particular time.

Like the interpretive process as a whole, however, the justification of interpretations is methodologically pluralistic. To illustrate: the most probative methods of justifying interpretations include (1) cross-validation and convergence of evidence; (2) demonstration of organized interlocking microstructures underlying interpretations (an example being the relation of an interpretation to the recurrent dynamic cycles identified by the RC approach); (3) indirect prediction and postdiction ("indirect" referring to classes of events rather than specific events); and (4) repetition of themes and patterns. The widely used methods of coherence and patients' responses to interpretations are less reliable, especially if used alone—the former because it is circular and the latter because the patient's responses themselves must be interpreted. When these two methods operate in concert with other, more probative justifying methods, however, cross-checking of their results can occur. Quantitative methods, including computer-assisted content analysis, also have a place in our pluralistic justifying approaches. Qualitative and quantitative methods can be combined advantageously both for process analysis and the justification of interpretations.

The RC approach and its pluralistic justifying methods require records, usually in the form of process notes, of the entire therapeutic process from completed treatments. Contrary to widespread belief, Freud did not categorically interdict process notes, but recommended only that therapists not attempt to take full notes such as a shorthand record. He saw no objection to brief notes "in the case of dates, the text of dreams, or particularly noteworthy events" (1912b, p. 113; see also 1909b). Wolfson and Sampson (1976) have demonstrated that process notes compare favorably with verbatim transcripts as representative samples of the total clinical data.

I employ a two-step procedure in making process notes. During therapy sessions I jot down very brief notes that provide a record of the sequence as well as the gist of the patient's associations; the importance of sequences will become evident below. Immediately or as soon as possible following each session, I dictate further details of what transpired during the interview, including my reactions, impressions, interpretive reasoning, alternative constructions, preliminary justifying attempts, and interventions (see Chapter 5 for a good example).

The RC approach exploits the decidedly redundant characteristics of the therapeutic process, which much of the time appears to follow a largely independent course. Although the latter concept has become controversial among some recent schools of psychoanalysis, Freud (1913) concluded that the analyst

> sets in motion a process, that of the resolving of existing repressions. He can supervise this process, further it, remove obstacles in its way, and he can undoubtedly vitiate much of it. But on the whole, once begun, it goes its own way and does not allow either the direction it takes or the order in which it picks up its points to be prescribed for it. [p. 130]

Employing a mainly ego psychological conceptual framework, the RC approach identifies sequential structures in the therapeutic process in terms of dynamic relations between conflicts and defenses. The therapist is thus alert to dynamic themes that may express and disguise the most highly activated and overdetermined conflict, on the one hand, and a sequential repertory of defenses against that current "composite conflict," on the other. The RC approach also goes a step further and attempts to identify recurrent *series* of conflict-defense relationships that repeat themselves in much the same sequence throughout the therapeutic process. To identify these recurrent series of sequences, the RC method employs a data processing strategy called "template matching," in which a previously constructed conflict-defense configuration is used as a template, model, and guide to identify similar such dynamic sequences elsewhere in the data of the therapeutic process.

As the investigator works backward toward the beginning of the case, the originally formulated template cycle from the end of the treatment is used as a model and guide to search for similar such dynamic cycles in the case material. Teller and Dahl (1986, 1993, Dahl 1988) have employed a somewhat similar method of validating reconstructions in their microanalytic Frame methodology.

For more detailed descriptions and illustrations of the RC approach and its multiple justifying methods, see Chapters 8 and 9 of my previous volume (Rubovits-Seitz 1998).

RELATIVISM (PERSPECTIVISM) AND THE INTERPRETIVE PROCESS

Postpositivist science emphasizes that all of our knowledge is conditional, that is, formulated within particular conceptual systems. Use of multiple perspectives is indigenous to the fields of human behavior, and the differences observed from diverse perspectives are both real and fundamental, systematic rather than random. Thus observations from different perspectives must be treated as different data rather than as approximations of the same data. Each school carves out its own special area, and no single reference frame is superior overall to the others. This is not an issue that can be decided on evidence; one can only assert the reasonableness and fruitfulness of a particular conceptual system for proposing interpretive hypotheses to explain given sets of data.

The relativistic aspect of knowledge, however, produces serious problems of communication between colleagues identified with differing schools of thought. We often try to translate other concepts and interpretations into our own conceptual framework in an attempt to understand them, but it is necessary to understand a hypothesis in the context of its own conceptual framework. If we interpret it according to our own way of thinking, we change its meaning, distort it, and interpret only a caricature. Spence (1982a) suggests that we must "adopt a colleague's metaphor" (p. 256) to understand his or her interpretive reasoning and conclusions.

The context-bound character of knowledge does not necessitate a complete relativism, however. Alternative knowledge claims within the same conceptual system can be assessed by comparison with each other in relation to the available data; thus some interpretive hypotheses within the same conceptual system can be accepted and others rejected. R. Miller (1987), a philosopher of science, points out further that diverse conceptual frameworks that generate different interpretations and explanations of the same phenomena within the various schools of a particular discipline (such as depth psychology), also do not constitute an epistemologic or methodologic crisis; for choice of a specific reference frame does not imply that its approach and results are valid, but only that it is capable of producing plausible hypotheses to interpret and explain the phenomena.

I apply these epistemologic concepts and limitations to the interpretations and justifications presented here. The interpretations that I have posited and attempted to justify do not and cannot claim to be the most plausible formulations that any and all schools of psychoanalysis might propose. The claims for my interpretations and their justifications must be and are considerably more modest than that. Namely, within the primarily ego psychological perspective that I employ (in patients with psychoneurotic pathology), the constructions that I have formulated and attempted to justify appear to be the most plausible ones when compared with alternative hypotheses formulated within a similar primarily ego psychological framework.

MY CONCEPTUAL-METHOLOGIC
ORIENTATION TO PSYCHOANALYTIC
PRACTICE AND INTERPRETATION

In my previous volume on interpretive methodology (1998), I described my orientation as primarily ego psychological, but also involving a considerable component of postpositivist relativism and pluralism. That description still applies, but due largely to the influence of Irwin Hoffman's seminal writings (see especially his 1994 essay, "Dialectical Thinking and Therapeutic Action," and his recent volume, *Ritual and Spontaneity in the Psychoanalytic Process: A Dialectical-Constructivist View* [1998]), I can be more specific at this point regarding the pluralistic aspect of my orientation. His writings have convinced me that, without fully realizing it, I have been not only an ego psychologist but also a "dialectical constructivist" all along: that is, I have adhered to certain basic psychoanalytic rituals, including the somewhat asymmetrical aspect of the analytic relationship, but at the same time have engaged with the patient in a way that is sufficiently spontaneous and self-expressive—though with a minimum of self-disclosure—that a bond of mutual identification could develop between the patient and me. As Hoffman (1994, p. 187) puts it, I have attempted in practice to find "an optimal position between psychoanalytic authority and personal responsivity and self-expression."

For myself, therefore—and I suspect for many if not most analysts, whatever their training and affiliations with the various psychoanalytic schools—I consider this orientation to be an important and necessary dialectical compromise in the practice of our "impossible profession." I believe also that it appropriately characterizes Freud's flexible and natural, though disciplined, approach to psychoanalytic technique (cf. Lipton 1977), and also that it has close conceptual-methodologic relations to the cogent clinical writings of the late John Klauber (1968, 1980).

Acknowledgments

I AM INDEBTED to several colleagues and friends who have given me encouragement and good advice in writing this book: Drs. George H. Pollack, Paul H. Meehl, and Robert L. Stewart. I am grateful also to Dr. Jason Aronson, and to the editorial and promotional staffs of Jason Aronson, Inc. I am most grateful to my wife, Randi Rubovits-Seitz, M.D., who has stood by without complaint for so long while I have been preoccupied with writing this book.

There are those who view the method of natural science as the only scientific one. As if it were not a scientific task to seek ways of investigation, of verification, of understanding [an individual's] personal peculiarities. We need to discover methods. There is a need of different ones for different problems, and often a combination of several is required for the solution of one problem.

Johann Droysen on "Art and Method,"
in his *Outline of the Principles of History* (1868)

The scientific method, of which so much is spoken for both good and ill, is whatever means may be appropriate for solving problems. . . . The working scientist brings to bear on these problems everything at his command—previous knowledge, intuition, trial and error, imagination, formal logic, and mathematics—and these may appear in almost any order in the course of working through a problem.

The 20th Century Harvard Report,
General Education in a Free Society

PART I

The Interpretive Process

CHAPTER ONE

The Interpretive Process As a Whole: Its Foundations and Fallibilities

During the first half-century of psychoanalysis, Freud and his followers assumed that their methods of inferring latent meanings and determinants were scientifically sound. Freud (1905a) claimed confidently and repeatedly that "it is easy to learn how to interpret dreams, to extract from the patient's associations his unconscious thoughts and memories, and to practise similar explanatory arts: for these the patient will always provide the text" (p. 116). He assured clinicians that free association provides a "plentiful store of ideas" that "put the therapist on the right track" of what is repressed; and that clinical data contain "such plain and numerous hints" that the doctor is able to understand the patient's unconscious meanings (1924, pp. 195–196; for similar such statements see Freud 1914, 1915, 1925, 1937b). (See also Leavy 1980, Rangell 1987, Rubinstein 1997, Shope 1987). Even at the end of his career, Freud (1937b) continued to insist that psychoanalytic methods of confirming interpretations are "in every respect trustworthy" (p. 263).

When analysts had difficulty agreeing on the interpretation of the same case material, Freud dismissed their disagreements with the ironic comment, "*Quot capita, tot sensa*"—"as many heads, so many opinions" (cited by Klauber 1968, p. 81). Freud's writings thus suggest that he did not fully appreciate the complexities, uncertainties, and unsolved problems of interpretation, which has contributed to the continuing tendency in

3

psychoanalysis and dynamic psychotherapy to underestimate the methodologic problems and limitations of clinical interpretation. In fairness to Freud, however, it should be noted that in one of his last writings he finally acknowledged the consensus problem in clinical interpretation:

> Our justification for making such inferences and interpolations and the degree of certainty attaching to them of course remain open to criticism in each individual instance; and it cannot be denied that it is often extremely difficult to arrive at a decision—a fact which finds expression in the lack of agreement among analysts. [1940, p. 197]

Nevertheless the uncertainties of clinical inference and interpretation did not begin to surface clearly in psychoanalysis until the 1950s when Edward Glover (1952) and Thomas M. French (1955), working independently of each other and employing different methods of investigation, reported disturbing indications that clinical interpretation may not be as easy or reliable as Freud had claimed. French was dismayed to find that individual analysts often react differently to the same clinical data, and Glover expressed alarm at the variability of conclusions based on interpretations. French referred to this limitation of interpretive methodology as the "consensus problem"; Glover called it the "Achilles heel" of psychoanalysis.

The reports by Glover and French influenced a group of psychoanalysts in Chicago to undertake a systematic investigation of the consensus problem. The research team included Thomas M. French, Louis B. Shapiro, Fred P. Robbins, George H. Pollock, Roy M. Whitman, Joseph G. Kepecs, William C. Lewis, and the present writer (Seitz 1966) who served as coordinator of the project. We worked together for over three years, attempting to interpret various amounts and kinds of clinical data, but were never able to achieve satisfactory consensus on the blind interpretation of the same case material. Since that time, numerous other investigators have documented the consensus problem (e.g., Bernardi 1989, Fisher and Greenberg 1977, Fossage and Loew 1987, Hunter 1994, Peterfreund 1983, Rosenbaum and Muroff 1984, Runyon 1981, Sklansky et al. 1966, Spence 1982a, Thomä et al. 1976, Weber et al. 1966, Werman 1979).

The consensus problem is not confined, however, to clinical interpretations by psychoanalysts and dynamic psychotherapists but applies
also to interpretive judgments in other clinical fields, and to the human
and social sciences generally (Bernstein 1988). Since investigators in all
of these disciplines have similar difficulties in agreeing on the interpretation of the same data (or texts), our problem does not appear to be that
clinical data are unusually obscure, but that interpretive methods in all
fields of human study suffer from limitations of reliability. It should come
as no surprise, therefore, that questions of how best to infer latent contents, and how to formulate and justify interpretive hypotheses in psychoanalysis and dynamic psychotherapy, remain unsolved.

This chapter presents a clinical illustration of the consensus problem, followed by discussions of the multiple factors that contribute to
this problem, some clinical implications of the problem, and the methodologic foundations of the interpretive process.

CLINICAL ILLUSTRATION

The case to be presented is from the volume *Methods of Research in Psychotherapy*, edited by Gottschalk and Auerbach (1966). The verbatim transcript of a tape-recorded session was included in the book so that
contributors to the volume could apply their respective methods to the
same clinical data. As it turned out, however, only four of over thirty
contributors utilized the Temple University Interview, the most detailed
and clinically focused of the four contributors being the Chicago Consensus Group (Seitz 1966).

Prior to presenting a verbatim transcript of the session, the patient's
analyst, Dr. Albert Scheflen, gave the following description of the patient and his analysis:

> The patient was a 35-year-old man who held degrees in several fields and
> had made brilliant but spotty contributions in still other fields of intellec-
> tual endeavor even when he was still an adolescent. He had, however, not
> developed any progressive or focused career line and hardly earned a liv-
> ing. Each accomplishment was followed by a period of severe depression
> and nonproductivity. He had no friends, no social or recreational life, and

no sexual experience. These difficulties brought him to analysis with a male analyst. In analysis he was extremely aggressive and rebellious. He denied hearing any intepretations and consciously tried to conceal any evidences of relationship or transference. Nonetheless his depression disappeared. He married, and by focusing his career activities he attained in three years a remarkable success, prestige, and income. These things, too, he attempted to conceal. He insisted upon dressing and acting like a laborer despite important professional status and considerable financial holdings. He retained various feminine elements of speech and mannerisms to conceal marked aggressiveness and his general manner belied his unusual intelligence and high education. The incongruity between his presentation of himself and his career attainments characterizes the interview reproduced below and is most likely to mislead the reader. This picture and his driving, unrelaxed competitiveness were features of his unresolved transference. After three years of analysis he was referred to a woman training analyst for consultation and she conducted a series of weekly psychotherapy sessions with him. One of these was filmed for the research, and the transcript of this session follows. [Scheflen, in Gottschalk and Auerbach, 1966 pp. 240–241]

The following is my abstract of the verbatim transcript of the consultant's session with the patient. (The members of the Chicago Consensus Group used the verbatim transcript in making their interpretations.) The abstract summarizes the principal manifest contents and themes of the session. P in the abstract stands for the patient, and C for the consultant therapist (Dr. Catherine Bacon). Al refers to Dr. Albert Scheflen, the patient's analyst; and the consultant therapist's interventions are enclosed in brackets.

P commented that being filmed was unusual, interesting, and fun—reactions that he attributed also to the way Al feels about being filmed. [C asked how he's been.] He evaded the question, continued talking about the experience of being filmed, which he compared with recording what goes on at a party. He also mentioned fantasies of being the center of attention which he enjoys, but feels "out of context" here. [Asked why,] he said because he doesn't know who will see the film and how they will react. He gets annoyed and tense without an audience from whom he can sense how he is doing. [C raised the question of whether he was disappointed that Al was not present at the session.] P agreed that he was disappointed, and saw this as one of his problems. Being uncertain of himself, he depends on cues from others too much. He conforms excessively. If Al were here he'd know what to do. [But that way you would leave yourself out a lot.]

He emphasized his strong "transference" to Al—so much so that one of the main blocks in his analysis has been conforming. If Al doesn't give him much to go on (voice trembling at this point) he gets mad because he doesn't know what to do. [Like the kid who wants to do what his father does?] Yes; but when Al once asked his advice about something, P was very pleased. Sometimes he tells Al rebelliously that he's not listening to him, but then he goes ahead and acts on what Al said. As much as he has changed and become more successful, he is still just Al's "dopey kid." Like in his session with Al the previous day, he was idiotic, and has been doing stupid things ever since. [You want Al here now to tell you that identifying with him is OK, and that you haven't really stolen anything from him. You feel guilty if you compete with him.] He feels that if people pay more attention to him in this film than to Al, then Al won't like him. He jokingly mentioned a fantasy of cutting Al's name off of the titles and putting his own name on the film. Subsequent associations are about his pattern of giving Al "top billing." He debates with himself whether he will ever catch up with Al, adding that it must be pretty obvious how competitive he is. [The question is why it bothers you.]

He explained that if you win, the men all crumple up. The men he's known just faded away and died if someone else won. [You're uncomfortable about what's going to happen to Al.] Yes. "I get pretty hostile thoughts, you know!" His associations then shifted suddenly from his own hostility to that of a man whom he and Al both know—a "real charlatan who palms himself off as being a lot more than he is." The man is trying to undercut Al, talks about all the mistakes Al's made; and he's also having a terrible fight with a very nice compassionate woman who internalizes her feelings and is about to explode from it. The man asked P to help him smooth out a problem with his boss, but P knows "the guy is going to cut me out underneath"—so he refused to do what the man asked. Now the man is confronted with either getting an analysis or losing his job—which gets him off of the nice woman's back, as well as P's.

[C made a series of interpretations at this point: (1) she connected the foregoing associations with his fear that if he is successful, his father will topple; (2) he has something like that going on with Al that he hasn't solved yet; (3) he wants Al around so P won't go too far—and it is important to know what his fantasies are about going too far; (4) a question arises whether his motivations toward the other man may include "rescuing mother."] P responded with some thoughts about Al that he had felt blocked about mentioning. [C encouraged him to say it.] P commented, in the manner of an aside, "Al might want to cut this part out." Al once told him that it was a long time after his own analysis ended before he realized that if his analyst didn't like someone, then Al would dislike and even get rid of the person; or if his analyst liked someone, Al would begin to like him, too, and would even hire the person. [End of session.]

Interpretations by the Chicago Consensus Group

To facilitate the comparison of interpretations, members of the Chicago Consensus Research Project always formulated their interpretations in terms of the following psychodynamic categories:

1. *Precipitant* of the session's principal conflict.

2. *Principal (thematic) conflict* of the session, the opposing motivations of which are referred to as:

    a. *Disturbing motive* (e.g., hostile-competitive feelings toward therapist [as father-figure])

versus

    b. *Reactive motive* (e.g., fear of retaliation [castration anxiety]).

3. Sequence of *defenses against and attempted solutions* of the thematic conflict.

Table 1–1 summarizes the (blind) interpretive formulations by individual members of the Chicago Consensus Group.

All five of the interpreters agreed that the precipitating situation concerned the patient's feelings and fantasies about the consultation, and the effect on the patient of Al's sudden and unexpected leaving. Three interpreters agreed that the disturbing motive of the session's thematic conflict was hostile-competitive feelings toward Al, while the other two participants each postulated different disturbing motives. Some agreements and overlaps occurred among the posited reactive motives, but there is even more disagreement in this category. The same applies to the category of principal defenses and attempted solutions.

Eight two-hour meetings were held at weekly intervals to discuss the various interpretations of this session; but rather than reaching more agreement during these discussions, more disagreements arose. Considering the entire Consensus Research Project, which continued for more than three years, the group as a whole modified their interpretations on the average only 30 percent of the time. Despite our consistent difficulties in achieving consensus, individual members did not change much over time in how frequently they modified their interpretations. Combining all of our attempted interpretations during the entire project, we found the most (but still little) agreement on disturbing motives and the least on defenses and attempted solutions, with precipitants and reactive motives being intermediate between the other categories.

Factors that Contribute to the Consensus Problem

Before focusing on methodologic factors responsible for the consensus problem in clinical interpretations, a word should be said about the ubiquity of methodologic problems in general science. Faust and Meehl (1992) point out that since scientific procedures are characteristically stochastic (probabilistic), exceptions occur in the findings of virtually any methodologic approach. There are no infallible methods in science.

> Successful scientists can vary tremendously in what they have done, successful and unsuccessful scientists may pursue the same methods, and the same scientist may succeed one time but not another. The world is stochastic not only in the linkages between scientific methods or strategies and outcome, but also in the connections between facts and theories, for

Table I-I
Summary of Interpretations in the "Temple University Interview"

Interpreter	Precipitating Situation	Disturbing Motive	Reactive Motive	Principal Defenses and Attempted Solutions
A	Al's absence from interview interferes with defense of pleasing Al by performance, and gives rise to anxiety about competitive feelings toward Al.	Destructive competitiveness toward Al.	Fear of punishment.	Maintain close, dependent relationship to analyst.
B	The consultation, with sudden, unexpected absence of Al.	Hostile competitive impulses toward Al.	Fear of inadequacy.	Identification with aggressor. Pseudo-rebellion. Pseudo-compliance. Self-depreciation.
C	Interview made him feel inferior, which he hoped to relieve by appearing superior to Al in the eyes of the woman consultant. Al's leaving frustrated this hope, left him feeling inferior, which activated hostile rivalrous feelings toward Al.	Hostile phallic-Oedipal rivalry toward Al (as father-figure) for the admiration and favor of the woman consultant (as mother-figure) with the fantasy of cutting off Al's penis and using it to gain superiority over Al.	Fear of retaliative castration from Al (father).	Self-abnegating reaction-formations. Dependent regression. Rationalization. Projection.

D	Disappointed that Al left because he wanted to impress him. In the absence of Al, he turns to the interviewer for cues.	Wish to please the woman interviewer who urges him continually to be aggressive.	Wish to remain on the good side of Al, who will know the content of this interview.	Denial of his successes and dependence upon Al.
E	Disappointed that Al left because he wanted to use this opportunity to continue a warm, younger colleague-type relationship with Al.	Passive homosexual feelings toward Al.	Shame.	Pseudo-aggressive protests.

the same set of facts can be covered with comparable plausibility by alternate theories. [p. 199]

Numerous factors contribute to the consensus problem in clinical interpretation: (1) the sheer numbers, complex interrelations, and instability of unconscious meanings and determinants; (2) the overdetermination of mental events (De Bea and Romero 1986, Litowitz 1978, Ramzy 1963, Rieff 1963, Waelder, 1930, Weber 1991); (3) the obscuring effects of repression and other defenses; (4) the diverse perspectives, background assumptions, and biases from which we view all phenomena (interpretive relativism); (5) the diverse methods of interpretation that clinicians employ; (6) the universal and apparently ineradicable problem of "confirmation bias" (see below); (7) ambiguities inherent in language, paralinguistic cues, imagery, and in our perceptions of all such phenomena; (8) limitations of interpreters' objectivity, which contributes to countertransference distortions; (9) multiple conceptions rather than a unified definition of meaning; (10) several coexisting layers of meaning, producing plurivocality of individual meanings; (11) the multiplace locations of meanings—in the patient, the interpreter, the clinical data, and the context; (12) dissimilarities between meanings and determinants in the individual case compared with generalizations from other cases; (13) limitations and distortions of memory on the part of both patient and therapist; (14) the circularity and self-confirmability of interpretations; (15) the inherently provisional nature of constructions, necessitating multiple revisions and alternative hypotheses; (16) obstacles to the comparison of alternative constructions; (17) inherent problems in the nature of clinical evidence; and (18) difficulties in justifying interpretations (concerning the latter problem, cf. Freud's [1911] concept that the whole analysis is needed for definitive interpretation of any fragment).

To elaborate on the preceding factors: Clinicians listen to patients in different ways, which contributes to differing interpretations of the same data. Peterfreund (1971) asserted that there is not much point in haggling over which observations or conclusions are right or wrong when modes of observation differ so widely and when tests for interpretive hypotheses also vary greatly or may even be nonexistent. Since the interpretive process means different things to different therapists, the results of their various approaches cannot be compared readily.

Peterfreund's remarks refer to a problem that is widespread in scientific investigations, namely, method effects. Fiske and Shweder (1986) report that method effects are so substantial that even slight changes in method produce major alterations in one's findings. Inevitably, therefore, since clinicians employ diverse methods of interpretation, their conclusions also differ; compare, for example, the striking differences in interpretive findings produced by Kohut's (1959, 1984) predominantly subjective method, and findings based on the traditional pluralistic approach to clinical interpretation, which employs both subjective and perceptual-cognitive methods (Rubovits-Seitz 1988a).

The Chicago Consensus Research Project included detailed studies of how experienced psychoanalysts formulate their constructions. We found that each clinician employs his or her own preferred varieties of data and methods of arriving at interpretations. One participant, for example, considered precipitating events the key to constructions. Another relied mainly on paraverbal cues. Another participant stressed empathic responses, and still another found patterns of verbal content the most revealing. These differences are not surprising, for construction is a highly creative process (see Chapter 6), and creativity shuns formulas. The Chicago group's findings also illustrate that interpreters tend to employ only limited varieties of data and methods, rather than utilizing the broad range of clinical data and interpretive methods that our pluralistic methodology offers (see Chapters 3, 4, and 5).

The fact that all knowledge is formulated within particular conceptual systems (perspectivism, relativism) produces serious problems of communication between colleagues identified with different schools of thought. In the Chicago Consensus Research Project, however, all members of the research team had been trained at the same institute in a primarily ego psychologic framework, which illustrates (1) that perspectivism is not the only factor responsible for the consensus problem; and (2) that the pluralistic nature of most interpretive approaches makes it possible for clinicians associated with the same depth psychological school to employ diverse methods and strategies, and thus to interpret differently.

Another important but neglected factor that contributes to the consensus problem is confirmation bias—a universal and apparently ineradicable tendency in human beings to overvalue their own beliefs and to resist giving up a favored viewpoint (see, e.g., Rothstein 1980, Rubovits-Seitz 1992, Tweney et al. 1981). For example, in the Chicago Consensus Research Project (Seitz 1966), after members of the research team had formulated their individual interpretations of selected case material, they received copies of all participants' formulations, providing an opportunity to revise their original interpretations in the light of colleagues' differing constructions. Most of the time, however, a majority of the investigators ignored other participants' formulations, declined to modify their interpretations, and insisted that their own original formulations were correct. Gedo (1984c) maintains that even if justifying tests were available, seasoned clinicians would refuse to alter their convictions on the basis of the test results, but would continue to base their conclusions on their own personal experiences.

Confirmation bias in the interpretive process often takes the form of becoming overcommitted to a particular construction, neglecting to question its correctness, being intent upon confirming it, and ignoring disconfirming data. Clinicians often focus on what they want and expect to find (Abraham 1986), and their communications to patients sometimes subtly (or not so subtly) foster confirmatory responses (Wilson Dallas and Baron, 1985).

Confirmation bias also contributes to interpretive fallibility by producing an overconfident and dogmatic attitude toward interpretations rather than a scientifically skeptical approach. The latter attitude accepts the limitations of interpretive inquiry with respect to both the reliability of its methods and the validity of its conclusions; for, as Brenneis (1999) puts it,

> we spend far more of our time mired in uncertainty than otherwise. In my experience at least, the state in which I spend the most analytic time is one of feeling that *something* is going on but I do not know what it is, other than to notice some almost ineffable tension between my patient and me. Periodically, we learn something, but never everything, about it. Even those moments that feel like an epiphany usually prove in retrospect to be some-

thing more than what I thought had been happening. It is often the case that what we feel the most sure of turns out to be a misleading partial truth. Gradually, our understanding comes into clearer resolution, and we have a sense of the work moving forward; but at any given moment, what we do not understand far outweighs what we do understand. [p. 91]

Foundations of the Interpretive Process

The historical origins of clinical interpretation include both medical and nonmedical roots. Present-day medical histories, for example, are similar in important respects to those written by Hippocrates in the 5th century B.C. (Leavy, 1980); both attempt to understand and explain illness in terms of antecedent events. For example, the clinical interpreter attempts to identify motivational causes as well as meanings of mental states. Medical diagnosis is a form of interpretation, and Freud's training in the case history tradition of clinical medicine predisposed him to a method of interpreting psychological states that bears the stamp of its Hippocratic origins.

The nonmedical roots of clinical interpretation derive largely, though not exclusively, from hermeneutics—the art and science of interpreting meanings in texts of all kinds, including spoken communications as in psychoanalysis and dynamic psychotherapy. Hermeneutic scholars have studied the principles, methods, and problems of interpretation for centuries. For example, Saint Augustine developed a method of biblical interpretation based on internal consistency, that is, interpreting a particular passage by its relations to the text as a whole (Pelikan 1968)—a strategy employed in hermeneutics and clinical interpretation to this day. Martin Luther insisted that the interpreter of Scripture must "experience" the text's meaning personally—a method of exegesis having some similarity to empathy. During the Middle Ages, hermeneutic scholars concluded that since meanings are multiple and complexly interrelated, a single method of interpretation cannot grasp or express meanings fully. To surmount that problem they devised a pluralistic system of interpretation (see also Efird 1984), which anticipated the emergence several centuries later of Freud's pluralistic system of clinical interpretation.

Modern hermeneutics views behavior (and texts) as expressions of an individual's inner life—a network of interrelated meanings in which part and whole meanings are interdependent. Some of the most appealing characteristics of the hermeneutic approach are that it recognizes and studies the difficulties of interpretation, makes no claim to having achieved a consistently valid interpretive method, and attempts constantly to improve interpretive methodology (Kermode 1985; see also Hoit 1995, Packer 1985, Phillips 1991, Rubovits-Seitz 1986, 1991).

During the 1870s, an interpretive method emerged in the human sciences that was based on the deciphering of signs—an approach that relied on clues suggested by inconspicuous details (Ginzburg 1989). Ginzburg includes Freud's interpretive methodology among the disciplines that have employed such an approach, because Freud insisted that "intimate details" are necessary to make psychoanalytic formulations conclusive (cited by Nunberg and Federn 1962, p. 172). Freud (1914d) wrote that psychoanalysis attempts to interpret "secret and concealed things from the despised and unnoticed features, from the rubbish-heap, as it were, of our observations" (p. 222).

Freud's Development of Clinical Interpretation

Freud's need for interpretive methods became imperative when he discontinued using hypnosis and hand pressure, and relied instead on free association; for understanding latent meanings and determinants in such novel, voluminous, and seemingly disconnected clinical data was not possible by use of observation alone. He had little to say, however, about the methodologic processes and problems of how to interpret such data; his writings give the impression that clinical interpretation is both easy and reliable (e.g., Freud 1905, 1914, 1915, 1924, 1925, 1937b).

Freud believed originally that applying his theoretical understanding (of psychological dynamics and structure) to the patient's associations was a proper and sufficient method of interpretation (Anzieu 1970, cited by Leavy 1980). His reliance on doctrinal interpretation did not last very long, however; by 1900 he had developed a more sophisticated inductive approach. Despite his positivist preference for objective empirical observation, Freud recognized relatively early in his work that subjective biases are inevitable, making pure empiricism impossible (see, for example, 1901). He acknowledged, for example, that he found himself interpreting whatever interested him most at a particular time (cited by Klauber 1968); and in a letter to Jung dated December 17, 1911, he wrote:

> My interest is diminished by the conviction that I am already in possession of the truths I am trying to prove. Such truths, of course, are of no use to anyone else. I can see from the difficulties I encounter in this work that I was not cut out for inductive investigation, that my whole make-up is intuitive. [McGuire 1974; abstracted by McGuire in *Psychology Today*, February, 1974, p. 87]

Since he could not eliminate subjective elements from his observations and interpretations, Freud's strategy was to harness and use them (Schlessinger et al. 1967). He extended the range of clinical observation and interpretation to include everything that went on in the patient and himself, thus making subjective experiences in both participants essential to interpretive methodology (Waelder 1962).

Inclusion of his own inner experiences as part of his clinical approach led to one of the most important sources of Freud's interpretive methodology, namely, his self-analysis (Anzieu 1975, Freud 1887–1902). During the early, most active period of his self-analysis, he based clinical interpretations as much or more on his own introspections as on external data from the patient (Meissner 1971). He considered the "subjective connection" (p. 280) between the patient's and analyst's unconsciouses to be fundamental. Freud's self-analysis also became the prototype of extra-therapeutic interpretive activity by the therapist, which continues and extends the interpretive work done during therapy sessions (cf. Tuckett 1994b).

Freud's (1900) early emphasis on subjective methods resulted also from his distrust of processing perceptual data preconsciously, which he considered analogous to the secondary revision of dreams. Gradually, however, he recognized that subjectivity itself could go too far (1887–1902, 1935). By 1915 Freud had reversed his earlier mistrust of processing perceptual data and acknowledged the necessity for cognitive processing and integration of clinical data from both the patient and himself (see also Coltrera 1983). Thereafter he continued to employ both subjective and objective (perceptual-cognitive) methods in his interpretive approach.

The role of theory in Freud's interpretive methodology underwent an evolution of its own. After realizing the limitations of doctrinal interpretation, he turned to a more empirical approach. From then on he was at pains to assure readers that he based his interpretations on extensive empirical observations rather than on his own theories. Despite his insistence that his observations and interpretations were free of theoretical preconceptions, however, it seems likely that deductive reasoning continued to play a role in Freud's interpretive approach (cf. Eissler 1963). His determined and repeatedly stated efforts *not* to read his own theories into patients' material contributed serendipitously, however, to an important development in interpretive methodology, namely, an anti-doctrinal, heuristic strategy of searching for unknown, unanticipated meanings and determinants that emerge unexpectedly during the interpretive process, and are unique to the individual patient.

Freud presented a highly condensed overview of his interpretive method in one of his encyclopedia articles (1922). His method consisted, first, of abandoning conscious expectations, reflection, or focusing on any particular content in the patient's associations. He surrendered himself to his own preconscious mental activity by assuming a state of "evenly suspended attention." Unfocused listening of that kind often made it possible to "catch the drift" of the patient's latent thoughts. He emphasized that the latter tend to emerge in the patient's associations like "allusions to one particular theme" (cf. the widely employed heuristic of "thematization," that is, searching for an underlying theme that runs like an undercurrent through all of a patient's material during a therapy session; see Chapter 5). Freud used the thematic meaning suggested by the patient's allusions to "guess" what was being concealed. He emphasized that his method of interpretation was not guided by strict rules, but left much to the sensitivity, imagination, and judgment of the individual clinician.

Post-Freudian Developments in Clinical Interpretations

The twentieth century witnessed a major paradigmatic shift in both the philosophy and the conduct of science. The previous positivist model defined knowledge narrowly as based on strictly empirical observation and as absolutely certain. Positivists evaluated human studies by the same standards. By the middle of the twentieth century, however, philosophers and scientists recognized that the logical-empirical paradigm could not provide a secure foundation for absolutely certain knowledge. A radical shift or "postpositivist turn" occurred, as a result of which human and social science methodologies have undergone extensive reexamination, leading to broader understanding of science and novel approaches to inquiry.

Unlike positivism, postpositivist science questions the notion of certain truth, challenges foundationalism, and holds that human beings, including scientists, have no direct access to truth. Methodologically, the postpositivist perspective maintains that there is no one correct method to follow. Science is not a process of following methodologic rules that lead to acceptable results. Science is a search to understand better, employing whatever methods are relevant to the problems being studied.

The postpositivist perspective has produced a growing trend toward less formalized, more pragmatic, eclectic, and qualitative approaches to scientific inquiry. Qualitative approaches collect and analyze data in a more flexible, discovery-oriented, open-ended manner. They do not exclude traditional hypothesis testing, however, but complement and go beyond it in a number of ways. Postpositivist approaches are more pluralistic than the traditional hypothetico-deductive methodologies. Rather than a single overarching epistemology, postpositivist science accepts multiple systems of inquiry, each of which contributes progressive approximations to more "truthlike" knowledge.

The futility of attempting to reduce scientific inquiry to a single encompassing method or model applies also to clinical interpretation. No such simplification is possible for a pluralistic, antidoctrinal, largely heuristic methodology such as clinical interpretation. The human and social sciences, including psychoanalysis and dynamic psychotherapy, do not lend themselves to all-or-none conceptualizations or methodologies; for the high levels of variability that characterize personality and behavior preclude such generalizations (Fiske and Shweder 1986).

Postpositivist science emphasizes also the inherent difficulties, limitations, and fallibility of knowledge seeking. An important implication of this for interpretive methodology is the heuristic of learning from error, that is, resigning oneself to the limited reliability of our interpretive methods; approaching the interpretive task with a high degree of skepticism—doubting one's facts, hypotheses, and whether the two fit together as one thinks they do; employing as many error-detecting, -correcting, and -justifying procedures as possible; and accepting the inevitable incompleteness and uncertainty of every interpretation that we make (see Chapter 7). Freud (1916–17) appears to have had something like that in mind when he wrote that finding satisfaction in approximations to certainty, and pursuing constructive work further despite the absence of final confirmation, is actually a scientific mode of thought.

The postpositivist perspective differs also in being problem- rather than method-oriented. One's particular conceptual system determines and shapes the methods one employs, rather than the other way around. All of our knowledge is conditional, that is, formulated within particular conceptual systems; but this context-bound characteristic of knowledge does not necessitate a complete relativism. The exaggerated relativist notion that one interpretation is as good as another goes to the opposite extreme from the previous positivist view that only absolutely certain knowledge is valid. A more balanced, middle ground between the extremes of absolute certainty and absolute relativism recognizes that science builds on the best beliefs that are available, but leaves all aspects of those beliefs open to revision or rejection. The task is to develop a methodology that avoids absolutism, on the one hand, but does not collapse into complete relativism, on the other.

Due in part to the continuing influence of Freud's positivism, psychoanalysis and dynamic psychotherapy have been somewhat slow to accept the shift in science from a positivist to a postpositivist perspective. Schafer (1996) observes that psychoanalysis has "lagged behind the times, the logical-positivist orientation still prevails, each psychoanalytic school claiming to be the only one that has got the facts 'right'" (p. 249). Other examples of persisting positivist attitudes include the widespread tendency to minimize the difficulties and fallibility of clinical interpretation; the tendency of some clinicians to overvalue initial constructions, which are only conjectures for the most part and thus the most uncertain step in the interpretive process (see Chapter 6); unsubstantiated claims about uniquely revealing varieties of clinical data and methods of construing latent contents; and the continued use by clinicians of doctrinal interpretation based on specific clinical theories.

Unlike the physical sciences, the methodologies of psychoanalysis, dynamic psychotherapy, and clinical interpretation do not derive from or depend on scientific laws, nomic universals, or even a formal theoretical structure. Rather, the only (more-or-less) solid referent to interpretive statements is their empirical bearing (McIntosh 1979). The grounding of interpretations is never entirely empirical, however, and individual constructions are not tied to any single set of observables but rely also on a network of additional, interdependent interpretations that undergo continuous, progressive modification.

To understand a particular latent content, therefore, the clinician must turn to wider contexts that precede and follow the data in question; and the additional contexts must themselves be interpreted. The grounding of clinical interpretations is thus neither scientific law, nomic universal, formal theoretical structure, nor even purely observed fact, but is largely a shifting, ever-unfolding context of *interpreted* events. Hence the cogent observation by Tuckett (1994a) that "interpretations rest on interpretations, rest on interpretations, rest on interpretations, etc." (p. 869). Fish (1989) argues similarly regarding textual interpretation that there are no grounds for interpretation that are not themselves based on other acts of interpretation (cited by Brooks 1994).

In a similar vein, Brenneis (1994) describes how previous experiences with a patient shape the clinician's subsequent constructions:

> The listening mind is always active; nothing registers in isolation. We generalize and our generalizations spread a web of anticipation. As my encounters with a given patient accumulate, my listening is more and more shaped until it is in a state of expectant readiness, tuned to certain particu-

lars and to certain general categories with greater and greater precision. My attention is never evenly distributed, but rather has been shaped and activated, both perceptibly and imperceptibly, in specific ways. [p. 40]

Brenneis concludes that, contrary to Freud's (1912) caveat regarding the dangers of selective attention, "you cannot but follow your inclination and, in fact, very often find exactly what you already know, because it is what your inclinations have led you to expect. This is not a falsification of the process, nor a subversion of listening, but the very essence of it" (p. 42). This viewpoint has roots in the "hermeneutic circle," and in Heidegger's (1962) and Gadamer's (1975) concepts regarding the pre-structure of understanding. Gadamer stresses that understanding arises out of our preconceptions; that one must distinguish between fruitful presuppositions and those that prevent seeing and understanding—that "the important thing is to be aware of one's own bias" (1984, p. 238), so that we can be sensitive to the discourse's quality of newness (see also Friedman 2000; and Palmer 1969, who defines understanding in terms of experience rather than conceptual knowing, because experience participates in every event of understanding and contradicts expectations).

Due to its reliance on a shifting, ever-widening network of experiences, as well as unconfirmed inferences and interpretations, uncertainty is inevitable in every interpretation that we make. The hermeneutic scholar E. D. Hirsch, Jr. (1967) considers this gap of uncertainty a defining feature of interpretation.

Guiding Concepts of Interpretive Inquiry

Clinicians tend to assume that psychoanalytic theory should tell us how to understand our patients' problems and meanings. Parsons (1992) observes, however, that experience seems to belie this: "When we are with our patients we seldom work things out so deliberately" (p. 103). As indicated previously, Freud's initial reliance on doctrinal interpretation gave way by 1900 to a more sophisticated, inductive approach. He wrote in 1912, for example, that the most successful results occur when one allows himself to be surprised by any new developments in the data, and responds to such developments with an open mind, free of preconceptions; for if the therapist follows his own expectations he will find only what he already knows. In a letter to Ferenczi in 1915, Freud wrote that theory should remain like a stranger who has not been invited into one's house (Gribinski 1994).

On the other hand, observation requires some background assumptions and basic concepts, which ideally are of a broad general nature to avoid forcing interpretations into preconceived conclusions (see, e.g., the methodologist Adriaan De Groot 1969). Interpretive approaches driven by specific clinical theories generate single rather than alternative interpretive hypotheses, and frequently interfere with the discovery of unique, personal meanings.

Rather than relying on specific clinical theories, therefore, clinical interpretation rests ideally on a relatively small number of basic, very general methodologic concepts, without which interpretation would be impossible (Rapaport 1944; see also Edelson 1984). According to Rapaport (1944), the basic methodologic or core concepts (background assumptions) of psychoanalysis that underlie Freud's interpretive system include the concepts of an unconscious mind, continuity, meaning, determinism, overdetermination, instinctual drives, conflict, defense, repetition, transference, and the importance of childhood experiences. Rapaport concluded that these basic, general concepts "cannot be abandoned without shaking the whole structure of psychoanalysis because they are rooted not in empirics but in the method itself" (p. 191). Examples of applying these basic methodologic concepts are illustrated and discussed in Chapter 2.

A number of writers (e.g., Blum 1983, Edelson 1975, Eissler 1968, Fenichel 1941, Klein 1989, Meissner 1984, Rangell 1985, Ricoeur 1970, 1974, Rosen 1977, Rubovits-Seitz 1987, Shevrin 1984, Thomä and Kächele 1987) have suggested that Freud's metapsychologic viewpoints also represent basic methodologic concepts or background assumptions that help to orient and guide clinical interpretations. Because of these vantage points, for example, therapists listen to patients with only partially unfocused attention. They listen attentively for undercurrents of conflict in the patient's associations; for manifestations of resistances to the recognition and communication of disturbing mental contents; for the relative strengths of interacting motives; for recurring patterns of response, childhood memories, and the repetition of past experiences in the present—trends in clinical data that encompass the full range of Freud's metapsychological perspectives: psychodynamics, psychoeconomics, psychogenetics, topography, and structure.

Not only do therapists listen more-or-less attentively for such nuances in clinical data, but also from the outset of every treatment they urge the patient to do the same. For example, Freud's (1913) instructions to patients regarding the fundamental rule encouraged them to pay particular attention to thoughts and feelings that they felt conflict about and resistance to revealing—an injunction based on a metapsychological (structuro-dynamic-economic-genetic) conception of psychopathology and treatment. Ricoeur (1970) thus concluded that metapsychology is not just a speculation or an ideology, but "determines the field of interpretation" (p. 433); and Eissler (1968) asserted that "in every interpretation that is given, a metapsychologic statement is implicit" (p. 168).

Clinicians also use a great deal of knowledge about human beings that does not belong to the methodologic core of psychoanalytic theory—core implying "what is most distinctive, central, and essential about psychoanalysis as a body of knowledge, not what is peripheral in it or merely consistent with it" (Edelson 1994, p. 33n). Much of the nonpsychoanalytic knowledge that clinicians employ in their interpretive methodology thus derives from commonsense psychology (see, e.g., Rubovits-Seitz 1998).

The basic methodologic concepts of psychoanalysis influence the formulation of interpretations decisively, but their effects are usually indirect and inconspicuous because a complex, hierarchical system of strategies and other operations mediates between these basic concepts and clinical data. In fact, clinicians seldom think about the fundamental concepts that underlie their interpretations. Most of the time they are preoccupied with the ceaseless flow of clinical data and with the numerous transformative operations that they must deploy in order to identify, formulate, justify, and communicate latent meanings and determinants. Applications of these various interpretive methods and strategies are illustrated and discussed in Chapters 2 through 9.

In addition to the aforementioned basic methodologic concepts and interpretive strategies, a wide variety of heuristics also guides interpretive inquiry. Heuristics are loosely systematic procedures of inquiry that give good results on the whole, but do not guarantee them in any particular instance. For example, the fundamental rule of psychoanalysis is a heuristic strategy that both guides interpretive inquiry and serves as a constraint to reduce unfruitful searches. Another example is the psychodynamic maxim that excessiveness implies defense, as in various types of protests. Heuristic strategies focus on relevant information, reduce complexity and ambiguity, and increase understanding of what is most important at a particular time.

Freud employed numerous heuristics in his interpretive work, many of which have been collected by Grinstein (1983)—for example, the thematization heuristic, that is, searching for a thread of continuity that links disparate data into a dynamic theme; the fractionation heuristic, used to get behind the secondary elaborations of dreams; the importance of context; focusing strategies—for example, on the point of sensory intensity in a dream, on affects, and on conspicuous omissions or areas of vagueness—the latter suggesting repression; focusing on events of the previous day in search of possible precipitants; focusing on similarities, contrasts, contiguities, and repetitions; and many others.

Peterfreund (1983) also described a large number of heuristic strategies that he found useful in interpretive work; and a volume edited by Groner et al. (1983), *Methods of Heuristics*, provides a useful review of heuristic methods employed in various other disciplines—many of which have parallels with widely used heuristics in clinical interpretation (see, for example, Rubovits-Seitz 1998). Examples of applying heuristic strategies in clinical interpretation are illustrated and discussed in all of the case reports and methodologic commentaries in the chapters that follow.

Functional Phases of the Interpretive Process

In his original Introductory Lectures, Freud (1915–16) described clinical interpretation as a sequential process consisting of four phases:

1. Starting points, which derive from observed circumstantial evidence such as analogies, context, the patient's character, and precipitants.

2. A suspicion or suggestion of an interpretation (the phase of construction).

3. A search for confirmation, first in the current context (the initial phase of justification).

4. Subsequent events that support one's suspicion (a further phase of justification).

The following brief case report, with methodologic commentary, illustrates the stepwise character of interpretive methodology, that is, the phases of construing, formulating, justifying, and finally communicating depth psychological understanding in sequential but overlapping stages.

CLINICAL ILLUSTRATION

A middle-aged professional man came for treatment because of a chronic psychosomatic gastrointestinal disorder. A long-standing marital problem emerged in the course of his therapy. He wanted more closeness with his wife, including tender physical contact and sexual intimacy, but she preferred a certain distance, separate bedrooms, and less sex. He had been brought up in a strict, stoical, discipline-oriented family in which emotional display of any kind was discouraged. Partly for that reason he had never been able to verbalize his frustrations to his wife; he assumed that she would find such complaints childish, demanding, and inappropriate. Repressed negative feelings toward his wife emerged slowly, painfully, and against considerable resistance. The latter included the rationalization that a mature person would rise above such feelings. Eventually, however, he became able to discuss the problem with his wife. She responded in her customary cool and detached manner, saying that they were close enough for her, and that what he wanted seemed possessive to her. In reporting this interchange with his wife he added, "Naturally, I dropped the matter after she said that." In subsequent associations he mentioned that he had developed a choking sensation in his throat during the past two days. He blocked for a minute, then recalled a childhood experience that had always puzzled him. The incident involved a summer-long separation from his family when he was 9 years old. He had been very homesick, eagerly awaiting his mother's return for him. When she arrived, however, rather than hurrying to meet her, he fled, hiding himself so effectively that no one could find him for over an hour. He had thought about that incident many times over the years but never understood why he ran away from his mother when he wanted so much to see and be with her.

I experienced a subjective reaction to his memories of the childhood incident, a slight constriction of my own throat, to which I associated a suppressed sob. I then recalled the patient's choking sensations following the discussion with his wife, and also the highly rational, antiemotional family atmosphere in which he had grown up. Putting these several sources of information together, I asked gently, "Were you afraid you might cry when you saw your mother?" The patient choked up suddenly and started to weep; but he collected himself and said that of course that must have been the reason he fled—to hide his tears of relief at being reunited with his mother.

I then reminded him that he had been feeling choked up since the discussion with his wife. Tears came to his eyes again, but this time his jaw was set and his eyes blazed through the tears. He expressed hurt and anger about his wife's apparent indifference to what he had told her. When the anger began to subside, I asked, "Can you see the parallel between hiding from your mother and dropping the matter with your wife? Both reactions involved defensive avoidance, that is, withdrawing from a disturbing emotional confrontation." He could see the parallel but not its implication.

I explained that the tears he was afraid for his mother to see must also have been angry tears—anger at feeling alone and lonely for so long. He began to weep again, this time with sobbing, following which for the first time he expressed bitter feelings toward his mother for her apparent indifference to his loneliness and hurt as a child.

Commentary

The following phases of the interpretive process can be identified in the foregoing clinical example:

1. *Prerequisite knowledge*, which included considerable information about the patient's childhood family life and character development, as well as knowledge about the long-standing problem with his wife.

2. Important *new data* that were generated during the session—both perceptual-cognitive and subjective methods of data gathering being used to observe and collect them. The new data included the discussion with his wife, his suppressed emotional reaction to the discussion, a related incident from childhood involving his mother, and previously unexpressed feelings of sadness and hostility toward both his wife and mother.

3. *Data processing* occurred rapidly and largely preconsciously, culminating in an interpretive formulation of conflict between his frustrated, angry, demanding wishes for closeness to his wife and mother, on the one hand, versus fear of disapproval and loss of dependence on these crucially important persons, on the other.

4. Some *justifying measures* were carried out during the session: (a) by checking how many and how coherently the data obtained from different sources by different methods fitted the interpretive hypothesis; and (b) by observing his reactions to the interpretation, for example, his intense weeping accompanied by feelings of both sadness and anger.

5. A characteristic process of interpretive *technique*, namely, communicating depth psychological understanding in fractionated steps or stages, rather than attempting to convey it all at once (see Chapter 8).

For purposes of illustration and discussion, I have expanded Freud's brief description of the interpretive process, dividing it into the following interrelated, overlapping phases:

1. Various types of *prerequisite knowledge,* including "competences," which are preliminary to but necessary for interpretive work—what Gombrich (1969) calls the interpreter's need for a "very well-stocked mind" (p. 71), including certain *general strategies* of approach to interpretation.

2. *Empirical strategies,* which include large amounts and numerous varieties of clinical data (Chapter 3), as well as multiple methods of generating, gathering, and observing the clinical data (Chapter 4); also methods of maintaining good clinical records of each case (Chapter 4).

3. *Data-selection and -processing strategies* that reduce the voluminous clinical data to a workable but adequate sample of relevant information, and cognitively transform the latter into unique personal meanings and determinants that are specific to the individual patient and patient–therapist dyad (Chapter 5).

4. *Strategies of construction* and *reconstruction,* which lead to tentative, alternative interpretive hypotheses (Chapter 6).

5. Stategies of *checking, revising,* and *rechecking* alternative constructions to determine the most plausible hypothesis at a given time (Chapter 7).

6. Methods of *justifying* the most plausible hypothesis. Over a dozen different methods of justifying interpretations have been proposed by Freud and other investigators (Chapter 7).

7. *Reformulating* the hypothesis verbally so that it can be conveyed to and understood by the patient—an aspect of interpretive and therapeutic technique (Chapter 8).

8. *Progressive modification* of an interpretation in response to feedback from and negotiation with the patient, as well as from further information as it accrues during the course of the ongoing therapeutic process (Chapter 7).

9. *Self-analytic reflection* on one's interpretive understanding of individual patients and on oneself in relation to patients, which occurs both during and outside of therapy sessions, and may lead to tenta-

tive working orientations and grounded hypotheses concerning individual patients, specific therapeutic dyads, and countertransference problems (Tuckett 1994b; for a clinical example see Kantrowitz 1999) (Chapter 9).

The next eight chapters of this book are organized in terms of the foregoing functional categories, illustrating applications of the guiding concepts in each phase of the interpretive process.

SUMMARY

Unlike the physical sciences, interpretive methodologies do not derive from or depend on scientific laws, nomic universals, or even a formal theoretical structure. Rather, the only (more-or-less) solid basis of interpretive judgments is their empirical bearing. The grounding of interpretations is never entirely empirical, however, but relies also on a network of additional, interrelated interpretations that undergo continual, progressive modification. The foundations of the interpretive process thus include a shifting, ever-unfolding context of interpreted events, which contributes to the uncertainty and fallibility of clinical interpretations.

Because of this and other problems, clinical interpretation is neither easy nor justified in every respect, as Freud claimed, but is difficult and fallible—what Kermode (1979, p. 125) calls an "impossible but necessary" task. To illustrate the limitations of the interpretive process, this chapter presented a clinical example of the consensus problem, that is, the difficulties that clinicians have in agreeing on the interpretation of the same case material (cf. Reppen 1995). Methodologic factors that contribute to the consensus problem were identified and discussed.

Neither learning more about interpretive concepts nor the use of justifying tests can eliminate the consensus problem, however; for the latter deals with the issue of reliability (consistency) of our methods rather than with the probity of our results. The more complex the phenomena studied, the less reliability can be expected, but even highly reliable methods do not guarantee the probity of results. The persistence of the consensus problem makes it all the more necessary to check, cross-check, and re-check the plausibility of our inherently fallible constructions.

In addition to delineating the problems and limitations of the interpretive process, this chapter reviewed the basic methodologic concepts that orient, inform, and guide clinical interpretations. The latter include a small number of very general methodologic concepts (or background assumptions), in contrast to specific clinical theories; a larger number of hierarchically organized strategies and operations that mediate between the basic methodologic concepts and clinical data; a still larger collection of interpretive heuristics that facilitate depth psychological understanding; and, finally, the numerous, interconnected, previous interpretations generated during the treatment.

For purposes of description and illustration in subsequent chapters, the interpretive process is divided into a series of overlapping functional phases, including (1) prerequisite knowledge, (2) general strategies, (3) empirical strategies, (4) data-selection and -processing strategies, (5) construction and reconstruction, (6) checking/justifying strategies, and the progressive modification of interpretations, (7) reformulating hypotheses verbally, and other communicative strategies, (8) self-analytic reflection on one's interpretive conclusions, and (9) the development of self-interpretive competence.

CHAPTER TWO

General Strategies of the Interpretive Process

$\mathcal{T}$ERMS SUCH AS *collaborative therapeutic relationship* and the *therapist's stance* have become so familiar in our clinical vocabulary that we sometimes lose sight of their original methodologic meanings and purposes. Both of these commonly used terms refer to general methodologic strategies of clinical interpretation and the therapeutic process, that is, strategies that facilitate the therapeutic and interpretive process as a whole in contrast to specific methodologic strategies that deal with particular aspects of interpretation and treatment. This chapter illustrates and discusses the general methodologic strategies of clinical interpretation. The next seven chapters then focus on specific interpretive strategies, which include the empirical, processing, constructive and reconstructive, justifying, communicative aspects of clinical interpretation, and the development of self-interpretive and self-analytic competences.

What is meant by interpretive strategies? I employ the term *strategies* in the same sense as Peterfreund (1983):

> When I speak of strategies I refer to plans that guide activity toward some goal and are implemented by specific procedures. Strategies are used in all walks of life, although we may not be aware of using them. Specifying strategies is useful for teaching; we can present the strategies that have served us best for any given purpose. More important, specifying strategies is scientifically useful in that specification can help us understand exactly what

we are doing. If desired goals are not attained, the problem may lie in the use of faulty strategies. [p. 70]

Peterfreund added that (1) strategies guide the therapist "to do the optimal thing at a particular moment—optimal in the sense that it is the best thing to do to foster the analytic process" (p. 74); (2) the fundamental purpose of such strategies is to generate and organize relevant information, reduce complexity and ambiguity, and increase understanding of the patient; and (3) the entire analytic process and all of the strategies we employ are "geared toward the goal of establishing unique, personal meanings" (pp. 145–146) in the individual patient.

The general strategies illustrated and discussed in this chapter include the following:

> 1. *Developing and maintaining a simultaneously collaborative but also dialectical therapeutic relationship.* Collaboration implies that "our pathway to what is unconscious is more likely to be reached when it is jointly discovered rather than unilaterally inferred" (Schwaber 1990a, p. 35). Dialectics, on the other hand, involves argumentation, the counterposing of opposites. The simultaneously collaborative and dialectical nature of the interpretive process can be compared with a debate; that is, like debaters, the patient and therapist agree collaboratively to engage in their dialectical struggle.
>
> 2. *Adopting the (somewhat paradoxical) aspects of the therapist's stance.* Freud's recommendations continue to provide the principal and in some respects paradoxical guidelines for the therapist's stance: patience, a nonjudgmental attitude, encouragement, empathy, tact, and tolerance of uncertainty, on the one hand; but, on the other hand, abstinence, anonymity, neutrality, a scientifically skeptical attitude, and restricting the expression of all thoughts and feelings to words. As in the case of the simultaneously collaborative and dialectical therapeutic relationship, some tension is inevitable between the diatrophic-empathic-tactful aspects of the therapist's stance, on the one hand, and the strategies of neutrality, abstinence, anonymity, and skepticism, on the other.

3. *Emphasizing a data-driven, in contrast to a doctrinal, approach.* A data-driven approach is intent upon discovering and understanding the patient's unique, personal meanings, rather than resorting to ready-made interpretations based on specific clinical theories. Interpretations based on specific clinical theories are tempting because they seem to offer rapid ordering of the data and quick understanding, but the order they impose is external to the patient. "They do not find the intrinsic order and organization potentially discoverable within natural phenomena" (Peterfreund 1983, p. 79).

4. *Attempting to understand both latent meanings and determinants.* Freud alternated between hermeneutic and explanatory discourse, between meanings and mechanisms—a bimodal approach that characterizes psychoanalysis, dynamic psychotherapy, and clinical interpretation to this day (Rangell 1987, Rycroft 1985). Relations between meanings and determinants are problematic, however. Not only are the two difficult to distinguish, but also there is some question whether meaning relations or thematic patterns in clinical data provide evidence of unconscious causal motives (Grünbaum 1993; see also, however, Rubovits-Seitz 1998).

5. *Adhering to a policy of methodologic pluralism.* The subject matter of depth psychology is too complex and too elusive for any single method of interpretation. "Meaning eludes all unilateral investigation" (Barthes 1977, p. 87). Multiple interpretive strategies and heuristics must be employed "because of the vastness, complexity, unpredictability, and multidetermined nature of the phenomena we confront in [depth psychologies], as well as the unbelievable amount of what is unknown and not easily knowable at any given moment" (Peterfreund 1983, p. 73).

6. *Combining holistic and particularistic perspectives.* Clinical interpretation pays close attention to the smallest details, but recognizes also that the whole meaning at a given time is greater than the sum of its various parts. The two perspectives are complementary: "Both conflate to a meaning that is otherwise incomplete and misleading" (Olinick 1984, p. 649).

7. *Implementing relativistic and progressive perspectives.* Relativism refers to the inherent limitation on understanding imposed by the fact that all knowledge is based on particular conceptual systems at a given time. The progressive aspect of understanding is a corollary of interpretive relativism; that is, interpretations involve a selection and progressive modification of an initially plausible construction, the justification of which is relative at every stage of the interpretive process.

The following case report is presented to illustrate both the basic concepts and general methodologic strategies of the interpretive process.

CLINICAL ILLUSTRATION

Karen was a 33-year-old married woman whose treatment began in a psychiatric hospital following a suicide attempt. She had taken a moderate overdose of tranquilizing drugs prescribed by her family physician. She was cooperative, only mildly depressed, and talked freely about a problem with her husband. His work required a great deal of travel, to which she had adjusted during their six years of marriage. In recent months, however, even when he was not traveling he often worked late at his office, not coming home until midnight. She had complained mildly to him about her loneliness, but he was not very sympathetic. In an interview with him at the hospital, he confided to me that he no longer found Karen interesting or attractive, but remained married to her out of a sense of duty. He denied any extramarital involvement.

Karen was intelligent, sensitive, and related well during her sessions with me. Her physical health had always been good, and she had no history of previous mental illness. She was devoted to her husband, who encouraged her own career in art. She had a small circle of friends with whom she visited regularly, but she spent most of her time working alone in her home studio. She loved her work and her home, did not want children, and, except for seeing so little of her husband, was generally satisfied with her life.

Karen's father had left her mother when Karen was 2 years old. She never saw or heard from him after that, and had no memory of him. Because her mother had to work to support the family, Karen and her older brother were left alone a great deal. Her brother resented having to look after his little sister, which he expressed by ignoring her. Between the ages of 6 and 16 she had looked forward to each summer, which she and her brother spent with their grandparents in another city. Her brother found other boys to play with during those summers, but there were no girls in the grandparents' neighborhood for Karen. For the most part, therefore, she spent the time with her grandparents, who were very fond of her, and she of them. Her grandmother was an invalid; but her grandfather was a kindly, good-natured, energetic man who became the companion, playmate, and father that Karen had never had.

Karen's twice-weekly dynamic psychotherapy began while she was in the hospital, and continued for three years on an office basis. The initial phase of her treatment focused on the problem with her husband. She confided eventually that she felt not only lonely but sexually frustrated. Earlier in their marriage she and her husband had enjoyed frequent, passionate, and exciting varieties of sexual relations; but he no longer seemed interested in sex. She continued to desire sex, partly for its own sake, but also because sexual relations were important to her self-esteem and to maintaining a feeling of closeness to her husband.

As the therapeutic process continued and deepened, she reported dreams that condensed the image of her husband with that of her brother, who had ignored and neglected her during childhood. She now recognized that her suicide attempt had been motivated by anger at her husband, and by hope that it would force him to be more involved with her. She recalled similar self-destructive attempts to gain her brother's sympathy and attention during childhood.

Early in the second year of her therapy, her feelings toward me became increasingly positive, idealizing me in much the same way that she had felt about her grandfather. During the weeks preceding the session to be interpreted, her dream imagery became increasingly erotic in character, and her fantasies included intense, pleasurable expectations that

I would respond erotically to her sexual feelings. [I raised the question whether she might be reexperiencing feelings toward me that she had felt toward her grandfather.] She then confided that her close and loving relationship with her grandfather had included frequent genital fondling of each other during the period when she was from 7 to 13 years old. She seemed relatively free of conscious guilt or shame about the sexual contact with him. She had rationalized to herself that she was entitled to the pleasure it gave her because she had been deprived of a father's and brother's love, and because she had received so little time and attention from her mother.

The feelings she described for her grandfather had both the quality and intensity of romantic love (cf. Fenichel 1945, Jones 1938). From the beginning of their mutual fondling, she had always been the one who initiated the sexual intimacy. Whenever she felt lonely for her mother or rejected by her brother during those summers, she would look for her grandfather, cuddle up to him, fondle his penis or place his hand on her genitalia, which would lead to five or ten minutes of mutual genital fondling. She stopped having sexual contact with her grandfather when she was 13 years old, which she associated with the onset of her menses. From then on, rather than seeking erotic contact with her grandfather, she masturbated while recalling and fantasizing about her previous sexual experiences with him. Even as an adult, her most exciting and satisfying erotic fantasies were based on pleasurable memories of sexual contact with her grandfather.

Confiding the childhood sexual experiences with her grandfather did not immediately lessen Karen's increasingly romanticized feelings toward me. [When I called attention to her coy and somewhat flirtatious behavior toward me], she readily admitted that she had a crush on me, that she envied my wife, imagined what it would be like to be married to me, and thought about me when she masturbated.

Appointment Preceding the Session to be Interpreted

During the phase of increasing erotic transference to me, Karen came in one day looking flushed and distraught, which was unusual for her. She blurted out that she was very upset about a cat in her neighborhood that had become pregnant. She went on at length about her concern for the animal and its pregnancy. [When she began to calm down, I asked why she was so concerned about a normal condition like pregnancy?] She replied with a tone of anxious pity that the cat was only a kitten, and seemed much too small to carry and give birth to a whole litter of young. She recalled feeling awed by the size of pregnant women's distended abdomens. She was glad that neither she nor her husband wanted children, because she would never want to feel like that.

Session to be Interpreted

Karen was still upset when she came for her next appointment. She started by saying in an anxious and slightly accusatory tone that the kitten was becoming gigantic—more distended every day. She continued talking about the pregnant kitten and its plight for some time. When her feelings of alarm had peaked and began to decline, [I asked what exactly was she afraid might happen]. She replied that she was "desperately afraid" the kitten's abdomen would become so distended from the babies inside that it would just burst, which would kill the poor kitten. She then recalled a dream from the previous night:

> I was driving a school bus, stopping along the way to pick up children. More and more children boarded the bus until there was no room for more. But more kept getting on, until finally children started flying out of the bus windows. I was terrified and didn't know what to do.

She had no idea what the dream might mean. She had never driven a school bus, and had never been responsible for a group of children. The children were very young, like nursery school or prekindergarten age. She recalled with surprise that she seemed to enjoy driving the school bus and picking up the children—until the bus began to get overcrowded. Then she felt terrified at what was happening and at her inability to stop it.

I asked: [Can you see a parallel between the overcrowded bus and the pregnant kitten?] She looked blank for a moment, then exclaimed suddenly: "Oh! Of course! So overcrowded with children that they 'burst out.' It's the same thing I've been afraid would happen to the kitten. So the school bus must represent the kitten." I commented: [But in the dream it was *your* school bus, and you were in the driver's seat, suggesting that the school bus refers to something about yourself and your body.] Karen blinked unbelievingly, then protested that she wasn't pregnant, never had been, and never wanted to be. [I reminded her that all kinds of strange things can go on in the unconscious—even disturbing dreams about pregnancy.] "But I don't *want* to be pregnant," she insisted. She could never stand the idea of being "bloated with babies," and she feared the process of giving birth. [What specifically do you fear about it?] The pain, the bleeding, the possibility that she might hemorrhage and die. She recalled a woman describing her birth canal being "ripped and torn" as the baby came out.

I then interpreted: [It is clear that you have a great deal of conflict about pregnancy and giving birth; but despite that conflict, when a woman loves a man very much, she may want to have his child.] "Well, I love my husband; but I certainly don't want to have his child!" [I understand that; but recently you said that you have a crush on me, that you envy my wife, and that you have wondered what it would be like to be married to me. Your romantic feelings toward me may include wishes to give me a child— or for me to give you a child.]

Karen paused and became reflective at that point. A blush appeared as she said, "My daydreams about being married to you sometimes picture you coming home from your office to me and our children. In those daydreams, the children are already there. The thought of being pregnant with them and giving birth to them didn't occur to me." I then interpreted further: [This is probably not the first time you have experienced intense conflict about wanting to have a child with a man you loved. The same conflict may have occurred early in your marriage when you felt very romantically toward your husband. And I suspect that the conflict first occurred during your loving and erotic relationship with your grandfather. If so, that might help to explain why you are so fearful about pregnancy and giving birth. The fantasy or prospect of becoming pregnant while still a child could make a young girl feel the way you've been feeling lately about the pregnant kitten.] Karen nodded slowly and thoughtfully.

Commentary

AUTHOR'S INTERPRETIVE FORMULATION

Precipitant: Her increasingly intense romantic-erotic grandfather transference to me.

Principal current (thematic) conflict: Wish to have therapist's (grandfather's) child, versus the fear that her body (as a child) was not large enough to contain and give birth to a child, but might burst open and kill her.

Principal defenses: (1) Repression and transference as defenses against remembering her feared childhood wishes for grandfather's child. (2) Disavowal of any wish for a child. (3) Projection of her conflict about pregnancy to the pregnant kitten, and to the dream image of an overloaded school bus.

Genetic antecedent: Her intense, prolonged, romantic-erotic relationship with her grandfather, which appears to have included a highly conflicted wish for a child from him.

BASIC CONCEPTS AND GENERAL INTERPRETIVE STRATEGIES OF THE ILLUSTRATIVE CASE

The following discussion focuses on the role of both basic concepts and general interpretive strategies employed in the illustrative case, starting with illustrations of the basic (general) concepts that inform and guide clinical interpretations. As indicated previously, the basic background assumptions of psychoanalysis, dynamic psychotherapy, and clinical interpretation include the concepts of an unconscious mind, continuity, meaning, determinism, overdetermination, instinctual drives, conflict, defense, repetition, transference, and the importance of childhood experiences (Rapaport 1944).

With respect to *unconscious* mental contents, I was alert to clues that might suggest latent meanings and determinants of Karen's panicky obsession regarding the pregnant kitten. In addition, when Karen protested that she had never wanted to be pregnant, I reminded her that "all kinds of strange things go on in the Unconscious, including disturbing dreams of pregnancy." The basic concept of *continuity* is illustrated by the fact that, until the parallels were called to her attention, Karen did not recognize the relations (continuities) between her anxiety about the pregnant kitten, her anxiety-laden dream of the overloaded school bus, and her romantic-erotic fantasies of being married to me and having children with me.

Reliving of the childhood romantic-erotic relationship with her grandfather in her relationship with me illustrates the basic methodologic concepts of *meaning, determinism, childhood experiences, repetition,* and *transference. Overdetermination* is illustrated by the fantasies and images of babies or children bursting out of both the kitten and bus—condensing fear of injury to herself from giving birth, and injury to the children from wishes to get rid of the phantasied pregnancy. (*Note:* A terminologic convention employed throughout the present volume spells unconscious phantasies with a "ph," and conscious fantasies with an "f.")

The basic concept of *instinctual drives* is illustrated in material about the erotic relationship with her grandfather and her associated wish to have his child—both transferred to me in the present. The dynamic theme of the session—wish to have therapist's (grandfather's) child, versus the fear of her abdomen bursting open—illustrates the concept of *conflict. Defenses* included (among others) repression of the conflict about wishing to be pregnant with grandfather's (currently therapist's) child, disavowal of any wish for pregnancy, and projection of the conflict to a pregnant kitten and to the dream image of a bus "bursting at the seams" with children.

Turning next to the *general strategies* that mediate between the basic concepts and clinical data, the therapeutic dialogue in the interpreted session was both *collaborative* and *dialectical*; compare, for example, the interchanges between Karen and me regarding the pregnant kitten, the meaning of the school bus, and her protests that she did not want to be pregnant.

With respect to the therapist's *stance,* my attitude and behavior toward Karen was patient, nonjudgmental, encouraging, empathetic, tactful, and tolerant of uncertainty, on the one hand; but on the other hand my stance also included abstinence, anonymity, neutrality, scientific skepticism, and restricting the expression of all thoughts and feelings to words.

Scientific skepticism (toward both the patient's productions and my own inferences) is illustrated by a possible discrepancy that I noted in my interpretation, namely, that the dream image of children bursting out of the overloaded bus windows might imply injury not only to Karen but to the children. This discrepancy was resolved subsequently with the emergence of further material dealing with Karen's defensive-aversive wish to get rid of the phantasied pregnancy.

With respect to a *data-driven* in contrast to a doctrinal approach, the interpretive work in this session was based on the therapeutic dialogue rather than on specific clinical theories; compare, for example, the parallel that I noted between the dream image of the overloaded school bus and Karen's obsession with the pregnant kitten. I also adhered to a policy of *methodologic pluralism*, that is, I employed multiple varieties of clinical data and multiple types of interpretive methods and heuristics. Examples of interpretive *heuristics* included the following: (1) my inference that the school bus represented the patient's own body was based in part on the heuristic that the central character or figure in a dream is the dreamer; (2) a related heuristic suggests that a bus and its passengers often symbolizes a pregnant woman or mother; (3) my inference regarding the children bursting out of the bus windows was based in part on a heuristic that objects passing through a window often symbolize birth (clinical and methodologic aspects of symbolism are discussed more fully in the following chapters).

My attempts to understand both *latent meanings* and *determinants* are illustrated by my questions about why Karen was so disturbed about the cat's pregnancy. Inquiry revealed that she was disturbed because the cat was only a kitten, and because she assumed that the kitten's pregnancy might cause its very distended abdomen to burst. Possible determinants of her fears and fantasies about the kitten were inferred from Karen's increasingly intense romantic-erotic grandfather transference to me (the precipitating cause), and by the history of her prolonged romantic-erotic relationship with her grandfather (the predisposing cause).

Applications of both *holistic* and *particularistic perspectives* are illustrated by the detailed interpretive inquiry into Karen's pregnant kitten obsession and school bus dream image, combined with the construction of a holistic interpretation (her own feared wish for pregnancy) that provided a common denominator for all, or at least most, of the clinical data. *Relativistic* and *progressive perspectives* are illustrated by Karen's repression of and hence inability to disclose a key conflict concerning the "love affair" with her grandfather: her repressed phantasies and fears of becoming pregnant with his child did not emerge until their transference reliving in her relationship with me.

FURTHER COMMENTARY ON THE GENERAL INTERPRETIVE STRATEGIES

Collaborative and Dialectical Relationship

The importance of collaboration goes beyond the patient's need for emotional support in order to confront inner conflicts. A collaborative approach is necessary also to generate meanings that are unique to the individual patient; to facilitate error-correcting feedback regarding the therapist's interpretations; and to encourage the development of the patient's ability to understand and interpret his or her own associations, dreams, fantasies, and other psychological material (Beiser 1984, Blank and Blank 1986, Gardner 1983, Gedo 1986, Kantrowitz et al. 1990, Kramer 1959, Schlessinger and Robbins 1983, Sterba 1934; see also Chapter 6).

The widely applied concept of therapeutic alliance also implies and involves collaboration between patient and therapist (see, for example, Friedman 1969, Kanzer 1975, Olinick 1980, Sandler et al. 1973, Thomä and Kächele 1987). Friedman (1969, 1988) points out, however, that a working alliance does not mean that the purposes of patient and therapist are, or ever could be, completely congruent and harmonious; and Weinshel (1984) notes that, rather than representing a constant structure, the therapeutic alliance varies at different times during the course of a treatment—which brings up the other, dialectical side of the therapeutic relationship.

Therapy is dialectical from the start. It begins with the patient's report of conscious thoughts and the therapist's basic assumption that consciousness is often false (Barratt 1984, Ricoeur 1970; see also Arlow 1969, A. Freud 1951, Gill and Hoffman 1982, for good clinical examples of interpretive dialectics). Brody (1990) writes in this connection: "The psychoanalytic process is one of continued interchange, stimulation, and response, creating and resolving successive conflicts, both interpersonal and intrapsychic: new positions with their own questions arise from the resolution of antecedent struggles" (pp. 35–36). In addition to the inevitable tension between patient and therapist, Hoffman (1994) describes a related dialectic based on an opposition of attitudes and participation within the therapist—between the standard, formal, reflective interpretive stance, on the one hand, and a distinctive form of self-expression, on the other.

The dialectical encounter between patient and therapist generates disturbing emotions in both. Therapy can be arduous because it involves struggles with resistances—in both participants (Anzieu 1970, Leavy 1980, Ricoeur 1970; see also Ramzy 1974, for a striking example). Patients usually welcome the collaboration but not the interpretive dialectics of therapy. For both reasons the therapist walks a tightrope between the collaborative and dialectical aspects of the interpretive process: too much or too little of either can interfere with the interpretive process and with therapy (see, e.g., Coltrera 1981, Friedman 1988; cf. also Akhtar's [2000] attempt to integrate these polarities, discussed further in Chapter 8 on interpretive technique).

The Therapist's Stance

Originally the methodologic rationale of the therapist's positive attitudes was to overcome the patient's resistance to confiding. French (1958, 1970), French and Wheeler (1963), and Friedman (1969) have proposed an additional, dynamically more complex rationale of the therapist's encouraging attitude—that it facilitates the emergence of old conflicted hopes that the patient had long since repudiated for fear of traumatic disappointment. Compare also in this connection Stone's (1961) concepts regarding a positive, encouraging attitude toward the patient; Sandler's (1960/1987) concepts regarding safety feelings; Gitelson's (1982) concept of the therapist's diatrophic presence; Weiss and Sampson's (1986) concept of patients testing the therapist to assess the safety of the therapeutic relationship and process; and Kohut's (1984) emphasis on an affirming attitude toward the patient. These various strategies appear to have in common the aim of encouraging the patient to hope that it is both safe and desirable to allow the emergence of disturbing thoughts and feelings, including conflicted old hopes, in the therapeutic situation.

Like so many of the terms and concepts of depth psychology, *neutrality* has several meanings, usages, and posited rationales (see, e.g., Franklin 1990). The general strategy of abstinence appears to be less stringent nowadays than it was during earlier periods of psychoanalysis (see, for example, Greenson 1967, Leider 1984, Stone 1961, Thomä and Kächele 1987); but most therapists, including self psychologists, still refrain from gratifying patients' transference wishes directly (see, e.g., Goldberg 1978). The strategy of anonymity on the part of the therapist is also less absolute than it once was. Freud's (1912) recommendation that the therapist be mirror-like and opaque to the patient now seems debatable. Anonymity does not require the therapist to hide his or her humanity (Cremerius 1984, Gay 1988, Hoffman 1983, A. Kris 1990a, Lichtenberg and Slap 1977, Lipton 1977, 1988).

Interpretive strategies related to the therapist's stance are grounded mainly in the basic concepts of psychoanalysis, dynamic psychotherapy, and clinical interpretation. The basic methodologic concept of transference, for example, provides the rationale for anonymity; that is, the analytic incognito facilitates both the development of transference and its demonstration to the patient (Freud 1912a). The rationale of abstinence, which is part of neutrality, rests on instinct theory and psychoeconomics; that is, the frustration of instinctual drives in the therapeutic situation maintains sufficient tension (suffering) to motivate the patient to "do work and make changes" (Freud 1919, pp. 162–163). Brody (1990) proposes also that the therapeutic situation involves both perceptual and need deprivations in order to increase the patient's experience of "what is already there"—"the residue of past experience" (p. 30). Friedman (1988) suggests that abstinence also facilitates demonstration to the patient that all conscious experiences, including the transference relationship, are only attributes of a more generic inner structure, the mind as a whole.

A Data-Driven Approach

As indicated previously, initially Freud's interpretive approach was predominantly doctrinal (Anzieu 1970, Dalbiez 1941), but by 1900 his method had evolved considerably and employed mainly inductive and heuristic strategies. Parsons (1992) observes that we tend to assume that our theory should tell us how to understand patients, but "we do not generally arrive at our interpretations by using theory to deduce what they ought to be" (p. 103). He notes the risk that theoretical preconceptions can close off possibilities of fresh discovery, and adds that we do not determine once and for all what our theory is but must continually refind it in our clinical work with patients.

Schwaber (1987b) asserts and illustrates that use of models and theories in clinical work profoundly influences what is interpreted. No matter which theory one espouses, the model tends to supersede the data and foreclose discovery of other, unanticipated meanings. All too often, inferences are based (deductively) on the model rather than (inductively) on the clinical data. Although a completely atheoretical orientation is impossible, we need an interpretive approach that asks questions not answered by a model—questions that often cannot yet be answered, and thus call for tolerance of uncertainty rather than inference from a model.

Schafer (1997) points out that the perspectivism of postpositivist science rejects the notion of a single grand theory that accounts for all of the data, questions, and problems within a discipline. Theory has lost the "grandeur, majesty, and mythic proportions" (p. 21) that it had for Freud and other early theorists. Yet some schools of psychoanalysis and dynamic psychotherapy continue to employ theory-driven approaches to clinical interpretation. Examples include Klein's and Kohut's interpretive approaches, both of which are doctrinally driven by their respective genetic theories of pathogenesis. (For critiques of such approaches, see Arlow 1991, Gergely 1992, Hamilton 1993, Paniagua 1985, Rubovits-Seitz 1988a, 1998.)

Whether theory has a place in clinical interpretation depends largely on the type of theory one employs. The basic concepts or background assumptions of psychoanalysis and dynamic psychotherapy are indispensable to clinical interpretation because they are very general and thus provide a broad conceptual framework that facilitates the discovery of alternative meanings and determinants. Specific clinical theories, on the other hand, tend to find only what they seek. Thus Loewenstein (1957) advised that therapy be conducted as though clinical theory does not exist, and Anton Kris (1983) stresses the necessity to hold our methods of interpretation independent of specific clinical theories (cf. Böhm 1999, regarding freedom from plans and programs).

Latent Meanings and Determinants

Since psychoanalysis has roots in both the human and natural sciences, Freud included subjective as well as objective data and methods in his interpretive approach, making psychoanalysis a methodologic hybrid—a scientific investigation of human subjectivity (Meissner 1971).

Clinicians focus on three main sources of meanings and determinants in clinical data: the patient's current relationship with the therapist, extratherapeutic experiences, and childhood experiences. Repressed meanings and determinants are typically multiple rather than single, complexly interrelated rather than separate, and changeable rather than fixed—characteristics that contribute significantly to the practical difficulties of clinical interpretation. Another problem is the temptation to think of meanings as concrete entities. Meaning, however, is only a construal, a surmise about a set of data—an interpretation of a possible relationship between the clinical data and the patient's unconscious mental processes at the time (Laffal 1965).

With respect to determinants, clinical interpretation is most effective in identifying precipitating factors of current conflicts, defenses, and their associated meanings—the precipitating event often having occurred during the previous therapy session. Predisposing factors of psychopathology are so numerous and varied, however, that interpretive inquiry cannot possibly identify them all. A major interpretive strategy for dealing with the latter problem rests on the basic methodologic assumption that childhood experiences (as well as genic factors) are of the greatest importance in the development of personality and psychopathology. On that basis, clinical interpreters focus particularly, although not exclusively, on predisposing factors associated with disturbing childhood experiences.

Relations between latent meanings and determinants are problematic, the two often being difficult to distinguish (Shope 1973; see also Rycroft 1969). Historically, clinicians have assumed that in causal systems such as psychoanalysis and dynamic psychotherapy, the meanings that one construes often suggest the nature of their determinants (Edelson 1988). The philosopher Adolf Grünbaum (1984) maintains, however, that the interpretation of meaning-relations in clinical data tells one nothing about underlying causal processes such as unconscious motives.

I have argued elsewhere (1998) in this connection that although meaning-relations alone may be insufficient *warrant* (proof) for establishing causal inferences, clinicians are justified in considering meaning-relations as possible clues to latent determinants during the discovery phase of the interpretive process, and in pursuing such clues further in the course of the ongoing therapeutic process. Moreover, if a particular type of thematic relation occurs repeatedly during the course of a therapeutic process, and if in addition it is associated with a specific and recurrent pathodynamic constellation, the possibility of a valid causal-thematic link increases correspondingly.

Methodologic Pluralism

Interpretive methods are necessarily pluralistic rather than monistic in approach. Davis (1978) observes, for example, that human thought itself is inherently plural; there is no one method applicable to all questions. The task, therefore, is to develop the multiple strategies and procedures necessary to deal with the many different problems presented to thought.

Most but not all approaches to clinical interpretation are pluralistic. Freud's interpretive method was distinctly pluralistic (Rubovits-Seitz 1988a, 1992). Gardner (1991) notes that even clinicians who stress a single approach (for example, Kohut 1959, 1984) "smuggle in" other methods. Emphasizing a single method, perspective, or variety of data can be useful if employed intermittently, as one among a number of approaches; but when applied continually and exclusively, a single method is less capable of identifying, clarifying, and specifying the plurality and interrelations of latent contents in clinical data. Diesing (1971) warns that overuse of a single method produces a distorted view; and Kaplan (1964) concludes that if a particular method comes to be regarded as the one avenue to truth, it is truth that suffers.

A pluralistic perspective applies also, of course, to the vantage points from which the analyst views the patient and the therapeutic dyad. Warren Poland (2000) asks, for example, "Are not separate people, cognizant of their separateness, even so still part of the same intersubjective field?" (p. 29). Clarifying the several meanings of the term intersubjective, he writes:

> Confusion can be minimized if we remember these different meanings of the same word and if we also respect the need to entertain simultaneously multiple points of view. We now can identify three relational points of view: one addresses an intrapsychic one-person psychology; a second looks at two-person psychologies based on the interaction of separate subjects; a third considers emotional interaction as the outgrowth of a single unified dyad. It may be simplest to divide relational points of view into person-separate and person-unified views, with the person-separate vantage point then examined from both one-person and two-person angles.
>
> Certainly everything so far said about the growing self-definition of the patient carrying with it recognition of essential separateness can be viewed from the person-unified, dyadic vantage point. However, recognizing the importance of all points of view, we realize that the presence of a dyadic viewpoint does not cancel the critical developmental shift in self-other distinction that can be seen from the one-person and interactive two-person perspectives. Unified field intersubjectivity does not undo individuality. [p. 30]

The pluralistic strategy offers clinical interpreters a number of advantages: (1) Each individual method of interpretation and variety of data has limitations, for which additional methods and types of data compensate. (2) Combinations of subjective and objective methods facilitate "entering into one's subject matter," as Diesing (1971) puts it, "while remaining detached enough to maintain objectivity" (pp. 209–210). (3) Interpretive versatility facilitates working with different kinds of patients, psychopathology, and clinical-dynamic circumstances. (4) Increased interpretive range and comprehensiveness are available. Spence and Lugo (1972) have demonstrated experimentally, for example, that shifting from one mode of listening to another makes it possible to pick up cues from both primary and secondary process sources. If the therapist employs only one mode of listening, he or she hears only part of the message (see also Spence and Grief 1970). (5) Pluralistic approaches compensate for the reduced redundancy in clinical data (due to neurotic repression) by generating, gathering, and processing larger amounts and wider varieties of clinical data (Spence 1968). (6) A pluralistic approach is congruent with the conceptual perspective of relativism, which eschews final closure or finiteness of interpretations, opting instead for progressive revisions and continual evolving of posited meanings and determinants—seeking approximations to truth that have no absolute end point of complete understanding.

Holistic and Particularistic Perspectives

Freud insisted that "our presentation begins to be conclusive only with the intimate detail" (Nunberg and Federn 1962, p. 172; see also Freud 1923); and in 1918 he wrote, "It is always a strict law of dream-interpretation that an explanation must be found for every detail" (p. 42, fn. 1). Thus clinical interpreters pay close attention to the smallest details, but recognize also that the whole meaning at a given time is greater than the sum of its various parts. The two perspectives are not contradictory, however, but complementary.

The interpretation of individual therapy sessions illustrates the strategy of employing both holistic and particularistic perspectives. The therapist listens for a "whole" (thematic) meaning that ties together everything the patient says; but to discover such a theme also requires close attention to, and integration of, the session's details (Klauber 1980).

Certain clinical strategies enhance the holistic character of interpretations—for example, viewing the patient as a whole; considering part meanings in terms of their interrelations with other parts; basing interpretations on the primacy of subject matter (clinical data) over theories and methods, that is, focusing on the specific person and phenomena being studied, rather than applying preconceived categories to the individual patient (Diesing 1971); and attempting to account for all of the clinical data rather than selectively emphasizing material that fits one's hypothesis.

Freud's interpretive approach achieved a balance between holistic and particularistic perspectives (Kazin 1966). A common error in interpretive work is excessive focus on whole meanings, while neglecting the numerous part meanings associated with individual elements of the clinical data (Abraham 1986). Olinick (1984) states, "Psychoanalysis is an unusual discipline in its insistence that the detail must never, even momentarily, be overlooked for the general principle nor the general for the detail" (p. 649; see also Eissler 1959, Forrester 1980, Levenson 1988).

Relativistic and Progressive Perspectives

Relativism asserts that there is not just one truth; there are *some* truths that hold within diverse conceptual frameworks and at particular periods of time. "Reality" is views, each of the various systems of inquiry representing a context (Polkinghorne 1983).

The instability of meanings contributes to the relativity of interpretations. Meanings are not stable, autonomous structures but changing, evolving entities. The therapist's acknowledgment that we really do not know the patient's inner life also contributes to interpretive relativism. Schwaber (1990a) observes, "It is this outlook which marked the entry of [depth psychologies] into the scientific era of relativity" (p. 35).

These and other complexities of meaning magnify the relativity of interpretations, in consequence of which interpretations must perform a synthetic as well as an analytic function—an ongoing integration of progressively shifting information and meanings from the patient and interpretive elaborations by the therapist (Freud 1911). Because of its synthetic function, Moss (1985) refers to interpretation as an organizing idea that gathers together, gives conceptual substance and a tenuous degree of permanence (structure) to the otherwise fleeting, evanescent words, affects, and hints at meaning that compose the therapeutic dialogue.

The progressive aspect of understanding is a corollary of interpretive relativity. We do not understand a meaning simply by attributing a particular unconscious motive to it, nor can a single communication by the patient express a meaning fully. Understanding requires diverse, redundant, progressive expressions of a meaning (Ray 1984). As in science generally, the interpretive process involves comparisons of alternative constructions in an ongoing search for progressive approximations to truth (Edelson 1988). Clinical interpretation is thus not only a cumulative body of knowledge, but a gradual process of understanding.

SUMMARY

The basic (core) concepts of psychoanalysis and dynamic psychotherapy—that is, concepts of the Unconscious, meaning, determinism, overdetermination, conflict, defense, transference, and the importance of childhood experiences—influence clinical interpretations decisively but only indirectly, because a hierarchical system of interpretive strategies mediates between the basic concepts and clinical data. Strategies are plans, implemented by specific procedures, that guide the therapist's interpretive activities. The fundamental purpose of such strategies is to generate and organize relevant information about the patient. Strategies reduce complexity, ambiguity, and uncertainty by increasing understanding of the patient's unique, personal meanings.

This chapter illustrated and discussed various types of general strategies, that is, strategies that facilitate the therapeutic process and clinical interpretation as a whole, in contrast to specific strategies that deal with particular aspects of interpretation and treatment. A case report was presented to illustrate the roles of basic concepts and general mediating strategies in the interpretive process. Following the illustrative case, the rationales of our general interpretive strategies were discussed.

The general strategies illustrated and discussed in this chapter include (1) developing and maintaining a simultaneously collaborative and dialectical therapeutic relationship; (2) adopting the (somewhat paradoxical) aspects of the therapist's stance; (3) emphasizing a data-driven, in contrast to a doctrinal, interpretive approach; (4) attempting to understand both latent meanings and determinants; (5) adhering to a policy of pluralistic methods; (6) combining holistic and particularistic interpretive perspectives; and (7) implementing relativistic and progressive perspectives.

$\mathcal{E}$mpirical $\mathcal{S}$trategies of the $\mathcal{J}$nterpretive $\mathcal{P}$rocess: $\mathcal{C}$linical $\mathcal{D}$ata

$\mathcal{E}$MPIRICAL COMPONENTS of the interpretive process consist of clinical data and the methods used to generate, collect, observe, and record the data. This chapter focuses on clinical data as empirical components of the interpretive process; the following chapter deals with the methods used to generate, collect, observe, and record the data.

Human and social scientists gain access to the ways people experience themselves and the world through the medium of human expressions, the richest source of which is language. Paralinguistic and nonverbal expressions, as well as the therapist's reactions to the patient, are also important sources of clinical data; but the most characteristic form of human science data is discourse (Polkinghorne 1983). The "talking cure" produced a new kind of therapist, one who wants to understand language. Every word, no matter how seemingly senseless or unsuitable, becomes clinical data that calls for interpretation and understanding (Thass-Thienemann 1968).

ILLUSTRATIVE CASE I

A 40-year-old, highly educated, single man came for treatment because of impotence and occupational instability. He spoke with an affected Oxford accent, dressed meticulously, and drove a large classic foreign car.

He was the only child of a doting and possessive mother, and a father who deserted the family when the patient was 7 years old. The session to be described occurred during the middle phase of the analysis. The patient's transference to me at that time was mainly positive, making it possible for me to be moderately confrontational in some interventions.

He began the session by saying (in a tone of self-satisfaction, and with a gesture of looking affectedly at the fingernails of one hand) that he had had an appointment with a very important person the previous day. [Did you notice the way you looked at your fingernails as you said that?] No; but he felt pleased with himself, as he always does, when he gets to see an important person. It makes him feel important, too. He hastened to add that he was not "syncophantic" (sycophantic), however, because after all he lives in the real world where one must get ahead as best one can. [Could you be rationalizing?] Without answering the question he paused briefly, then continued in a self-explanatory manner, describing at length his lifelong feelings of physical inferiority. He was never chosen for the school teams, and has never mastered a sport. Instead he developed himself intellectually, about which he knows he tends to be snobbish.

He fell silent for about a minute, then asked what did I mean previously about looking at his "nose?" [I asked about looking at your fingernails.] Oh. I thought you said "nose." [What comes to mind about looking at your nose?] Well, it would have to be longer for me to see it. Pinocchio! His nose got longer when he lied. (Blocking set in.) [Do you lie?] He admitted with considerable embarrassment that he had not been truthful to the important person yesterday. He did what he always does when he "toadies up" to people: He says whatever he thinks they would like to hear, what would impress them. He also tries to make himself seem as much like the other person as possible. [You said earlier that you were not "syncophantic"; did you notice the slip?] What comes to mind is the media term "sync"—trying to be "in sync" with people. He feels he can bullshit almost anyone that way. [Do you do that here?] I try, but it doesn't get me very far. He senses that I value honesty, so usually he tries to be honest here; but his habit of trying to impress people interferes with his ability to associate freely. He can't lie back and just say anything. He has to "steer" his associations along lines that he thinks might please or impress me, and make himself seem clever, witty, urbane. [You seem conflicted, however, about some of the ways you try to gain favor with me and other people. Are those traits you want to change in yourself?] Yes; but what I would like to change even more is the doubts about myself that make me lie and show off and suck up to people the way I do.

Commentary

This clinical example illustrates the convergence of multiple clues from several varieties of clinical data—a gesture, a misperception (cf. Faimberg, 1997, cited by Spence 1998), a slip of speech, a suggestive tone, an image of Pinocchio, associations to the foregoing, and others—which, taken together, suggest a dynamic theme of craving affirmation from people, especially father figures (the analyst in his current transference) versus the shame about needing such approval, and about some devious ways of trying to obtain it. At the end of this patient's three-year treatment, some narcissistic traits were still evident in his personality and behavior; but he was more comfortable with himself, and had become both potent and occupationally stable.

ILLUSTRATIVE CASE 2

This patient's therapeutic discourse included a short poem that he had written, which became an interpretable part of the clinical data. The patient was an adolescent who had dropped out of high school because of a drug problem (marijuana). He had been in twice-weekly dynamic psychotherapy with me for six months at the time of the session to be interpreted. (A more detailed report of this case was published in Seitz 1974.)

Preceding Sessions

During the previous several weeks Jim had been more depressed and withdrawn than usual. He denied using more marijuana, but I suspected that he was smoking more "dope" than he admitted because his "pot paranoia" had increased (i.e., the fear that police were watching him, and that he might get "busted"). During the immediately preceding week he had been even more depressed and uncommunicative, but by active questioning I discovered that his mother, too, had been more depressed, withdrawn, and irritable recently. A change in her condition (cancer) necessitated her return to the hospital for additional x-rays and other tests. In the immediately preceding session [I had interpreted to Jim that his own increased depression seemed related to his mother's condition, but that it wasn't clear whether it was his mother's withdrawal from him, irritability toward him, or both, that was disturbing and depressing him].

Session to be Interpreted

He seemed somewhat less lethargic and a bit more communicative during this session. He started with an excuse for being a few minutes late. He had to drive his mother somewhere, which was out of the way, and he has to pick her up after he leaves here. She says that since he's not in school and doesn't have a job, he should make himself useful by helping her whenever and however he can. He muttered something that I couldn't understand. [I couldn't hear that.] Nothing. Not important. He said that he had written a poem recently, but then fell silent. [Do you feel like telling or showing me the poem?] He reached in his pocket and pulled out a crumpled sheet of paper that he handed to me. He had scrawled the following lines on the paper:

> Rushing through the back door
>   slamming the screen on my mind.
>   JIMMY, I TOLD YOU NOT
>   TO SLAM THAT DOOR!
> Rushing down the depth of my mind
>   licking the paper passport, to where?
>   JIMMY, DON'T EAT BEFORE DINNER!
>   IT'LL BE READY IN A MINUTE!
> Rushing through a maze of thoughts,
>   wiping nose drips on my sleeve.
>   JIMMY, HOW MANY TIMES HAVE I TOLD
>   YOU TO USE YOUR HANDKERCHIEF?

Mellowing on the sweet-sour smoke, lids low,
   irises black, and warm sweet peace.
     JIMMY, IT'S YOUR TURN
     TO SAY GRACE!
Good God, Sweet God, rush on through
   and take me along.
     JIMMY!

[What are your thoughts about the poem?] He didn't know. He used to write poems before he got depressed. This is the first one he's written in a couple of years. He just writes what comes to his mind, doesn't plan it or try to make sense out of it. [You don't see any pattern or meaning in this poem?] No. I just wrote what came to my mind—like stream-of-consciousness writing. [That's surprising, because it seems to tell a story.] It does? I don't think so. [Are you putting me on?] No, no! I mean, I agree it's about something—like about smoking dope. But naturally I'd write about that, since that's the main thing I do and think about. [But isn't it also about some*one*, some person?] Uh, maybe. I guess it's mostly about me—like what I think about when I smoke dope. [When you smoke you think that you shouldn't slam the door, and that you shouldn't eat before dinner, and should use a handkerchief instead of your sleeve, and should say grace at dinner?] (He blocked for about two minutes.) [What were you thinking?] Nothing. [Your mind was blank after my question?] Not exactly. I don't know why I write those things, or why I wrote them in big letters.

[At that point I interpreted to Jim that the alternate stanzas in upper-case letters sounded like his mother talking to him, nagging and scolding him; and that slamming the door, leaving the house, not using a handker-chief, and smoking dope were not-so-subtle ways of being angry at her, which he can't seem to express directly.]

Jim seemed to listen more attentively than usual to my interpreta-tion. When I finished, he was silent for a minute, then said with a tone of irony that in his home "You don't mouth off to mother!" [Why not?] Because if you do you get the "deep freeze." She freezes you out for days at a time, which he finds harder to take than her nagging and hollering. It's annoying when she yells, but he tunes it out. The "cold treatment" is really "nothingsville!" [So your depression and "nothing feeling" may be a reaction to her withdrawal from you?] He nodded thoughtfully. [And provoking her is your way of getting back into contact with her?] He nodded again. [And pot is your antidepressant?] He nodded. [That's interesting, because pot makes you withdraw, too—shutting her out as you did in the poem. You turn the tables on her by doing the same frustrating things to her that she does to you.] He was silent for a minute, then murmured *"Damn her!"* as the session ended.

Commentary

Jim's poem illustrates that clinical data can take many forms. Although a somewhat unusual example of therapeutic discourse, it was clearly a relevant and appropriate communication that fitted into the context of the recent and current sessions. It might even be construed as Jim's response to the interpretation that I made at the end of the immediately preceding session—that his increased depression seemed related to his mother in some way, but I wasn't sure whether it was a reaction to her withdrawal from him, nagging him, or both.

Among the multiple meanings contained in the poem, the two most recognizable patterns are the references to his drug use and to his mother's nagging. Jim made his mother's nagging even more conspicuous by printing her remarks in upper-case letters. The exaggerated nature of this hostile caricaturing of his mother alerts the interpreter to its possibly defensive function. Another example is the prominent material about pot smoking. He mentions "rushing" four times in the poem, placing this drug culture term conspicuously at the beginning of the first three stanzas. Repetition is one of the common devices in literature, dreams, and even in conversation for emphasizing a particular idea, making it more apparent. Its prominence does not necessarily mean that the recurrent content is the dynamic theme of the session, however, but may imply a defensive function.

The thematic conflict of this session (supported by detailed retrospective analysis of the entire therapeutic process) was hostility toward his mother for her withdrawal from him versus the dread that if he expressed the hostility openly she would withdraw all the more (separation anxiety). Two of his major character defenses for dealing with that conflict appear in the session (including the poem). One is a passive-aggressive, basically restitutive attempt to regain at least an abrasive form of contact with his mother by provoking her, and the other is his defensive introjection of his mother's frustrating withdrawal from him (identification with the aggressor; cf. his slamming out of the house, leaving his mother behind, and his withdrawal into a drug-induced narcissistic state).

Prognostically, Jim's writing and showing the poem to me were promising therapeutically. In addition to further opening up of important conflicts and defenses, writing poetry was also a constructive, sublimative outlet for those conflicts. Jim's treatment with me lasted for two years, during which he overcame his depressive symptoms, gave up drugs, and made substantial gains in his capacities for love and work. In addition to obtaining a job, he began dating. Eventually he met, fell in love with, and lived with a young woman artist with whom he appeared to be compatible.

CLINICAL DATA

Empirical Data

As in other fields of science, the empirical data of psychoanalysis and dynamic psychotherapy are *observable* phenomena—what the patient actually (manifestly) says and does during therapy sessions, and what the therapist introspectively perceives in his or her own reactions to the patient's material. Phenomena such as the "atmosphere" of a session (Duncan 1990), symbolic meanings, transferences, resistances, unconscious fantasies, and the like employ, but are not themselves, empirical data because they are based on inferences from the data.

Although therapists are more concerned with unconscious than with conscious or preconscious meanings and determinants, the interpretive process nevertheless begins with what the patient actually says and does during therapy sessions. Freud (1911) stated, "It is of the greatest importance for the treatment that the analyst always be aware of the surface of the patient's mind at any given moment" (p. 92). (For further discussions of the analytic surface, see also Kramer 1989, Paniagua 1985, 1991).

Sklansky et al. (1966) report in this connection that the most frequent interventions by therapists deal with manifest meanings, such as asking the patient to clarify what he or she meant by certain associations (see also Lipton 1982, Gassner et al., 1986, Peterfreund 1975). It is imperative that the therapist understand the patient's conscious meanings accurately; otherwise even a slight misunderstanding of what the patient actually says and means can lead to major distortions in one's interpretive conclusions. For example, a shy, inhibited young woman with a psychosomatic disorder referred to a "disk jockey" in a dream. Mistakenly thinking that she meant the kind of jockey who rides horses, her venerable foreign-born therapist interpreted competitiveness with men. The patient was too timid to correct the therapist, who occasionally referred back to the "jockey dream" in subsequent sessions. The mistake was carried forward repeatedly, therefore, to new material and interpretations.

Unlike the self-explanatory "brute data" demanded by J. S. Mill's model of natural science, the data of the human and social sciences, including psychoanalysis and dynamic psychotherapy, are ambiguous, plurivocal, and unstable (see Peterfreund 1983). What they lack in precision, however, human science data make up for in richness and relevance to the ways that human beings actually experience themselves and the world (Polkinghorne 1983). Thus despite the variability and uncertainties of such data, they nevertheless represent meaningful, information-bearing, code-using phenomena that exhibit such properties as wholeness, coherence of parts, structure, determinacy, and interpretability (Rogers 1981).

Freud (1901) emphasized that what we are looking for in the therapeutic process is unconscious material, but that to discover it we have to follow a long path through a complicated series of associations. The question then arises: Where is the unconscious material to be found in clinical data? Does everything the patient says during free association contain latent meanings, or is unconscious material found in some associations but not in others? Freud's (1912) answer was unequivocal: "Every single association, every act of the person under treatment . . . represents a compromise between the forces that are striving towards recovery and the opposing ones" (p. 103). In his paper, "The Unconscious," Freud (1915) wrote that the Unconscious exerts a constant influence on the Preconscious, which seems consistent with his earlier statement that every single association represents a compromise between the two systems.

Varieties of Clinical Data

Inquiry in the human and social sciences requires large amounts and wide varieties of data, partly because the variability of phenomena in these fields is much greater than in the physical sciences (cf. Chassan 1957), and also because the construal and justification of latent meanings and determinants often depend on the recognition of relations and patterns (e.g., repetitions) in the data (Polkinghorne 1983).

The clinical literature contains many suggestions regarding specific types of data that individual investigators consider particularly revealing—the most noteworthy being Freud's (1900) reference to dreams as the "royal road" to the Unconscious. I maintain, however, that there is no *via reggia*. All varieties of clinical data work together to produce contextual meanings. It is not the dream alone, for example, but the timing, context, and manner in which the dream is told, the patient's extensive and varied associations to the dream, and the therapist's equally diverse responses to the associations, including inferences, which suggest its possible latent meanings and determinants (Freud 1913, Grinstein 1983, Kris Study Group 1967).

Thus no particular type of data lends more credibility to an interpretation than others. No single variety of clinical data, nor any particular combination of data types, constitutes a *sine qua non* of interpretive relevance. Although a single element of clinical data sometimes provides the initial clue to a possible construction—an odd choice of words, a slip of speech, a gesture, a catch in the voice, a suggestive dream image—one does not construct latent themes from a single clue (Dowling 1987, Rangell 1987).

Empirical data produced by patients include *verbal reports* of experiences including thoughts, memories, perceptions, feelings, impulses, urges, and desires; *images* in dreams, fantasies, and daydreams; *"process"* data dealing with how verbal language is used, how the patient relates to the therapist, and shifts in content, direction, mood, or emphasis; *language usage* such as idioms, tropes, clichés, and slang; and *verbal relations* including parallels, contrasts, contiguities, analogies, repetitions, and sequences. With respect to tropes, Arlow (1979) notes the use of metaphor in all science, and refers to clinical disciplines such as psychoanalysis and dynamic psychotherapy as "metaphorical exercises"—mutual communications of metaphors between patient and analyst (cf. also Shengold, 1981; but see also G. Klein 1973, Leites 1971, Schafer 1976, Stoller 1971, who object to their use and especially to their reification). Rangell (1985) argues, on the other hand, that if one avoids confusing ideas with things, reification does not occur.

Paraverbal data produced by patients include the prosodic features of tone, pitch, and melody, rate and rhythm of speech, and variable smoothness of delivery. *Nonverbal* data from the patient include posture, gait, gestures, facial expressions, and repetitive movements. *Affective* data may reveal themselves either directly or indirectly.

Additional empirical data *generated by the therapist* include his or her introspectable reactions to the patient, for example, thoughts, associations, memories, perceptions, feelings, impulses, urges, desires, images, moods, affects, fantasies, dreams, kinesthetic and motor phenomena, and vegetative reactions—specifically as these relate to the patient. Countertransference phenomena are not empirical data, but inferences from the data. Schafer (2000) believes that as analysis progresses, mutual processes of projective and introjective identification produce an interpenetration of analyst and patient so that all clinical data are a mixture of the two.

The Basic Interpretable Unit of Clinical Data

The basic interpretable unit of clinical data refers to the minimal amount and variety of empirical data required for depth psychological interpretation. The basic unit must achieve a balance between an adequate sample of clinical data, on the one hand, and an amount that can be assimilated and processed fairly rapidly and completely, on the other. Information theorists point out, for example, that one of the major difficulties in complex forms of problem solving results from the relatively large number of possible solutions that must be considered. An important approach to solving complex problems, therefore, is to "reduce the size of the problem space so that it can be searched in a reasonable time" (Newell et al., 1962, p. 105). In the case of clinical interpretations, the individual therapy session usually provides both an adequate and manageable amount of data for construing latent meanings and determinants that are dynamically most active and emergent at a given time (cf. Freud 1913, French, 1952, 1954, 1958a, b, Gill and Hoffman 1982, Rangell 1987)—keeping in mind, however, that as in the interpretation of a dream, the data of a therapy session must be understood also in the larger context of the ongoing therapeutic process, especially other recent sessions (Freud 1911b; see also Shapiro 1994). Each session provides a unique current sample of clinical data that to some extent stands on its own, while simultaneously mediating between the preceding and subsequent sessions of the therapeutic process.

The methodologic significance of the foregoing conclusion is this: If one views the entire therapy session as the usual unit of interpretable data, differences in the specific varieties of empirical data become less important. No one type of clinical data is singled out and interpreted in isolation from the rest, for meaning is defined in terms of contextual relations among the various data. The diverse data of a therapy session serve as "commentaries" on and contexts for each other (Rogers 1981), which contribute to their joint as well as respective meanings and provide a network of interrelated meanings on which to base alternative constructions (cf. Rapaport 1944, Wittgenstein 1967). Hence Michels' (1983) conclusion that "there is nothing the patient thinks, says, or does that does not serve as a basis for interpretation" (p. 65; see also McDougall in Raymond and Rosbrow-Reich 1997). To illustrate: Conigliaro (1997) emphasizes the following heuristic sequence in his approach to dream interpretation: first, understanding the dream *session*; then, within that context, attempting to understand the dream; and, finally, responding to the dream.

Sources of Clinical Data

The construction of alternative hypotheses necessitates the acquisition of as much information as possible (Arnoult and Anderson 1988). To that end, patients in psychoanalysis and dynamic psychotherapy are encouraged to employ the method of free association, which generates voluminous amounts of clinical data; and therapists augment their patients' associations still further by employing the complementary strategy of "freely hovering attention." The latter process is discussed in the following chapter.

Freud is usually credited with originating the method of free association, but Zilboorg (1952) notes that Francis Galton (1879–80) had described the method earlier, and had used it effectively on himself. Galton concluded that free associations "lay bare the foundations of man's thoughts with curious distinctness and exhibit his mental anatomy with more vividness and truth than he would probably care to publish to the world" (p. 162).

Freud's rationale for employing free association was fairly complex and changed over time. Combining his assumptions about psychic unity, the dynamic nature of the unconscious, and the concept of associations based on latent wishes, Freud (1893) theorized originally that repressed ideas can influence waking thoughts by association—for example, by increasing the vividness of certain conscious thoughts and thus the patient's conscious communication of free associations necessarily reveals unconscious connections (1900, 1912). That line of reasoning led to the concept of "unconscious thematism" that Freud postulated in spontaneous associations (Dalbiez 1941), and to the methods of free association by the patient and evenly suspended attention by the therapist (Rapaport 1944).

Freud (1900) proposed an additional rationale for free association by comparing the patient's renunciation of reflection with the state of falling asleep; that is, "involuntary ideas" emerge under both conditions. Reduction of conscious control that organizes and directs waking thought results in the emergence of more dream-like, imagistic thought and associations (Waelder 1960). Blum (1976) thus refers to free association as a "regression in the service of analysis" (p. 320); and Edelson (1988) notes that free association involves a special state of mind in which connections among mental contents are much more extensively influenced by primary processes than in ordinary states of consciousness.

Rosner (1973) describes the nature of free association this way:

> A thought presents itself to the patient. This thought stimulates another thought, which stimulates another thought (c, d, e, . . . , z). These thoughts are related to each other, each exerting an influence on succeeding thoughts. These thoughts proceed from the "top down"—i.e., from the more ego-controlled to the less ego-controlled, from the more defended to the less defended, from the more conscious to the less conscious. [p. 558]

> Psychoanalytic technique is based on the [further] assumption that there is a connection between each succeeding session (if not in manifest, then in latent content). Thus the content, affects, and ideas from one session can be the stimulus for the idea that presents itself at the beginning of the next hour. . . . The Zeigarnik (1927) effect demonstrates that a quasi tension state is aroused so that the subject returns to an interrupted task in order to relieve the tension. Similar tensions may be aroused in the therapeutic session. A tension continues from one session to the next because of unfinished business to be continued or completed at the following session. [p. 560]

Drawing on Gestalt concepts regarding the development of insight, Rosner continues:

> Thoughts lead to other thoughts by means of similarity. Whether it be on the manifest and/or latent level, the connecting link is that of similarity. The Höffding (1901) function demonstrates that for recall to occur, the way must be prepared by the selective effect of similarity. . . . When, in [treatment] a patient is talking about a contemporary situation, e.g., with his boss (c) and then with his teacher (d) and this, in turn, leads to ideas about his father (b), the association takes place by means of similarity. . . . It is probable (though untested) that the Höffding function does not operate only for conscious thoughts. Henle (1961) [a Gestalt psychologist] points out that in order for repressed material to emerge in dreams and symptoms the memory traces must still be intact. Rather, there would seem to be a disturbance in the interaction between process and trace which

is based upon similarity. This interaction is the basis for recognition. [p. 565]

In his comprehensive survey of the literature on free association, Mahony (1979; see also Kanzer 1972) concludes that Freud's writings on free association did not progress very far beyond his early concepts that suspension of conscious purposive ideas results in their replacement by concealed purposive ideas; that conscious associations are displaced substitutes for suppressed, deeper ideas; and that superficial associations may disguise either the contents of or connections between deeper thoughts (cf. Freud 1900).

Freud's comparison of renouncing reflection with the state of falling asleep, however, and its implication of a "controlled regression" (discussed further below), presaged a gradual shift in his later thinking about the rationale of free associations in the interpretive process. As he moved from an id (prestructural, topographic) to an ego (structural) psychology, he began to conceive of free association in terms of the need to generate large amounts and wide varieties of clinical data in order to facilitate the inference and interpretation of unconscious meanings and determinants (see, e.g., Freud 1929, Kanzer 1972, Loewenstein 1971). Leavy (1980) considers the latter view a much more sophisticated conception of both free association and depth psychological interpretation than the earlier more mechanistic and linear analogy of free association as a chain of ideas leading step by step to underlying meanings.

In later writings (e.g., 1925c), Freud claimed the following advantages for free associations: providing an inexhaustible supply of data; exposing the patient to the least amount of compulsion; avoiding the introduction of expectations by the analyst; a saving of labor for both patient and analyst; maintaining contact with the actual current situation; and guaranteeing that no factor in the patient's neurosis would be overlooked.

Loewald (in Panel 1971) suggested that free association has the added advantage of making multiple meanings appear more clearly. Loewenstein (in Seidenberg 1971) noted, on the other hand, that one of the limitations of free association is the use of the method by some patients as resistance—for example, by giving meticulously precise accounts of symptoms and life history. In another type of resistance, the patient jumps from one thought to another, expressing emotions easily but being barely intelligible—that is, giving expression without description. In the illustrative case presented in the next chapter, the patient's odd way of free associating included the latter type of resistance, and yet the brief phrases that he strung together could be interpreted not only as resistance but also as disguised expressions of latent conflicts and defenses.

Reis (1951) compared interpretations of dreams with and without associations to elements of the dreams. Somewhat surprisingly, interpretations based on the dream imagery alone largely agreed with those based on imagery plus associations. Reis concluded, however, that free association to the elements of a dream adds important information to what can be derived from manifest contents alone (cited by Fisher and Greenberg 1977). Stoller (1979) comments: "More and more I think success in analysis depends on the patient's need to be honest" (p. 65).

Anton Kris (1982) has revived (controversially) Freud's (1893) original concepts that psychopathology involves limitations to the freedom of associations, and that an important aim of treatment should be to focus on and reduce such limitations. Kris notes the varieties of free association and therapeutic discourse that occur in the clinical situation, and describes differences in the form, quality, style, modality, and functions of free associations. To account for these differences, he attempts to correlate the varieties of free associations with their underlying "organizing principles"—for example, internal conflict, an emerging memory, enduring traits of character, and others. He concludes that much of the time

> the analytic hour does not yield a sharply definable single determinant. In such hours one can delineate, nonetheless, a number of trends at work determining the free associations. One of the ordinary tensions in the analytic process is the conflict between a focus on one main determinant of the associations or several operating at once. [pp. 10–11]

The case reports presented in the following chapter illustrate, however, that despite the differences in form, quality, and style of discourse, the patient's associations in each case appeared to support Freud's (1923a) conclusion that unconscious thoughts emerge in the associations as "allusions to one particular theme" (p. 239). The thematization or "focalization" of psychodynamics in free associations, dreams, and other clinical data is illustrated and discussed further in the following three chapters.

Freud (1931) referred to free association as "the most important contribution made by psychoanalysis, the methodologic key to its results" (p. 403; see also 1922; Barratt 1990). The case reports in this and subsequent chapters illustrate that the interpretive process relies on numerous varieties of free associations and other clinical data that tend to converge on a common theme.

SUMMARY

This chapter has focused on certain empirical components of the interpretive process, namely, the many varieties of clinical data, and the basic interpretable unit of clinical data. (Empirical methods of clinical observation are discussed and illustrated in the following chapter). The empirical data of depth psychological therapies consist of observable phenomena—what the patient actually says and does during therapy sessions, and what the therapist perceives introspectively in his own reactions to the patient's material. No single variety of clinical data, nor any particular combination of data types, constitutes a *sine qua non* of interpretive relevance. All varieties of clinical data are probative at different times, in various combinations, and in diverse contexts.

To generate and gather as much information as possible, patients in psychoanalysis and dynamic psychotherapy are encouraged to employ the method of free association, which produces voluminous amounts of often highly relevant clinical data. Therapists augment patients' associations still further by employing the complementary strategy of "freely hovering attention." Freud's reasons for considering free association the key to psychoanalysis, and his rationale for employing free association and evenly suspended attention, have been reviewed.

Two case reports have been presented to illustrate some of the many varieties and sometimes unusual types of free associations that clinicians encounter in their interpretive work. The illustrative cases also demonstrate Freud's (1923a) concept that unconscious thoughts emerge in the patient's associations as "allusions to one particular theme" (p. 239). Typically, interpretations derive from multiple varieties of clinical data that converge on a common theme.

In clinical practice, therapists tend to base their interpretations largely, although not entirely, on the data of individual therapy sessions. That is, therapists attempt to identify, formulate, and justify latent meanings and determinants that, for the most part, are immanent and thematic in the data of immediate and recent therapy sessions. The individual therapy session thus appears to represent the basic unit of interpretable data.

CHAPTER FOUR

Empirical Strategies: Methods of Observing and Recording Clinical Data

$\mathcal{B}$REUER AND FREUD's (1895) *Studies on Hysteria* introduced a new kind of clinical observation in psychiatry. Charcot's approach with patients, by contrast, was somewhat distant and aloof; but Breuer and Freud listened attentively and painstakingly to the language and stories of their patients (Grubrich-Simitis 1995; cf. also Fiumara 1990, who reports the relative lack of such studies in the human sciences generally, the latter being devoted mainly to listening rather than focused on expressive activities).

The therapist's field of empirical observation includes the patient's verbal reports of experiences (Ricoeur 1977), paraverbal and nonverbal accompaniments of the patient's verbal reports, and what the therapist is able to perceive introspectively in his or her own conscious reactions to the patient's material. We do not observe drives, defenses, transferences, and the like; we observe the patient's speech and overt behavior, and our own consciously introspectable responses. Everything else is inferred (Meehl 1973), which includes the interpretive activities of data processing, construction, and justification—discussed in Chapters 5 through 7.

The social science methodologist Paul Diesing (1971) notes that the main problem with observation is observer bias. All of the observer's theories, hypotheses, interests, experiences, and beliefs affect his perceptions and interpretations. This does not mean that observations are to be discarded as invalid, but the problem of biases must be taken into account by comparisons with observations from different perspectives.

ILLUSTRATIVE CASE

This case provides an opportunity to compare an earlier psychotherapeutic phase of the patient's treatment with a later analytically oriented approach that emphasized free association.

The patient was a 60-year-old, depressed college administrator whom I shall call "the professor." He was referred to me for psychotherapy after he had failed to respond to pharmacotherapy and electroconvulsive therapy (ECT). The depression developed insidiously during his mother's terminal illness a year previously, and became full blown within a month after her death. His symptoms were classically depressive, with melancholy mood, tiredness, anorexia, and insomnia (early morning awakening). Other symptoms included handwashing and other compulsive rituals, premature ejaculation, and hypochondria focused on his heart. He described himself as a "virtual cardiac cripple" due to frequent anginal attacks, but a report from his internist indicated that his cardiac function was normal. Despite his symptoms he had continued working, but for the most part he simply hid in his office with the door closed and got very little work done.

His past personal history suggested that he was sensitive and over-reactive to experiences of feeling burdened by demands and expectations of him. He was the youngest of three sons whose parents had immigrated to this country from Eastern Europe. His father had become very successful in business—so much so that he had little time for his family. He encouraged his older sons to work at his business from early ages, but insisted that the patient remain at home as companion and helper to his mother. In other words, he was assigned the role of "daughter" in the family—a role that we came to recognize had been a great burden to him.

His mother was severely neurotic: depressive, compulsive, and hypochondriacal about her heart—the latter keeping the patient alarmed and guilty about her health throughout his childhood. Worst of all, she burdened him with bitter weeping and complaints about his father's neglect of her. He envied his brothers, but was resigned to his own fate in the family. He did well in school, was shy socially, had few friends, and had never developed any hobbies. He was very inhibited sexually, not having had sexual relations until after marriage, and then finding himself impotent. Despite his sexual problem, the marriage appeared to have been relatively stable. He was very dependent on his wife and passively accepted her leadership of the family. The couple had managed to have several children, all of whom had had fairly extensive psychiatric treatment.

When I first saw the professor, it did not occur to me that an analytically oriented approach might be applicable. He seemed too ill for that. My plan for his therapy was to promote the development of rapport, and then to use the leverage of his positive transference for therapeutic manipulation of defenses. Within the first few months of treatment a positive transference became evident, and a possible strategy for manipulation of defenses presented itself. I learned that he had not mourned his mother's death. He denied that her death was that meaningful to him, insisting that he had lost any love for or attachment to her years ago. Yet an occasional comment or slip of speech suggested that he felt guilty about not grieving.

[I reminded him that even though he had become disenchanted with his mother in later years, he had never stopped behaving conscientiously and dutifully toward her. Whatever she asked of him, he did. I then asked him what she would expect of him now, after her death?] He replied that she would expect him to say the Kaddish prayers. [In that case, I advised him firmly, you had better say them.] He protested that he had not been in a temple for years, and wouldn't know how to do it. [Then get a regular member of the congregation to teach you, I insisted.] Dynamically, I was depending on the power of his positive transference, and his identification with his mother's expectations of him, to motivate him in a direction that might activate mourning.

After several weeks of obsessive procrastination and alternating ambivalence, he finally acquiesced to my urging that he do what his mother would expect of him. He attended early morning services at a temple where an old "regular" helped him with the Kaddish prayers. Within two weeks

grieving about his mother set in, and after another couple of weeks a remission of his depression ensued.

Following the remission of his depression, I did not see the professor for about a year. The remission might have lasted longer had it not
been for the occurrence of another life experience that struck his Achilles heel of feeling burdened. The college where he held an administrative
position had expanded his department, more than doubling his work load
and responsibilities. He slid slowly and inexorably into another depression, and returned to me again for help. It now appeared that although
activating the delayed mourning about his mother's death had relieved
one aspect of his pathology, his hypersensitivity to feeling burdened had
not been touched and would continue predisposing him to depressive
episodes as long as it remained unresolved.

At that point I began wondering whether a more uncovering, analytically oriented form of treatment might have a chance of reaching and
resolving, or at least reducing, his "burdensome mother" complex. [I discussed the possibility with the professor], who, after obtaining his wife's
approval (!), agreed to a trial period of analytically oriented psychotherapy.

His method of free associating was unusual. Rather than speaking
in sentences expressing more or less complete thoughts, as patients generally do during free association, his thoughts were almost entirely in the
form of brief phrases consisting of no more than two or three words. The
phrases themselves were strung together in what seemed on the surface
to be a random sequence. I found this style of free associating both baf-
fling and intriguing. In twenty-five years of practicing psychoanalysis and
dynamic psychotherapy, I had never heard free associations of that kind.
On the one hand, it seemed consistent with his compulsiveness generally
and, more specifically, with his meticulous way of choosing words. On
the other hand, there was something inventive and somewhat playful about
this style of thinking and communicating, which seemed out of character
for him—less compulsive, less conforming than his habitual way of thinking, speaking, and acting.

The professor himself was surprised and more than a little disturbed
by his odd way of free associating. On questioning, he stated that he had
never experienced such persistent phrase-making previously, although he

recalled that when not depressed he often enjoyed playing word games, punning, and picking up on the subtle nuances of words and phrases that other people used. He also indicated that many of the phrases that came to his mind during free association were unfamiliar to him, and often made no sense to him. One of the reasons that he felt disturbed by thinking and speaking in that way was because it did not seem fully under his control, whereas characteristically he attempted to control his thoughts and speech very carefully.

The following example of his unusual style of free associating illustrates both the surface obscurities and interpretable latent contents of his speech and thought stream. He did not pause very long between the phrases—no longer than one would between sentences in normal speech. In other words, the phrases were strung together with surprising rapidity:

> Cloudy sky . . . ominous portents . . . closed mind . . . Pandora's box . . . obligatory clause . . . necessarily close . . . close-closed . . . pitty-pat . . . perfect harmony . . . parallel patterns . . . peas in a pod . . . P's for penises . . . protected part . . . desultory danger . . . demon detective . . . cardinal clue . . . secret suspicion . . . murder will out . . . dastardly deed . . . rapacious rascality . . . rotten rat . . . dirty deal . . . difficult decision . . . close down . . . hush money . . . safety first . . . outrageous fortune . . . clamorous demands . . . permanent punishment . . . peaceful settlement . . . closed book . . . case closed . . . pious purity . . . disgusting solution . . . dishonest doings . . . Holy cow . . . promise anything . . . morganatic marriage . . .

[I interrupted the professor at that point to ask if he knew what a "morganatic marriage" is]. He had the feeling that he knew what it means, but could not remember it. [I took a dictionary from the shelf and read the definition: "A type of marriage in which the spouse and children of the marriage do not share in a wealthy or aristocratic person's estate or titles."] The professor saw at once a connection with his mother's estate. She had drastically reduced the inheritances of her children to a minimum in order to establish and endow a foundation in her own name. The professor had denied repeatedly that he resented his mother's doing that, or that he felt burdened by her appointing him to the difficult and demanding position of managing the foundation.

The foregoing associations, however, appeared to suggest how much the professor struggled intrapsychically with attempts to repress his ambivalence and guilt toward his mother regarding her estate, his reduced inheritance, and the responsibilty for managing her foundation. Allusions to her estate and the foundation appear in phrases like "hush money," "outrageous fortune," "dirty deal," and "morganatic marriage." Some possible genetic origins of the guilt-laden ambivalence toward his mother are suggested by phrases like "dastardly deed," "rapacious rascality," "clamorous demands," "rotten rat," and "murder will out"—that is, avaricious, acquisitive, oral-sadistic feelings and fantasies toward his mother and her estate.

The initial associations of "cloudy sky," "ominous portents," "closed mind," and "Pandora's box" suggest anxiety and conflict between the demands of the analytic process to open up his mind ("Pandora's box") versus keeping it safely closed (repressed). He appeared to allude further to this conflict in his associations of "desultory danger" (desultory meaning "passing aimlessly from one thing or subject to another," as in free association); "demon detective" (the analyst); "cardinal clue" (which may be revealed to the "demon detective" by free association); and "secret suspicion" (which may imply that he thinks the analyst might already suspect what he is hiding). Immediately following the latter series of associations, which suggests a dynamic connection by its contiguity, his next thought was "murder will out," accompanied by references to "dastardly deed," "rapacious rascality," and "rotten rat," which appear to be self-judgments of crime and guilt ("permanent punishment").

Commentary

Some strategies that contributed to the latent meanings that I have posited in the professor's free associations include (1) the important factor of the *context* in which the associations occurred, that is, we had been exploring how he felt about the reduction of his inheritance, and about his mother's burdening him with the management of her foundation; (2) the *analogic similarities* between some of his free associative phrases and their possible affective connotations, for example, the possible allusions of the initial four phrases to anxiety and conflict about opening up his mind versus keeping it "closed"; and (3) the *sequential contiguities* between certain groups of phrases, for example, the suggestive contiguity between the phrases "desultory danger," "demon detective," "cardinal clue," and "secret suspicion," on the one hand, and the immediately following group of phrases "murder will out," "dastardly deed," "rapacious rascality," and "rotten rat," on the other.

To illustrate the professor's ability to use and to benefit from a free associative approach, an analytic type of therapeutic process developed with the gradual unfolding of a transference neurosis, including interpretable resistances and defenses, and some effective working through of conflicts and defenses on both transference and genetic levels. For example, an important phase of working through occurred in the context of a negative transference to me, which developed in association with feeling competitive toward other patients for my favor. In a dream during that period he was trying to get elected to a high position, but he was afraid that the opposition would discover information about his depression, "which was created—I mean treated—by you." The slip implied that I had caused his depression. In the course of therapeutic work on this slip, intense ambivalence toward me emerged in the form of the following transference phantasies: (1) My casual lifestyle and clothing made him doubt that I could be a "top-flight analyst" (cf. he had always felt that his mother was inferior because of her lack of education and the unstylish clothes she wore). (2) I had prolonged his depression by using a long-term method of treatment that benefited me financially (cf. he felt exploited by his mother for her own advantage). (3) He felt he could not express such negative feelings toward me because I might then withhold the emotional support and care he needed (cf. he had always felt unable to speak up or complain to his mother for fear of losing her support and favor). The implication that I had "created" his depression thus appeared to represent a displaced and projected transference to me of repressed hostile blame toward his mother for his suffering.

As the working-through process continued, now on a genetic as well as transference level, he began to develop new insight into his extensive identifications with his mother and her neurotic behavior: One of the hardest things for him to face, he said, was the realization of how much like his mother he was—even to his "*verkrempt*" (downcast, scowling) facial expression. He realized now that he had always assumed a fake smile, trying to cover up a *verkrempt* look, so people would not think him sad, lonely, or neurotic like his mother. He also made a connection at this point between his handwashing compulsion and a similar symptom of his mother's, that is, her obsession with germs and compulsive cleaning. Soon after this he recognized his identification with his mother's cardiac hypochondria.

As further signs of improvement appeared, he referred to the "machine tool progress" of his treatment, because it "grinds slowly but with great precision." He began to experience hope that this form of treatment might help him overcome his symptom of impotence. Compare, for example, the following dream: He and a girl went to a garage to get a "Passover car," some kind of mechanical toy. Every time they played with it the toy car could do more and more. It came out of a tunnel, a small opening. He and the girl had a lot of fun with it. But it could not be controlled perfectly; it would run down. They ran it across the lawn, and someone made a derogatory remark about it; but he and the girl demonstrated that it could go even farther and do even more. His associations to this dream included resentment toward his wife, who at times expressed exasperation at his premature ejaculation, and also toward his mother for treating him like a daughter rather than appreciating his masculine potential.

OBSERVING AND RECORDING CLINICAL DATA

Methods of Clinical Observation

Various types of observational strategies are available to interpreters, their differences being based on the following factors: (1) the sensory modality of observation, that is, whether auditory, visual, or mixed; (2) the relative objectivity or subjectivity of observations; (3) the number of observational methods employed; and (4) whether observations are focused or unfocused. These differences are discussed separately.

Auditory, Visual, and Mixed Observation

We tend to think of our perceptual activities in the therapeutic situation as predominantly auditory (cf. Bernfeld 1941, Edelheit 1969, Isakower 1939, Lilleskov in Panel 1977), but a substantial amount of visual observation also occurs—for example, of nonverbal communication in the form of posture, body movements, and gestures (see Birdwhistell 1970, Dittman and Wynne 1961, Ekman 1965, Jacobs 1982, 1994, Lilleskov 1977, Kanzer 1961, Mahl 1987, Mahl and Schulze 1964, Scheflen 1973). More will be said about auditory perception in a later discussion of listening strategies; the present discussion focuses mainly on visual and mixed observation.

Anthony (in Lilleskov 1977) writes that "a stream of communication, nonverbal and verbal, flows from every person at every moment as a function of self-expression, information, and interaction." As development proceeds, "the verbal system gradually assumes predominance while the nonverbal one undergoes recession"; but "complementarity is involved, with each modality proffering a commentary on the others" (pp. 694–695). George Mahl, a pioneer in the study of both vocal and nonverbal behavior, reports that many nonverbal actions observed during depth psychological treatments are not just alternative ways of remembering in the service of resistance, as Freud maintained, but are integral to recollection and verbalization. He describes the following sequence associated with such phenomena: "A person talking about one thing performs an action that is not obviously related to what he is saying; he then spontaneously mentions something else that is thematically linked to the the first topic and clearly related to the former action; the action has anticipated the verbalization" (in Lilleskov 1977, pp. 696–697; see also Mahl 1987). Mahl illustrates this sequence with the following clinical example:

> Near the end of the third year of his analysis, a young man worried aloud about anticipated criticism of his marital life from his mother, removed the pillow from under his head, and placed it against the wall for about a minute before replacing it. Two sessions later he recalled an episode in adolescence when his mother discovered him masturbating against a pillow and punished him by taking away his pillow for years. The analysis of

this episode and related conflicts involved very significant aspects of his life and analysis. [In Lilleskov 1977, p. 697]

Mahl concludes that "the frequency with which one can observe the regular progression from a bodily expression to primitive ideation to eventual verbalization suggests that these are some of the usual transitional stages in the process of something becoming conscious" (p. 699). He suggests that if the therapist observes some nonverbal behavior that is unusual for a particular patient, it can be useful to ask himself: "'Will I hear something that will make this nonverbal behavior comprehensible?' These observations of nonverbal behavior can be used fruitfully if the analyst waits and does not jump in on it as a resistance" (p. 705).

Furer (in Lilleskov 1977) cautions against the assumption that nonverbal behavior is a more primitive form of communication merely because it develops earlier than speech. He points out that nonverbal actions may reflect the highest levels of thought and language. Kanzer (1961) notes similarly that some therapists mistakenly assume that all nonverbal communication is preverbal, whereas both verbal and nonverbal communications can express a continuum of mental contents from archaic to advanced. In addition, Birdwhistell's (1970) investigations of gestures have led to the discovery of parallels between kinesic and language structures. The kinesic system employs forms that are very similar to words in language: body behaviors that function like sounds combine into complex units like words, or into longer structures like sentences or even paragraphs. Also like words, the same body movements can be used to communicate different meanings; thus a specific movement does not always express the same meaning.

Turning to the psychophysiology of perception, in a psychoanalytic study of the visual function, Barglow and Sadow (1971) cite George Klein's (1959) concept that perception is the end product of a four stage sequence: stimulation; registration; ordering of sensory events according to a preexisting memory framework; and, finally, perception, which emerges passively into consciousness as an image, percept, action, or verbalization. According to the alternative "analysis-by-synthesis" model, however, human perception is not just stimulus- or data-driven, but shifts rapidly back and forth between centrally generated expectations, on the one hand, and confirmations or disconfirmations based on incoming stimuli, on the other—a process of very rapid "generate-and-test cycles" (Dennett 1991, Neisser 1967). Applying the latter model to our perceptions of patients in the therapeutic situation, our clinical observations are not based solely on what patients say and do, but result also from a stream of preconscious anticipations that are checked against and modified by the patients' speech and actions (cf. Smith 1995). The latter model of clinical observation is analogous to Holland's (1978) description of the reading process: "We 'predict' our way through a text, eliminating alternatives to produce a single interpretation" (p. 193). The "analysis-by-synthesis" model appears to be applicable also to the interpretive phases of data processing, construction, and justification (discussed in Chapters 5, 6, and 7).

Other recent studies of human perception (e.g., Massaro 1998, Massaro and Storch 1998) suggest that visual information is often combined with auditory inputs in the brain, resulting in impressions that only seem auditory. We think we *hear* the message because spoken language is usually heard. Thus in speech perception utterances are inferred from a confluence of audible, visual, and other contextual sources of information—which in the therapeutic situation produces a mixed form of observation.

OBJECTIVE VERSUS SUBJECTIVE METHODS

Objective types of observation employ perceptual-cognitive methods, as in naturalistic observation, perception guided by general guiding concepts (background assumptions), and various focused forms of observation (discussed below). Subjective forms of observation include introspection, empathy, controlled regressive listening, phenomenologic experiencing, and various combinations of these several strategies. The therapist monitors both his objective observations of and subjective reactions to the patient's productions by the method of introspective self-observation. Arlow (1979) maintains, for example, that Freud "focused on the inner experience of the analyst as the guidepost to the proper understanding of the patient's mental life" (pp. 196–197). Rycroft (1969) suggests in this connection that clinical observation might best be classified as a "transitional activity" (in the sense of Winnicott's [1971] "transitional realm"), because it mediates between subjective and external reality, between selfhood and otherness.

In his history of scientific psychology, D. B. Klein (1970) emphasized that it is not always possible to establish a sharp line of distinction between the subjective and the objective, for all facts are not necessarily facts of material or physical existence. The concept of a scientific fact has both subjective and objective implications. Loewald (1970, cited by Teicholz 1999) anticipated postmodern, including intersubjective, viewpoints when he wrote that "to discover truth about the patient is always discovering it with him and for him as well as for ourselves and about ourselves. And it is discovering truth between each other, as the truth of human beings is revealed in their interrelatedness" (p. 65).

The subjective method of *empathy* has a long history in psychoanalysis, dynamic psychotherapy, and the interpretive process. Freud (1905) alluded to it early in his writings, and restated its importance in later works (1921, 1925). The method has received added emphasis during the past several decades by Kohut (1959), Greenson (1960), Beres (1968), Beres and Arlow (1974), Basch (1983), and others. Additional writings on the subject appear in the volumes edited by Lichtenberg et al. (1984). Recently Kainer (1999) has stressed the imaginative aspect of empathy.

Kohut's (1972–76) description of the empathic method coincided closely with the traditional psychoanalytic approach, that is: "We think ourselves into another person by various cues that we get from him, then we reconstruct his inner life as if we were that other person. In other words, we trust the resonance of the essential likeness of ourselves and the observed other" (p. 228; see also Rubovits-Seitz 1999). Although at times Kohut stressed the uniqueness and centrality of empathy (e.g., 1972–76, 1984), at other times he was more circumspect about its role in the interpretive process, delimiting its function to data collection and observation (e.g., 1971).

Spencer and Balter (1990) point out that both free association by the patient and evenly hovering attention by the therapist involve *controlled regression*—usually to the same general regressive level. They propose that both subjective and perceptual-cognitive methods of observation operate at a partially regressed level, which enhances the field of observation by providing clues to latent contents and how the latter affect manifest content (1990; see also Edelson 1988, Kanzer 1961, Olinick 1980, Poland 1984, Seidenberg 1971). Weinshel (in Raymond and Rosbrow-Reich 1997) describes his altered state during analytic work as like a dream while awake. Peterfreund (1971) suggested that the therapist's controlled regression enables him or her to fill in the patient's associations with a large amount of additional information from other sources—for example, from the empathic participant relationship with the patient; the therapist's own emotions, fantasies, and memories; empathy with other figures in the patient's life; and reactions to oneself as participant observer.

Factors that encourage partial regression in the patient include the basic rule to suspend the critical faculty, use of the couch, limitations of the patient's vision and motility, the therapist's relative silence and divulging relatively little about himself (in the traditional analytic approach)—all of which put the patient in a more child-like position in relation to the therapist (Kanzer 1961, Waelder 1960). The extent of the patient's regression is limited, however, by the requirement of verbalizing associations to the therapist—the "need to remain comprehensible" (Kris 1956, p. 450). The partial regression induced in the patient involves a shift away from purposeful reflection toward fantasy, which changes the formal qualities of thought from logical thinking to more dream-like imagery—a "primitivization of ego functions" (Kris 1950, p. 312; see also Balter et al. 1980).

Less is known about how therapists bring about such a state in themselves. Freud had nothing to say about this aspect of clinical observation. Leavy (Panel 1971) suggests that there is a "readiness" in the therapist's mind "and also an activity" to allow the patient's associations to be dissolved, and imagistic elements to be fragmented and then reconstituted in new syntheses. The mental activity alluded to by Leavy presumably includes (1) a partial suspension of the therapist's critical faculty, similar to the mind-set of patients during free association (cf. Reik 1937, 1949); (2) adopting a relatively unfocused mode

of listening (discussed below); (3) a shift in the analyst's defensive organization (Reik 1933, Smith 1995); (4) setting aside conscious expectations, which increases the potential for curiosity, surprise, and
discovery (Smith 1995); and (5) listening empathically. Regarding the
latter, Bachrach (1993) reports that the capacities for adaptive regression and for empathy are related; and Olinick (1980) stresses the regressive aspect of empathy itself.

Phenomenologic observational approaches employ mainly subjective
strategies, for example, phenomenologic experiencing of the patient as
"other," which utilizes but is not the same as empathy (Palmer 1969; see
also Thompson 1980, regarding the receptive function of the therapist).
Another phenomenologic approach to observation is descriptive, that is,
describing the phenomena more and more completely. A more radical
phenomenologic-existentialist approach is rarely applied by clinicians, and
only with certain types of patients. The method involves taking everything the patient says at face value, identifying with those appearances,
and accepting the patient's point of view completely. "Advocacy and a
partial identification with the patient replace everything that is objective,
rational and scientific" (Havens 1974, p. 9; cf. also Schwaber 1983a,b,
1986, 1995).

PLURALISTIC VERSUS MONISTIC OBSERVATIONAL APPROACHES

Due to the fact that the subject matter of depth psychology is so
complex, most observational approaches employ a pluralistic strategy.
Friedman (1988) stresses that "complex meaning requires complex attention" (p. 122); and Schafer (1970, cited by Friedman 1988) asserts
that the patient's associations should be looked at in as many ways as
possible. Freud's approach, for example, was decidedly pluralistic (Eissler
1963, Meissner 1971, Rubovits-Seitz 1988a). A smaller group of approaches employs a monistic approach that emphasizes a single observational method—e.g., Kohut's (1984) insistence that empathy is the only
useful method of clinical observation. An increasing number of Kohut's
followers, however, now accept that "information obtained through external observational methods should be recognized, correlated, and inte-

grated with empathically-derived theories" (Leider 1989, p. xiv; see also Basch 1984a,b, Galatzer-Levy 1991, Goldberg 1988, Lichtenberg 1981, Shane and Shane 1993). Emphasizing a single strategy of observation can be useful if employed intermittently, as one among a number of methods; but when applied continually and exclusively, a single approach is less capable of identifying the plurality and interrelations of latent meanings and determinants. Levenson (1981) points out, for example, that there is no one right way to hear the material. In addition, pluralistic approaches serve as checks on each other and compensate for the limitations of individual strategies.

FOCUSED VERSUS UNFOCUSED OBSERVATION

Freud's (1923a) strategy of "evenly suspended attention" is a largely, though never completely, unfocused form of observation (Gardner 1991, Reik 1949). The therapist listens simultaneously with partially focused attention for clues to conflict, manifestations of resistances, the relative strengths of interacting motives, and repetitions of past experiences in the present (cf. Smith 1990). Shapiro (1991) emphasizes that we also listen attentively for words and meanings that have affective valence.

Another common form of focused observation is pattern-seeking, often suggested by parallels, contrasts, contiguities, and repetitions in the data. For example, Strenger (1991) describes a widely used method of focused observation (and inference) for recognizing two levels of intra-psychically determined, idiosyncratic patterns in the patient's ways of thinking, feeling, and acting. First,

> the information the patient provides about his behavior, feelings and thoughts in his daily life. The analyst comes to know quite a bit about his patient's habitual ways of leading his life, and he can scan this information for recurring indications of relatively inflexible, subjectively determined patterns. Second, he does the same with the patient's fantasies, feelings, expectations, wishes, etc., which relate to the analyst himself. These may be voiced explicitly (and the patient is encouraged to do so), or they may be implied by the way the patient talks and relates to the analyst. [pp. 78–79; see also Edelson 1984, Rubovits-Seitz 1998, Spence 1995]

Langs (1978) proposes three levels of focused listening: (1) manifest content, which necessarily engages much of the therapist's attention; (2) latent contents in the form of so-called type I derivatives, which link present material with unconscious fantasies and past experiences; and (3) latent implications in the form of type II derivatives, which concern the patient's unconscious perceptions of here-and-now interactions with the therapist. Only the first of these three postulated levels represents empirical observation, however; the second and third levels are inferential and thus involve data-processing operations.

Listening Strategies

Freud (1923a) wrote that unfocused listening often makes it possible to "catch the drift" of the patient's latent thoughts. A number of writers since Freud (e.g., Diamond 1983, Edelson 1988, Kanzer 1961, Olinick 1980, Peterfreund 1971, Poland 1984, Seidenberg 1971, Spencer and Balter 1990) have suggested that the therapist's evenly hovering attention involves a mental state of controlled regression that facilitates experiencing events more as the patient experiences them. Freely hovering attention in a state of partial regression involves a reduction of discursive, linear thinking, allowing the therapist to listen more nonlinearly to the patient's "presentational" symbols (Langer 1942) metaphors, and other figures of speech (Leavy 1980). "Presentational" symbols contain multiple meanings condensed in a single analogical expression that is understood intuitively, nondiscursively, as a whole. The processing of clinical data, including metaphorical expressions, is discussed in Chapter 5.

Arlow (1979) describes the operation of evenly hovering attention this way: Sooner or later the therapist's initially unfocused, passive-receptive mode of listening is disturbed by the intrusion of a thought, feeling, or fantasy-image, which the therapist notices (introspectively) because at first it seems to differ from what the patient had been saying. Soon after experiencing the response, however, the therapist may recognize a meaningful relation between the intruding content and the patient's associations (see Kern 1978, Ross and Kapp 1962 for clinical examples).

The Sandlers (1998) emphasize that the method does not involve "'clearing of the mind' of thoughts or memories, but, rather the capacity to allow all sorts of thoughts, daydreams, and associations to enter the analyst's consciousness" (p. 50) while listening to the patient.

An experimental study by Spence and Grief (1970) concludes that evenly hovering attention may involve a process called "listening away" or partial listening. When we listen with evenly suspended attention we do not focus sharply on what the patient says; we half-listen to the patient, and half-listen to our own reactions and associations. Isakower (1992) suggests, for example, that evenly distributed attention hovers between what comes from the patient and what comes from the analyst. Partial listening of that kind, according to Spence and Grief, appears to facilitate the perception and registration of subliminal stimuli, which have more direct access to preconscious and unconscious mental processes in the listener. The gestalt concept of "restructuring interval" has some similarity to "listening away"; that is, insight often occurs when the clinician is not focusing on the immediate interpretive problem, which may result in a spontaneous (preconscious) restructuring of the problem (Rosner 1973; see also Chapter 6).

Another experimental study recorded electroencephalogram (EEG) activity during listening (Alpert et al. 1980). Clues were more likely to be recalled if the listener was in an alpha-wave state indicative of relaxation and unfocused attention. Clues were recalled even better by listeners engaged in more right hemisphere activity, presumably utilizing more imagistic, parallel processing, primary process thought.

Therapists' listening strategies have been addressed by a number of writers, beginning with Reik (1937, 1949; see also Heimann 1977, Lothane 1981). Listening in psychoanalysis and dynamic psychotherapy is generally believed to be of a special kind—with the "third ear," as Reik (1948) put it—and therapists do seem to listen more searchingly than anywhere else in life. There is something in our attitude, however, that goes beyond mere listening and passive availability. The silently listening therapist also transmits the message: "More! Go on! There is much more to tell about all this!" The therapist's silence and waiting patiently are thus an "expectant" form of listening, that is, an expecta-

tion that further associations will tend to clarify the patient's underlying problems.

Freedman (1983) emphasizes the "temporal" aspect of listening,
that is, as Freud (1923a) observed, listening is a process; thus what one
hears is often not understood until later. Freedman describes the "structure" of the listening process as a complex sequence of rhythmic alterna-
tions (or oscillations) between phases of receptiveness that are open to
multiple alternatives, followed by phases of distancing and restructuring
that involve a narrowing of attention, a reduction in the number of possible meanings, and an emphasis on objectification. Quantitatively, however, the clinician spends much more time (consciously) in the receptive
phase than in restructuring—the latter being mainly a form of preconscious processing (see Chapter 5).

Because we are better at describing how we ought to listen than
how we actually do listen, Brenneis (1994) has studied his own listening
process. He agrees with Gardner's (1991) observation regarding the idiosyncratic nature of listening, because "every mind is unique, not only by
content, but also by process, only a segment of which we consciously direct
and only a portion of which we consciously apprehend" (Brenneis 1994,
p. 31). Smith (1995) observes similarly that "we do a disservice to our
students and to ourselves with any idealisation of analytic listening, a
process which seems to me far more diverse and idiosyncratic than we
commonly acknowledge" (pp. 76–77).

Brenneis (1994) has identified two principal forms of listening in
himself: one mode that is mostly outside of awareness, automatic, and
highly personal involves "tagging and sorting" what he hears, and antici-
pating what he expects to hear. Superimposed over that form of listening
is a more conscious and directed mode in which he listens through "fil-
ters" that attempt to capture what he regards as clinically relevant material such as associations suggesting transference. Brenneis suspects that
the patient gradually identifies with the therapist's ways of listening, which
promotes the development of a capacity to listen to him- or herself with
a more open mind (see Chapter 9.)

With only a few exceptions—which include Kohut (1959, 1984),
who sometimes insisted that empathy is the only valid way of listening to

patients; Paul Gray (1973, 1982, 1994), who emphasizes an observational (but perhaps also partly and preconsciously inferential) focus on the immediate and detailed workings of the ego in its defensive activities against specific drive derivatives; and Schwaber (1983a,b, 1986, 1987b, 1990a,b, 1992), who stresses a sustained focus on the patient's perceptual reality, that is, how the patient perceives and experiences relationships and events—most of the writings on listening strategies have emphasized the strategy of pluralism (Rubovits-Seitz 1998). Pine (1988) proposes, for example, that the therapist's evenly hovering attention is informed and guided by the four overlapping perspectives of drive, ego, object relations, and self. Each perspective adds something to clinical understanding, and each is relevant to interpretive work.

Noting that the concept of multideterminism is one of the most important basic assumptions of psychoanalysis, Peterfreund (1983) pointed out that "any clinical example may require the use of multiple strategies, just as it may require invoking multiple working models. And, as with the working models, the strategies are not sharply or clearly differentiated. They overlap and interrelate, a reflection of the multifaceted nature of the phenomena that we observe" (p. 142). Rogers (1984) stresses the importance of listening "differentially," in both focused and unfocused modes. Focused listening, for example, is more context-supplying, bringing context to the patient's associations from the therapist's interpretive competence and experience.

Spence (1982a) concludes that "we have not yet arrived at a model of clinical listening which does justice to the intricacies of the process" (p. 152). He distinguishes between active and passive listening, and argues that passive free-floating attention is effective only when the patient's associations are relatively well-organized rather than fragmentary. The more usual fragmentary nature of the material produced by free associations (cf. the patient's brief phrases strung together in the illustrative case above) requires a more active, constructive (inferential) kind of listening. Spence asserts also that clinical listening is strongly influenced by the basic concept of continuity, which keeps us on the lookout for sequences, patterns, and coherence. Other variations in listening proposed by Spence include focusing alternatively on form and content (1982a), listening "to" versus listening "through" the patient's words (Spence 1980a,b); and listening "vertically" for hidden meanings as opposed to "horizontally" for repetitions of previous themes (Spence 1987).

Schwaber's (e.g., in Schuken 1990) method of listening involves a shift in outlook. The therapist does not assume that he or she already understands the patient's meanings but asks rather than tells, and raises questions about affects—in that way leaving room for the patient's experiences, which may not match the therapist's observations and expectations. Schwaber suggests that such an approach promotes autonomous reflection and interpretive collaboration by the patient.

In an evaluation of Schwaber's approach from the standpoint of Gadamer's (1975) hermeneutics, Phillips (1991) concludes that her method is valid and useful as long as it is viewed as one among a number of perspectives that contribute to interpretive methodology. Phillips emphasizes the "double hermeneutic" aspect of clinical interpretation; that is, clinical data are preinterpreted first by the patient, and then are reinterpreted secondarily by the therapist from the standpoint of his or her own interpretive competence. Gadamer's concept of a "fusion of horizons" suggests that the interpreter must employ his or her own perspective in attempting to understand the patient's horizon of meanings or self-interpretations, while also viewing the patient from the patient's own horizon. The differing horizons enter into dialectic dialogue with each other, which transforms both, leading to some degree of "horizonal fusion."

Herbert Schlesinger (1994) describes three modes of listening that he suggests, taken together, comprise the sense of evenly hovering attention. He believes that the clinician listens not only to receive information and to maintain contact, but also to prepare for the communication of interpretations to the patient (see also Ogden 1997). Thus therapists must appreciate the complexities of listening, which include the ability to listen in several modes at once. One such mode is listening contextually, much as one would listen to a close friend or family member; but if one listened only in that mode, most depth psychological information would be missed. Listening also in a "decontextual," naive, deconstructive mode tends to counteract the limitation of contextual listening. The third mode is listening for intention rather than content—that is, for the patient's purposes in saying what he does, which is revealed mainly by the way he says it. The latter mode involves listening for clues to transference. Free floating attention involves allowing one's attention to drift imperceptibly among these several modes of listening.

Additional writings on multiple listening perspectives and strategies include Chessick (1989, 1992), Cohen and Alpert (1981), Frederickson (1998), Hedges (1991), Kainer (1984), and Silverman (1986). An unresolved problem in the proposals of multiple listening perspectives is how to deal with and employ the different listening "channels" and strategies. Hedges (1983) writes in this connection:

> Uncritical eclecticism destroys the unique and powerful contribution which each style of listening has to offer. The emerging problem has become how to integrate the crucial contributions of many into a comprehensive and consistent framework while avoiding the pitfall of dilution through eclecticism. [pp. 1–2]

Hedges' way of dealing with this problem, which seems both clinically and methodologically sound, is to apply particular listening perspectives to the specific types of patients, or to the specific phases of the therapeutic process in the individual patient, in which each perspective is most effective. Some writers, however (e.g., Pine 1990, Silverman 1986) view their several perspectives as complementary and integratable. Chessick (1989), on the other hand, writes that his five proposed channels "contradict each other in fundamental ways, and they cannot at present be reconciled because they reflect profound disagreement about the nature of humans and the nature of knowledge itself" (p. 24). Golland (1991) is critical of the latter view; but from the standpoint of clinical practice, Chessick's argument is persuasive (cf. Schlesinger's 1994 for the concept that free floating attention drifts among several listening modes).

Clinical Records

Clinicians and clinical investigators have debated the issue of clinical records ever since Freud's (1909b, 1912b) early comments on the subject. Contrary to widespread belief, Freud did not categorically interdict process notes, but recommended only that therapists not attempt to take *full* notes such as a shorthand record. He saw no objection to brief notes "in the case of dates, the text of dreams, or particularly noteworthy events" (1912b, p. 113; see also 1909b).

In his report of the Rat Man (1909b), Freud cautioned that note taking might distract the analyst's attention to some extent from the patient's ongoing free associations. He elaborated on this point in his first paper on technique (1912e). With this problem in mind, I limit my own note taking *during* therapy sessions to jotting down the briefest notations regarding the gist and sequence of the patient's material and my interventions. At any time during the session, if I notice that writing is interfering with my listening to the patient, I suspend the note taking temporarily until I feel fully focused again on the patient's productions. I use the very brief notes as soon as possible after the session to guide my dictation of a more complete record of what transpired.

Chassan (1956) noted long ago that a practical approach to recording clinical data would be for therapists to make brief notations at the end of each interview—a form of process notes. Wolfson and Sampson (1976) have demonstrated that process notes compare favorably with verbatim transcripts as representative samples of clinical data (see also Argelander 1984). Garduk and Haggard (1972) note the difficulty of identifying specific affects in verbatim typescripts. Spence (1979) believes that process notes are actually better than verbatim recordings because process notes contain references to the therapist's inner responses. In Joyce McDougal's (1980) case report of a patient named Paul, for example, she presents a process account of the interchange between the patient and herself, but also includes in parentheses her own inner experiences and reasoning that led to her interpretations (see also Argelander 1984, Dewald in Panel 1973, Rubovits-Seitz 1998).

Despite the controversies concerning clinical records, their value seems evident. Greenacre (1975) reported that going back and reading her notes helped her recognize connections that she had not seen originally. Fisher and Greenberg (1977) point out that for psychoanalysis and dynamic psychotherapy to be accessible to scientific scrutiny, "All that is necessary is that there be clear and repeatable bookeeping about what is being observed" (p. 9). Elsewhere I (1998) have described and illustrated the use of clinical records in the posttherapeutic justification of interpretations from completed cases (see also Merendino 1985, Mergenthaler 1985, Renneker 1960, Rubovits-Seitz 2000, Spruiell 1984, Tuckett 1994b, Wallerstein and Sampson 1971).

SUMMARY

This chapter has focused on further empirical strategies of the interpretive process, namely, various methods of observing clinical data, and of making clinical records.

Various types of observational strategies are available to interpreters, their differences being based on several factors: the sensory modalities involved (i.e., whether auditory, visual, or mixed); the relative objectivity or subjectivity of observations (i.e., perceptual-cognitive methods in contrast to introspection, empathy, and phenomenologic "experiencing"); the number of observational distinctions between the two. Constructions are not necessarily concerned exclusively with early life experiences, but also deal with current pathodynamic issues; and according to traditional (hermeneutic) usage in other interpretive disciplines, construction is defined as a relatively discrete phase of the construal process in which the interpreter attempts to formulate a tentative overall or "whole" (thematic) meaning of the current data being studied. Reconstruction, by contrast, is a gradual process in which crucial childhood events are not reproduced as recollections, but have to be constructed gradually from diverse data.

Construction draws on all of the mind's capacities, in particular a back and forth focus on parts and whole, which is the principal processing operation of hermeneutics. The hermeneutic focus on interdependent relations of part and whole meanings is based on the concept that the whole is derived from and constituted by the parts, the latter being delineated and integrated by the whole. Freud employed the part-whole principle in his concept that the meaning of any fragment depends on the meaning of the whole. The meaning one seeks to understand is grasped first in a tacit sense before it is known more fully.

The complexities, difficulties, and limitations of the interpretive process are such that there can never be a method or model of correct construction, because the psychology of understanding cannot be reduced to a systematic procedure, and there is no way of assuring a right "guess" by means of rules and principles.

Guesses about the underlying "whole" or thematic meaning of a given set of data are attempts to discover an explanation that can tie together coherently all of the data studied at that time. In casting about preconsciously and imaginatively in search of the best explanation, we consider various possibilities and choose the one that seems to account for the data most completely and coherently. Our goal is to discover the underlying thread of continuity in the patient's associations; thus we necessarily listen with an ear tuned to sequence and coherence, and a sensitivity to continuity and coherence can be viewed as essential aspects of our clinical interpretive competence.

Ideally, we do not simply apply some preexisting clinical theory to the data—which would be a form of doctrinal interpretation. Rather, our preconscious data-processing and constructive operations are imaginative, original, and creative; they attempt to construct the best explanation of the data, whatever that may be, whether it is part of psychodynamic theory or not. Thus we should not look to Freud or the leaders of other therapeutic schools for all of the answers, but rather should cultivate receptivity in therapy sessions and create our own low-level, first-order interpretive theories; for the best explanation of a given set of data may come from commonsense rather than from one of our numerous clinical theories.

CHAPTER FIVE

Data Processing Strategies and Operations: Examples of Cognitive Transformations

$\mathcal{H}$AVING GENERATED, collected, and observed large amounts and wide varieties of data, the clinical interpreter is then faced with the crucial but elusive task of processing the data in search of clues to latent meanings and determinants. The philosopher Hans Reichenbach (1951) commented about this phase of scientific inquiry:

> Knowledge begins with observation: our senses tell us what exists outside our bodies. But we are not satisfied with what we observe; we want to know more, to inquire into things that we do not observe directly. We reach this objective by means of thought operations, which connect the observational data and account for them in terms of unobserved things. [pp. 176–177; for a very similar commentary focused specifically on psychoanalysis, see Freud, 1940a, pp. 196–197]

In clinical interpretation, the "thought operations" that Reichenbach refers to are called "cognitive processing." The scope of the term "cognitive" is much broader, however, than just thought processes. Holt (1964) writes that the term cognitive "comprises perceiving, judging, forming concepts, learning (especially that of a meaningful, verbal kind), imagining, fantasying, imaging, creating, and solving problems"—in other words, "all aspects of symbolic behavior, in the broad sense" (pp. 315–316; see also Meehl 1960).

An important implication of cognitive processing is that depth psychological understanding does not come about from direct perception of unconscious meanings and determinants, which Freud (1912b) had assumed in his early "telephone analogy," or from a highly developed "attunement" to latent mental contents (cf. André Green, in Raymond and Rosbrow-Reich 1997), but is achieved mainly by an indirect process of inferring unobserved things from our diverse empirical data. Meehl (1973) points out, for example, that aside from what a patient actually says and does during therapy sessions, everything else is inferred. As Freud (1901) put it: "We are looking for unconscious material"; but "in proceeding from the ideas that enter the mind of the person who is being questioned to the discovery of the disturbing element, we have to follow a longer path, through a complicated series of associations" (p. 58). He later described the process of finding the "disturbing element" in the "complicated series of associations" this way:

> We fill in what is omitted by making plausible inferences and translating it into conscious material. In this way we construct, as it were, a sequence of conscious events complementary to the unconscious psychical processes. The relative certainty of our psychical science is based on the binding force of these inferences. [Freud 1940a, p. 159]

The data processing phase of clinical interpretation is thus referred to by some writers as "the inference process" (cf. Meehl 1973, Tuckett 1995, Woodard 1992). With respect to the range of inferences employed in clinical interpretation, Clippinger (1977) notes that a rule-governed approach to data processing would restrict the kinds of inferences that could be made—hence the advantage of flexibility in cognitive processing. A flexible approach, which can generate any number and variety of inferences, may result in more frequent incorrect interpretations; but speakers and listeners regularly make incorrect inferences and then correct them as additional information is acquired (cf. Grice 1975, Rubovits-Seitz 1998; see Chapter 7).

Some Problematic Aspects of Studying Data Processing

The cognitive processing of clinical data is arguably the most important but also the least understood aspect of the interpretive process. One of the reasons that data processing is poorly understood is because many or most such mental activities operate outside of awareness, making them difficult to study (Edelson 1980, Green 1974, Kris 1951, Reik 1949). The behavioral science methodologist Adriaan De Groot (1983) comments in this connection:

> What happens mentally is itself, in some respects, fuzzy, ambiguous, undifferentiated, undecidable. Such ambiguity need not harm the problem-solving process[, however]: on the contrary, it may be highly economical—the heuristic being, *never think more explicitly than is needed.* [p. 128; the clinical uses and functions of heuristics are discussed more fully later]

Another source of difficulty in studying cognitive processing is that it occurs at different levels, which are not autonomous but interactive. Both speech and comprehension, for example, rely on separate "modules" operating at different levels—a complex, interactive organization and functioning. Johnson-Laird (1983), a cognitive scientist, writes:

> Three phenomena—different kinds of organization, dependence on context, and interaction between levels of processing—all point to one essential, though hardly novel principle: *mental processes occur in parallel.* There are different levels of organization because separate processes can operate on different levels simultaneously; at a given level, one processor works on one item whilst others work on its context; and communication between processors at different levels allows them to interact. [pp. 452–453; see also De Beaugrande 1980, Posner 1973; see also, however, Prideaux 1985]

The complexity of processing operations is illustrated further in additional experimental findings by cognitive and information scientists. Michael Posner (1973) has presented evidence, for example, that the external world is coded in terms of multiple representational modalities (visual, auditory, kinesthetic), and that much of our cognitive processing is based on the interaction of multiple such codes, which must be coordinated. Allen Newell (1973) reports:

> Much of what goes on in information processing is control. Almost every operation in a large complex program does nothing except arrange things so something else can do something. This appears to hold for both humans and computers. . . . The decoding hypothesis is in fact a form of the same

magician's trick, in which the actions that take time are not the apparently productive part . . . , but a preparatory piece of housekeeping. In short, [processing] methods are mostly control, so that any theory of [processing] methods must operate within an explicit theory of control. [pp. 520–521; for clinical applications, cf. Horowitz 1993; also Kris's (1956a) observation that the processing of clinical data is often a long drawn-out process, based on many preceding sessions of preparatory work; and Freud's (1923a) aphorism that the meanings of what we hear during an analysis are usually not recognized until later on]

Still another problem of clinical data processing has been described by Einhorn and Hogarth (1986), who note that in the course of collecting, observing, and processing clinical data, therapists identify numerous cues to latent meanings and determinants. In attempting to sort out and classify the multiple cues, the therapist faces a daunting mathematical problem in the sheer number of possible cue combinations that might be relevant. Ten pieces of information (cues) extrapolates, for example, to nearly ten million different possible combinations of cues. Thus to reduce the number of interpretive hypotheses to a manageable number, some constraints on cues, combinations of cues, and alternative constructions are necessary.

Most of what psychoanalysis and dynamic psychotherapy have learned about the processing of clinical data has been based on intuitive impressions rather than on systematic investigation (see, e.g., Spence 1979). The clinical literature on data processing is thus relatively limited; but a considerable amount of information on this subject is available to us from other disciplines. Investigations of perceptual processing, language processing, communication, cognitive science including cognitive psychology, information processing, research in complex problem solving, artificial intelligence, as well as the philosophy and sociology of science, among others, provide numerous suggestive parallels with data processing in our own fields (cf. Edelson 1980).

With respect to the relations and differences between concepts of mental processing in psychoanalysis and cognitive science, Weinberger et al. (2000) emphasize the basic conceptual differences between the two; for example, psychoanalysis holds that there are two kinds of unconscious processing, while cognitivists insist on only one. For this reason, Weinberger et al. doubt that a conceptual integration of the two approaches is feasible, but they hold out the possibility of an integration of methods: "Cognitive science needs to attend to the insights into affect offered by psychoanalytic theory to become a complete science of human functioning; psychoanalysis needs the methods of cognitive science to rigorously test its claims" (pp. 149–150).

Semiotic Aspects of Data Processing

Freud is usually given credit for inventing the method of clinical interpretation but, as occurs in most scientific discoveries, his development of clinical interpretation had precursors. The historiographer Carlo Ginzburg (1989) notes, for example, that during the 1870s a method emerged in the human sciences that was based on semiotics, that is, on the deciphering of signs of various kinds. The method was essentially an interpretive approach that relied on clues suggested by inconspicuous details in human science data—an approach that is intrinsic to semiotics, and was invented by the American philosopher and polymath, Charles Sanders Peirce (pronounced "purse") (1931–1935), who also was the founder of the school of pragmatism (cf. Smith 1978, Thayer 1982; see also Joseph Brent's [1960] biography of Peirce). Ginzburg includes Freud's interpretive approach among the disciplines that have employed a semiotic approach, because Freud's method focuses on minor details that serve as clues that are interpreted as signs of crucial, concealed aspects of the mind (cf. Freud 1914b).

The relation between semiotics and our strategies of clinical interpretation is only beginning to be explored systematically, but holds considerable promise (Kettner 1991, Rubovits-Seitz 1998, Shapiro 1991). A defining feature of semiotics, for example, is interpretation, because the essential function of a sign is referral, that is, representing or standing for something other than itself; and the meaning of a sign, what it stands for, must be interpreted by the receiver of the sign. To illustrate: a thermometer is a type of sign because it stands not only for itself but for something in addition to itself, namely, the surrounding temperature.

When the thermometer is read, a third factor enters in, that of interpretation. Umberto Eco (1985) points out that a characteristic feature of signs is that they stimulate their own interpretations.

Royce (1965) emphasizes the distinction between sign and symbol. The former, however, which like a symbol stands for something else, involves only a one-to-one relationship with what it indicates (cf. the thermometer). The symbol, on the other hand, can stand for a wide variety of things under different circumstances. For example, depending on the context at the time, an image of a snake may represent symbolically a penis, a sneaky despised person or act, a lurking danger, a hostile impulse to bite or to encircle and compress, an unattractive or promiscuous woman, a derogatory reference to a Caucasian by a black person, a temptation to use drugs or alcohol, or urination (snakes hiss = piss). In addition, many different images can symbolize the same thing (Arnheim 1969); for example:

> According to Freud, the human mind groups, at the level at which dreams are made, sticks, umbrellas, knives, steeples, watering cans, serpents, fishes, nail files, hammers, zeppelins, and the number three. Another group of dream items comprises pits, hollows, caves, bottles, boxes, chests, pockets, ships, gates, and mouths. This grouping is made because of a vital concern with the organs of reproduction. More specifically, the grouping is not based on just any attribute objects happen to have in common with the genitals but on those crucial to the sexual interest, namely, pointedness and the capacity to rise and pour *versus* concavity, receptivity, etc. [pp. 204–205]

Erwin Singer (1970) believes that symbols are inevitably expressive in purpose (cf. symbolic language), even when they express the desire to repress. He suggests that correct interpretation of the inner state of another person requires that the interpreter be empathically aware of similar states in himself, and also be able to conceptualize himself as symbolizing such states in similar cognitive terms. The cognitive part of Singer's proposal has some similarities to Edelson's (1975) earlier concept that the interpreter must be able to reconstruct preconsciously the speaker's mental processes of expressing/disguising the speaker's (e.g., patient's) utterances. Singer argues further that although symbols, like signs, stand for something else, the something else tends to be specifically an inner mental state; or, as Fromm (1951) put it, symbolic language is that in which the world outside is used as a symbol of the inner world.

The semiotic aspects of interpretive processing appear to include also certain subjective signal phenomena that alert the clinician to potentially important clues. To illustrate, Smith (1995) considers surprise a crucial affective ingredient of the therapist's listening, attention, and data gathering; but his clinical examples suggest that surprise is also part of data processing—a factor in the selection of data for processing. Smith cites a personal communication from Arlow (1992), for example, that "an unusual word, a striking figure of speech, an irrelevant reflection, an observation out of context, an intrusive thought, a strange metaphor (or any metaphor), all of these occasion surprise and curiosity [in the therapist]" (Smith 1995, p. 76; see also Diesing 1971, Gould 1983, Reik 1937, 1949, Spence 1982b).

Holland (1975), on the other hand, emphasizes the limitations of subjectivity in interpretive work. He suggests that to reduce the domination of subjective factors in interpretation, the therapist must focus on similarities within the patient's thoughts, feelings, and actions rather than on similarities between his own and the patient's reactions.

Clinicians differ in their ability to recognize signs of, or clues to, latent meanings in clinical data. In an experimental study, for example, Spence et al. (1974) found that clinical sensitivity to clue words was significantly correlated with the therapist's amount of clinical experience.

Since semiotics is part of the larger field of communication, it is useful also to consider some parallels between clinical discourse and interpretation (cf., e.g., Cherry 1957, Wachtel 1993, Watzlawick et al. 1967). In the psychology of communication, the perception, assimilation, and understanding of messages involves a process of recoding that, as we shall see, is involved also in the interpretive processing of clinical data. One form of communicative recoding groups information thematically, applies a new name to it, and then remembers the new name rather than the original information. Recoding is thus a powerful method of increasing the amount and complexity of information that can be processed, stored, and recalled. Because recoding must be accomplished rapidly, it cannot be carried out consciously but must be performed preconsciously or unconsciously.

The most common kind of recoding is translation into a verbal code, rephrased in one's own words (cf. Prideaux 1985, regarding the ubiquity of paraphrase). Another common form of recoding utilizes imagery (cf. Arlow 1979, Gardner 1983, Heimann 1977, Leavy 1973; for clinical examples see Kern 1978, Ross and Kapp 1962, Rubovits-Seitz 1998). Johansen (1986) points out in this connection that, very early in his theorizing, Freud (1900) anticipated just such a semiotic perspective on psychological processing, namely,

> memory systems constructed according to different semantic and syntactical principles which inscribe the experiences in the psyche according to at least two different semiotic systems, one mainly iconic and the other mainly symbolic—pictorial and other kinds of perceptual representations on the one hand and linguistic representations on the other. In this perspective the psychical apparatus is . . . a device that can transform inputs from the outside and from the body into different sign systems, store this information, recall it, combine it, select from it, transform it from one type of sign system to another, create new meaningful chains of signs on the basis of what is actually stored, and so on. [Johansen 1986, pp. 520–521]

Cognitive Processing in the Clinical Interpretive Process

In the data processing phase of clinical interpretation, selected clinical data and information from both patient and therapist are subjected to multiple, complexly interrelated data processing operations that transform the data and information into unique personal meanings and determinants that are specific to the individual patient. These transformative operations are the pivotal axis of the interpretive process.

The general cognitive requirements of clinical data processing appear to be associated with a special kind of intelligence called "psychological mindedness." Isaacs (1939) illustrated this capacity long ago with the story of a 5-year-old boy who said, "I don't like dreams—they are horrid"; then, after a pause, he added, "And another thing—I don't have any!" Isaacs maintained that anyone with psychological mindedness immediately understands the boy's denial, and concludes that because his dreams are horrid he *wishes* he didn't have any.

If one attempts to delineate the various components of psychological mindedness, the principal elements appear to include an unusual kind and degree of interest in, curiosity about, alertness to, ability to empathize with, and capacity to transform analogically, abstractively, symbolically, and metaphorically, certain specific types of phenomena, namely, intrapsychic and interpersonal events that deal with feelings, attitudes, motives, and relationships in oneself and in other people. The cognitive transformations of these particular types of intrapsychic and interpersonal events may be similar to or the same as those involved in thinking generally, that is, perception of similarities among phenomena, abstraction of analogies, and construction and comprehension of symbolic representations such as communicable metaphors (Rubovits-Seitz 1988b).

Some of the most commonly employed operations in the processing of clinical data include contextualization, pattern seeking, thematization, restructuring, reversal, visualization, fractionation, abstraction, deconstruction, classifying, completion, imagination, intuition, and inference. These and other methods of data processing are usually combined with each other rather than operating singly. Close study reveals further that even individual processing strategies are actually compound operations.

The multiple methods and operations of cognitive processing illustrate and are consistent with the basic investigative strategy of pluralism, which is necessitated by the multi- or overdeterminism of mental events. That is, multiple complexly and simultaneously interacting cognitive mechanisms are required to process the extensive, diverse, and overdetermined data generated by both patient and therapist in the therapeutic process.

Just as clinicians differ in every other aspect of the interpretive process (cf. Seitz 1966), they differ also in their methods of processing clinical data. Diamond (1983) has demonstrated empirically, for example, that experienced therapists differ from novices in their methods of clinical data processing. Experienced therapists wait longer before formulating an interpretation, attempt to synthesize a particular trend or theme from several perspectives, and formulate more psychodynamically and transference-oriented interpretations than less experienced therapists, who formulate interpretations more quickly, focus on contents closer to the surface, and generate fewer psychodynamically and transference-oriented interpretations.

The most frequent and important clinical processing strategy is use of context (Laffal 1965). Freud (1900) recognized early in the development of psychoanalysis that correct interpretation can be arrived at only from the context at the time (see also Cavell 1988, Rubovits-Seitz 1998, Wollheim 1993b). Freud appears to have been strongly influenced regarding the importance of context by Hughlings Jackson's view that context is "everything," that "words in sentences lose their individual meanings" (Greenberg 1997, p. 146, cited by Hoffman 1999).

The importance of context in interpretation has been demonstrated experimentally by the work of Bransford and Johnson (1973) on the role of visual processing in language comprehension. Their findings show that linguistic data cannot be processed effectively without access to additional information. "The interpretation of any utterance is possible only when we can find relevant context in our conceptual knowledge about the world" (Trabasso 1973, p. 439). For example, enrichment of a patient's material by related information from the therapist's associations, which include previous interpretations during the treatment as well as general knowledge, is a frequent form of contextualization in the interpretive process (cf. Levenson 1988). It is important to note, however, that although context is necessary to understanding, at times it can be biasing and misleading (cf. Miller 1967).

With respect to the various sources of context, children do not begin with an internal store of knowledge, so their processing relies more on extraction of information from regularities of occurrences in external inputs. Adult processing, by contrast, rests on minimal external inputs that are used to access and operate on highly organized internal structures (Trabasso 1973). The importance of matching highly organized internal knowledge in long-term memory with sensory inputs is a key concept also in Norman's (1969) model of memory and attention.

CLINICAL EXAMPLES OF
COGNITIVE TRANSFORMATIONS

Rather than attempting to describe all of the clinical interpretive processing operations, I have selected several important and problematic examples to discuss and illustrate in some detail, namely, pattern seeking, thematization, and clinical inference.

Pattern Seeking

A case reported by Ramzy (1974) illustrates the role of both analogic and repetitive patterns in the formulation of a transference interpretation. The patient became intensely disturbed about the possibility of losing his cleaning lady at a time when a separation from the analyst was imminent. Ramzy suspected that the patient's acute disturbance about losing his cleaning lady was a displacement from deeper concern about the coming separation from him. He based that surmise on having observed and construed similar such reactions in the patient when previous separations had occurred—a repetitive pattern—and also on a pattern of suggestive analogic parallels between the cleaning woman and the therapist; that is, both were in the paid service of the patient, both carried out personal services for the patient, and both seemed to be leaving him.

Commentary

Most clinicians probably would agree that Ramzy was on fairly firm ground in his construction, but Donald Spence (1982a) has mounted a forceful critique of such pattern matching in interpretive work. In discussing Ramzy's case, for example, Spence cautioned that we should not assume that our selected link is either demanded by the material or is the only choice available. It is merely the analyst's association to the patient's material, and may be off the mark. The vast majority of clinicians and scholars in related disciplines, however, feel considerable confidence in and continue to employ such methods. The philosopher Donald Davidson (1986) points out, for example, that "as interpreters, we work our way into the whole system, depending much on the pattern of interrelationships" (p. 314).

In a more recent publication, Spence (1991) appears to have reversed himself. He now suggests, in keeping with a concept proposed by Greenwald et al. (1986), that clinicians should focus on the conditions under which a given phenomenon makes its appearance—for example, a male patient provokes arguments with his father only when his mother is present. That processing strategy takes both the clinical episode and its context into account, focusing on a series of patterns rather than simply a series of events. Spence acknowledges that this form of interpretive inquiry makes recurrent patterns our basic unit of clinical significance, and establishes pattern matching as our essential clinical activity (for further critiques of Spence's views on pattern matching, see Brooks 1994, Cheshire 1975).

Grünbaum (1984, 1986, 1990, 1993) has raised another, possibly more serious, problem regarding pattern seeking in the processing of clinical data. Focusing on Freud's view that symptoms have meanings by virtue of their motivational causes, and drawing on (unspecified) arguments from the philosophy of science, he maintains that patterns of meaning—what he calls "meaning kinships" or "thematic affinities"—*never* indicate unconscious motivations. In Ramzy's case, for example, Grünbaum would insist that the analogic similarities between the cleaning lady and therapist would have no causal-motivational relevance to the patient's intense disturbance about losing his cleaning lady.

Grünbaum's critique bears directly on the issue of pattern matching and the probity of clinical interpretations, because the identification of various types of thematic relations and patterns in clinical data is one of the most widely used methods of attempting to construe unconscious motivations (Cheshire 1975). Traditionally, we have assumed that meaning relations suggest the nature of their determinants (Edelson 1988). Grünbaum's argument thus challenges a basic methodologic concept and long-established interpretive practice in psychoanalysis and dynamic psychotherapy.

With respect to the extensive debate on this and related issues that Grünbaum's critiques have stimulated, I have reviewed these debates at some length in a chapter of my previous volume, *Depth-Psychological Understanding* (1998), where I concluded that we should not summarily dismiss Grünbaum's critique, as some psychoanalysts and dynamic psychotherapists have done, but should consider carefully and investigate the questions he raises.

General Aspects of Pattern Matching

The methodologist Abraham Kaplan (1964) describes two principal ways of achieving understanding in science—either by fitting something into a known pattern, or deducing it from other known truths. In the former, the unknown is identified with something known by its place in a network of relations. The social scientist Donald Campbell (1966) believes that all scientific knowledge is gained by a process of pattern matching; and the psychoanalysts Rosenblatt and Thickstun (1994; see also Margolis 1987) postulate that the widespread use of intuition in science also may be based on preconscious or unconscious forms of pattern recognition.

Arnheim (1969) writes: "To understand an event or state of affairs scientifically means to find in it a pattern of forces that accounts for the relevant features of the system under investigation" (p. 193). He adds that pattern seeking does not ignore the context from which the pattern was drawn. On the contrary, patterns are found "by those whose boldness in extracting the similar from the dissimilar is matched by their respect for the contexts in which the similarities are found" (p. 193); for nearly all such cognitive processing is carried out with constant reference to the phenomena they describe.

With respect to the clinical rationale of pattern seeking, De Beaugrande (1980) points out that meanings rarely occur as isolated elements in human experience; nor is meaning carried by individual words or phrases, but by complex conceptual-relational patterns or contexts, called semantic networks. Thus to grasp a speaker's (or writer's) meanings, serial processing of single words and sentences is not sufficient; the transformative processes by a listener (or reader) necessarily employ multiple mechanisms that operate simultaneously on complex contextual patterns, that is, by interactive parallel processing of semantic networks.

De Beaugrande (1980) concludes that pattern matching is the basic form of data processing; in fact, it is possible that our propensity for pattern making and pattern seeking is "hard wired." Margulies (1984), for instance, cites an unpublished report by Kenneth Weiss on the literature of primate art. Given art materials, would chimpanzees produce recognizable forms?

> Whatever the interpretation of the data, they were not random scribbles; they reached for pattern completion and produced a humanly recognizable sense of form and balance. By innate design primate egos, minds, and brains organize . . . experience and establish patterns of perception. [p. 1029]

Freud (Breuer and Freud 1893–1895) hit upon the interpretive strategy of pattern seeking very early in the development of psychoanalysis and clinical interpretation. He recognized a number of patterns in the associations and memories of his early patient, Elisabeth von R.; for example, "She produced a whole number of scenes . . . beginning with her early childhood. They seemed to have in common . . . some injury done to her, against which she had not been able to defend herself" (p. 172). Freud (1900) later cited Aristotle to the effect that "the best interpreter of dreams was the man who could grasp similarities . . . from the misshapen picture." Mahony (1989) believes that Strachey's translations obscure or ignore Freud's ability to discern unifying patterns among the most diverse data and to evoke these patterns through his use of language. Meehl (1995) writes,

> In psychology, such diverse thinkers as Allport, Cattell, Freud, Murray, Skinner, and Thurstone—who one sometimes thinks could hardly have had a meaningful conversation with each other because of their vast differences in method and substance—all had the maximizing of orderliness in the material as their guiding principle, and all wrote explicit methodological passages to that effect. [p. 269]

Elsewhere Meehl (1992, p. 414) writes, "If you want to achieve a causal understanding of the world, do not adopt a policy of attributing replicable orderliness to mere coincidence."

Arlow (1979) describes multiple processing methods, all of which involve relations or various kinds of patterns in clinical data: context, contiguity, congruence (usually analogic similarity), contrast, configuration (the form and sequence of associations), convergence, and recurrence of themes. The types of relational patterns identified most frequently in clinical interpretive work include contextual, part-whole, repetitive, sequential (including contiguities), analogic, causal (including motivations), and oppositional relations. Repetition of themes, analogic similarities, contiguities, and contrasts are among the most frequent types of relations that clinicians employ in data processing and construction. They provide heuristic guides to which data are most relevant, and suggest how to construe the latent meanings of those data (Rogers, 1981).

The search for relations and patterns in clinical data employs an array of cognitive operations that are mainly preconscious, and include scanning, focusing, selecting, sorting, ordering, classifying, comparing, trial and error matching, analysis and synthesis, abstracting, intuition, imagination, visualization, restructuring, inductive and deductive inference, and hypothesis formation (see Peterfreund 1983 for clinical examples). A corollary heuristic of pattern finding indicates that the larger the pattern the better (Reiger 1975); for example, the narrative strategy of data processing attempts to identify a coherent, story-like structure that encompasses essentially all of the clinical data.

Neil Cheshire (1975) considers analogic similarities the mainstay of pattern matching in particular and of clinical data processing generally. Analogic relations can be elusive and highly variable; for example, the following example reported by Duncan (1989): "Images of human decomposition arose at a point when the patient was deliberately suppressing and hiding anger at [me]. . . . A decomposing corpse was what she was imaginatively making of her analyst at that moment" (pp. 695–696). Einhorn (1988) notes that how such hypotheses are generated from the processing of clinical data is not well understood. Various aspects of similarity such as analogy and metaphor seem most likely. Speaking generally, when attempting to explain something that is not understood, one searches for a similar, often simpler, phenomenon that is understood.

Bronowski (1978) gives the example of Isaac Newton "thinking of likeness between the thrown apple and the moon sailing majestically in the sky. A most improbable likeness, but one which turned out to be (if you will forgive the phrase) enormously fruitful" (pp. 109–110).

Since analogic forms of pattern matching are so common (though controversial) in clinical interpretation, they need to be considered more thoroughly. Analogies, including metaphors, are employed not only in proverbs, poetry, jokes, parables, and myths, but also in science—"to help clarify obscure concepts or understand phenomena that are difficult to observe" (Paniagua 1982, p. 509; see also Gould 1983). Freud (1933) used figurative analogies a great deal—noting, however, that "analogies decide nothing, but they can make one feel more at home" (p. 72).

Metaphorical analogies can be good or bad, but not true or false, because they are not intended literally. Another form of analogy—isomorphisms—are not just figurative comparisons but imply literal similarity; thus they can be assessed as correct or incorrect. In psychoanalysis, for example, "the central isomorphic assumption is that transference phenomena recapitulate the passions and conflicts experienced with parents in early life. This is not a figurative 'as-if' analogy; this belief implies a causal connection and is meant literally, not metaphorically (Paniagua 1982, pp. 512–513).

Thematization

Thematization is the concept that a dynamic theme runs like an undercurrent through all of the data at a given time, for example, within a specific therapy session, or over a series of sessions. This strategy is closely related to pattern seeking, the pattern in this case being sequential (thus both synchronic and diachronic).

Freud (1923, p. 239) observed that the patient's associations tend to emerge as "allusions to one particular theme"; and John Klauber (1980, p. 196) noted that therapists routinely and actively search for a thematic pattern that gives "interdependent relevance" to everything the patient says. The focal-conflict theory of clinical interpretation proposed by Thomas French (1952, 1954, 1958a,b), and elaborated by the German investigators Helmut Thomä and Horst Kächele (1987), also are based largely on the concept of thematization. Along similar lines, Robert Waelder (in Guttman and Guttman 1987) asserted that sooner or later the therapist discovers that the varied and seemingly disconected contents are part of a pattern that characterizes the patient's personality. "They fit together, complete each other, support one another, make each other possible" (p. 61); and finally the therapist realizes that "all these pieces are held together by something they have in common: they serve the same purpose, or they fight against the same danger, or they express the same desire or hope or fear" (p. 61). And when the therapist sees that, he or she then recognizes this common denominator in all of the data being studied.

Paula Heimann (1977) stresses the thematizing heuristic that, although the patient's conscious interest at times focuses on the therapist, the patient him- or herself is the central figure in most of the associations. The therapist thus tries not to initiate themes, but follows the patient's lead. Both patient and therapist employ thematizing methods, in different but reciprocal ways (Pine 1985). The productive processing that underlies the patient's free associations includes a thematizing mechanism, and the therapist's listening or receptive processing also is guided by a strategy of alertness to an underlying self-referential theme in the patient's discourse (for a good clinical example, see Spielman 1999).

The processing strategy of thematization can be used also to illustrate the hierarchical relationship between the background assumptions of psychoanalysis and clinical interpretive strategies. That is, thematization rests on three of the basic concepts (guiding assumptions) of psychoanalysis: (1) the existence of unconscious mental processes, (2) the continuity, and (3) the determinism of mental events. The clinical interpreter thus assumes that the patient's free associations are influenced by depth psychological disturbances that act as significant determinants of the patient's associations; and the clinician makes the further assumption that since the patient's free associations derive in part from a currently activated unconscious complex, the associations necessarily involve continuities with each other and with the determining source of unconscious disturbance.

Thematization also illustrates the compound nature of data processing procedures, because it involves not only theme tracing but also repetitive and analogic forms of pattern seeking—as in the following clinical example.

CLINICAL ILLUSTRATION OF THEMATIZATION

A young man came for treatment because of difficulty in sustaining relationships with women. After about two years of analytically oriented therapy he announced suddenly that he had become engaged to a woman he had dated for only a few months. With the interpretive heuristic in mind that genuine structural changes occur only slowly during treatment, whereas sudden changes are usually defensive, I doubted (silently) that he had adequately resolved his conflicts about a close and sustained relationship with a woman; rather than expressing the doubts, however, I decided to wait and see what developed.

Soon after the engagement, he began a session by extolling the "joys of marriage," and indicating how lucky he felt that Beth had accepted his proposal. His associations continued along those lines so effusively that I commented: ["You sound very certain about your future with Beth. Do you ever have any doubts about it, or wonder whether there are any problems that might arise?"]. He seemed surprised by my question; but his initial gush of associations began to slow down, and at that point he remembered a dream from the previous night: "I was escaping from prison in Nashville, and was trying to escape to Memphis."

His associations to Nashville were about a former girlfriend, Betty, who lived in Nashville and from whom he had fled because she "smothered me with love." He paused for a moment, then interjected that his present fiance, Beth, "is also very loving." His associations to Memphis were about Elvis Presley, who came from that city. He admired Presley for his fame, fortune, and especially his free-loving lifestyle. He sometimes imitated Presley as a joke. Recently he teased Beth that they should go to Memphis for their honeymoon and visit the Elvis Presley museum.

[I asked about his associations to escaping from prison.] He recalled with a trace of embarrassment that he had told the dream to Beth, who was upset by it. She thought it meant that he felt imprisoned by their engagement and wished to escape. He protested to her that he had no such feeling, that the dream was about a former girlfriend from whose clutches he had escaped. But Beth remained uneasy, and became even more disturbed when soon after that discussion he made a slip and called her Betty.

Commentary

The theme that appeared to run through this entire session was the issue of the patient's engagement—more specifically, his unacknowledged ambivalence about the engagement and coming marriage (see Chapter 7, for the justification of this interpretive conclusion). In hermeneutic terms his conflict about engagement and marriage to Beth can be viewed as the whole (or thematic) meaning of the session, which, if correct, should account for and integrate the part meanings of all the individual associations. As Ricoeur (1977) puts it, the interpretive explanation attempts "to reorganize the facts into a meaningful whole which constitutes a single and continuous history" (p. 861) or theme. For example, in clinical interpretation some associations may represent disguised expressions of the thematic problem or whole meaning. Other—in fact, most—associations usually point to various defenses against and attempted solutions of the thematic problem, and still other associations may derive from secondary problems based on ego-alien aspects of the defenses and attempted solutions themselves (Rubovits-Seitz 1986).

Although most of the practical problems of interpretation are concerned with inferring the part meanings of individual associations, the uncertainty of interpretations results mainly from the necessity to guess initially about the whole or thematic meaning of the session (see Chapter 6, for the conjectural component of interpretive constructions).

Thematization as a method of cognitive processing makes the understanding of clinical material both easier and more difficult—easier because it reduces the "search space" for latent meanings and determinants to the principal dynamic theme at a particular time, and more difficult because the dominant theme of a therapy session is the most intensely defended against and its disclosure the most tenaciously resisted. In addition, thematization implies that not just any construction can be considered acceptable, because it postulates that only one set of meanings and determinants—the dominant dynamic theme of a therapy session—can be considered the most plausible interpretation at a given time.

Like any generally useful data processing heuristic, however, the search for thematic unity in clinical data can be misused; for example, doctrinal interpretation may be imposed on the data but rationalized as a unifying theme. Meehl (1983) offers this perceptive metaphor: "We want the [therapist] to *discern* the 'red thread', not to spin it and weave it in" (p. 360). Doctrinal interpretations often betray themselves by accounting for only a few suggestive elements of the clinical data while ignoring the rest (cf. Abraham 1986; and for a clinical illustration of this common error, see Rubovits-Seitz 1988a). Ideally, therefore, clinical interpretations do not attempt to promote the theories of a particular psychoanalytic school, but represent an open-minded inquiry into latent meanings and determinants that are part of a unique, complex, momentary truth about a specific patient at a given time.

Before leaving the subject of thematization, we should ask whether thematization is compatible with the basic depth psychological concept of overdetermination, or are these two concepts contradictory? In his treatise on the scientific methodology of psychoanalysis, Rapaport (1944) wrote:

> When you talk about overdetermination you are not talking about a psychological indeterminacy, but about something which is a direct consequence of our method of going at psychological events, because the meaning of an event is the psychological continuity into which it fits, and these continuities are always multiple. . . . When you are faced with the question of what is . . . the main determinant, there is no answer. It is a question of which of these various levels of continuity now play such a role that the patient can be brought, without too much anxiety, to understand better the event under discussion. There is no primary determinant, and if somebody claims that the issue of reality is primary, surely that is not true; that is only one level of the continuity of meaning. There are several levels, and if you neglect them, so much the worse for you. [p. 216]

Somewhat similarly, Rothstein (1987) questions attempts to determine a unidimensional dynamic basis of dreams, rather than seeking multiple, overdetermined meanings. The question thus arises whether the search for a thematic meaning of a therapy session, dream, or other segment of data is inconsistent with the principle of overdetermination. My answer is that the two are not inconsistent but complementary; that is, the thematic meaning is primary precisely because it is the most condensed, overdetermined, composite disturbance at the time.

A number of clinical concepts in psychoanalysis and clinical interpretation deal with the operation of thematizing mechanisms in both data production and in interpretive processing, which together generate what might be called a "composite conflict," that is, a conflict that not only is the most highly activated latent disturbance at a particular time, but also involves a confluence or final common pathway of multiple, related, overdetermined motivations. For example, my concept of the principal current (or thematic) conflict coheres with a number of related clinical concepts, including Freud's (1916–1917) intersection of forces; Hartmann's (1939) concept of a hierarchization and thematization of ego activities; French's (1952, 1954, 1958a,b) focal conflict; Levine and Luborsky's (1966) core conflictual relationship theme; Peterfreund's (1983) most pressing determinant; Thomä and Kächele's (1987) focus; Malan's (1963) and also Balint et al.'s (1972) focal therapy; and the widely employed concept of a "dynamic theme" in individual therapy sessions. The coherence of these various viewpoints suggest that the concepts of overdeterminism and thematization are both compatible and complementary.

Employing a combined psychoanalytic and information theory model, for example, Peterfreund (1983) pointed out that multideterminism does not mean that at any given moment it is quite acceptable to take up any of the possible meanings that may be present. At any given time, "only one or a few of the determining factors for the phenomenon is dominant, at the forefront, more discernible, 'hotter,' and more available for discovery" (p. 141). Thus it is the task of interpretation "to find out what is the most pressing, most urgent, most 'highlighted' determinant at the given moment. This task is pivotal in psychoanalytic therapy" (p. 142).

Clinical Inference, and a Method of Investigating Data Processing

I turn now to the role of inference in cognitive transformations, and a clinical method of investigating data processing. More than a century-and-a-half before Freud, Christian von Wolff (1679–1752) appears to have been the first to state explicitly that nonconscious factors must be inferred from those that are conscious—a conclusion that he reached while extending and clarifying Leibniz's conception of unconscious mental processes: "Insofar as something further exists in us than we are conscious of, we must bring it to life by *inferences* from that of which we are conscious, since otherwise we should have no ground to do so" (cited by Whyte 1960).

The psychoanalytically informed experimental cognitive psychologist Matthew Erdelyi (1999) places Freud also in the tradition of Helmholz (1867), who proposed the concept of unconscious inference for the complex interpretations by which human beings achieve coherent depth perceptions from shifting stimuli. Freud extended the concept of unconscious inference from the phenomena of depth perception to "the more unruly domain of depth psychology" (p. 610), where motives are involved. Thus "Freud, in effect, extended the problem of sight to the problem of insight" (p. 611). Erdelyi notes further:

> Once more, the context was seen as the decisive molder and sifter of perception, though Freud incorporated a number of additional ideas, such as dream work, primary-process thinking, and symbolism to his psychological palette. Still, the overriding principle of psychological perception (insight, interpretation) was context according to Freud. [p. 611]

> Meaningful, complex stimuli have surface (manifest) as well as deep (latent) contents; . . . context both gives and hides meaning. Further, and this is a critical point, interpretation (perception, insight) is not untrammelled. Interpretation is highly constrained. It is not, as some Postmodernists would have it, a semantic free for all. Context reduces semantic degrees of freedom, often to $df = 1$. [p. 614]

Erdelyi illustrates such constraints with the following example: A graffito in a Greenwich Village café, depicting two crudely drawn cubes with the scribbled caption, "Picasso's Balls," suggests the interpretation that a Cubist like Picasso has cubically shaped testicles. The relevant context (the caption below the two cubes), is not just physical, however, but also is psychological; that is, without the additional contexts from memory—that Picasso was both a Cubist and a rake—there is no latent content to understand.

Erdelyi suggests further that in the production of both art and clinical interpretations, "the unconscious plays a deep role both in generating content and shaping style. For, in addition to the artist's conscious planning and craft, a shadowy realm within the artist gurgles up, in transformed guises (and disguises), to give substance to the artist's creations" (pp. 614–615; cf. also the creative process of generating clinical interpretations). Erdelyi adds:

> The artist, according to Freud, is that breed of human who, without losing control over the id, is yet capable of voluntarily and playfully regressing to id processes and merging the brutal vitality of the id with the civilizing constraints and craft of the ego. It is a tricky, even dangerous game; the artist is a juggler of worlds (Freud 1908). [p. 623; cf. also, once again, the creative process involved in clinical interpretation]

> Freud's synthetic genius was to perceive these phenomena as general themes of human cognition: We recover unconscious memories in distorted, disguised, yet often astonishingly creative forms, in a variety of psychological media from dreams, daydreams, and free associations, to jokes, symptoms, and religious ideas. [p. 617; for experimental illustrations confirming these concepts, see Fisher 1954, 1956, Pötzl 1917],

Important as clinical inference is in the methodologies of psychoanalysis and clinical interpretation (see, e.g., Woodard 1992), however, it is only a necessary and not a sufficient cause of therapeutic change. Freud (1916–1917) wrote:

> *Our* knowledge of what is unconscious in the patient is not equivalent to *his* knowledge of it; if we communicate our knowledge to him, he does not receive it *instead of* his unconscious material, but *beside* it; and that makes very little change in it. . . . The repression must be got rid of—after which the substitution of the conscious material for the unconscious can proceed smoothly. [p. 436; italics are Freud's]

Einhorn (1988) notes that the clinician first looks backward to discover determinants of present behavior, using backward inference to connect prior causes with observable effects. Backward inference depends on skills of construction (see Chapter 6), that is, causal thinking, which includes hypothesis formation and change, linking variables in causal chains, assessing the strength of such chains, and considering alternative explanations.

In his philosophical analysis of psychoanalysis, Roland Dalbiez (1941) concluded that the factors of de-repression and interpretive inference are reciprocally causative in exposing the repressed:

> To suppose that the unconscious can only be reached by *inference* and not by *de-represssion* . . . would be a serious mistake. An analysis which ended merely in inferences would be a failure. Skillful technique [in communications to the patient] must bring about the reintegration in the conscious field of memories hitherto incapable of voluntary evocation. [Vol. I, p. 400; see also Vol. II, p. 93]

In addition, inferring latent entities in clinical data should not be thought of as a separate or independent processing mechanism; it is merely one among a wide variety of interrelated cognitive transformations employed in interpretive processing—the combined operations of which help the therapist and patient to identify inner conflicts and defenses that need to be de-represssed, channeled into talk, and understood more thoroughly and deeply in terms of childhood antecedents—emphasizing again that the interpretive process is concerned not only with latent meanings of mental events, but also with their unconscious determinants.

In an unpublished monograph, "The Psychoanalytic Inference Process," Woodard (1993) notes a tendency to underestimate the complexities of the processes by which clinical inferences are made. Ramzy (1963, 1974), for example, proposed that, despite the overdetermined nature of clinical data, clinical inferences follow purely logical rules; and Luborsky's (1984) guided inference manual gives the impression that the Core Conflictual Relationship Theme (CCRT) method solves the problems of clinical inference. Schafer (1959), Spence (1968, 1981), and others argue, however, that the therapist's understanding depends on a very broad context of information about the patient that is built up only gradually over time, thus contributing eventually to better-informed and more effective inferences (cf. also Edelson 1978, Loewenstein 1957, Ramzy and Shevrin 1976, Stern 1983, Waelder 1939). Examples of interpretive inferences are included in the case report (below); the case report also illustrates a clinical method of investigating data processing.

In an empirical investigation by Diamond (1983), therapists had great difficulty in identifying and reporting the processing operations they employed in listening to audiotapes of therapy sessions. Edelson (1978; cited by Woodard 1993) points out that interpreters cannot be aware of such processes, and can only gradually become aware of them *with prompting*. In the method of studying data processing to be described, immediately following each therapy session the therapist employs brief process notes to prompt him- or herself to recall as much as possible about such processing mechanisms. The method to be described for the investigation of data processing thus involves the retrospective "naturalizing" or "unpacking" of therapy sessions as soon as possible following each appointment. The terms "unpacking" or "naturalizing" refer to a process of elaborating on and adding significant details to the record of a session. The method of unpacking therapy sessions is available to every clinician, but requires a record of the therapeutic process. A naturalized text has the advantage of more closely approximating completeness and closure of a session's dynamics, including the therapist's cognitive activities. A particular context, by itself, does not have the "closure property" of an unpacked session, because every context can be further amplified and clarified by being placed in other contexts (Seung 1982). Jonathan Culler (1982) asserts similarly that "total context is unmasterable, both in principle and in practice. Meaning is context-bound, but context is boundless" (p. 123; cited by Rogers 1987).

Spence (1981, 1982a) suggests that the unpacking process should attempt to explain virtually everything that occurred during a session, but I have made certain revisions in the naturalizing process proposed by Spence. Unpacking every therapy session and everything that occurs within each session may be the investigative ideal, but is not feasible for most clinicians and investigators because the naturalizing of therapy sessions is very time consuming; in my experience it may take as long (or even longer) to unpack a therapy session as to conduct one. For that reason I have focused most of my naturalizing activities on "critical dynamic episodes" (French 1952, 1954, 1958a,b) within particular sessions. On the other hand, I attempt to unpack "good therapeutic hours" (Kris 1956, Peterfreund 1983) as completely as possible (for a clinical example employed in a case report, see Rubovits-Seitz 1988b).

The following brief case report illustrates both the method of naturalizing a therapy session, and the role of inferences in cognitive transformations.

ILLUSTRATIVE CASE

The clinical material to be presented is from a single therapeutic encounter with an acutely psychotic patient in a mental hospital. Although some psychoanalysts and dynamic psychotherapists do not treat psychotic patients, the case to be presented offers certain advantages for purposes of the present discussion: It is a good example of investigating data processing activities by the method of naturalizing the record of a therapy session, and it also illustrates the role of inferences in clinical data processing. In addition, since relatively little background information and clinical context about the patient were available, the therapeutic experience and its unpacking can be presented very briefly. The case is not paradigmatic in any way, but is an example of the occasional heuristic value of the unusual case in science.

The data processing methods appropriate to psychotic patients are similar in many respects to those that we use with nonpsychotic patients, but interpretive technique differs considerably. As Eissler (1951, 1953) and others have observed, psychoanalytically informed treatment of psychotic patients often requires greater use by the therapist of the primary processes, and also what Eissler called the need at times to "talk metapsychology" to the schizophrenic patient—both of which occurred in the present case.

The clinical encounter will be described first, just as it happened, without any attempt to explain the dynamics of the interaction or my clinical reasoning. Then I shall describe the subsequent unpacking of the session, with special attention to preconscious processing operations. I emphasize the *preconscious* nature of the processing activities because, as Sandler et al. (1997) observe, "It is remarkable how often we underestimate or even ignore the major role of the Preconscious, and speak or write as though there were only two systems—i.e., the Unconscious and the Conscious" (p. 85n; see also Kantrowitz 1999).

Case Report

I was asked to see a recently admitted, agitated and assaultive, powerfully built man in his middle twenties on the acute ward of a mental hospital. The ward staff and other patients had been terrorized by the patient for hours. He had injured a psychiatric aide and another patient who had tried to help him. Taking several strong attendants with me, I observed the patient from a safe distance. He was shouting incoherently, was wide-eyed, and was making threatening gestures with the leg of a chair he had smashed. I listened with unfocused attention to his incoherent ranting for five or ten minutes, but was unable to sense or understand any particular trends in his wild verbalizations. I then called out to him in a loud voice that could be heard above the din of his own shouting: "Here I am! What do you want me to do?" He seemed to shout something in my direction but it was not coherent enough to understand. I called back: "Talk sense so I can understand you! Tell me what you want me to do!" He stopped shouting for a moment, looked straight at me, then cried out coherently in a tone of anguished bitterness: "I have thrown my mother and my sister in the ashcan and all I have left is my Daddy!" Almost instantaneously I found myself calling out to him in a tone conveying unmistakable medical authority: "Then you had better get your mother and sister back, because without them you are having a severe mental breakdown!" He argued vehemently against my suggestion. We had a shouting match about whether he should do as I urged. Intensely abrasive contact between us was clearly established at that point. He denounced and cursed the women in his family and extolled the virtues of his "Daddy." I insisted that he *needed* his mother and sister, even if they had been mean and rotten to him. After about 15 minutes of such shouting back and forth, he capitulated suddenly, calmed down, and dropped the club he had been brandishing. He sauntered toward me slowly, saying now in a conversational tone: "Alright, Doc—alright already! Maybe you're right. Maybe a bad mother is better than no mother at all." The crisis was over, and his psychotic episode did not recur.

Commentary

Turning to the unpacking of this therapeutic encounter, during the clinical incident I experienced two conscious subjective reactions that, together with very rapid preconscious processing, appeared to facilitate the favorable therapeutic outcome—an example of subjective reactions operating in concert with other processing methods. The first subjective reaction occurred when I first saw the patient, who was wide-eyed, shouting incoherently, and wielding his club; I noticed with surprise that rather than feeling mildly apprehensive and vigilant as I often do with belligerent paranoid patients, my immediate reaction was a twinge of compassion for him—a concerned wish to help him, to relieve his obvious distress. Although the compassion puzzled me momentarily, it was dispelled quickly by a rapid series of thoughts that in retrospect (i.e., upon subsequent unpacking of the episode) I was able to recognize as a form of inferential reasoning, the premises of which included specific clinical observations and psychodynamic heuristics. The clinical inferences can be expressed for present purposes in the form of syllogisms:

First Inference
The major premise of the first inference was the psychodynamic heuristic that excessiveness implies defense.
The minor premise was the clinical observation that his aggression seemed excessive.
My conclusion, therefore, was the deductive inference that his aggression was probably defensive.

Second Inference

The major premise of the second inference was the psychodynamic heuristic that defensive aggression often wards off anxiety.

The minor premise was the conclusion of the first inference, that is, this patient toward whom I feel compassion is defensively aggressive.

My conclusion was that my compassion for the patient was probably a response to his underlying panic.

These inferential processes were not reasoned out consciously or deliberately during the encounter, of course, but appeared to have occurred preconsciously. At the time of the episode, only the two conclusions flashed through my mind in response to feeling surprised by my twinge of compassion for the patient. The two conclusions thus represented self-interpretations of my subjective response—illustrating that subjective reactions themselves do not provide direct interpretive answers, but require and undergo preconscious processing in which their meanings are constructed (cf. Kohut 1971, 1972–1976, 1984, who insisted that subjective reactions are not interpretations; they are introspected clinical data).

Further unpacking of the first subjective response suggested that my preconscious recognition of the patient's underlying anxiety was not based entirely on inferences, but resulted also from direct clinical observation of the patient's wide-eyed look, which I perceived (or apperceived) as a sign of panic. My conclusion that panic underlay his overt aggression thus resulted from the combined operations of a clinical observation, a subjective response, two psychodynamic heuristics, and some inferential processing—illustrating that clinical observation and preconscious processing operations tend to be complexly interrelated.

A second subjective response occurred when the patient shouted in a tone of bitter anguish that he had thrown his mother and sister in the ashcan and that all he had left was his "Daddy." My subjective response was a slight twinge of caution, a warning signal, which I did not understand initially. In unpacking the experience afterward I was able to reconstruct the following possible steps in my reaction. First, I had to distinguish the signal of caution from the more familiar feeling of vigilance toward combative paranoid patients. No, it was not that kind of caution. Was it a response to his bitterness and anguish? No, that seemed to elicit compassion. My thoughts settled on what might be called a "marker" word, "Daddy," and its regressive implications. Little children call their fathers Daddy. I then recalled that within seconds of experiencing the caution signal, the possibility crossed my mind that his panic might be homosexual in origin. A decision was made instantaneously and preconsciously—preconscious because I was not aware of making the decision, but found myself assuming an authoritative stance toward the patient and telling him in a commanding tone to get his mother and sister back.

In naturalizing this sequence I was able to fill in some of the mental processes in myself that appeared to have occurred without conscious registration during the episode. The word "Daddy" had seemed regressive, what a young child would call his father. The intensity and excessiveness of those feelings seemed to imply a defensive function—but against what? Saying that his father was "all I have left" sounded as though he might fear the loss of all primary attachments, which would plunge him even further into a psychotic state. That might explain his anguish about getting rid of his mother and sister. Thus holding on to his father with such passionate intensity may have been a desperate effort to ward off the terror of catastrophic anxiety activated by the loss of attachments to his mother and sister. The defensively intensified attachment to his father, however, may have produced the additional terrifying complication of homosexual incest, with its associated dread of injury and punishment.

The final phase of unpacking focused on the dynamic reasoning that led to the specific style and content of my interventions, including my interpretation that getting rid of his mother and sister was causing his mental breakdown—an example of what Eissler would call "talking metapsychology" to the patient—and framing the interpretation in a forceful, authoritative manner.

The preconscious processing that underlay these clinical decisions appeared to include the following inferential reasoning: How could I help the patient reduce the homosexual panic, the aggressive defense against it, and the even greater dread of imminent mental collapse? Intuitively and preconsciously I appeared to have hit on an integrative solution—a single interpretation that attempted to reduce the intensity of both anxieties; that is, the homosexual panic from defensive overattachment to his father, and the threatened catastrophic anxiety from loss of primary attachments to his mother, sister, and the possibly threatened loss of his desperately overintense attachment to his father. Urging him to reinstate the attachments to his mother and sister attempted to relieve the catastrophic anxiety and reverse the psychotic regression by reactivating the lost attachments to the women in his family. At the same time, urging him to get the women back had the additional purpose and function of reducing the defensive overattachment to his father, and thus of decreasing the homosexual panic.

A probable reason for the authoritative tone of my interpretation— an example of what Eissler would call the use of primary processes with a psychotic patient—emerged at this point in the unpacking process. My subjective response of caution now appeared to have been directed against the initial subjective reaction of compassion; that is, the caution warned me not to act compassionately toward the patient, because it might aggravate his homosexual panic, for he had attacked a psychiatric aide and another patient who approached him in a friendly manner in their attempts to help him. Thus the forceful, authoritative tone of my intervention attempted to contact the patient in a way that corresponded narcissistically with his own overt aggression, rather than in a manner that might be construed as seductive.

The reader's attention is called to the consistent use of qualifying terms in presenting the results of my efforts to naturalize this therapeutic encounter. My reason for doing so is that the findings of this clinical method are not simply facts but are largely surmises, attempts to interpret the additional data generated by the unpacking process. The subjective nature of this method makes it more than usually susceptible to the projective fallacy. That is, the therapist or investigator who employs this method may unwittingly read later thoughts into his earlier responses in order to rationalize or justify subjective reactions and interpretive choices (cf. Meehl 1983). If these limitations are kept in mind, however, one can learn a great deal about data processing from the systematic unpacking of therapy sessions.

SUMMARY

This chapter has focused on a central phase of the interpretive process, the data processing strategies and operations that cognitively transform clinical data and information into latent meanings and determinants that are unique to the individual patient at a given time. Rather than attempting to review all of our diverse processing operations briefly and superficially, I have selected several important and problematic examples for more detailed discussion and illustration: pattern seeking, thematization, and inference. A clinical method of investigating data processing, the retrospective "unpacking" or "naturalizing" of therapy sessions, has been described and illustrated. I have indicated also that we can learn a great deal about this subject from various other disciplines whose methods of studying cognitive processing supplement our own.

Students sometimes ask, "Do we really need such detailed knowledge of the preconscious processes that underlie our clinical interpretations? Will it make us better interpreters?" The short answer is yes. The long answer tells why, namely, the more we can learn about methods of cognitive transformation, and the more we are able to make that information part of our clinical interpretive knowledge base, the more likely we are to draw on and use that knowledge preconsciously (intuitively) in the depth psychological understanding of our patients.

CHAPTER SIX

Strategies of Construction and Reconstruction

CONSTRUCTION IS CLOSELY RELATED TO and a sequel of cognitive processing. Processing activities bring current clinical data into contact with as much relevant information as possible, including previously accumulated information about the patient, related information from other patients, the therapist's own experiences, and from human life generally (Peterfreund 1971). Clinicians draw on a great deal of knowledge about human beings (including, for example, commonsense psychology) that does not belong to the core of psychoanalytic theory (Rubovits-Seitz 1998). Conceptual enhancement of current and previous data from the patient leads to interpretive hypotheses (constructions) of possible latent meanings and determinants.

The definitions of construction and reconstruction are somewhat confused in psychoanalysis because Freud (1937b) used the terms interchangeably. Moore and Fine (1990) also define reconstruction and construction as synonymous, referring to both as formulations about repressed experiences in the early life of the patient. From the standpoint of the interpretive process, however, construction differs from reconstruction in two important ways: First, constructions are not necessarily concerned exclusively with early life experiences, but also deal with current pathodynamic issues. Second, according to traditional (hermeneutic) usage in other interpretive disciplines, construction is defined as a relatively discrete phase of the construal process in which the interpreter attempts to formulate a tentative overall or "whole" (thematic) meaning of the current data being studied. Reconstruction in clinical interpretation, by contrast, is a gradual process about which Freud (1918) wrote that crucial childhood events "are as a rule not reproduced as recollections, but have to be divined—constructed—gradually and laboriously from an aggragate of indications" (p. 51; see also Jacobsen and Steele 1979, Moore and Fine 1990). Citing Kris, Schwaber (in Malin 1982) makes the further interesting suggestion that if we could include the peculiarities of the parents' personalities in our reconstructions, an essential and sometimes crucial set of pathogenetic factors would be added.

Thus from the standpoint of the interpretive process, I distinguish between constructions and reconstructions—only the latter dealing specifically with formulations of repressed experiences from the patient's early life (see also Lichtenberg in Malin 1982).

A CLINICAL ILLUSTRATION OF CONSTRUCTION

Rachel was a 25-year-old law student who had been born and raised in Israel. She now lived in the United States. She came for treatment because of depression and anxiety, which began two weeks previously in response to learning about the worsening of her father's health problems. While tearfully describing her concern about her father, she blurted out with great agitation that another reason she was so upset was because of something terrible she did recently. While browsing in a bookstore she absentmindedly put a book of Hebrew poems in her book bag. A security guard observed her do that and arrested her for shoplifting. She insisted that she had no idea why she did it; she had never done such a thing before, and had no memory of putting the volume of poems in her book bag. The store threatened to prosecute her for theft, and she lived each day in dread that it would do so.

She was the eldest child in an orthodox Jewish Israeli family. An elderly grandmother who lived with her family had told Rachel repeatedly as a child that her family were disappointed that she was not a boy.

She worked hard to prove her worth, and became an outstanding student as well as a tireless helper at home. She was closest to her father throughout childhood because he took more interest in her intellectual development, encouraged her, and was more warm and loving than anyone else in the family. In recent years her father had developed colon cancer, for which he had undergone surgery. He did better for a while, but recently had begun to lose weight and had become very weak. He had been admitted to the intensive care unit of a hospital in Israel, and was being considered for further surgery.

For the first several weeks of her therapy, Rachel talked mostly about problems in her current home situation. Her husband's widowed father had come from Israel to live with them during the past year. Her husband and father-in-law expected her to wait on them almost in the manner of a servant; more immediately, they had refused her request to take the time and funds to visit her sick father in Israel. Her husband's first loyalty was to his own aging father, not to her or her father, and he was unsympathetic toward her complaints. Rachel had become fairly Americanized from living in this country for half-a-dozen years, and felt her position in this family to be demeaning and humiliating. She had been tempted to leave her husband, but feared its effects on her sick father, who would be disappointed and concerned if Rachel's marriage failed.

Session to be Interpreted

Rachel started the session by saying that she felt less anxious and depressed, because her father was in somewhat better condition now. She had decided that despite her husband's and father-in-law's refusal to support her plan to fly to Israel for a visit with her father, she would go anyway. Her husband and his father controlled the family finances, however, and they insisted that her duty was to them. Her husband told her that such a trip would cost too much, and that his old father needed her help here. She told this in her usual rather bland and long-suffering tone [which I called to her attention, and asked how did she really feel about her husband's attitude?] Instead of answering my question directly, she replied that she made arrangements to study late with a classmate so she would have an excuse not to go home that night. [I asked why?] She said that she didn't want to "cause a fuss" with her husband in front of his old and strict father. She was so determined to defy them, however, that she had gone ahead and made plane reservations to Israel. But then she talked to a woman friend from Israel about her plan, and the friend convinced her not to go through with it.

[What happened then?] "I was up all night studying, and had classes all the next day, so I was out on my feet. When I went home the second night I went straight to bed, and the next morning I left early for school." [Was this going on at the time you were arrested?] She paused briefly and then suddenly began laughing hysterically, and was unable to stop for several minutes. [What's so funny?] "I suddenly re-called that my father loves Hebrew poems." [Why is that funny?] She didn't know—it just suddenly popped into her head and she started laughing. No, it isn't funny and she doesn't understand the laughter. [Just think out loud about it.]

Tearfully and nostalgically she recalled an earlier time when her father was ill, and she read Hebrew poems to him. He enjoyed it, and it seemed to make him feel better. [So the book of poems is associated in your mind with your father, and with wanting to make him feel better?] More tears flowed, followed by an unusually forceful statement that she wished she had gone ahead and taken the money from the family funds and used it to go to Israel. [So another common denominator between wanting to take the money and taking the book of poems was breaking rules about taking something that you felt was forbidden.] She saw this parallel quickly and spoke excitedly about how intense the urge was to take the money from family funds, something she had never done before. [I then made the following interpretation:

> You must have been furious at your husband, but the anger at him never really surfaced directly. Instead you became passively aggressive toward him by avoiding him and depriving him of something he wanted, namely, your companionship and care. The anger and aggressive defiance toward him that you had been holding in may have slipped out indirectly and sym-bolically when you took the volume of Hebrew poems for your father and put it in your book bag.]

In her response to the interpretation she said that not confronting her husband about the issue now reminded her of something else about her father. When her mother called her from Israel and told her that her father was in the intensive care unit, her mother said that this time her father seemed to have "given up fighting." Rachel now felt that she had done the same thing when she avoided the confrontation with her husband. [Noting her recognition of an identification with her father, I interpreted further:

> It now occurs to me that slipping the book, which you associate with your father, into your book bag seems symbolically similar to putting a loving image of your father inside yourself—internalizing it, that is, identifying with him. That kind of identification often occurs as a way of trying to hold on to someone whom a person fears he or she might lose.]

Rachel wept profusely at that point, saying finally that that is why she needed so desperately to go to her father when he was in the intensive care unit. She was so afraid he would die before she had a chance to see him and be with him and comfort him one more time. The possibility of losing him is the hardest thing she has ever had to face. She doesn't even know whether she can stand it and recover from it; and whenever he seems a little better, as he does at present, she feels so relieved.

Commentary

RETROSPECTIVELY DERIVED FORMULATION OF THE SESSION

Applying the recurrent cycles (RC) approach—that is, starting at the end of Rachel's treatment and working backward interpretively to the beginning of the case—I found a recurrent subcycle throughout her therapeutic process that involved a conflict of loyalty toward father figures versus mother figures. The recurrent loyalty conflict had childhood roots in having to choose between differing expectations of her on the part of her parents. For example, her father felt that Rachel's allowance should be increased because she did so many chores around the house, but her mother insisted on a minimal allowance. When Rachel served as baby-sitter for the younger children, making it unnecessary for her parents to hire someone for that purpose, her father felt they should pay Rachel, but her mother insisted that taking care of the younger children was a family duty for which Rachel should not be paid. Her mother exhorted Rachel to save rather than spend her meager allowance, and she often complained to Rachel that her father was extravagant. Her father countered with complaints to Rachel that her mother was stingy. Her parents regularly played out their disagreements with each other by confiding to Rachel their disagreements and mutual resentments, competing in that way for influence on her.

Rachel usually took her father's side in such matters but she paid a price for doing so, for her mother reacted with criticism followed by sullen withdrawal from Rachel. The latter experiences were particularly frustrating to Rachel because her mother was not very available generally, and the further withdrawal made Rachel feel almost completely cut off from her mother. Both Rachel's and her father's tendencies to defer to Rachel's mother appeared to be based on fear of provoking angry withdrawals on her mother's part. One of the long-term effects of those experiences on Rachel was a defensive identification with or introjection of her mother's frustrating pattern of withdrawing in anger: Rachel herself developed a pattern of withdrawal when angry.

Detailed study of the recurrent loyalty conflict pattern in Rachel's treatment also revealed two major recurrent compromise formations, both of which appeared to have been reactivated in the recent loyalty conflict between her husband (as a mother figure) and her sick father. The first was the aforementioned withdrawal pattern, which served as a compromise between her angry feelings and her fear of alienating a mother figure. By withdrawing she expressed her hostility passively, with less risk of the mother figure's retaliatory withdrawal.

The other compromise formation dealt with conflict between impulses to defy a mother figure versus fear of her alienation and withdrawal. In this compromise she would defy the mother figure, but in surreptitious ways that were not readily observable. Rachel's father had provided a model of and warrant for such a compromise, because he sometimes purchased items without informing Rachel's mother. To illustrate this pattern in Rachel: in compliance with her mother's exhortations to save money, Rachel dutifully put her allowance in a piggy bank; but from time to time, when the need was great, she would extract coins from the bank without her mother's knowledge. Another example: she was not above borrowing money, clothing, toys, and sweets from friends and siblings, which she sometimes did not return or repay. Her character pattern of mooching was thus a way of getting what she wanted without spending money (cf. also in this connection her taking the book without paying for it).

Rachel's conflict with her husband over money to visit her sick father activated both of these characterologic compromise formations: the withdrawal pattern, which dealt with conflict about anger at her husband, and the secret defiance pattern, which attempted to get what she wanted without her husband's (mother's) knowledge.

Formulation of the Described Session

Precipitant(s) of the Principal Current Conflict

In addition to the external factors of her father's illness and her husband's insensitivity toward her, the following intrapsychic factors also appeared to be involved as precipitating factors:

I. Rachel's anxiety about her father's illness was so intense that she urgently needed to be with him and her childhood family in order to control the anxiety. Her husband's objections undercut her principal method of dealing with the anxiety, namely, her lifelong character pattern of helpfulness to her family, based in part on both sublimated and warded-off dependent aggression. Part of the (inhibited) rage at her husband resulted, therefore, from (a) frustration of reactivated dependence on her father, and (b) increased separation anxiety produced by her husband's interference with one of her principal characterologic mechanisms for coping with such anxiety.

2. Another intrapsychic precipitant of the current conflict (inhibited rage at her husband) was transference to him from her frus-

tratingly penurious mother, whose restrictions on spending money and other pleasures had left a wellspring of potentially transferable negative feelings in Rachel toward any and all stingy and controlling mother figures.

PRINCIPAL CURRENT CONFLICT

The principal current conflict is hostility toward her husband (as mother figure) for frustrating her reactivated dependence on her father and interfering with her coping pattern of helping her family, versus fear of alienating her husband (mother figure), and provoking his withdrawal from her.

DEFENSES AGAINST THE PRINCIPAL CURRENT CONFLICT

1. Passive-aggressive withdrawal from husband, which included active mastery of anxiety about his (i.e., mother's) possible withdrawal by withdrawing herself.

2. Surreptitious defiance (e.g., making plane reservations, planning to take money from family funds, and shoplifting).

3. Reaction formation (dutifulness).

4. Masochistic submission, with self-pity.

5. Outbursts of exaggerated and displaced emotion (uncontrolled laughter and weeping).

6. Rationalization of her own motives.

FORMULATION OF THE SHOPLIFTING SYMPTOM

I considered several related motives and meanings of the shoplifting symptom. Overdetermined meanings of the Hebrew poems included an iconic image of her father, a memory of how to make him feel better, and a symbolic enactment of an identification with her father's having "given up fighting." Taking (or "stealing") the book appeared to represent a substitute for angrily taking money from her husband, and putting it in her bag may have enacted symbolically an internalization of her father in an attempt to hold on to and feel close to him, rather than feeling separated from or losing him. Still another overdeterminant of the shoplifting symptom was her character pattern of mooching as a way of getting what she wanted without spending money. Each of these posited constructions derives from actual clinical data during the session, as well as from relevant clinical concepts of psychoanalysis and clinical interpretation.

TESTING THE CONSTRUCTIONS AGAINST ALL OF THE SESSION'S DATA

Virtually all of the described session's data appear to reflect defenses against or attempted solutions of the previously mentioned principal current conflict. Her associations will be reviewed and interpreted sequentially:

1. She feels guilty that she did not go to Israel to be with her father: Since she is conscious of that guilt, one can assume that the guilt is probably not part of the principal current conflict, because that conflict is always unconscious. I suspected, therefore, that the guilt was foregrounded defensively as a substitute for more disturbing feelings.

2. Her uncontrolled sobbing: Defensively exaggerated and displaced emotion; a "hysterical" mechanism to avoid the more disturbing feelings associated with the principal current conflict (see the next associations).

3. She discloses for the first time the events surrounding the conflict with her husband about visiting her sick father: She had employed isolation and intellectualization to ward off these disturbing feelings.

4. She said she felt "stunned" by her husband's opposition: An ambiguous word that said little about her actual feelings, but might imply a massive warding off of intense emotion.

5. She tried to persuade her husband, but he was adamant: A rational but essentially unemotional response on her part.

6. He accused her of selfishness: Her failure to turn this accusation back against her husband is striking. She absorbed the allegation without defending herself or retaliating—a submissive masochistic defense, due to fear of provoking her (mother figure) husband's withdrawal.

7. She considered asking her mother for money, but decided not to: Possibly a rationalization, although in view of past experiences with her mother concerning money, the decision may well have been nondefensively rational.

8. Her secretly making plane reservations, and her plan to take money for the trip from family funds: Enactments of her character pattern of secretly defying mother figures.

9. Her taking her friend's advice not to defy husband, not to take the money, and not to go to Israel: Another rationalization, concealing her underlying fear of confronting and possibly alienating her husband (as mother figure).

10. Her more uncontrolled weeping: see item #2 above.

11. She responds to increased interpretive pressure about her true feelings toward her husband by describing her two-day avoidance of him: An evasive but interpretable answer to the therapist's question about how she really felt.

12. Her hysterical laughter in response to the therapist's interpretation of anger at her husband: Exaggerated and displaced emotion, by which she avoids the hostility toward her husband by substituting a relevant but tangential connection between the book of poems and her father.

13. Her attachment to her father, and pattern of being helpful to him: This relates to an overdeterminant of the shoplifting symptom, but it also serves a defensive function of avoiding the principal current conflict of anger at her husband versus fear of alienating him.

14. Her self-critical statement that she should have taken the money: She reproaches herself for being intimidated by her husband, and defensively turns the anger against herself.

Since all of the data of the session appear to be explained adequately by the posited construction, that formulation can be considered (tentatively) the most plausible interpretation at the time. On the other hand, more definitive posttherapeutic justification might reveal incompletely explained data (see Chapter 7 for discussion and illustration of posttherapeutic justification).

SOME GENERAL ASPECTS OF CONSTRUCTION

Freud's Views on Construction

Near the beginning of his first encyclopedia article, Freud (1923a) presented a short section entitled "Psychoanalysis as an Interpretive Art." In that single, seldom-quoted paragraph Freud abstracted over a dozen key elements dealing with his method of construction, namely: (1) psychoanalysis is an *art* of interpretation; (2) the aim of such interpretation is to discover deeper, hidden meanings in the patient's associations; (3) one of the methods that the analyst uses for this purpose is to listen with "evenly suspended" rather than focused attention; (4) what the therapist listens for is the "drift," that is, the gist, essence, or theme of the patient's associations; (5) in favorable circumstances the undercurrent meanings emerge indirectly in the form of "allusions"; (6) the allusions are to "one particular theme," of which the patient is unaware; (7) the therapist then "guesses" the central theme or motif from the allusions in the patient's material (see The Role of Conjecture in the Process of Construction, below); (8) unfavorable conditions, such as excessive resistance, can make it impossible to grasp underlying meanings; (9) rather than following strict rules, construction leaves considerable leeway to the therapist's "skill and tact"; (10) "impartiality and practice" in interpretation contribute to "trustworthy results"; (11) confirmation depends on repetition of results in similar cases; (12) even though this approach to construction lacks a definitive theoretical basis, and thus is largely an ad hoc process, it has been found useful; and (13) in fact, this method is still used, although with better understanding of its limitations.

Freud's interpretive method may have had more of a theoretical basis than he realized, however. Most of the interpretive strategies and concepts that he described are similar to, or in some cases are identical with, the centuries-old theory of interpretation known as hermeneutics. Hermeneutics is the theory and exegesis is the practice of interpreting meanings in texts of all kinds, including spoken communications (including the therapeutic dialogue). The principal difference is that what Freud described represents mainly the initial or constructive phase of the interpretive process, which is largely a guess about the overall or whole meaning of a particular text or set of data (cf. Forrester 1980, for a critique of Freud's later method of construction).

Natterson (1991) observes that the analyst never knows with certainty whether an interpretation is correct, because he or she never knows all of the factors that contribute to the situation. "So the analyst makes a sophisticated guess, prepares for the high probability of error, and expects a flawed but constructive consequence of the interpretation" (pp. 118–119). Poland (in Weich 1986) thus concludes that all interpretations conveyed to the patient are really trial interpretations. Weich (1986) agrees, and proposes the concept of a "good enough therapist" (see also Kumin 1989). Eagle (1984) suggests the related concept of a "good enough interpretation."

Freud (1900) indicated that it is impossible to give specific instructions about the method of arriving at a symbolic interpretation, because "success must be a question of hitting on a clever idea, of direct intuition" (p. 97). Symbolic relations define or treat one thing in terms of another. The highly developed symbolic function in humans conserves resources and storage of information by grouping comparable things together and interpreting new experiences according to representations of *types*; but the richly variegated possibilities of symbolic relations make such processing less reliable (de Beaugrande 1984).

In "An Outline of Psychoanalysis," Freud (1940) referred to both the necessity for and the limitations of construction in clinical interpretation:

> In our science as in others the problem is the same: behind the attributes (i.e., qualities) of the object under examination which are presented directly to our perception, we have to discover something else which is more independent of the particular receptive capacities of our sense organs and which approximate more closely to what may be supposed to be the real state of affairs. We have no hope of being able to reach the latter itself, since it is evident that everything new that we have inferred must nevertheless be translated back into the language of our perceptions from which it is simply impossible for us to free ourselves. But herein lies the very nature and limitation of our science. [p. 196]

Considerable controversy has occurred, however, concerning the methods involved in construction (cf. Diamond 1983). Reik (1937, 1949), for example, carried Freud's recommendations regarding freely hovering attention to an extreme, arguing emphatically against use of the intellect by therapists. Fenichel (1941) disagreed, insisting that a balance between cognitive and subjective methods is needed. Ramzy (1963, 1974) went to the other extreme, proposing that clinical inference follows purely logical rules. Schafer (1959), Spence (1968, 1981), and others disagree, arguing that the therapist's understanding depends mainly on a broader context of information about the patient that is built up gradually over time.

The Role of Conjecture in the Process of Construction

According to Glaser and Strauss (1967), construction should be concerned with generating first-order, low-level theory, and should be grounded inductively in actual observations as much as possible, rather than in other sources such as coincidence, conjecture, speculation, common sense, fantasy, deductive inference, and so on. Their argument can be questioned, however, because it rests on an idealized premise of theory resulting from pure stepwise induction, rather than involving a significant amount of imaginative guesswork.

In his informative essay on "Epistemological Aspects of Psycho-analytic Interpretation," for example, the philosopher of science Gregorio Klimovsky (1991) points out that

> in an interpretation the psychoanalyst formulates a proposition; he enunciates what logicians call a *declarative sentence*—that is, something the psychoanalyst can be right or wrong about. In most cases, the affirmation that constitutes the interpretation has a hypothetical character, because the truth or falsity of what is being said is not known. Of course, this is not directly so for the patient; but it is not known by the therapist either. The interpretation is characterized to a considerable extent by conjecture. [p. 473]

Some controversy continues, however, concerning the roles of detailed observation versus intuition in positing constructions. Citing the work of Loewenstein, for example, Yale Kramer (1989) maintains that clinical judgment "is not a magical or mystical process dependent upon some transcendent intuition of the well-analyzed therapist. . . . Loewenstein's approach was practical and empirical. For him the solution was to be found through meticulous examination of the objective data that emerged in the analytic setting" (p. 338). Another example of this kind was Karen Horney's contention that a discrepancy or inconsistency is "as definite an indication of the presence of conflicts as a rise in body temperature is of physical disturbance" (cited by Paris 1997, p. 5). Paul Gray's (1986, 1994, 2000) and to a lesser extent Fred Busch's (1999) methods of "close process monitoring" also emphasize observation over interpretation. Other writers (e.g., Arlow 1979, Donnel 1983, 1985) have stressed the intuitive, creative, aesthetic aspects of construction, and Gribinski (1994) asserts that "to guess and to construct are synonymous" (p. 1011). Rangell (1985) writes that "informed speculation *precedes* discovery and proof" (p. 86, emphasis added).

With respect to intuition, Laughlin (1997) summarizes the studies of Bastick (1982) on the nature of intuition, emphasizing the following characteristics: the nonlogical, gestalt nature of such experiences; the suddenness, unexpectedness, associated affect, and ineffability of the insight; the relationship between intuition and creativity; confidence in the process, while at the same time realizing that an intuitive insight may be incorrect. Harbort (1997) describes intuition as a mix of psychological constructs including imagery and narrative formation, with an underlying basis of experience. Bergson (1946) noted that experience presents a "flow" of phenomena—that is, reality "flows," and we flow with it (cf. Duncan's [1989] application of a similar concept to the clinical interpretive process).

Intuition makes it possible for one to employ experience, personal knowledge, and creative faculties, including self-reflection, pattern recognition (Margolis 1987), and worldview components, in dealing with the uncertainties of problems. It mediates between the particulars and the generalities of experience, thus facilitating both intention and will to act (e.g., intending and deciding to communicate an interpretation).

Based on studies of how physicians arrive at their interpretations of medical diagnoses, and drawing on Ricoeur's (1976) concepts of interpretation, Harbort (1997) concludes that speculation *precedes* the actual process of interpretation. He writes that one of the primary factors in the art of interpretation is

> making the initial guess at a starting point for understanding of a patient's complex, dynamic set of interrelated problems. Choice of a starting point for interpretation, however, is not [clinically] part of the process and it certainly is not objective. The skill orientation of the physician often determines his or her starting point, and the process of interpretation begins thereafter. "The act of understanding is at first a genial (or a mistaken) guess and there are no methods for making guesses, no rules for generating insights. The [clinical] activity of interpretation commences when we begin to test and criticize our guesses" (Ricoeur 1976, p. 81). [p. 133]

In contrast, I include the conjectural aspect of construction as an integral step in the clinical interpretative process.

Hermeneuticists emphasize the complexities, difficulties, and limitations of the interpretive process—for example, that there can never be a method or model of correct construction, because the psychology of understanding cannot be reduced to a systematic procedure, and there is no way of assuring a right guess by means of rules and principles (Hirsch 1967). Similarly, the method of interpretive inquiry called *Verstehen* (Jaspers 1962; see also Ehrlich and Wisser 1988), which was introduced originally in the human and social sciences, is difficult to describe logically, but it has influenced our approach to clinical interpretation. The method appears to draw on all of the mind's capacities, in particular a back-and-forth focus on parts and whole, which is the principal processing operation of hermeneutics. Polkinghorne (1983) stresses that the meaning one seeks to understand is grasped first in a tacit sense before it is known more fully (cf. Moustakas 1990, Polanyi 1966). The cultural historian, Jacques Barzun (1956), notes also that the investigator "selects his material not by fixed rule but by the *esprit de finesse* that Pascal speaks of, the gift, namely, of seeing a quantity of fine points in a given relation without ever being able to demonstrate it" (p. 393).

The hermeneutic focus on interdependent relations of part and whole meanings is based on the concept that the whole is derived from and constituted by the parts, the latter being delineated and integrated by the whole. Freud (1911b) employed the part-whole principle in his concept that the meaning of any fragment depends on the meaning of the whole, but he subsumed part-whole relations in clinical data under the principle of determinism rather than associating it with hermeneutics (cf. 1916–1917). In fact, Freud appeared to ignore the discipline of hermeneutics (Kermode 1985, Rubovits-Seitz 1998).

Hermeneutic theory views part meanings as implications of the overall meaning; that is, the whole meaning implies certain part meanings but not others. Drawing of correct implications depends on a correct "guess" about the posited whole meaning. Although most of the practical problems of interpretation are problems of implication, the uncertainty of constructions results from the necessity to guess initially about the overall meaning (cf. Kermode 1979). A parallel between the interpretation of therapeutic discourse and the psychology of ordinary communication illustrates this process. In his book on the psychology of communication, Miller (1967) describes a listener's communicative task in the following way (the rapidity of the process suggests that it occurs preconsciously, for the most part):

The listener begins with a guess about the input information, on the basis of which he or she generates a matching internal signal. The first guess is often wrong, which leads to another such guess. The cycle of guessing, mismatches, and corrected guesses recurs until a satisfactory match is obtained. The efficiency of this process depends largely on the quality of the initial guess. If the initial guess is close, the iterative process is completed rapidly; if not, the listener may not be able to keep up with the flow of speech. Initial guesses are like predictive hypotheses about what incoming messages will turn out to be. Advance postulates make it possible to attune one's apperception to certain interpretations while rejecting others. [Rubovits-Seitz 1998, p. 121]

The hermeneutic concept of "fore-understanding" (*Vorwerständnis*) also contributes to conjectures about the "whole" meaning in the constructive process (Friedman 2000, Gadamer 1975). Kermode (1979) points out that we sense the genre of what the speaker says, and that without such fore-understanding of the whole we could not understand the parts. What appears to make fore-understanding possible is some degree of redundancy in the message, which reduces the range of possible meanings. On the other hand, Shoshana Felman (1987) cites Lacan's caveat that analysis has no use for knowledge given in advance: "What the analyst must know is how to ignore what he knows" (p. 81). Similarly, Hundert (1989) cites Piaget's conclusion that insights are achieved only when people are able to decenter themselves from the usual schemas with which they assimilate their world (see also Edward Jones 1986).

It will repay us at this point to examine still more closely the source and nature of the guesses that are involved in attempting to identify the underlying whole or thematic meaning of a therapy session. Guesses of this kind are not extraneous to cognitive processing and construction, but are integral to it. Conjectures of this kind are often wrong, of course, which necessitates a series of rapid "generate-and-test cycles" that alternate between guessing and checking in search of a thematic meaning that *can* unify all, or at least most, of the clinical data. The social science methodologist Paul Diesing (1971) points out that in actual practice interpreters do not rest satisfied with their first guesses, but think up as many alternative conjectures as possible, often very rapidly (see also Brenman 1984).

Each guess is tested, and those that survive are tested some more; "testing and revision is a continuous process" (pp. 145–146; see also Meehl 1954, Oskamp 1965).

On a vastly smaller scale, such guesses can be compared with what Einstein (1934) referred to as "free inventions of the intellect" (p. 15). which he maintained are indispensable to the method of theoretical physics. He explained that "there is no logical bridge between phenomena and their theoretical principles"—that "only intuition, resting on sympathetic understanding of experience, can reach them" (p. 4). Freud (1915) made a similar point in his comments at the beginning of "Instincts and Their Vicissitudes." Like Einstein, Freud stressed that everything depends on such guesses not being arbitrarily chosen, "but determined by their having significant relations to the empirical material"—relations, however, "that we seem to *sense* before we can clearly recognize and demonstrate them" (p. 117, emphasis added; cf. also Polanyi's [1966] "tacit knowing": the capacity to sense the wholeness of an object, event, or experience from our understanding of its parts). Vague but perceivable elements combine with imperceptible aspects of experience to produce a sense of wholeness, so that the tacit dimension underlies and guides intuition in the form of conjectures or "hunches."

In a similar vein, the scientist E. O. Wilson (1998) describes the Darwinian basis of the scientific method, noting that scientific theories are a product of "informed imagination." Investigators try to think of every possible way to test a hypothesis, using multiple competing hypotheses and devising tests that will eliminate all but one (cited by Pollack 1999).

Another philosopher of science who stressed the role of imaginative conjectures in scientific work was Karl Popper (e.g., 1963), who argued that theories (including interpretations as first-level theories) cannot be induced from facts alone; they can be created only by an imaginative leap beyond particular instances in order to find a better explanation. We learn by conjectures and refutations, so that progress results from making bold, imaginative guesses, followed by careful, critical assessment of alternative hypotheses (Berkson and Wettersten 1984).

Some clinicians (e.g., Schwaber 1983b, 1987b, 1990a) have criticized the conjectural component of the clinical interpretive process as an unjustified inferential (inductive) leap, but such a criticism seems inapposite because the conjectural leap involved is not based solely on inductively extended perceptions, but also involves imagination, abstraction, intuition, and both inductive and deductive inferences. According to Watanabe (1977), for example, interpretations are not based entirely on perception of extant patterns, but also on the therapist's skill, for the facts that he or she elicits and interprets arise in part from that skill. Harbort (1977/87, 1997) comments in this connection: "This embodiment of the skill in the practitioner rather than in the sciences that he utilizes is what elevates diagnostic medicine from a taxonomic science to an interpretive art" (p. 133).

Another concept should be mentioned in connection with the conjectural aspect of our search for whole meanings in the process of construction: Guesses about the underlying whole or thematic meaning of a given set of data are attempts to discover an explanation that can tie together coherently all of the data studied at that time. In casting about preconsciously and imaginatively in search of the best explanation, we consider various possibilities and choose the one that seems to account for the data most completely and coherently. Hofstadter (1982) suggests that the most creative explanations are often imaginative variations on a theme (see also Fischer 1986). The philosophy of science literatures dealing with this issue refer to this process by two names that mean essentially the same thing: inference to the best explanation (Brody 1970, Harman 1965, 1973, 1986) and abduction (Eco 1990, Kettner 1991, Peirce 1901, 1931–1935, 1958).

Peirce described abduction as a process of considering a large number of observations (cf. a therapy session), and allowing the observations themselves to suggest a first-order, low-level theory (inference or interpretation) that would explain them. Peirce viewed abduction as the source of novelty in ideas, but as having no real probative force in its own right, because the hypotheses generated by abduction are essentially guesses. On the other hand, interpretive hypotheses are not just wild guesses, but represent sophisticated conjectures, informed by observations and by the (often intuitive) recognition (sensing) of some general feature or relationship within the data. The process of abduction cannot be formalized, however, because there is no consistent logic of guessing in the discovery process (see also Hirsch 1967, Smith 1978).

Freud also used the term "guess" (*zu erraten*) when writing about this phase of the interpretive process (Gribinski 1994)—imaginative guessing or conjecturing being a necessary step in data processing and construction. Gribinski believes that Strachey's translations of *zu erraten* attempted to downplay the role of guesswork in clinical interpretation by using euphemistic, scientific-sounding terms such as "to detect and explain."

Abduction or inference to the best explanation is thus a highly important concept, which applies methodologically to all fields, including interpretive disciplines such as our own; it represents yet another basic similarity that binds psychoanalysis and dynamic psychotherapy to general science. Marshall Edelson (1988) points out, for example, that depth psychological therapy relies extensively on inference to the best explanation, and that Freud employed reasoning of this kind frequently in his case histories.

We should note also that this type of inferential reasoning or abduction is exploratory—a process of trying out various possible explanations, including quite novel ones, to account for the data as completely and coherently as possible. Ideally, we do not simply apply some pre-existing clinical theory to the data, which would entail the fallacy of doctrinal interpretation. Rather, our preconscious abductive data processing operations are imaginative, original, and creative; they attempt to construct the best explanation of the data, whatever that may be, whether it is part of psychodynamic theory or not. In this connection, Paula Heimann (1977) has called attention to a tendency by some therapists to underestimate the power of our imaginative capacities in cognitive processing and construction (cf. also Kainer 1999, who emphasizes the imaginative aspect of empathy; and Lafarge 2000, who stresses the analyst's effort to imagine the inner world of his or her patient). Andresen (1983) suggests cogently that we should not look to Freud for all the answers, but rather should cultivate receptivity in therapy sessions and create our own low-level, first-order interpretive theories; for the best explanation of a given set of data may come from common sense rather than from one of our numerous clinical theories (cf. Rubovits-Seitz 1998; see also Lord et al. 1979).

The point I am making is not a critique of psychoanalytic and psychodynamic theories themselves, but of their misuse in our interpretive work. Compare, for example, Freud's (1912) insistence that the most successful results occur when we allow ourselves to be surprised by any new developments in the data, and respond to such developments with an open mind, as free of preconceptions as possible. He suggested that in our interpretive work theory should remain like a stranger who has not been invited into the house (cited by Gribinski 1994). In other words, it is to a clinician's credit as an interpreter if he or she is open-minded and inventive enough to construct nondoctrinal explanations of our rich, ambiguous, overdetermined data. As Harbort (1997) concluded, for example: "For the purposes of problem-solving, the 'stem' of analogic reasoning used as an entry point into [interpretation] cannot be restricted too much or the human problem-solver will be unable to realize his full potential" (p. 133). This does not mean, of course, that anything goes interpretively, for, as emphasized previously, the criteria of the best, the most plausible, construction is how completely and coherently it can account for all (or at least most) of the data at a given time.

The preceding argument concerning the importance of seeking nondoctrinal constructions should not be taken to mean, on the other hand, that highly original interpretations are readily and easily available. The work of Roland Fischer (1986), referred to previously, suggests in fact that the number of themes available for construction is limited. He notes that interpretations are constructed largely according to specific plots involving past complementarities between biology and history, as recorded in myths, fairy tales, and narrative fiction—the codified human interpretive repertoire. Fischer argues further that this limitation applies to science generally:

> The recurring themes of science appear to be embedded in tropes that in time evolve in complexity and sophistication; not the themes [, however,]

but the compelling nature of the tropes makes us believe that the solution of a problem is imminent. . . . The myth of the "eternal return" appears as . . . "eternally returning" stories and *themata* that are constantly rewritten, reformulated, and retroped by and for passing generations [and also for individual patients]. . . . Their nature and meaning mark the limits of self-knowledge. [p. 26; cf. Freud's concept of repetition compulsion]

The repertoire of *themata* consist largely of wish-fulfilling self-interpretations that are the [basis] of narrative fiction. . . . The themes and stories are constantly rewritten . . . with but slight variations within a change in style begun by others. . . . The greatest freedom of interpretation—based on a large variety of plots and scenarios—prevails in those states of consciousness that cluster around the "I" state of daily routine [equivalent to Freud's ego]. In these states . . . we are free to vary the "content" of consciousness, a content directed toward action in the sensible world "out there." As we move away from the "I" state toward the "Self," . . . the universe that appears in these states of consciousness has to be interpreted in a "less-action"-minded and more stereotyped and predictable manner. [p. 21]

In a perceptive essay, "Peirce's Notion of Abduction and Psychoanalytic Interpretation," Matthias Kettner (1991) notes similarly that abduction does not specify how our hypotheses originate—in fact, "is indifferent as to whether explanations get introduced into the realm of the reasonable by a selective-eliminative procedure among explanation cadidates or by genuinely cooking them up from hitherto non-explicit potentially explanatory resources" (pp. 164–165). In other words, the sources of our abductions are multiple and varied.

Construction Versus Extraction
of Latent Meanings and Determinants

Studies of language processing suggest that listeners (including therapists) preconsciously construct rather than merely extract meanings from what is perceived. The role of construction in language processing is illustrated, for example, by the ubiquity of paraphrase; that is, we usually recall the gist rather than the actual wording of what we hear (Prideaux 1985). We also recall more than was actually heard, because the meaning representations that we construct include not only what we actually heard but also the inferences we drew from what the speaker (or patient) said. We fill in the blanks preconsciously to produce a complete and coherent meaning (Bransford and Franks 1971); and once such inferences have been placed in memory, they cannot be distinguished from that part of the meaning representation that is based on what was actually said—a finding that has important implications for misunderstandings in the clinical dialogue.

Abstraction, however, is one of the cognitive operations involved in construction (see, e.g., Kelly 1955). Arnheim (1969) defines abstraction as the drawing of essentials from organized wholes in which certain features are more crucial than others. Spinoza emphasized similarly that to express the innermost essence of something, one must avoid taking individual properties for the thing itself. In clinical interpretation we attempt to abstract the central dynamic theme of a session's data in the form of a construction. Arnheim cites the following illustration of abstraction by a writer who asked what the following had in common: "The Manhattan skyline, the gridiron town plan, the skyscraper, the model-T Ford, the constitution, Mark Twain's writing, Whitman's *Leaves of Grass*, comic strips, soap operas, assembly-line production, and chewing gum" (p. 172). A first abstraction suggests that all of the items are concerned with "what is American about America." A further abstraction, however, elicits a more subtle and essential trait that is common to all eleven items, namely, "a concern with process rather than product." According to Arnheim, abstraction often involves "the ability to wrest a hidden feature from an adverse context" (p. 70).

One of the inherent problems of human data processing and construction is the limited and unreliable human capacity for searching our vast memory stores. The ability to form symbolic relations, however, which defines one thing in terms of another, is highly developed in human beings. The capacity for symbolizing conserves resources and memory storage by grouping comparable experiences/memories together, and interpreting new experiences according to representations of already existing types.

Another problem concerns cross-situational consistencies of behavior. We assume that the way patients act in the therapeutic situation also characterizes their personalities and behavior generally, including outside of the therapeutic relationship. Thus we listen to the patient's associations about extratherapeutic experiences with two inevitable biases: one is to view such material as a displaced transference resistance; and the other is that our inner model of the patient, the template against which all associations are compared, is a product very largely of experiences with the patient in the therapeutic situation.

Language also contributes to our thinking of human behavior in trait terms. English, for example, contains approximately 18,000 trait or traitlike terms, almost 5 percent of the lexicon; but our vocabulary for labeling situations is meager and awkward. Intuitively, cross-situational consistencies seem logical and likely, but empirical research has failed to support the assumption (Bem and Allen 1974). The variety of situations in which investigators observe people is surprisingly limited, both in representativeness and extent. In addition, a particular clinician's presence can evoke a consistent mode of responding.

De Beaugrande (1980) notes that continuity, access, and economy are basic principles or postulates of data processing and construction. In this context, "continuity" refers to relations among stored mental contents, and relations of new experiences with old. "Access" refers to retrievability and "spreading activation" among related contents. "Economy" refers to efficiency of mental effort and storage by grouping comparable experiences together, and by constructing the largest possible pattern to deal with maximal data at the same time (Reiger 1975). The efficiency of data processing and construction is facilitated also by the fact that participants in discourse, including clinical discourse, rely on probable occurrences based on multiple varieties and patterns of clues.

Returning to the phenomenon of paraphrase, the ubiquity of this linguistic phenomenon illustrates further that meaning is not carried by words or phrases but by conceptual-relational patterns. Unlike logic and linguistic formalism (rule ordering), human communication (i.e., language in use) thrives on uncertainties, exceptions, and unexpected events (De Beaugrande 1980). The concept of semantic networks is useful in describing integrative and interactive models of communication. Meanings characteristically form multiple, interlocking, configurational groupings, so that cognitive processing and construction address themselves to patterns and pattern matching (Colby and Parkinson 1974, Pavlidis 1977). A perfect match is not necessary, according to Reiger (1975); a reasonably good fit is adequate. But listeners construct the largest possible pattern to maximize the amount of data covered at one time (De Beaugrande 1980).

The central problem in understanding discourse is the issue of continuity, or connectivity, within the data. The continuity is not manifest, however, so the interpreter must link data to other data. Theoretically, an ideal language model would employ the same procedure for both the production and comprehension of discourse (or written texts). Mapping of meanings between surface and underlying structures would then be symmetrical in both directions, but an arrangement of that kind is not plausible in human communication. The mapping of meanings is asymmetrical in both discourse and textual communication. Listeners and readers construct much of the meaning that they hear or read, and the ubiquitous phenomenon of paraphrase demonstrates that they do not end up with exactly the same material that the speaker or writer expressed. Persons engaged in discourse make important changes in the material presented to them; and when the original material is rerepresented to them they do not shift toward the actual message but retain their own modified versions, preferring the latter to the original (Kay 1955).

Listeners also vary considerably in how much of the original communicated material they process, store, and recover. They employ whatever is necessary and accessible to achieve a narrative-like continuity (see Kartiganer 1985, for Freud's use of narrative construction in his report of the Wolf Man). The continuity principle thus serves as a powerful constraint on the number of possible interpretations for a given discourse. For that reason and others, Bouchard (1995), De Beaugrande (1980), Ricoeur (1974), Rogers (1984), and I (1986) have questioned the radically relativist claim that an infinite number of plausible interpretations can be construed for a given discourse or text.

Construction and Coherence in the Interpretive Process

Depth psychologies assume that the plurivocal meanings of clinical data are interrelated in various ways, for example, associatively, contextually, hierarchically, thematically, synchronically, diachronically, topographically, and structurodynamically. In the process of clinical interpretation, coherence refers to the degree of internal consistency that a construction or reconstruction is able to impart to clinical data and their overdetermined meanings. De Beaugrande (1980) distinguishes several varieties of coherence: (1) surface connections, called "cohesion," which are sequential in nature; (2) underlying connections, called "coherence," which are conceptual rather than sequential; and (3) "planning" connections, each component of which relates to some interactive or communicative plan.

The logic of coherence as a criterion of internal consistency rests on its relation to the basic concept (background assumption) of continuity. That is, to the extent that an interpretive hypothesis exhibits a potential for organizing meanings coherently, we assume that it reflects one of the most characteristic features of clinical data and of meanings themselves, namely, their continuity. Atkinson (1978), a historian, defines coherence similarly as "comprehensiveness with unity, nothing relevant omitted, everything irrelevant excluded" (p. 131). Ego psychology views coherence as an achievement of "that special functional control and integration that we know under the name of a synthetic, or better, organizing function" (Hartmann 1951, p. 34).

Freud's view of the clinical process has significantly influenced the way we listen to patients. That is, our goal is to discover the underlying thread of continuity in the patient's associations; thus we necessarily listen with an ear tuned to sequence and coherence, and a sensitivity to and search for continuity and coherence can be viewed as essential aspects of our clinical interpretive competence (Spence 1982a). Like the historian, the clinician is allowed considerable latitude in reconstructing the past to make it cohere with the present (Einhorn 1988).

The popularity of coherence in interpretive work is partly subjective, however—the satisfaction of a logically consistent explanation in contrast to the unsettling effects of ambiguity and incoherence. Einstein (1934) wrote, for example, that to be left with two explanations for the same set of phenomena is intolerable to any orderly mind. Similarly, the structural (or pattern-model) approach of the social sciences views the world in terms of relationships rather than things—an orientation that corresponds with the structurodynamic perspective in Freud's system, which also formulates clinical data from the vantage points of functional relations, patterns, organization, or structure of the behavior studied. The structural viewpoint maintains that interpretations should illumine not only individual mental contents but also the organized continuity of all relevant meanings at a given time. The hermeneuticist E. A. Hirsch, Jr. (1967) notes, for example, that in practice we are always relating our understanding to something else, and that usually we cannot even understand the data without perceiving such relationships, for we cannot artificially isolate the construction of one meaning from all those related meanings that accompany it. Since meaning is a structure of component meanings, construction has not done its job when it simply enumerates what the component meanings are. The interpreter must also determine their probable structure.

Coherence is applied in the constructive phase of the interpretive process by the therapist's scanning of the associations heuristically and noting that different elements of the data cohere with each other in some manner, for example, by similarity, contrast, repetition, or sequence. Coherence becomes even more important once a tentative whole meaning (e.g., thematic conflict) has suggested itself to the therapist, for at that point the interpreter undertakes a more systematic review of the clinical material to determine whether the data as a whole fit together coherently in terms of the initial construction. The gradual shaping of a more definitive construction depends even further on coherence, to assess the "goodness of fit" produced by each trial revision of the construction. The adequacy of the final construction is assessed by its ability to integrate the individual data and meanings of the entire session into a coherent whole.

Coherence is invoked even more stringently as a criterion of internal evidence in the justification of interpretations (see Chapter 7), but coherence is used also in the context of discovering (constructing) unconscious meanings and determinants. Its use differs, however, in these two phases of the interpretive process. For purposes of construction, it is not necessary to account for all of the data, some of which are not even available yet. The degree of internal consistency needed at this stage is only a rough approximation between a tentative hypothesis and the major, most evident meanings of the clinical data. Even very rough equivalences such as posited analogic patterns may be good enough at this point for the purposes at hand (Colby and Stoller 1988). When used for purposes of justification, however, the criterion of coherence is applied to all of the data, with particular attention to how all of the details (the individual associations and their part meanings) fit together, and how they fit with the thematic or whole meaning represented by the construction.

Some contemporary philosophers of science define truth as that which forms a coherent whole (coherentism), a viewpoint that has some relations to a growing movement in a number of fields called constructivism. During the past decade or two a number of writers have introduced constructivist concepts into psychoanalysis and dynamic psychotherapy (e.g., Barratt 1984, Hoffman 1991, Loch 1977, Ricoeur 1977, Schafer 1983, Spence 1982a, Steele 1979, Stern 1985, Viderman 1979). Constructivism is based on the postpositivist perspective that any so-called reality is a construction of those who believe they have investigated and discovered it—actually an invention whose inventor is unaware of having invented it, but who assumes that the reality exists independently of him- or herself.

Stern (1985) observes that for the constructivist, regularity is substituted for truth. Unlike the empiricist, who holds that meanings can be found only in observations, constructivists insist that one cannot know reality apart from the operations used to interpret it. All we can do is judge how well a regularity accounts for experience, that is, how good the fit is. "Reality is understood as a constraint on our constructions, not as a match for them" (p. 204).

On the other hand, discarding the older viewpoint based on the match of knowledge and reality does not mean that reality itself is nothing but our construction of it. Manicas and Secord (1983) have summarized the arguments by some philosophers of science (e.g., Bhaskar 1975, Harré 1972), who accept the critique of empiricism, but who hold that there is a natural world external to us. Because the natural world is so complex, however, composed of so many interrelated strata, no single understanding of a phenomenon is adequate.

The latter view of knowing and the known is called the Realist theory of science, or Fallibilist Realism—a viewpoint that incorporates the constructivist point of view but rejects the notion of pure self-reference. Thus constructivism does not necessitate a complete relativism, although it should make one reconsider any claims of certainty. Varela (1984) argues for a perspective of "participation and interpretation, where the subject and the object are inseparably meshed" (p. 322).

In his later writings, Merton Gill (e.g., 1984, 1991, 1994) adopted the social-constructivist perspective (recently renamed dialectical constructivism) of his collaborator, I. Z. Hoffman (1991, 1994, 1998, 1999). "Social" implies that the approach is based on a participant paradigm in which the therapist as well as the patient is involved, and that each participant shapes the other. "Constructivist" indicates that each participant "reads" the other from his or her own perspective. The social component of this paradigm was anticipated by Balint (1965), Ferenczi (1925), Racker (1968), Schafer (1983), and Sullivan (1953).

Reconstruction

Freud (1937b) described a prototypical example of reconstruction in the following way: A reconstruction "lays before the subject of the analysis a piece of his early history that he has forgotten, in some such way as this":

> Up to your nth year you regarded yourself as the sole and unlimited possessor of your mother; then came another baby and brought you grave disillusionment. Your mother left you for some time, and even after her reappearance she was never again devoted to you exclusively. Your feelings towards your mother became ambivalent, your father gained a new inportance to you . . . and so on. [p. 261]

This prototypic example of reconstruction by Freud is based on a very common, almost universal, childhood experience; but in his case histories of the Wolf Man, Rat Man, and others, Freud postulated a variety of much more highly specific, including idiosyncratic, infantile, and childhood experiences that had been repressed, but that were reconstructed in the course of the patients' treatments.

An example of a highly specific reconstruction in the current clinical literature has been reported by Freeman (1998):

A depressed young man as an adolescent had the masturbatory fantasy of a woman inserting and then withdrawing objects from her vagina. This fantasy was linked to a series of dreams which the author interpreted as memories of early childhood visual experiences that were mentally represented but had never been conscious. As a child he shared his parents' bedroom and may have seen his mother remove a used Tampax, discard it, and insert another. This reconstruction resulted in a dramatic improvement in the patient's depression. [cited by Gillett 1999, p. 305]

Sometimes reconstructions are possible even in small children. For example, I reported the case of a young child with trichotillomania, who pulled out her hair and tickled her nose with it only when nursing from a nursing bottle (Seitz 1950). I surmised reconstructively that a conditioning factor that may have contributed to this symptom might have been earlier breast nursing by a mother with hirsute nipples. The child's mother reported that she had breast-fed the child for only two weeks, but examination of her breasts revealed a ring of coarse hairs around each nipple. The reconstruction was tested further by preparing a rubber nipple with hairs around its base that would brush against the child's upper lip and nose when she nursed from a bottle. As predicted, when the hairy nipple was used she did not pull out her hair, but when a regular nipple was used the trichotillomania recurred.

CLINICAL ILLUSTRATION
OF RECONSTRUCTION

I reported the following case to the Chicago Psychoanalytic Society on January 24, 1967.

The patient was a 31-year-old, single, high-achieving woman doctor who developed a major depression (dysthymic disorder, *DSM* 300.40) when her mother died of breast cancer. She had grown up in a highly intellectual, hyperrational, matriarchal household that included, in addition to her parents, her maternal grandmother and aunt. She was the "white hope" of the three adult women, who lived through her vicariously. Her brother was born on her first birthday, following which she was expected to behave much of the time as another competent, if miniature, adult in the family.

Soon after her psychoanalytic treatment began, the depression became so severe that she was unable to work for the next two years. She stayed at home and kept house for her father, came for her analytic appointments four times a week, but had no contact with friends or colleagues during that period. We agreed to continue her analysis without medication, electroconvulsive therapy, or hospitalization, if possible. A prolonged period of therapeutic regression appeared to be necessary to work through the narcissistic, symbiotic, and dependent pathology produced by her brother's birth so early in her life, the premature pseudo-maturity demanded of her following her brother's birth, and the narcissistic relationships with her on the part of her mother, aunt, and grandmother.

During the fourth year of her treatment, a transference development, combined with an enactment based on an identification with her mother as frustrator, led to the following important reconstruction. A new wave of negative transference toward me had developed, this time with angry accusations that I was "inconsistent" with her—that I was tolerant of her infantile feelings, but also expected too much of her. [I asked in what specific ways she felt I had expected too much of her?] She replied that I expected her to be "completely honest" in what she said, no matter how difficult it was to talk about certain things. She then recalled that her mother was a stickler for honesty. Her mother was scrupulously honest, and expected her to be the same.

[I asked whether she might be perceiving me as her mother in that regard.] Absolutely not, she insisted. Her mother was 105 percent consistent! She noticed the protestational quality of what she had just said and became reflective about it. She then recalled her mother urging her to be precocious in various ways, but interfering with her carrying out the precocious activities by doing them for her. When she became frustrated and angry at her mother for doing that, her mother "reasoned away" such feelings with careful, rational explanations, leaving the patient with the feeling that she was not justified in feeling frustrated or angry.

Additional material during the same phase of negative mother transference included a theme of entitlement to special favor, which she "acted in" toward me by refusal to accept responsibility for and pay her already greatly reduced fee. [I commented that her attitude and behavior about the fee seemed inconsistent with her ideals of honesty and fairness.] After an intense, angry protest that my interpretation undermined her self-confidence, she calmed down and began to recognize other forms of inconsistency in herself, especially regarding honesty. [I commented that so many of her attitudes and behaviors seemed to be based on identifications with her mother that I couldn't help wondering whether there was some inconsistency in her mother regarding honesty and fairness.] At the time of that session, however, she was unable to recall any examples.

Soon afterward, while attempting to extend the mortgage on her family home, she discovered with horrified amazement that her mother had embezzled family funds for some obscure purpose of her own. As a result, ownership of the family home was in jeopardy, and large sums had to be repaid to avoid serious legal consequences. In this context she reported the following dream: "In one part of the dream the man I was engaged to appeared; in another part a co-worker on a research project. In both parts of the dream I was on the defensive—something about money, what I had done with some money, and why I was so mysterious about it."

Her spontaneous associations to the dream were about feeling disturbed recently when she found some pictures of her mother and herself. The pictures made her realize how much alike they were. She also felt disturbed recently when she discovered more ways that her mother had hidden her "funds filching." In the dream, however, she herself was on the spot about how some money was handled. "I'm furious at my mother about the money business, and about her always making such a big deal about honesty and fairness when all the while she was 'dipping into the till' for her own selfish reasons. Yet in the dream, instead of being mad at her, I seemed to *be* her."

Another reconstruction during this patient's treatment dealt with infantile experiences of toilet training. The reconstruction was based largely on transferences to me and a severe psychosomatic symptom during recurrent phases of anal regression. The transferences were of two types, both hostile. They alternated between passive-aggressive, stubborn refusal to follow the basic rule, and overtly hostile, sadistic attacks on me for what she felt was my "pressuring" her to "open up." During the passive-aggressive, withholding phases she became so severely constipated that she did not move her bowels for a week or more at a time. During the sadistic phases, she not only blasted me with invective, but also "blasted" away on the toilet, which at those times became stopped-up from her huge amounts of accumulated feces.

[I offered the reconstruction that her toilet training experiences may have been excessively strict and possibly too early during her infancy.] Support for the reconstruction came from both confirmatory clinical data and from a reliable, extratherapeutic source of information. When she was able eventually to ask her father about her toilet training, he told her that he recalled it clearly: Her grandmother had insisted to her mother that the patient be completely toilet trained by the time her brother was born (on her first birthday). Intratherapeutic evidence came from confirmatory clinical data such as the following dream—the first dream of her analysis in which she was openly and directly angry at her mother:

> I had missed out on going to dinner with my parents, so they were taking me out another time to make it up to me. At the restaurant mother and I went to the john together; but when I came out of the toilet booth, mother was gone. I looked for them in the restaurant, but they weren't there. It seemed heartless for them to have left me. I went home and found them there. Mother said it was too bad I had missed out again. I was so frustrated and angry I could barely talk, but I did anyway. I said angrily to mother: "Why did you do that? I thought we went out to dinner for *my* sake." I told her how hurt and angry I felt, and asked her: "What did I do? All I did was go the john."

Based on the dream imagery, the context in which it occurred, and her associations, we concluded that her question at the end of the dream may have referred to some of her earliest feelings of frustration and rejection by her mother, that is, at times when she had accidents during her premature toilet training, and perhaps also if she took too long on the "pottie."

General Aspects of Reconstructions

Despite the differences between constructions and reconstructions, there are a number of similarities between the two, for example, both employ

the constructive strategy of imaginative guessing (i.e., since reconstructions do not replicate childhood experiences exactly, they necessarily involve a constructive aspect [cf. Loch 1989]), both must avoid the doctrinal
fallacy of imposing specific clinical theories on the data, and both formulate alternative interpretive hypotheses that are then subjected to checking, revising, and rechecking in order to determine the most plausible
interpretation at the time. In addition, as Etchegoyen (1991) observes,
since one's past is reflected in each of a person's acts, there cannnot be a
categorical difference between interpreting the past or present (cf. also
Malcolm 1986).

Edelson (1988) points out that rival reconstructions are not necessarily from paradigms of differing psychoanalytic schools, but just as often
are based on alternative formulations within the same paradigm (cf., for
example, the consensus problem, discussed and illustrated in Chapter 1).
In addition, a study of "the good therapy hour" by Orlinsky and Howard
(1967, p. 624) found that both patients and therapists associated a "good
hour" with the patient's discussion of "childhood experiences with family members, and feelings about them," suggesting the importance of
genetic factors in both constructions and reconstructions.

Brenman (1980,) summarizes some of the various factors that influence an analyst to choose one reconstruction rather than another.
Such choices may be based on the analyst's insights and development,
or his biases, past training, and personal pathology, or on the patient's
attempts to influence the analyst in a particular direction (see also Blum
1980).

Arlow (1991) warns that reconstructions are particularly prone to
doctrinal interpretation, that is, use of a specific genetic model of infantile psychology to guide reconstructions of a patient's associations. Examples include Klein's (1975, 1992, 1993) and Kohut's (1972–1976,
1977, 1984) interpretive approaches, which are doctrinally driven by their
respective theories of pathogenesis (see, e.g., Rubovits-Seitz 1988a, 1998).
Arlow refers to this type of reconstruction as "foisting upon the patient's
associations an interpretation based upon a model concept of pathogenesis" (p. 544; cf. also Lafarge 2000), and Paniagua (1985) notes that
use of specific psychogenetic theories in interpretations all too easily be-

comes indoctrination. For example, Colby and Stoller (1988) Jacobsen and Steele (1979), Mahony (1986), and Steele and Jacobsen (1978) conclude that Freud's reconstructions in the cases of the Rat Man (1909b) and the Wolf Man (1918) included tendentious use of doctrinal and genetic fallacies (cf. also Etchegoyen's [1991] reanalysis of Freud's [1900] "*Non Vixit*" dream, illustrating a possibly overlooked preoedipal problem). Rangell (1985) notes further that transference is but a way station toward reconstructive insight, and that "attention to the transference neurosis alone, without a relentless establishment of its links to the past, is a technical error of many analyses today" (pp. 87–88).

In one of his final publications, Freud (1937b) proposed that frequently the therapeutic process is unable to recover repressed traumatic experiences from childhood, but that a sense of conviction about the correctness of a reconstruction "achieves the same therapeutic result as a recaptured memory" (pp. 265–266)—a conclusion that makes reconstruction sound suspiciously like a "faith cure." A number of writers (e.g., Crits-Christoph et al. 1988, Eagle 1980, Edelson 1992a,b, Reed 1995; Rogers 1984, Rubovits-Seitz 1998, Sherwood 1969, Silberschatz et al. 1988, Thomä and Kächele 1987) argue, on the other hand, that for depth psychological therapies to make scientific as well as therapeutic claims, the criterion of interpretive accuracy must be retained.

SUMMARY

Freud used the terms *construction* and *reconstruction* interchangeably, referring to both as formulations about repressed experiences during infancy and childhood, but this chapter distinguished between the two. Constructions are not necessarily or specifically concerned with early life experiences, but represent a relatively early phase of the interpretive process in which the clinician attempts to formulate a tentative overall or whole (thematic) meaning of the current data being studied. Reconstructions, on the other hand, deal specifically and exclusively with formulations of repressed experiences from early life. There are a number of similarities, however, between constructions and reconstructions, for example, both include genetic factors and both employ construction.

Freud referred to his method of construction as lacking a theoretical basis, but most of the interpretive strategies and concepts that he employed were similar to or identical with the hermeneutic theory of interpretation. Freud did not realize the similarity of his interpretive approach to that of hermeneutics, however, because he ignored hermeneutics. Determining the interdependent relations of whole and part meanings is the principal processing operation of the hermeneutic theory of interpretation. The whole is derived from and constituted by the parts, the latter being delineated and integrated by the whole.

Freud's acknowledgment that constructions employ informed guesses about underlying meanings and determinants rather than being based exclusively on systematic, stepwise inductions from the clinical data, is similar to both hermeneutics and semiotics. The nature of such guesses—called abduction or inference to the best explanations—was discussed in this chapter; such conjectures employ imagination, abstraction, intuition, and both inductive and deductive inferences.

Abduction or inference to the best explanation applies to all scientific fields, including interpretive disciplines like psychoanalysis and dynamic psychotherapy, and thus constitutes a procedure that binds clinical interpretation to general science. The process of abduction cannot be formalized, however, because there is no consistent logic of guessing in the discovery process. Freud (1900) concluded, for example, that it is impossible to give instructions about the method of arriving at a symbolic interpretation, for success requires "hitting on a clever idea, of direct intuition" (p. 97).

The initial conjectural phase of constructions has the purpose of seeking an overall or whole meaning of the data studied. For example, when the clinician gains an impression about a general theme or type of meaning emerging in a therapy session, the interpreter's conception of the overall meaning provides a basis for preliminary understanding of specific details. The initial impression about a possible whole meaning functions heuristically in the interpretive process, not only influencing but largely determining everything else that the interpreter understands.

Comparison of clinical interpretation with language processing suggests that listeners (including therapists) preconsciously construct rather than merely extract meanings from what is perceived. The central problem in understanding discourse is the issue of continuity, or connectivity, within the data. The continuity is not manifest, so the interpreter must link data to other data. Listeners (and readers) construct much of the meaning that they hear or read, and the ubiquitous phenomenon of paraphrase demonstrates that they do not end up with exactly the same material that the speaker or writer expressed.

As it does in every phase of the interpretive process, coherence also plays an important role in the constructive phase of interpretation. Coherence, a corollary of the core concept called the continuity principle, means that the parts of a whole constructed meaning are not only connected but cohere in a self-consistent way that omits nothing relevant.

This chapter also included clinical illustrations of construction and reconstruction, followed by commentaries on related, relevant issues.

CHAPTER SEVEN

Strategies of
Justification, Error Detection,
Error Correction, and
Progressive Modification

CLINICIANS' DIFFICULTIES in agreeing on the interpretation of the same case material (see Chapter I) confront us with the limitations of our interpretive methods. Limitations are unavoidable because the grounding of our interpretations is neither scientific law, nomic universal, formal theoretical structure, nor even purely observed fact, but is largely a shifting, ever-unfolding context of interpreted events. Thus there is always an element of uncertainty in every possible aspect of interpretation, which Hirsch (1967) maintains is a defining feature of interpretation.

The limitations and uncertainties of the interpretive process make errors inevitable and frequent in our clinical interpretive work. Numerous factors contribute to the problems and difficulties of interpretation, among them the following: (1) the sheer numbers, complex interrelations, and instability of unconscious meanings and determinants; (2) the obscuring effects of repression and other defenses; (3) the diverse perspectives, background assumptions, and biases from which we view all phenomena (interpretive relativism); (4) special limitations of interpreters' objectivity, in particular confirmation bias and countertransference; (5) limitations of memory on the part of both patient and therapist; (6) ambiguities inherent in language, in nonverbal and paralinguistic accompaniments, imagery, and in our perceptions of all such phenomena; (7) multiple conceptions rather than a unified definition of meaning; (8) several coexisting layers of meaning, which produce plurivocality of individual meanings; (9) the multiplace locations of meanings—in the patient, the interpreter, the clinical data, and the context; (10) dissimilarities between meanings in the individual case compared with generalizations from other cases; (11) the circularity and self-confirmability of interpretations; (12) the inherently provisional nature of constructions, necessitating multiple revisions and alternative hypotheses; (13) obstacles to the comparison of alternative constructions; (14) inherent problems in the nature of clinical evidence; and (15) difficulties in justifying interpretations (Rubovits-Seitz 1998).

For these and other reasons, clinical interpretation is not easy (Freud 1905a, p. 116, 1913, p. 140) and "trustworthy in every respect," as Freud (1937b, p. 263) claimed, but is difficult and fallible. Even the language we use to discover, construct, formulate, and justify latent mental processes limits as well as facilitates what can be perceived and understood in patients' associations (Viderman 1974), for language, including paralinguistic and nonverbal cues, serves purposes of concealment as well as revelation. In addition, every person draws differently from the repertory of verbal, paraverbal, and nonverbal devices (Labov and Fanshel 1977). Thus language can serve as the "persistent seduction, the central resistance" (Spence 1982a, p.62) of therapy, because it so readily replaces the patient's primary inner experience with words and paraverbal accompaniments, all of which are inherently ambiguous.

The preceding problems are examples of so-called method effects in scientific inquiry, that is, the methods we use decisively to influence and constrain what we can observe and understand. The methods one uses to solve a scientific (including interpretive) problem are thus an important part of the problem itself (Fiske and Shweder 1986, Fox 1963, Hooke, 1963).

Freud's view that interpretation is easy and trustworthy persists, however, in a widespread tendency by clinicians to underestimate the difficulties and fallibility of our interpretive methodology. I. A. Richards insisted, by contrast, that "the only proper attitude toward a successful interpretation is to view it as a triumph against odds" (cited by Hirsch

1967, p. 164); and Kermode (1979, p. 125) observes wryly that interpretation is an "impossible but necessary" task.

"Damage control" thus becomes an important part of the interpretive process, that is, systematic use of error-detecting, error-correcting, and justifying procedures. To accomplish this, ideally the accuracy of interpretations would have to be linked by systematic feedback to the data and cues that led clinicians to specific constructions. Although we lack such an ideal method, we can employ the indirect approach of learning from error (Berkson and Wettersten 1984, Polkinghorne 1983); that is, since errors are inevitable, the interpreter can use his mistakes as error-correcting feedback.

To deal with errors realistically, one must attempt to recognize mistakes when they occur and, if possible, put them to some use in the interpretive process. For example, we attempt to recognize and utilize countertransference distortions as potential aids to understanding, and the same basic error-correcting strategy of learning from one's mistakes applies to all types of clinical errors (see, e.g., Peterfreund 1983). As Kramer (1989) observes, depth psychological therapy at its best is a process in which mistakes are put to good use.

I (1998) distinguish between justification *during* therapy sessions and more definitive justification *after* completion of the treatment. The former is necessarily limited, consisting mainly of attempting to determine the most plausible among alternative constructions at a given time. For that purpose the therapist checks how much of the data a construction can account for, modifies the construction so that it accounts for more of the data, and rechecks the revised construction to determine whether it now covers most of the data. If not, the original construction is discarded and replaced by a different hypothesis.

The process of checking, revising, and rechecking constructions usually generates several promising modified hypotheses. The final step is comparison of these revised alternate hypotheses (De Groot 1969, Edelson 1988). The principal selection criterion at this phase of the justifying process is internal evidence, that is, which of the alternative hypotheses accounts most consistently, coherently, and comprehensively for the largest number of data.

More definitive justification of clinical interpretations requires additional posttherapeutic investigation based on a record of the entire (completed) therapeutic process, which the therapist or investigator can study retrospectively and systematically in as much detail as necessary. The latter, more extended and detailed justifying process can employ multiple, increasingly exacting justifying procedures, including micro-analytic methods of studying the clinical data (for detailed descriptions and illustrations of these methods, see Rubovits-Seitz 1998).

CLINICAL ILLUSTRATION
OF JUSTIFICATION DURING TREATMENT

This example draws on a case report presented in Chapter 5 of a patient I referred to as an "Elvis wannabe." To review the case briefly, the patient, who had problems sustaining relationships with women, announced suddenly and relatively early in his treatment that he had become engaged to his present girlfriend, Beth. When he extolled the "joys of marriage" effusively, I commented that he seemed overly certain about how the relationship with Beth would work out. He then recalled a dream in which he "escaped from prison in Memphis, and tried to escape to Nashville." His associations to prison in Memphis were about a former girlfriend, Betty, "from whose clutches I had escaped" because she "smothered me with love." He paused and added reflectively, "Beth is very loving, too." His associations to Nashville were about Elvis Presley, whom he admired and sometimes imitated, because of his "fame, fortune, and free-loving life-style." He had joked to Beth that they should go to Nashville for their honeymoon and visit the Elvis Presley museum. He mentioned with embarrassment that he had told the dream to Beth, who was upset by it. She thought it meant that he felt imprisoned by his relationship with her, which he protested was not the case, but Beth remained uneasy, especially when he made a slip and called her Betty.

Commentary

The theme that appeared to run through this entire session was the issue of the patient's engagement, more specifically, his unacknowledged ambivalence about the engagement and coming marriage. To justify this construction during the patient's treatment, I checked whether the posited underlying theme could account for and integrate all of the session's individual associations, including dream images. The patient's initial associations, in which he extolled the joys of marriage and stressed how lucky he felt to be engaged to Beth, appeared to fit the posited theme as a defensive protest against latent ambivalence about the engagement (cf. also the heuristic that "excessiveness implies defense").

A digression is needed at this point to explicate the definition and role of heuristics in scientific, including interpretive, work. Heuristics are loosely systematic procedures that give good results on the whole, but do not guarantee them in any particular instance. Meehl (1992), for example, stresses the importance of recognizing the stochastic (statistical) nature of heuristic guidelines. They are part of the prerequisite knowledge that informs and guides interpretive work, and thus helps to reduce unfruitful searches. The advantages of heuristics in solving complex problems, including depth psychological interpretations, are that they involve methods appropriate to the problems they deal with, and because they are based on relevant factual knowledge about particular problems.

To illustrate, a heuristic method that I employ extensively, both during the treatment process and in the posttherapeutic study of patients' records, involves starting at the end of a dream series, therapy session, or completed treatment—where dynamic trends tend to be clearer and thus easier to interpret—and then seeing whether inferences about the later material help to account dynamically for the earlier clinical data (Rubovits-Seitz 1998). Drawing on Hegel's conceptualizations, Ricoeur (1974) suggests a possible rationale of this heuristic: every figure receives its meaning from the one that follows it; thus the truth of one moment resides in the subsequent moment, and intelligibility proceeds from the end to the beginning.

Returning to the patient, I checked his associations further. When I commented how certain he seemed, and asked whether he ever felt any doubts about marrying Beth, he reacted with surprise, his effusive rush of associations slowed down, and he then recalled a dream from the previous night. These reactions appeared to fit the posited dynamic theme as a momentary weakening of the overcompensatory defense—a conclusion that is suggested also by an interpretive heuristic that weakening of a defense produces changes in the form or content of associations, which may include the recall of "forgotten" material such as a dream.

In telling the dream he used the term "escape" twice—escaping from prison in Memphis, and trying to escape to Nashville—a repetition that fits the posited dynamic theme as a hoped-for solution to the underlying problem. He had managed to escape from a previously confining relationship with Betty, which appeared to serve as a basis for hoping that he might be able to escape again, this time from Beth. We note also that in his associations to the dream, he unwittingly equated Betty and Beth by the contiguity of his references to the two women (cf. Freud 1900), that is, he said that Betty had "smothered me with love," followed immediately by a pause and the reflective afterthought that Beth, too, "is very loving."

The dream imagery of escaping from confinement in prison further supports the dynamic theme by its analogy with a confining relationship, which Beth herself sensed when he told her the dream. The prison metaphor also could imply guilt, suggesting that he may have been continuing his relationship with Beth in part because of some pressure from his conscience to fulfill his commitment to her.

The dream statement that he was "trying to escape to Nashville" elicited associations about his imitation of Elvis and admiration of his "free-loving lifestyle," which fits the dynamic theme of ambivalence about his engagement, and the hope of returning to his own free-loving bachelorhood.

It is worth noting in this connection that Elvis represents an iconic metaphor in these associations; for a great deal of data processing in depth psychological therapies is directed toward understanding the latent meanings of metaphors and other tropes by the heuristic of analogic relations (cf. Leavy 1980, p. 73). Studies by cognitive linguists suggest, in fact, that metaphor is not only a fundamental way that humans think, but some investigators suggest further that *most* of our thinking occurs in the form of common metaphors (Gould 1983, p. 19; Holland 1999, p. 358; Lakoff and Johnson 1980).

The patient's embarrassment upon recalling that he had told the dream to Beth, and that she was upset by it, had the quality of his feeling "caught in the act"—or in this case caught in the unacknowledged fantasy—of wishing he could get out of the engagement and marriage. Despite his denial to Beth, his slip in calling her "Betty" provided still further support for the posited thematic problem. Since all of the data from the reported session have been accounted for coherently by the dynamic theme of ambivalence about the engagement, we are justified (partially and tentatively) in considering the posited construction the "inference to the best explanation," and thus the most plausible interpretation at the time of that session. More definitve justification would depend, however, on detailed posttherapeutic study of the entire therapeutic process.

CHECKING CONSTRUCTIONS DURING THE TREATMENT: SOME GENERAL STRATEGIES

Error-Detecting Strategies

Error detection begins with the expectation that one will make mistakes. That mind-set increases the clinician's alertness to discrepancies between his or her constructions, on the one hand, and *all* of the clinical data (rather than selected data that support one's hypothesis), on the other (Einhorn 1988, French 1958). The clinician who accepts the inevitability of errors doubts everything that goes into his proof: doubts his facts, his hypotheses, and whether the two fit together as he thinks they do (Larrabee 1964).

Acceptance of errors and recognition of discrepancies are crucial strategies not only in clinical work but in all scientific and interpretive activities. Darwin (1888) wrote that he could not recall a single hypothesis that did not have to be modified or abandoned eventually. Gordon's (1982) description of deciphering ancient scripts also emphasizes the importance of recognizing errors. He writes that decipherers make inferences that seem to fit some pattern inherent in the text, but the inferences may or may not be correct. Such guesses are necessary, but to be successful they must take into account the realities, or at least the probabilities, of the text to be deciphered. Even then, Gordon stresses, most of the guesses are wrong. Wrong guesses are usually exposed as incorrect by the fact that they lead to impossible combinations when applied elsewhere in the text. Guesses must be made, but for every correct guess, many wrong ones must be scrapped. Thus a prime quality of both the cryptanalyst and clinical interpreter is flexibility.

This line of reasoning coincides closely with Karl Popper's (1959, 1963) thesis that conjecturing and the likelihood of errors are inherent in all forms of inquiry. One of the fundamental ways that human beings learn is by trial and error, or conjectures and refutations, but although it is imaginative and creative, the conjectural approach to understanding is also very fallible. To avoid the ever-present problem of confirmation bias, Popper proposes that the tests of hypotheses must take the form of falsification, for it is relatively easy to obtain confirmations of almost any theory, including interpretations, but a truly genuine test of a theory attempts to refute it (for a good example see Eccles 1974, cited by Rubovits-Seitz 1992).

Error-Correcting Strategies

Error-correcting strategies comprise a process of continuous, increasingly exacting evaluations of clinical interpretations. Because constructions are essentially conjectures about the whole (thematic) meaning of the data being interpreted, the hermeneuticist E. D. Hirsch, Jr. (1967) recommends that the interpreter (1) check how much of the data a construction accounts for, (2) modify the construction to account for more of the data, and then (3) recheck the revised construction to determine whether it now covers most of the data. If not, the interpreter must consider discarding the original construction and replacing it with a different hypothesis. The process of checking, revising, and rechecking constructions usually results in several promising hypotheses.

The next step is comparison of *alternative* hypotheses, which requires a criterion for selecting among the competing constructions (see Edelson 1988). The principal selection criterion is internal evidence, that is, which of the alternative hypotheses accounts most coherently and comprehensively for the largest number of data.

The operations of checking, revising, comparing, rechecking, and selecting interpretive hypotheses derive from three basic strategies of the human and social sciences: comparison of alternative hypotheses, testing competing hypotheses against all of the data, and use of disconfirming tests (cf. De Groot 1969, Polkinghorne 1983). In the series of operations described above for clinical interpretations, each revised construction constitutes an alternative hypothesis; competing hypotheses are tested against all of the clinical data, and each discarded construction represents a disconfirmed hypothesis.

At this point in the error-correcting process, the clinician has selected what appears to be the most plausible interpretive hypothesis from among various competing constructions. During the actual therapeutic process itself, this is essentially as far as the error-correcting process goes. An additional phase of the error-correcting process includes justifying procedures, only some of which can be employed during the course of a treatment. Other, more definitive justifying methods must await a record of the completed treatment. The record of a completed treatment makes it possible to employ multiple justifying procedures, including microanalytic methods.

MORE DEFINITIVE JUSTIFICATION BASED ON POSTTHERAPEUTIC STUDY OF THE ENTIRE THERAPEUTIC PROCESS

A good example of posttherapeutic justification, which identified and clarified an interpretive error during the early phase of an analytic process, is presented in Chapter 10.

Further Aspects of Posttherapeutic Justification

The posttherapeutic phase of interpretive justification requires a record of a completed therapeutic process, which can be studied in as much detail as necessary. Systematic, retrospective study based on the record of a completed treatment employs more varied, complex, detailed, and probative methods of justification.

Like the interpretive process as a whole, the justification of interpretations is pluralistic. The most probative methods of justifying interpretations include cross-validation and convergence of evidence, demonstration of organized interlocking microstructures underlying interpretations, indirect prediction and postdiction (of classes of events), and repetition of themes and patterns. The widely used methods of coherence and patients' responses to interpretations are less reliable, especially if used alone—the former because it is circular, and the latter because the patient's responses themselves must be interpreted. When these methods operate in concert with other, more probative justifying methods, however, cross-checking of their results can occur. Quantitative methods, including computer-assisted content analysis, also have a place in posttherapeutic investigations of the therapeutic process. Qualitative and quantitative methods can be combined advantageously for both process analysis and the justification of interpretations (for accessible descriptions of these various justifying methods, see Rubovits-Seitz 1998; for more detailed descriptions, see Holt 1978).

The method that I employ for posttherapeutic justification of interpretations is the recurrent cycles (RC) approach, an adaptation of Thomas French's (1952, 1954, 1958a,b) method of investigating the therapeutic process, which is described in the preface of this volume.

Justifying Strategies

Justification of interpretations is the final, most difficult, and least utilized step in the error-correction process—the latter in spite of Freud's scientific interest in methods of justifying interpretations. His concepts and strategies of interpretive justification included or anticipated a number of methods employed in contemporary human and social science methodologies (De Groot 1969, Diesing 1971, Kaplan 1964, Polkinghorne 1983). To illustrate, Freud's (1923) jigsaw puzzle model of interpretive justification implied a coherence rather than a correspondence theory of truth and justification (Davidson 1986; but see also Hanly 1990). It also anticipated the importance of small-scale, microstructural evidence in the justification of interpretations, that is, the complex interrelations of part meanings associated with individual elements of the clinical data. Freud insisted, for example, that "our presentation begins to be conclusive only with the intimate detail" (Nunberg and Federn 1962, p. 172). Edelson (1984) writes similarly that what should be given special weight is the emergence of circumstantial detail, having a high degree of specificity and idiosyncratic nuance, in reports of fantasies, experiences, and other data. It is these data, Edelson continues, that in the end prove to be the most relevant to the search for probative evidence (see Cheshire 1975, Davidson 1986, Hirsch 1967, Rubovits-Seitz 1986, 1987, 1998, Seitz 1968, Teller and Dahl 1986).

Another prescient aspect of Freud's justifying approach was its pluralism. Human and social science methodologies build redundancy into their justifying checks as a substitute for infallibility of individual methods (Diesing 1971). Multiple checks reduce errors (Popper 1963), and two proofs are better than one (Polya 1945). Grünbaum's (1984, 1986, 1993) critiques of Freud's (1915–1917) justifying approach focus on the so-called tally argument, but that was only one of Freud's suggestions regarding justification—one to which he was not deeply committed, and which he did not continue to employ or defend (see Rubovits-Seitz 1998).

Freud's justifying approach included (1) use of internal evidence, mainly coherence, encompassing the vast network of observations and interpretations from the entire therapeutic process (Freud 1923); (2) all of the various (mainly indirect) responses to interpretations—remission of symptoms representing only one such response (1915–1917, 1937); (3) postdiction (1920); (4) prediction of similar findings in other cases (e.g., 1919, 1922); (5) external validation (1909). The pluralistic nature of Freud's justifying approach also includes the potential for (6) cross-validation based on multiple samples and varieties of clinical data, drawn from many episodes and phases of the analytic process; and (7) convergence of evidence from diverse justifying methods.

For fuller discussion of the foregoing and other methods of justifying interpretations, see Rubovits-Seitz (1998). Both the science and the therapy of depth psychological treatments benefit from such methods, for there is a closer association than is generally recognized between the accuracy of clinical interpretations and therapeutic effectiveness (cf. Crits-

Christoph et al. 1988, Eagle 1980, Rubovits-Seitz, 1998, Silberschaltz et al. 1988, Thomä and Kächele 1987).

Progressive Modification of Clinical Interpretations

Constructions and reconstructions always involve a selection and progressive modification of an initially plausible interpretation, the justification of which is relative at every stage of the therapeutic process. The numerous revisions and reshaping of constructions, and the filling in of reconstructions, result from two main features of the interpretive process: (1) the gradual weakening of defenses, with consequent emergence of previously repressed memories and mental processes; and (2) detection and correction of previous interpretive errors in the case.

CLINICAL ILLUSTRATIONS OF PROGRESSIVE MODIFICATIONS

For a summarizing example of progressive modifications in a completed analysis, see Rubovits-Seitz (1998). The following are two additional examples from the clinical literature illustrating the process of progressive modifications of interpretations. The first is a slightly abbreviated paraphrase of a clinical vignette by Duncan (1989):

> We had come to refer to it as The Funny Thing, in the sense of odd, peculiar. I would say something or fail to say something, fail to understand something or understand something only too well, and suddenly Ms. K. would totally despair of me. The analysis was hopeless; I would never understand her. It was the same each time. Afterward, she would not mention it, as though nothing had happened. I tried to understand what set it off, but it rang no meaningful bell in my emotional self-knowledge. Eventually these incidents linked up in the material with a delusional aspect of Ms. K.'s mother, who would suddenly take some seemingly neutral event as having aggressive intent, and would put a construction and importance on it that seemed crazy to everybody else. On those

occasions her mother was impervious to reason, and would behave in very eccentric ways. All this helped us to understand The Funny Thing as properly inside of Ms. K. With working through it gradually went away.

Gedo (1984) reported a similar case in which the patient's emotional outbursts were like assaults on him, causing him to distance himself by becoming more formal. Gedo formulated the assaults originally as transference repetitions of childhood feelings toward a parent; but in the course of further therapeutic work they discovered that the patient was not repeating childhood feelings and behavior of her own, but of an early childhood caregiver toward her.

These examples illustrate the progressive modifications of interpretations as treatments proceed.

SUMMARY

The limitations and uncertainties of the interpretive process make errors inevitable and frequent in our interpretive work. These limitations are examples of method effects, which occur in all forms of scientific inquiry, for the methods we use decisively influence and constrain what we can observe and understand. Damage control is thus an important part of interpretive methodology, that is, systematic use of error-detecting, -correcting, and -justifying procedures. We lack an ideal method for this purpose, but can employ an indirect method of learning from error, which involves use of one's mistakes as error-correcting feedback.

Error-detecting strategies begin with the expectation that we will make mistakes, which increases the clinician's alertness to discrepancies in his or her interpretations. Since it is relatively easy to obtain confirmations of almost any theory, a truly genuine test of an interpretive hypothesis must attempt to refute it.

Error-correcting strategies include continuous, increasingly exacting evaluations of clinical interpretations. During the treatment process itself, the interpreter can check how much of the data a construction accounts for, can modify the construction to account for more of the data, and then can recheck the revised construction to determine whether it covers all, or at least most, of the data. If not, the original construction is considered falsified, is discarded, and is replaced by a different hypothesis.

The next step is comparison of alternative hypotheses; the principal selection criterion is which of the competing constructions accounts most coherently and comprehensively for the largest number of data. This is as far as the error-correcting process goes during the actual treatment of patients. Other, more definitive methods of justifying interpretations must await a record of the completed treatment.

Freud's concepts and strategies of interpretive justification included or anticipated a number of methods employed in contemporary human and social science methodologies. He emphasized the importance of small details in the search for probative evidence, and a pluralistic approach to justifying interpretations. Freud and other writers have proposed over a dozen different justifying methods, which in the order of their relative probity include cross-validation based on multiple samples and varieties of clinical data drawn from many episodes and phases of the therapeutic process; convergence of evidence from diverse justifying methods; organized interlocking microstructures underlying interpretations, as in the RC method; indirect postdiction and prediction (of classes of events); repetition of themes and patterns; coherence (i.e., internal consistency and comprehensiveness); the patient's responses to an interpretation; quantitative methods; external evidence; justification by observation and implication; and ruling out the improbable.

This chapter illustrated and discussed the process of justification during treatment, more definitive justification posttherapeutically, and progressive modification of interpretations in the course of the therapeutic process.

CHAPTER EIGHT

Strategies of Interpretive Technique: Verbal Reformulation and Communication of Interpretations

CLINICIANS TEND TO THINK of interpretation mainly in the context of therapeutic interventions, that is, the communication of depth psychological information to patients; but the interpretive process is primarily a form of *inquiry*, an attempt to gain understanding of the patient in depth. Another way of putting this is that the therapeutic role of interpretation has less to do with the communication of depth psychological information to patients than it does with the more basic function of promoting the clinician's *understanding* of the patient's (and therapist's) inner mental life in the therapeutic relationship and process (Rubovits-Seitz 1998).

The therapist's understanding of the patient and his or her reactions to the patient is communicated to and perceived by the patient not only through formal interpretations, but in multiple ways—many of which are probably subliminal. The extent to which, and exactly how, such understanding achieves therapeutic effects is not fully understood. Some writers (e.g., Fonagy and Target 2000) suggest that it may enable "the patient to find himself in the therapist's mind and integrate this image as part of his sense of himself" (p. 870); but other possible factors may be involved also in this subtle and complex process between patient and therapist.

I have found it useful to differentiate between interpretive methodology and interpretive technique. Interpretive methodology is the broader concept; it includes the construal and justification ("discovery") phases of the interpretive process, on the one hand, and interpretive technique—the criteria of communicating depth psychological information to patients—on the other. A vast literature has accumulated on problems of interpretive technique, while relatively little attention has been paid to our methods of seeking, construing, formulating, and attempting to justify latent meanings and determinants (for the latter, see Rubovits-Seitz 1998).

FREUD'S VIEWS ON REFORMULATING AND COMMUNICATING INTERPRETATIONS

Freud's explanation and rationale of reformulating clinical interpretations in words and communicating the latter to patients can be summarized in the following way: He noted (in 1910) that the continued existence of neurotic structures depends on their distortion, which prevents their recognition by the patient. When the riddle they present is solved, communicated to, and accepted by the patient, they no longer are able to exist, which he compared with "evil spirits whose power is broken as soon as you can tell them their name—the name which they have kept secret" (p. 148).

To the doubts of critics that "anything can be done about the illness by mere talking," Freud argued that "words were originally magic and to this day words have retained much of their ancient magical power. . . . Words provoke affects and are in general the means of mutual influence" between people (1916–1917, p. 17).

Freud (1915) added the following proviso, however: "A moments's reflection shows that the identity of the information given to the patient with his repressed memory is only apparent. To have heard something and to have experienced something are in their psychological nature two quite different things, even though the content of both is the same" (pp. 175–176). To deal with this problem he proposed the further technical concept of "working through":

> The first step in overcoming the resistance is made . . . by the analyst's uncovering the resistance, which is never recognized by the patient, and acquainting him with it. . . . [But] one must allow the patient time to be-

come more conversant with the resistance with which he has now become acquainted, to *work through* it, by continuing, in defiance of it, the analytic work according to the fundamental rule of psychoanalysis. [p. 155]

ORGANIZATION OF THIS CHAPTER

To organize and abbreviate the present discussion of interpretive technique, I have divided the subject into the following categories or topics:

1. *verbal reformulation* of interpretive hypotheses;

2. *whether* (and why) to communicate interpretations;

3. *what* (including how much) to communicate;

4. *when* to communicate; and

5. *how* to communicate interpretations.

Dividing the subject in this way is useful also in reviewing and comparing the differing views of various writers and clinical schools regarding these specific aspects of interpretive technique.

CLINICAL ILLUSTRATION OF VERBAL REFORMULATION AND THE COMMUNICATION OF INTERPRETATIONS

The following case, described more completely in Rubovits-Seitz (1988b), illustrates the collaborative nature of both the discovery phase of interpretive methodology, and also the phase of interpretive technique.

John was a 30-year-old single man, the youngest of three sons in a wealthy southern family. He came for treatment because of inferiority feelings, occupational instability, and lack of a love life. His eldest brother was the "fair-haired boy" of the family— successful, married, and had children. The second son had been less successful, and was killed in an auto accident 10 years previously. John was overprotected by his mother, partly because he had been born with several congenital defects, most of which were corrected surgically during his childhood. His father was gruff toward John and took less interest in him than in his older brother. As a result, John had turned all the more to his mother for acceptance and affection. His father complained frequently that his mother was making a "sissy" of him.

In his teens he made a serious suicide attempt, and was hospitalized for about a year. His conscious reason for attempting suicide was fear of facing his father about getting caught and expelled from school for forging his father's signature on an excuse from gym classes. In the course of our therapeutic work, however, we found that his unconscious reason for the suicide attempt was intense attraction toward a handsome boy in his gym class. He felt that his father's direst prediction about him— that he would end up homosexual—had come true.

He had been in analytic therapy for a couple of years, and was progressing slowly but steadily in understanding his inner conflicts, defenses, and childhood traumatic experiences. In recent sessions he had been preoccupied with his father' coming to town to discuss family business. During the previous year he had convinced his father to let him handle the investment of some family funds. In an effort to outdo his father by achieving greater returns on the investments, he had speculated in the market and lost money. Knowing that his mishandling of the funds would be reviewed during the coming visit, he anticipated his father's arrival with dread.

In this context of events, he started a session by asking: "Did you know that the bridge near here is called 'suicide bridge'?" Recently he had experienced a return of his old height phobia, which started in his teens, went away while he was in the hospital at age 17, but returned after he left the hospital and went to visit an older woman whom he had met at the hospital. She lived in a high-rise building, and while looking down from her apartment his height phobia recurred. Coming over the high bridge near my home on the way to his appointment, he felt the height phobia again.

He wondered why he had the height phobia. As a boy he liked to climb trees. A son of the family who later bought John's childhood home hanged himself in the tree John used to climb. Asked about his reaction to that, he replied: "He succeeded, dammit!" [You wish you had?] "Sometimes, because then I wouldn't have to face problems." [What problems at present?] "I'm not sure—maybe facing my father about the money I lost in the market. I haven't told him about it, but it will come up in our discussions next week. [This is beginning to sound like what happened just before your suicide attempt.] He responded with surprise: "Right! I was afraid to face him then, too, for fear he'd be furious. That reminds me of a bunch of dreams I had last night." (What appeared to remind him of the dreams was the association about fearing his father—cf. the manifest content of the first dream. The connection he made here illustrates his growing ability to think and reason associatively.)

> *Dream 1:* "I was trying to hide from someone I was afraid of. I became a statue in a fountain, but turtles kept nipping at my pants legs."
> *Dream 2:* "David Stockman, who is in charge of the budget office, [in President Reagan's administration in the 1980s], attempted suicide by swallowing a bunch of pins."
> *Dream 3:* "I was living with an older woman whose husband was dead. I think it was the older woman in the hospital whose apartment I visited."
> *Dream 4:* "There was a statue covered with ice. I was chipping the ice away. The ice was falling off in big chunks."

He began associating to the dreams spontaneously:

Associations to Dream 1

There was a fountain at the mental hospital with a statue in the middle of it. I wasn't just pretending to be a statue—I *was* a statue. Turtles live a long time and have a thick shell—both like my father! That dream sounds like trying to hide from my father, but he catches me anyway.

Interpretation of Dream 1

[A statue sometimes represents a dead person. You tried to escape from guilt and fear of your father by death. Have you been thinking of doing that again because of guilt and fear about the investments?] "Yes!" he blurted out. "It has crossed my mind. But I wouldn't actually do it now—at least, I don't think I would . . . but, uh . . ."

Associations to Dream 2

". . . on the other hand, that second dream about David Stockman swallowing the pins could be *me!* My mother says I look like him—but she prefers Ronald Reagan. [She prefers the "old man," eh? What about the pins?] "Pins remind me of a man's sperm. They look like sperm cells." He then recalled an earlier dream of swallowing semen, which occurred when his father was visiting and slept in the same room with him. "But how could swallowing my father's sperm be suicidal?"

Interpretation of Dream 2

[Perhaps by killing off your manhood to keep from competing with him.] "Competing with him about the investments? About mother? I wonder if the investments, my father's money, represents mother to me. I tried everything to get control of the money, and then tried to outdo my father with it! [You also "took some liberties" with it.] "Yeah, I did, didn't I? I took some liberties with Mother, too—like giving her those long passionate kisses during my teens. I was afraid for Father to know about that, too!"

Associations to Dream 3

"That reminds me of the next dream about living with the older woman whose husband had died. She tried to make a husband out of her son. Maybe she'd have done that with me, too."

Interpretation of Dream 3

[Maybe that's why the height phobia returned when you visited her. You probably felt you were getting in over your head with her—which you must have felt with your mother, too. What about the last dream?]

Associations to Dream 4

"Chipping the ice off the statue seems like what I do in treatment. I chip away at the coatings that cover up my feelings and find out what's underneath. Lately I seem to be chipping away pretty fast and deep. In the dream what lies under the ice is someone dead—*me!* Hmm. I'm getting the feeling that my old suicidal thoughts must have been stronger and lasted longer than I realized!" [Right; and why do you think that is?] He was quiet for a minute, then said: "Guilt! Guilt about wanting to get rid of my Dad; guilt about wanting to get his money; guilt about wanting to outdo him with Mother; guilt about wanting Mother all to myself; and guilt about wanting sex with her. So guilty I should be given the death sentence!"

Commentary

The following is my unverbalized formulation of the patient's dynamics at the time of the session: The *principal current conflict* (PCC) or thematic conflict appeared to be phallic-oedipal rivalry with his father versus guilt and fear of his father's wrath. The conflict appeared to have been precipitated by his father's upcoming visit, during which his mishandling of some family funds was certain to be discussed. The principal defense mechanisms against and attempted solution of the thematic conflict appeared to be:

Avoidance mechanisms
(a) Hiding the truth from his father
(b) Symptoms: height phobia; suicidal thoughts

Displacement, substitution, and *projection*
(a) From outdoing father with mother to outdoing him with money
(b) From Mother to older woman whose apartment he visited
(c) From his own suicidal urges to memories of the boy who actually hanged himself, and to the "suicide bridge" from which other people had jumped to their deaths

Reaction formation: latent homosexual fantasies toward his father

Masochistic, self-punitive mechanisms
(a) Motivated failures
(b) Denying himself a love life
(c) Turning aggression against himself (attempted suicide and sui-
     cidal thoughts)

Attempted solution: Attempting to understand and resolve the suicidal
thoughts via depth psychological treatment.

We now turn to (a) the verbal reformulation of these posited dynamics; (b) whether (and why) to communicate interpretive hypotheses;
(c) what (and how much) to communicate; (d) when to communicate;
and (e) how to communicate interpretations.

Verbal Reformulation of the Postulated Dynamics

Relatively little verbal reformulation of the previously described session
was necessary because the session flowed associatively and dynamically,
from beginning to end, with such clarity and spontaneity that both John
and I seemed to experience a sense of inevitability about its momentum
and its meaning (cf. Chapter 9). Our collaboration in the therapeutic
dialogue (cf. Leavy 1980) was unusually effective and satisfying. For all
of these reasons I believe the session represented a "good analytic hour,"
which Kris (1956) described. The "good hour" occurs in patients who
are well advanced in analytic therapy:

> It may come gradually into its own, say after the first ten or fifteen min-
> utes, when some recent experience has been recounted, which may or may
> not refer to yesterday's session. Then a dream may come, and associations,
> and all begins to make sense. In particularly fortunate instances, a memory
> from the near or distant past may present itself with varying degrees of
> affective charge. . . . When the analyst interprets, sometimes all he needs
> to say can be put into a question. The patient may well do the summing
> up by himself, and himself arrive at conclusions. Such hours seem as if
> prepared in advance. [p. 255]

Peterfreund (1983) evaluated the significance of "good hours" in
the following way:

The good hour is one wherein patient, therapist, as well as competent observers would agree that something important happened, something "true," "real," or meaningful, both cognitively and affectively. Often, these are dramatic hours, but they need not be. Good hours are especially important because so many of our sessions are murky, uncertain, confused, and it is often difficult to know what has happened. The good hour is akin to a successful experiment which has given clear-cut, valid, unambiguous results. [pp. 67–68]

I believe the session described was a good analytic hour. Such sessions were not rare in John's analysis but occurred several times a year during the latter half of his therapeutic process (cf. Chapter 9 regarding the development of John's self-interpretive competence).

Prior to verbal reformulation, clinical experiences are registered mentally in a basically ambiguous form, but reformulating the raw material into language gives it structure, organizing it along specific communicable lines. Herbert Schlesinger (1994) suggests in this connection that even during the listening phase of the interpretive process, the clinician's aim is not only to receive information and to maintain contact, but also to prepare for the communication of interpretations to the patient (see also Ogden 1997).

Not just any language will do for verbal reformulation, of course, since the therapist's aim is to convey depth psychological information that will be understandable and useful to the patient. Thus consideration must be given to what kind of language would best convey the therapist's interpretive impressions (e.g., of the most plausible hypothesis at the time, which the therapist has been occupied silently in construing). The choice of language to be used is guided by multiple factors, including the dynamics of the therapeutic process at that particular time; previous experiences with the patient, which suggest the kinds of language to which he or she is most responsive; use of simple, nontheoretical language, including the patient's own words and metaphors when possible; and the additional criteria discussed below, namely, whether (and why), what (and how much), when, and how to communicate interpretations.

Rangell (1985) emphasizes the limitations of specific clinical theories in reformulating and communicating interpretations. A different view is stressed by Etchegoyen, a Kleinian clinician and scholar. In the preface of his *Fundamentals of Psychoanalytic Technique*, for example, Etchegoyen (1991) surveys the major previous writings on psychoanalytic technique, and states:

> Like most authors, I think the union of theory and technique is indisoluble in our discipline, so that no matter how involved we become in one, we pass to the other without realizing it. I have tried to show in every chapter in what way the two are linked, and in the same way I have done my best throughout the book to make people realize how the problems are grouped, and how they influence each other. [p. xxiv]

Like Rangell, however, I have attempted to disconnect the interpretive process from its traditional linkage with specific clinical theories, and have argued that adherence to a data-based rather than a doctrinal approach is one of the surest ways to improve clinical interpretation (for a review of numerous other writers who have favored a nondoctrinal approach, see Chapters 1 and 2 and Rubovits-Seitz 1998).

Ruth Malcolm (1986), another Kleinian analyst, emphasizes that, ideally, the analyst should reformulate and communicate his interpretations to the patient only verbally.

> In order for the interpretations to be alive and to bring emotional conviction to the patient they have to be [formulated] in terms of the immediacy of the relationship to the analyst. On the other hand, the analyst, when formulating them, should keep in mind the notion that it is the patient's past that is expressed in his unconscious fantasies. . . . At some point this past should be made explicit for the patient and linked to his actual present experience. [p. 436]

Brockman (1998) proposes a more psychotherapeutic approach for dealing with the "primitive psychobiological sense of danger" during early phases of treatment with patients having severe forms of pathology. He suggests the metaphor of a map for reformulating interpretations: "The therapist will tailor-make his moves, depending on a specific data-derived 'map' variously to soothe, contain, advise, set limits and encourage (even as these might foster dependence, gratify the transference or allow splitting and displacement)" (p. 214; cited by Caston 2000, p. 184).

Margulies (2000) calls attention to the limitations of verbal refor-mulation. Citing Gadamer's (1976, p. xxxii) phrase, "the infinity of the unsaid" surrounding our words, Margulies notes that we are "constantly up against our limits of articulation" (p. 77):

> And so too with the psychoanalytic situation; both analyst and analysand actively engage in their inarticulateness, ask themselves to express not-fully-known experience in an attempt that can only partially succeed, and one that never really stops. [p. 77; cf. Gadamer's (1976, p. 17) related concept, the "infinity of dialogue," which is only interrupted, never concluded]

Whether (and Why) to Communicate Interpretations

In the illustrative session presented above, the patient was doing so well in interpreting and understanding his own material that my decision and aim were simply to encourage and reinforce the associations, self-observations, and self-interpretations that he was producing (cf. Chapter 9). Some other clinical situations in which the therapist stands back and decides not to communicate interpretations are presented by Poland (2000) in his essay on witnessing. Levenson (2000) notes regarding two of Poland's clinical examples that

> he stopped trying to act therapeutically and gave his patient space. In the first case, it was a spontaneous response to the patient's crisis; in the sec-ond, he felt he had done his work and was standing back to allow the patient to experience his own desolation. . . . We have all had moments when we simply give up, let go, "open the fist" in the Zen phrase, and then to our surprise the patient becomes productive. [pp. 67–68]

Theodore Reik (1949, 1968) postulated that the dynamics of the therapeutic situation are based fundamentally on the therapist's silence. He proposed that the process really begins when the patient realizes that the therapist's silence is deliberate, that he intends not to speak. At that point the patient feels the need to do the speaking himself in order to change the therapist's silence. Racker (1958), on the other hand, consid-ered Reik's view coercive and persecutory. Anzieu (1970), differing from Freud, maintains that the analyst's interpretations divert patients' consciousness, making them focus more on the functioning of their own psychic realities.

Kleinian analysts, who appear to communicate interpretations more frequently than analysts of other schools, base their decision of whether (and why) to interpret on the appearance of anxiety in the patient. Melanie Klein stressed that interpretations should be based on the patient's anxiety level ("point of urgency"). She felt that the patient's point of urgency obliges the analyst to interpret without delay (Etchegoyen 1991).

Although she focuses her interpretive work on here-and-now transference events, the Kleinian analyst Malcolm (1986) also believes it is important, sooner or later, to link the interpretation of the present to the historical past. She explains the rationale of the strategy this way: "I think the main reason for doing this is that, by connecting the historical past with the past as it appears in the transference, we enable patients to gain a sense of the continuity of their lives" (p. 441); in that way the ego becomes better integrated and stronger. She illustrated this approach with the case of a young man who was seriously ill, and who often

> would respond to her interpretations by saying "yes" in a rather mechanical way. His mechanical way of saying "yes" made her feel isolated, which led eventually to her having an image of a baby crying, trying to communicate something, and being responded to with a mild "yes, yes, dear"—an automatic response of a mother who was present but emotionally absent or incapable of resonating to her baby. Malcolm assumed that the patient was employing projective identification both as a defense and as a communication, and that this was based on an early relationship to his mother, the nature of which had remained frozen in him and separated from other parts of his personality. (To simplify her actual, rather complicated and potentially confusing interpretation to him): She told him that his lodging a bit of himself in her was done both to get rid of the part of himself that felt so unhappy and lonely (a frequent complaint of his), and also to make Malcolm know how it feels when not listened to or understood properly. [p. 435]

Schafer (1997) emphasizes the necessity of constructing and communicating interpretive narratives, which he considers the crux of psychoanalytic truth: "The narrativity of knowledge is not a cause or a prescription; it is an observation of what has always been the case and is obviously the case today" (p. 191). Jacobson (2000) notes critically, however, that the preceding view departs from Schafer's usual pluralism; it attempts to make clinical interpretation an exclusively hermeneutic, narrative process, leaving no room for a complementary objectivist or natural science perspective.

Discussing Warren Poland's (2000) concept of the analyst's "witnessing and otherness," André Green (2000) argues that a certain "distancing" on the therapist's part is necessary to prevent the analyst from being "overwhelmed" emotionally by the patient's discourse:

> I call this move the *objectivization of subjectivity*. But this does not mean the analyst's view is objective. It is an approximation of what the analyst believes is in the patient's mind, an approximation that can always be questioned, revised, or even canceled. . . . Whether it will precede [a communicated] interpretation or not is a different question. Usually . . . the interpretation will mature in the analyst's mind. Interpretation is less the result of a deliberate search than an outgrowth of analytic communication that combines the discourse of the patient's and the analyst's listening-witnessing. [p. 60]

In contrast to debating with oneself whether to make an interpretation to the patient, Roche (1989) emphasizes the importance of spontaneity in communicating interpretations; he argues that "truly creative interpretations are not only usually bold but often also surprise those who make them; it is not unusual for us to realize what we have said to our patient only after we have expressed them" (p. 345). Klauber (1980), McLaughlin (1988), Duncan (1989), and Hoffman (1994, 1998) have made much the same point.

What (and How Much) to Communicate Interpretively

Etchegoyen (1991) reviews the evolution of Freud's conceptions of interpretation and how it works in the therapeutic process. He compares Freud's view with Anzieu's and concludes that Freud's was more "intellectualist," while Anzieu focused more on affect.

With respect to *what* is interpreted, the content varies, of course, depending on the dynamics of the therapeutic process at a particular moment. Anna Freud (1968) mentioned that theoretical issues also influence what is interpreted. Thomas M. French (1958b, 1963) stressed the value of attempting to thematize and understand what he called the "focal conflict" at a particular time: "The analyst should not be content with fragmentary bits of insight. His constant aim should be to understand how different trends and themes in the patient's associations fit together into a single intelligible context" (1958b, p. 207).

French (1963) applied the same clinical principle to the technique of communicating interpretations to patients; he suggested also that therapists interpret to patients at the level of the focal conflict:

> The patient should be much better able to understand and assimilate an interpretation that has to do with the problem with which he is already preoccupied. This is a well-recognized principle of education. . . . To the patient an interpretation is a stimulus. Interpreting the focal conflict often activates it more intensely and centers the patient's reaction even more sharply on the analyst and on what the analyst said. . . . If [by contrast] the analyst should interpret some conflict which at the moment is at the periphery of the patient's interest, then the effect may be to activate a competing focus and thus to make the patient's [responses to the interpretation] much more difficult to understand. [pp. 212–213]

Describing the Ulm process model of psychoanalytic technique, Thomä and Kächele (1987) adopted French's concept of the focal conflict and its communication to the patient. They defined the focus as the interactionally formed focus of the therapeutic process—an "ongoing, temporally unlimited focal therapy with a changing focus" (p. 347). They reviewed the further developments of French's concepts in their own work, in the work of Malan's (1963) focal therapy workshop, and in Balint and colleagues (1972). Thomä and Kächele illustrate their concepts and methods in a second volume, *Psychoanalytic Practice: 2. Clinical Studies* (1990).

Continuing the discussion of what (and how much) to interpret, Eissler (1953) introduced the concept of technical parameters, by which he meant whatever intervention a particular case requires in addition to the basic model technique of interpretation only. He proposed several situations in which to use parameters: (1) when the basic model technique is insufficient, (2) when the parameter is employed minimally, (3) when it can be dispensed with eventually, and (4) when the effect of the parameter on the transference can be resolved later by interpretation.

Etchegoyen (1991) questions whether analysts can be objective enough to decide that the basic model technique is insufficient, and believes that the best way of helping patients is to remain faithful to one's own particular technique.

Eissler (1958) later introduced the concept of pseudo-parameters, that is, devices used when interpretation arouses insuperable resistances. If a pseudo-parameter can make the interpretive point more or less imperceptibly—for example, in the form of a timely joke—it might be useful. Etchegoyen (1991) opposes the use of any such a device "on the sly," however, as manipulative.

According to Racker (1958), the various therapeutic schools differ most on *how much* to interpret—an issue that involves conflict for the therapist between interpreting and silence. Freud was very active; he asked questions, illustrated his assertions with quotations from Shakespeare, made comparisons, and so on. Lacan (1958a), on the other hand, compared the analyst with the dummy in bridge. Etchegoyen (1991) writes: "The problem of *how much* to interpret is of singular importance because it confronts us with two different, and at times opposed, techniques. The amount of interpretation has more to do with the analyst's theories than his personal style or the patient's material" (p. 342).

In the illustrative case above, the patient was doing so well in free associating, self-observation, and self-interpretation, that the questions of what and how much to interpret were not major issues of interpretive technique (cf. also Chapter 9).

When to Interpret

With respect to *when* to interpret, Etchegoyen (1991) believes that the patient's influence—for example, his manifest and latent demands on the analyst—is more important than the analyst's theories and personal style. Loewenstein (1958) emphasized a somewhat different timing of interpretations, namely, "at the right moment," when the patient is "ready to receive it." He acknowledged, however, that it is difficult to define what that moment is. Many analysts appear to believe that the right moment is when a resistance interferes with the flow of associations.

Concerning the illustrative case above, the sequence of conflict-defense relations in the reported series of dreams is instructive. Defenses predominated in the first two dreams of the series (mainly avoidance mechanisms of hiding from his father in the first dream, and avoiding facing his father by suicide in the second dream). The underlying conflict did not emerge until the third dream in the series. Early in a session (or dream series, or treatment as a whole), the available data are still limited, defensively obscure, and more difficult to understand. Because of the tendency for defenses to predominate prior to emergence of the principal current (thematic) conflict, it is often useful to hold off on formulating and communicating the underlying conflict until a session has proceeded far enough that the latter has begun to reveal itself more clearly.

Note also the collaborative nature of the therapeutic work in the reported session, and the patient's ability to interpret many of his own associations, which illustrates the development of promising self-interpretive competence in the patient, and the value of encouraging such development in the patient by the therapist (cf. Chapter 9).

How to Interpret

Freud (1912b) recommended that the analyst relate to the patient and make his interpretations on the model of a surgeon, that is, with an attitude of emotional detachment. He discouraged bringing one's own individuality into the relationship and interpretations, argued against educational activity, and cautioned about intellectual discussions. In his paper, "Beginning the Treatment," Freud (1913, p. 139) emphasized the importance of facilitating (1) "a proper *rapport*," and also (2) the patient's attachment to the treatment "and to the person of the doctor"—by giving the patient time to develop such feelings, and by exhibiting "a serious interest in him."

Freud (1910c) also cautioned the clinician "not to rush"; and similarly, in a letter to Fliess, he commented on some parallels between clinical interpretation and Jakob Burkhardt's (1898–1902) *History of Greek Culture*: "For the way in which one should comport oneself in the work of interpretation: The result is not at all to be forced; a gentle attentiveness with regular diligence leads further" (Freud 1985, p. 342).

In his paper, "Transference Love," Freud (1915) emphasized again the necessity to carry out the treatment in abstinence, but added: "I do not mean physical abstinence alone, *nor yet the deprivation of everything that the patient desires, for perhaps no sick person could tolerate this*" (p. 165; emphasis added). Here Freud opened the door slightly for some important changes in technique that were to develop following his death.

Around the middle of the twentieth century, at about the same time that the scope of indications for psychoanalysis widened gradually (cf. Stone 1954), questions inevitably arose about Freud's "surgical analogy" regarding the analyst's stance. In a landmark treatise on *The Psychoanalytic Situation*, for example, Leo Stone (1961) reviewed and questioned the "overzealous and indiscriminate application of the crucial and essential rule of abstinence" (Stone 1967, p. 3). He did not argue against the importance of abstinence itself, but only its overuse in disturbed patients who often require warmer, more human responses from the analyst in order to tolerate the anxiety and frustrations of the analytic situation.

As the strictures of abstinence were loosened gradually, some conservative traditional analysts (e.g., Eissler 1953) resisted such changes by emphasizing a "basic model technique" relying solely on the communication of interpretations to patients. Even Eissler (1958) agreed in a later publication, however, that "pseudo-parameters" (devices used when interpretation arouses insuperable resistances) may be necessary.

A related development that began at around the middle of the twentieth century was growing interest in countertransference phenomena (Blum 1986, Giovacchini 1989, Heiman 1950, Jacobs 1986, 1991, Little 1951, 1981, McDougall 1979, Racker 1953, 1968, Searles 1965, 1987, Tower 1956, Winnicott 1949). Theodore Jacobs (1991) observes that this aspect of therapeutic technique actually has origins in Anna Freud's (1954) caveat that therapeutic "technique was not designed for the defense of the analyst," but enjoins the analyst to consider privately "*all* that passes within him for its informational value in terms of the patient"

(p. xiv). In this way "we are able to turn to the interactional level of analysis, not as an avoidance of depth psychology, but with a fuller realization of the implications of unconscious functioning in each of the parties, each with his own unconscious" (p. xiv). "My concern is not with this phenomenon in a narrow sense. It is, rather, with the experiences of the analyst as they resonate with, comment on, and illuminate those of the patient" (p. xxii).

Jacobs notes also that this approach is not concerned only with

> the words exchanged between patient and [therapist], but the underlying messages that accompanied these communications . . . transmitted through tone and syntax, vocal quality and inflection, posture and movement . . . feelings, attitudes, and values of which neither patient nor [therapist] is consciously aware. This level of communication serves to modify, punctuate, emphasize, or contradict the words spoken by each [p. xxi; see also Jacobs (1996) and below regarding the related semiotic perspective, which emphasizes messages transmitted through signs such as tone, vocal quality, inflection, kinesthetic cues, and syntax, as well as words].

The depth psychological interactive perspective implicit in the wider use of countertransference in the interpretive process probably contributed, in turn, to the growth of interest in (object-)relational, intersubjective, and dialectical constructivist viewpoints. Influential contributors to *object-relational* views have included Lawrence Friedman (1975), Otto Kernberg (1976, 1988), Spruielle (1978), Vann Spruiell (1979), and others. Kernberg (1988) attempts to integrate ego psychological and object relations theories, but a fundamental assumption of the more recent and *radical relational approach* advocated by Greenberg and Mitchell (1983) and Mitchell (1997) is that everything in the therapeutic process can be cast in a relational perspective, focusing on the immediate therapeutic interaction. "It elevates the virtues of an [exclusive] interpersonal perspective over any intrapersonal considerations" (Meissner 1998, p. 420). In a review of Teicholz's (1999) volume on postmodern psychoanalytic views of self and relationship, however, Vida (2000) argues that "the relational element has always been part of psychoanalytic practice (see Lipton 1977), even if not made explicit in practice" (p. 982).

An *intersubjective* approach emphasizes the dyadic, collaborative nature of the therapeutic relationship, including candid expressions of feedback—even if these involve very negative feelings—between the two participants. It views psychoanalysis as a two-person psychology, and questions the traditional authoritative position of the analyst in one-body (intrapsychic) theories such as Freud's. Where the classical paradigm emphasizes the analyst's objectivity and the patient's transference, the intersubjective approach recognizes that transference and countertransference inevitably commingle. The intersubjective approach differs also from the objectivist paradigm by emphasizing and confirming the patient's point of view, through dialogue and some self-disclosure by the analyst.

Analysts and dynamic psychotherapists who are pluralistically inclined attempt to employ both traditional and intersubjective models; they try to identify clinical situations in which it is best to interpret transference, and others in which it is better to engage in dialogue. The two paradigms can become confused, however, with the intersubjective approach being used in the service of transference-countertransference enactments (Beng 2000).

Jacobs (1999) has reviewed the history of self-disclosure in psychoanalysis and dynamic psychotherapy, and evaluates whether it is an error or an advance in therapeutic technique. He concludes that most depth psychological therapists consider it questionable; but although it cannot be prescribed at this time as a general technique, further clinical experience with self-disclosure may reveal that in selected cases and clinical situations it may be found useful.

The *dialectical constructivist* approach is associated mainly with the writings of Irwin Z. Hoffman (e.g., 1983, 1994, 1998). He has drawn on the work of Bollas (1987), Ehrenberg (1992) Jacobs (1991), Levenson (1983), Mitchell (1988), Modell (1990), Natterson (1991), Ogden (1986), Racker (1968), Searles (1965), and Tanzer and Burke (1989) to develop a theory of therapeutic and interpretive action that he calls dialectical constructivism (formerly called social constructivism [Hoffman 1992]). Hoffman's therapeutic and interpretive approaches emphasize spontaneity and self-expression (though not the degree of self-disclosure used in the intersubjective approach); but at the same time he stresses that the analyst's effectiveness is enhanced also by adherence to certain psychoanalytic rituals, including abstinence and the asymmetrical aspect of the therapeutic relationship. He refers to this double demand on the therapist's functioning as "struggling to find an optimal position relative to the dialectic between formal [clinical] authority and personal responsivity and self-expression" (p. 187).

Concerning his conclusion that "some acceptance by the patient of the recognizably technical aspects of the analyst's behavior is essential" (1994, p. 192), Hoffman notes that

> classical technique, especially when practiced in a rigid way, is a familar target of criticism for its seeming coldness. I would say it is actually a scapegoat, a whipping boy, for a problem that cuts across most of the major theoretical positions. . . . It is more difficult but equally important to locate the expression of [problems] in points of view that advertise themselves explicitly as warmer or more "human" alternatives to the classical position. Self psychology is one such point of view. The central principle of technique in self psychology is "sustained empathic inquiry." Can conformity to such a "benign" principle cast a shadow . . . on the analyst? I think it can. [p. 191; see also Slavin and Kriegman 1992]

Hoffman (1994) cites what he considers an excellent example of dialectical thinking in an account by Mitchell (1988) of the optimal posture of a therapist dealing with narcissistic issues in the transference. Mitchell notes regarding a patient inviting the therapist to participate in a "mutually admiring relationship":

> Responding to such an invitation in a way that is [therapeutically] constructive is tricky, and difficult to capture in a single formula. What is useful most frequently is not the words, but the tone in which they are spoken. The most useful response entails a dialectic between joining the analysand in the narcissistic integration and simultaneously questioning the nature and purpose of that integration—both a playful participation in the analysand's illusions and a puzzled curiosity about how and why they came to be so serious, the sine qua non of the analysand's sense of security and involvement with others. [p. 205]

Hoffman concludes further that the therapeutic and interpretive attitudes which are "most integrative and authentic must be an alloy of doubt and openness. . . . The work requires an underlying tolerance of uncertainty and with it a radical, yet critical kind of openness that is conveyed over time in various ways, including a readiness to soul-search, to negotiate, and to change" (p. 215).

As I have indicated in the preface of this volume, my own conceptual-methodological orientation to clinical practice and interpretation includes significant aspects of Hoffman's dialectical-constructivist approach. In addition, I subscribe to a view of relational aspects in psychoanalysis and clinical interpretation suggested by Meissner (2000a), who suggests that what we need and seek

> is a theory of the self as an *open* system—but if we are to have an open system, it should be a system that continues to maintain its own inherent organization, structure, stability, coherence, constancy, identity and integrity. If we open such a system to the influence of others in the form of relatedness, intimacy, attachment and affiliation, we do not have to destroy it in the process. [p. 192]

Before concluding this section on "how" to interpret, I turn to a *semiotic* perspective on depth psychological therapies and clinical interpretation. In Bonnie Litowitz's and Phillip Epstein's informative volume, *Semiotic Perspectives on Clinical Theory and Practice* (1991), Litowitz notes, "Freud had little to say about discourse directly. He did warn about the dangers of one-sided interpretation" (p. 100), however. Freud (1900) wrote, "In the process of transforming a thought into a visual image a peculiar faculty is revealed by dreamers, and [a therapist] is rarely equal to following it with his guesses. . . . [One needs] the creator of these representations . . . to explain their meaning" (p. 361 fn). Litowitz adds:

> Psychoanalysis provides a window on the semiotic functioning of the human mind. Psychoanalysis also provides the best description we have of a psychic syntax—the types of psychological signs, the rules for their formation and expression—seen most clearly in descriptions of the dreamwork and case studies. This knowledge becomes a part of one's competence that is applied to the act of interpretation or reading of new signs. . . . Meanings are created over time through *dialogue* with others and can, therefore, only be interpreted through negotiated discourses. . . . The critical move from the earlier talking cure to the importance of a transference

neurosis is evidence that Freud felt the *dialogic process* had to be reengaged within the analysis for understanding to take place. He concluded that it is not sufficient for repressed material to escape repression by hooking up with verbal expression. . . . The systematic regressions of transference neuroses provide insight and understanding precisely because they reenact patients' roles in dialogues from earlier periods in their lives with the analyst as significant others. . . . For example, in exploring Little Hans's all important substitution of a horse for his father, Freud explains why a horse. It seems that Hans's father used to play at horses (play "horsey") with him. Similarly, the Wolfman's anxiety about wolves could be traced to a fairy-tale about seven little goats who were devoured by a wolf, just as the father in play jokingly used to threaten to gobble the Wolfman up (1926). [pp. 101–102; emphases added]

Further contributions to a semiotic perspective on clinical interpretation have come from Victor Rosen (1969/77, John Gedo (1986), Wilma Bucci (1985, 1989), Björn Killingmo (1990), and Matthias Kettner (1991). Rosen had theorized that the principal form of communication between parent and infant is a signal-sign system, including the cry of hunger, the smiling response, gestures, babbling, and mimetic behavior—all of which are superseded but not replaced completely by the later development of language. On the basis of experiments in cognitive psychology, Bucci postulates that verbal and nonverbal contents are coded and stored separately (cf. also Paivio 1986, and Johansen's [1986] proposal of two different semiotic memory systems—one being perceptual, pictorial, or iconic, the other involving symbolic linguistic representations).

On the basis of their clinical experiences, both Gedo and Killingmo have suggested the related concept that it may not be possible to activate or modify affects deriving from presemantic levels solely by the verbal content of interpretations. It may be necessary to approach such affects by intonation and enactments, which might serve as presemantic "semiotic supplements" to verbal-symbolic interpretations.

SUMMARY

The technique of clinical interpretation consists, first, of verbal reformulation, and then communication of interpretive understanding to patients in depth psychological treatments. The communication of interpretive understanding is not necessarily, or even usually, conveyed through formal interpretive statements to the patient, however. The patient gains such insights in multiple ways, some through the therapist's understanding, others by self-understanding (see the following chapter) or both.

Freud's views on formulating and communicating interpretations have been reviewed; he suggested the model of a surgeon's emotional detachment for the communication of interpretations to patients. He indicated, however, that he did not mean by abstinence that one should deprive the patient of everything, which no sick person could tolerate.

After presenting an illustrative case report, including commentaries on interpretive technique in the case, the remainder of the chapter discussed the subject in terms of the following categories: (1) verbal reformulation of interpretive hypotheses, (2) whether (and why) to interpret, (3) what (and how much) to interpret, (4) when to interpret and (5) how to interpret. The views of various clinical schools (traditional, object relations, more radical relational theories, the intersubjective approach including self-disclosure, and dialectical constructivism) as well as the author's own preferences and practices were reviewed in discussing the several categories of interpretive technique. A semiotic perspective on interpretive technique may be useful, especially in certain types of cases, for example, in patients having predominantly presemantic fixations.

CHAPTER NINE

Development of Self-Interpretive Competence

*I*N ONE OF HIS relatively early writings, Freud (1910) wrote:

> No psychoanalyst goes further than his own complexes and internal resistances permit; and we consequently require that he shall begin his activity with a self-analysis and continually carry it deeper while he is making his observations of his patients. Anyone who fails to produce results in a self-analysis of this kind may at once give up the idea of being able to treat patients by analysis. [p. 145]

Much later, in "Analysis Terminable and Interminable," Freud (1937a) concluded that psychoanalysis changes the ego, resulting in less defensive activity and freer intrapsychic communication (see also Freud 1918). This statement corresponds with observations by a number of later investigators that, as defensive activity diminishes during the course of an analysis, conflict-defense patterns become clearer and easier to interpret.

Freud (1937a) concluded also, however, that infantile conflicts have an unusual tenacity, cannot be resolved completely, and thus may be revived again posttherapeutically. These considerations led him to speak of analysis as interminable and to propose that analysts might need to be reanalyzed at intervals—a possible alternative being a continuing self-analysis. In the same essay, Freud said about training analyses:

> We hope and believe that the stimulus received in the learner's own analysis will not cease to act upon him when that analysis ends, *that the processes of*

ego transformation will go on of their own accord and that all further experience will be made use of in a newly acquired way. [The italicized part of this quotation differs from Strachey's translation; it represents a more literal translation of the German original by M. Kramer 1959, pp. 17–18. For other views by Freud on self-analysis, see 1912, 1914a, and his 1936 self-analysis of a disturbance of memory on the Acropolis]

The preceding views by Freud concerning the importance of self-analysis in the training analysis gradually came to be applied by a number of psychoanalysts to patients generally, not only to candidates in psychoanalytic training. One of the earliest and most influential of these writings was by Maria Kramer (1959). In her pioneering study, "The Continuation of the Analytic Process After Psychoanalysis (A Self Observation)," she reported a self-analytic process in herself that she described as occurring spontaneously, extending over a period of months, and resulting in the resolution of persistent problems that had not been resolved during her therapeutic/training analysis or in previous deliberate attempts at self-analysis. On the basis of her self observations, she postulated the existence of an autonomous self-analytic ego function that she called the autoanalytic function. She concluded, "Self-analysis plays an important part in any analyst's work, but finds its limitation in the power of the resistances which blind the self to the correct interpretations. The autoanalytic function can lead to insight even if active attempts have failed" (p. 25).

MARIA KRAMER'S CLINICAL ILLUSTRATION OF SELF ANALYSIS

Maria Kramer (1959) drew on Freud's (1937a) comments about training analyses in a pioneering study of her own (spontaneous) self-analytic experiences. She wrote:

> In reviewing the knowledge gained about my unconscious in this spontaneous way, I found a remarkable continuity in the material. Though the episodes of insight were often separated by considerable periods of time, the new material discovered was either a further elaboration of the problem last dealt with, or approached conflicts which were closely related to

it. The spontaneity of the emergence of this material gives evidence that the analytic process can become an autonomous, non-volitional ego function which automatically deals with whatever is most strongly cathected in the unconscious. [p. 19; cf. in this connection Freud's (1936) self-analysis of his disturbance of memory on the Athenian acropolis, which also appeared to have involved only partially successful active attempts to analyze the event, but resulted in more complete insights which emerged gradually over an extended period of time]

Kramer illustrated her thesis by describing three experiences related to the same unconscious conflict, but separated by several months (for reasons of discretion, she used the language of psychodynamics in reporting some of the more personal details of her self-analysis):

The first [experience] consisted of intermittent feelings of estrangement which were not frightening but uncomfortable enough for me to try to analyze them. I told myself that these feelings must be a defense against some anger or hostility. I repeatedly tried to associate, to find a correlation in the situation in which these feelings occurred, but no answer came. After a while the feelings disappeared.

In the second episode, several months later, I was troubled by the appearance of a compulsive thought, disturbing in character and annoying by its insistence. Again I tried to analyze it, associating to its manifest content with no success. Then [spontaneously] one day I became aware of a fleeting feeling of guilt, and suddenly I realized the reason for the guilt and also the meaning of the compulsive thought. I became aware that the feeling of guilt and the compulsive thought, though apparently unrelated to each other, had been caused by the same unconscious conflict. This conflict had also been the source of long-standing inhibitions which I had not understood until then. The guilt was due to oral aggressive impulses and was accompanied by fear of retaliatory punishment by the archaic superego. The preceding compulsive thought had focused on restitution as an attempt to deny the guilt. The awareness of this conflict was followed by the disappearance of the compulsive thought, the guilt feeling and the inhibitions.

The third episode occurred after a further lapse of several [more] months. One day I became angry with a person, and this anger was very persistent. I tried not to think of it, to distract myself in various ways, but the anger did not disappear. Finally, I stopped myself from attempts to evade the disturbing feeling. Thereupon the thought came to mind, "I couldn't possibly be so angry with *this* person." Almost simultaneously, it became clear from whom the affect had been transferred and what the original situation must have been in which the anger was generated and repressed. At the same time, the anger itself increased to an intensity I had never previously felt. It then became clear to me that this was the affect [associated with] the oral aggressive impulse. This affect had remained repressed while the impulse content had become conscious in the preceding episode. During the process of working through, ramifications of the consequences of this conflict into many other areas of my life became clear, and the physical symptom, present for years, gradually diminished and finally disappeared.

Kramer (1959) compared the spontaneous operation of her autoanalytic experiences with the dynamics of a "good hour," which Kris (1956) had described as material emerging "as if prepared in advance outside of awareness" (p. 447). Kris had explained the phenomenon as a result of the crumbling of a resistance structure, about which Kramer commented: "We see, therefore, that after decrease or crumbling of defenses, there is dynamically no difference between the process of a 'good analytic hour' and the post-analytic experiences here described" (p. 23). An example of Kramer's having used a *self-interpretive* strategy to deal with a defense can be seen in the third episode of her self-analytic experiences: She said about the persistent anger at a person: "I tried not to think about it, to distract myself in various ways, but the anger did not disappear. *Finally, I stopped myself from attempts to evade the disturbing feeling* [emphasis added]. Thereupon the thought came to mind, 'I couldn't possibly be so angry at *this* person.'" Thus by opposing the defensive evasion, new insight into the source of the transferred anger emerged. I make a point of Kramer's self-interpretive activity because it bears on the question of whether the so-called autoanalytic function is completely autonomous, which Kramer had concluded.

Kramer added the following further relevant memories of experiences that had preceded the self-analytic activities:

Not until I was reviewing the material for the purpose of writing this paper, did I realize that a dream I had following my mother's death had also revealed an aspect of this conflict. Here is the dream: I was offering my mother five bishop's caps for dinner. In Vienna [Kramer's original home], bishop's cap was the name given to the rear end of a cooked fowl. This part of the chicken had been my mother's favorite, and whenever chicken was served this piece was passed on to her. My association to the bishop's caps was the fact that I was suffering from hemorrhoids at the time. The dream had been neutral in feeling tone, but this association struck me as very amusing. The idea that I was mourning the death of my mother with a painful rear end provoked me repeatedly to laughter. I understood the dream as a peace offering, and assumed it was due to an increase of general guilt following my mother's recent death. . . .

There had been another association that had remained unexplained. To the number five [bishop's caps] I associated the Tetons, the mountain range where I was spending my vacation at the time of the dream. The name Tetons was given to the mountains by the French explorers who discovered them and who compared the five peaks of the range to tits. . . . I know now that in this dream I offered my mother part of myself as restitution for the same oral aggressive impulse, the analysis of which I have described. [pp. 20–21]

OTHER POST-FREUDIAN CONTRIBUTIONS TO THE METHODOLOGY OF SELF-ANALYSIS

Helen Beiser (1984) presented another example of self-analysis, and reviewed the literature on this subject—including Freud's (1887–1902) self-analysis as described and illustrated in his letters to Fliess; Karen Horney's (1942) seldom-cited, largely theoretical volume entitled *Self-Analysis*; Maria Kramer's (1959) earliest report in the post-Freudian psychoanalytic literature of personal self-analytic experiences; Gertrude Ticho's (1967) interviews with colleagues, which revealed varied motives and methods of self-analysis; and related reports by Myerson (1960), Fleming (1971), Hatcher (1973), Engel (1975), Baum (1977), and Calder (1980). Beiser (1984) concluded that "the consensus seems to be that self-analysis is valuable and should be available in some form to *all* patients post-analytically" (p. 5; emphasis added)—especially, but not only, to analysts.

At about the same time as Beiser's report, Schlessinger and Robbins (1983) published their volume on follow-up studies of patients who had completed successful analyses. They concluded:

> Our findings in the successful analytic cases we studied paralleled the results of Pfeffer (1959, 1961, 1963) and Norman et al. (1976). [As Freud observed in 1937a, cf. also Spitz 1994] psychic conflicts were not eliminated in the analytic process. The clinical material of the follow-ups demonstrated a repetitive pattern of conflicts. Accretions of insight were evident but the more significant outcome of the analysis appeared to be the development of a preconsciously active self-analytic function, in identification with the analyzing function of the analyst, as a learned mode of coping with conflicts. As elements of the transference neurosis reappeared and were re-solved, the components of a self-analytic function were demonstrated in self-observation, reality processing, and the tolerance and mastery of frustration, anxiety, and depression. The[se] resources gained in the analytic process persisted, and their vitality was evident in response to renewed stress. [pp. 9–10]

On the basis of her literature review, Beiser (1984) had noted that most authors do not describe the actual process of self-analysis; but Schlessinger and Robbins (1983) reported the following method employed by some of their patients:

> [Some] former patients reported that in confronting problems they would use a "benign presence" externally or in fantasy to facilitate efforts at solution of conflict. A particular friend, a spouse, or the remembered presence of the analyst served as a useful catalyst. These descriptions underlined the significance of the analytic alliance as a matrix for the analytic process, and for the acquisition and consolidation of a self-analytic function. [pp. 9–10; Cf. also in this conection Freud's early comment to Fliess about difficulties he was having with his self-analysis: "I can only analyze myself with the help of knowledge obtained objectively (like an outsider)" (referred to in 1914a, pp. 20–21, n. 2)

Myerson (1965) and also Hatcher (1973) investigated how self-analysis is carried out by studying the process of self-observation in themselves. They proposed similar distinctions between two types or modes of self-observation. The simpler of the two—experiential or reality-oriented self-observation—has the function of facing the immediate flux of experiencing and reporting what is visible to the inner eye, especially concerning one's relationships with key figures. The more complex, depth-oriented mode of self-observation—reflective self-observation or psychoanalytic insight—includes the capacities to suspend attention, to recapitulate in fantasy earlier efforts at mastery, to observe such efforts in an autonomous manner, to reexperience qualities of the mental state prominent during such attempts at mastery, and to reinterpret the experience through a deep acceptance of one's own reactions.

Both Myerson (1965) and Hatcher (1973) consider reflective self-observation the key to both the self-observing process and insight. Contents that emerge in the experiential phase are identified as elements in a larger, unifying context. The search for and identification of such contexts is the essential feature of the reflective self-observing process, the most relevant feature of which is its degree of intrapsychic focus—an increasing appreciation of the self's contributions to experience, so that the locus of explanation shifts from the outside to the inside (see below, the development of self-interpretive competence in the author's patient, John).

Hatcher (1973) suggests that a considerable amount of early therapeutic work in treatment is directed at modifying experiential self-observation. Miller and colleagues (1965) have reported various ways that therapists attempt to help patients observe themselves more consistently and effectively: exhorting patients to use their self-observational capacities; interpreting obstacles to self-observation; actively instructing patients in self-observation; and the therapist's use of him- or herself as an illustration and model of self-observation. Stern (1970) has proposed a technology that he calls "therapeutic playback" in which a patient with a relatively undeveloped capacity for self-observation may relisten to selected sessions on a tape recorder, which is said to facilitate the patient's listening to himself more reflectively, and thus to augment his self-observing skills, but (perhaps predictably) the method has not caught on with clinicians.

Kantrowitz and colleagues (1990a,b,c) suggest that the concept of self-analytic competence developed during analysis and used as a termination criterion should be reevaluated. In the Boston Outcome Study of Psychoanalysis, for example, no evidence was found that attainment of a self-analytic function was related to the stability of therapeutic gains or the extent to which the transference neurosis had been resolved. The authors added, however, that almost all the patients in the Boston study valued self-understanding, and that the majority of patients reported developing the capacity for self-analysis. The investigators concluded that the limited variability in the sample may have prevented any relation of self-analytic competence to therapeutic outcome from showing. Some patients in the study described continuing their self-analytic work through analysis of dreams or in imaginary conversations with the former analyst or another imaginary listener, with the aim of acquiring further insight; others evoked memories of the analyst or another imagined listener to attain a sense of comfort or support. Thus, according to the reports of patients in this study, it appears that there are different ways to attain improved functioning and to gain a sense of well-being through the use of the analytic process.

A volume edited by Barron (1993) reviews and evaluates various models of self-analysis. A quantitative study by Heaton and colleagues (1998) compared therapist-facilitated and self-guided dream interpretation; their findings support the view that therapists play a critical role in making the interpretive process meaningful and useful to patients. Although dream interpretations by therapists were preferred by patients and led to greater therapeutic gains, additional evidence also supported the efficacy of self-guided interpretation. A number of previous investigations cited by Heaton and colleagues (1998, p.120) demonstrate that many people benefit from self-help materials. Recently, Jason Zack and Clara Hill at the University of Maryland have developed an interactive computer program for self-guided interpretation of dreams—an approach that includes such psychodynamic features as exploring possible "triggers" of dreams, and associating to individual dream images.

THE PRESENT THESIS: DEVELOPMENT OF SELF-INTERPRETIVE COMPETENCE

I postulate that the self-analytic function, which most writers on the subject consider an important outcome of a successful analysis, may result largely from patients learning in the course of their treatments how to apply clinical interpretive methods to their own associations, dreams, fantasies, slips of speech, and other interpretable data. That is, as the therapeutic process progresses, gentle but steady encouragement by the therapist appears to reinforce the patient's motivation toward self-mastery, which facilitates a learning process in which more and more of the therapist's specialized interpretive competence is acquired and used with increasing effectiveness by the patient.

I postulate further that one can observe the patient's coding and recoding of such information as the therapeutic process unfolds over time. During early phases of the treatment the patient is relatively unfamiliar with the conventions (or "code") of clinical interpretation, but as the therapeutic dialogue progresses, the patient gradually learns some of the key interpretive conventions of depth psychology, and becomes increasingly able to anticipate the therapist's interpretations and to apply the conventions to his or her own associations (cf. Rubovits-Seitz 1998, Schafer 1983, Schlessinger and Robbins 1975).

I argue also that learning the conventions of clinical interpretation in the course of the therapeutic process is a significant factor in the patient's development of both self-interpretive and self-analytic competences—the former appearing to be a prerequisite of the latter. Thus with encouragement from their therapists, patients learn how to talk more freely about increasingly personal, conflicted thoughts and feelings. They also learn how to listen to themselves, to observe their own thoughts and actions, paying particular attention to slips, repetitions, omissions, overstatements, parallels, contrasts, and contiguities in a systematic search for hidden meanings and determinants. They learn that images that occur in fantasies and dreams are important vehicles of the mind for mediating unconscious thoughts, feelings, conflicts, and defenses—and that images, as well as metaphors, often represent something other than their manifest appearances.

Patients also learn to expect and to investigate the myriad emotional resistances that must be overcome to discover important hidden meanings and determinants. They learn to connect present-day patterns of behavior with relevant childhood experiences, but not to expect repressed memories to be remembered directly because repressed memories tend to return mainly by being relived toward persons in the present. Patients learn also that hidden meanings and determinants are not simple or clear-cut but are usually complex and multiple—that understanding necessarily comes about gradually, which necessitates patience and diligence in the process of self-discovery. Peterfreund (1983) thus concluded that "most activities performed by a therapist can be performed by a patient, and often much better" (p. 196).

To support these hypotheses, I draw on several sources of evidence. One source is something that I suggest every therapist can observe in the course of his or her clinical work, namely, that patients tend to become increasingly capable of interpreting their own associations, fantasies, dreams, slips of speech, and so forth, as a treatment proceeds. As Schafer (1983) puts it:

> Interpretation is more than uncovering; it is discovering, transforming, or creating meaning, too. . . . This means that [patients] learn as well as admit, discover as well as recover. And . . . by introducing the new, one may throw much previous knowledge and understanding into a new light. [p. 87] . . . Within the interaction between [therapist and patient], there develops a mutual construction of two . . . second selves. The self of the person in [treatment] is not identical with what it is in the outer world. It is within this mutual construction that personal experience can become possible that will at times transcend in richness and intensity what is ordinarily possible. [p. 292; cf. also Gill 1984, 1991, Hoffman 1991, 1998]

A related source of evidence for the present thesis is an observation by Marmor (1962): "Depending upon the point of view of the [therapist], the patients of each school seem to bring up precisely the kinds of phenomenological data which confirm the . . . interpretations of their [therapists]" (p. 289). An often overlooked interpretation of this view is that patients are capable of learning different codes or conventions of clinical interpretation, depending on the specific schools of psychoanalysis and dynamic psychotherapy with which their particular therapists are identified.

Still another source of evidence is Thomas French's finding (1952, 1954, 1958a,b; see also Rubovits-Seitz 1987, 1992, 1998, Seitz 1968) that the recurrent dynamic cycles that characterize a well-going therapeutic process are completed more rapidly as an analysis proceeds. My own studies of this phenomenon suggest that the major reasons for the speeding up of cycles as an analysis progresses are the respective learning processes that take place in the therapist and patient. That is, in a well-going therapeutic process, the therapist becomes steadily more familiar with the patient's particular genetic and dynamic patterns, including sequential patterns or cycles, and the patient becomes increasingly knowledgeable about, confident, and effective in employing the methods of free association, self-observation, and clinical interpretation.

CLINICAL ILLUSTRATION OF THE DEVELOPMENT OF SELF-INTERPRETIVE COMPETENCE, IN THE AUTHOR'S PATIENT "JOHN"

This clinical example is the same illustrative case presented in Chapter 8, the case of John. I add details of that case here, illustrating the present thesis regarding the development of self-interpretive competence.

First, I should add that John had multiple left-hemisphere–mediated cognitive deficits, including a speech disorder. He had a full-scale IQ of 107, which is within the average range of general intelligence. The report that I published on John, "Intelligence and Analyzability" (1988b), concluded that, contrary to what many writers have claimed, treatment with depth psychological methods may not depend on relatively high *general* intelligence. Rather, the cognitive requirements of such treatments may be associated primarily with that special kind of intelligence called "psychological-mindedness," which may be partially independent of general intelligence (see, e.g., Rubovits-Seitz 1988b, 1998, regarding "commonsense psychology)."

From the time of his suicide attempt at age 17 until his treatment with me at the age of 30, John had been in therapy almost continuously. Presumably because of his limitations, the therapies had been primarily supportive rather than exploratory. When I first saw him and heard the history of his life, I too assumed that his treatment would have to be considerably less that than psychodynamic or analytic. His somewhat awkward, unsophisticated, adolescent manner, in addition to his difficulties with language, even pronunciation, made it fairly easy to underestimate him. It was only after he had been in treatment with me for about six months that I began to sense more potential in him for a depth psychological approach. After six months of therapy, therefore, I explained free association to him and asked whether he would like to try it. He said that he would, so his appointments were increased and from that point on his sessions consisted of free association, study of his dreams, and depth psychological interpretive inquiry.

He had little difficulty in adjusting to the changes in his treatment. My talking much less than before occasioned reactions and comments from him, but actual disturbance about the changes was minimal. He seemed at home with free association—if anything, more relaxed and spontaneous than when we had talked more conversationally.

Early in the second year of this analytic therapy, John was awarded a prize for stimulating the most new business in his company. The following dreams and their interpretation became a turning point in his treatment:

> *Dreams:* "A woman at work wanted to kiss me but I was afraid the boss would see us, so I told her not to kiss me when he was around." In another dream, "I was angry at the Pope for backing Iran."
>
> *Associations:* He recalled his father telling his mother that she was making a sissy of John by petting and pampering him and keeping him around the house so much. During his teens he once

kissed his mother very passionately, which startled her. Afterward he was afraid she might tell his father. Associations to the Pope backing Iran brought out anger at his father for not rescuing him from his mother, by whom he felt he had been "held hostage."

Interpretation: [I commented interpretively that in the first dream he blamed his mother for holding on to him, and in the second dream he blamed his father for not rescuing him from his mother. Perhaps he blames *them* to avoid feeling blame himself.] He responded sheepishly that he had to admit that the kiss was his own idea; and he probably could have gotten away from his mother if had really wanted to. But the truth is that he liked being with her.

Note that *I* did the interpreting of these particular dreams and their associations. Note also that my interpretation drew on the basic concept of *defense*—that he blamed his parents to avoid painful feelings of self-blame. From later developments in his treatment, it appeared that he understood both the interpretation and the basic concept underlying it, and as a result was able to apply them to at least some of his subsequent free associations and dreams with a minimum of interpretive guidance from me. More will be said later about techniques of helping patients develop self-interpretive competence.

From this point on in his treatment, John took increasing responsibility for his own problems, behavior, and treatment. Following the preceding episode, John began to associate more freely, became more adept at observing his own associations, and took increasing interest in attempting to interpret his own productions. During the next several months, for example, an important defense against his competitive feelings and fantasies became evident to both of us, and he was as quick to recognize the pattern as I. The pattern was a need to fail—what Freud (1916) called the character pathology of being "wrecked by success." For example, soon after receiving the award for new business, he very nearly got himself fired for failure to attend required meetings at his company. He connected that behavior with another manifestation of the self-defeating tendency, namely, job hopping—never staying with a job long enough to compete for advancement. He also coupled that insight with a childhood pattern: Having been a sick child, he found he could obtain considerable attention from his family by appearing unable to compete. A year later in his treatment he added the still further insight that by being sickly he could often have his mother to himself.

During the third year of John's analysis he showed even more self-interpretive capacity—illustrated by the series of dreams and their associations, which included a number of self-interpretations, in the "good therapeutic hour" described in Chapter 8. In the first dream of the series, for example, he was trying to hide from someone he feared, but turtles kept nipping at his pants legs. He concluded on his own that the dream sounded as though he was trying to hide from his father, but that his father caught him anyway. In addition, his associations to the turtles noted that they have a thick shell and live a long time—both of which reminded him of his father. His associations to and interpretations of the turtles demonstrate that he had learned the important role of *analogic similarity* in the interpretation of symbols. Neil Cheshire's book, *The Nature of Psychodynamic Interpretation* (1975) refers to such analogies as the key to clinical interpretation (see the section below, however, on the conventions or code of clinical interpretation, which appear to include much more than any single key; see also Rubovits-Seitz 1998).

When I asked him during that session whether he had been thinking about suicide again, he acknowledged that he had, but denied that he would do it now. Then it occurred to him spontaneously that, on the other hand, the second dream of the series about David Stockman committing suicide by swallowing pins could refer to himself, because his mother had said that John looked like Stockman. Here one can see that he had learned the important interpretive heuristic that the central character in one's dreams and associations is often oneself. Further associations about the pins reminding him of sperm cells because of their shape, which reveals again his growing ability to look not only for analogic similarites but also for similarities of all kinds in his attempts to interpret his dreams and associations.

He then recalled an earlier dream of swallowing his father's sperm, which occurred when his father was visiting and slept in the same room with him. He wondered how swallowing his father's sperm could be like a suicide attempt? (Here we see an example of his using relection in search of a possible analogy.) His reflection led to recalling that what he feared most when he attempted suicide in his teens was not his father's reaction to the forgery of an excuse from gym classes, but his father's reaction to John's homosexual feelings.

Note here how well he is free associating, observing his own associations, and attempting to interpret them. To recapitulate, the series of associations reviewed in the preceding paragraph led from the dream about David Stockman committing suicide by swallowing pins, to recognizing that David Stockman was a disguised image of himself, then recalling a previous dream of swallowing his father's sperm, which led to his wondering what the connection might be between doing that and his suicical thoughts, followed by remembering that what he feared most about his father's reaction to his evading his gym class prior to his suicide attempt was his intense attraction to a handsome boy in that class.

[At this point, because he seemed so close to an insight about a connection between his homosexual feelings and self-destructive feelings, I raised the question whether swallowing his father's semen might represent a symbolic killing off of his masculine competitive feelings toward his father.] He thought about the interpretation, and concluded, "Yes, competing with him about investments, and about Mother." He then wondered (insightfully) whether the investments and his father's money were like his mother to him, yet another example of John seeing a cogent analogy. "I tried everything to get control of the money, then tried to outdo my father with it." [I reminded him that he also "took some liberties" with the money.] "Yeah, I did, and I took some liberties with Mother, too, which I was afraid for Father to know about"—illustrating his ability to recognize parallels between the present and the past.

His next associations continued the same theme by recalling the third dream of living with the older woman whose husband had died. He now added further relevant associations to that dream and the woman (mother figure) in it: "I happen to know that she tried to make a substi-

tute husband of her son. Maybe she would have done that with me, too"—
at which point an insight dawned on him suddenly. He said, "Oh!
No wonder the height phobia returned then." [To reinforce his self-
interpreted insight, I agreed with the dynamic parallel that he was suggesting and added that, as with his mother, he may have felt that he was
getting in over his head with her.] He responded, "For sure! Like the time
I kissed Mother so long and it made her all flustered. I was *scared to death*
[note the allusion of this phrase to the theme of suicide, illustrating again
how revealing his associations had become] that she'd tell Father and they'd
both punish me for it."

John's associations to dream 4 about a statue covered with ice and
his chipping the ice away in large chunks led to his self-interpretive understanding that the imagery referred to his chipping away in his analysis at
the thick coatings that cover up his feelings, and finding out what is underneath. He then added the insight that what he had uncovered in this session by "chipping away" was that "what was under the ice was someone
dead—*me!*" He concluded on his own at that point that his old suicidal
feelings had lasted longer than he realized.

[Asked why he thought that the suicidal feelings had lasted so long?],
he became thoughtful for a while, and then responded insightfully that it
was because of guilt—toward his father for wanting to get rid of him,
for wanting to get his money, for wanting to outdo him with his mother,
for wanting his mother all to himself, and for wanting sex with her: "So
guilty I deserve the death sentence!" (Note that here I did not make an
interpretation for him, but raised a question that gave *him* a chance to
reflect and to make an interpretation himself, which is one of the ways
that psychoanalysts and dynamic psychotherapists help patients to learn,
develop, and practice self-interpretation.)

In the follow-up sessions with John after his treatment was completed, he free associated well, observed his own associations, and continued to show considerable ability to interpret and understand latent
contents in his own associations and dreams, which suggests that the gains
in self-interpretive competence acquired during his treatment had been
retained and were continuing posttherapeutically.

THE CODE (CONVENTIONS)
OF CLINICAL INTERPRETATION

What are the conventions or code of our interpretive methods? Clinicians differ in their answers to this question, but most appear to agree that there is no strict code; rather, as Freud (1923a) insisted, clinical interpretation is not based on rules but leaves much to the sensitivity, imagination, and judgment of the individual clinician (see also Goldberg 1988, Hartmann 1951, Rubovits-Seitz 1998). The methodologist, Adriaan De Groot (1969) indicates that the same applies to the behavioral sciences generally: interpretive activities "are not subject to any hard and fast logical or methodological rules" (p. 35).

This is not to say, however, that our interpretive methodology lacks grounding. Goldberg (1985) maintains that clinical interpretations are grounded largely in specific clinical theories. I have questioned that view (1998), suggesting alternatively that the grounding of clinical interpretations consists of (1) the relatively small number of basic general concepts (or background assumptions) of psychoanalysis—the concepts of an unconscious mind, continuity, meaning, determinism, overdetermination, instinctual drives, conflict, defense, repetition, transference, and the importance of childhood experiences (Rapaport 1944); (2) a relatively large number of frequently useful psychodynamic interpretive heuristics—loosely systematic methodologic procedures that give good results on the whole, but do not guarantee them in any particular instance; they are part of the prerequisite knowledge that informs and guides scientific (including interpretive) work, thus reducing unfruitful searches; (3) the grounding of the interpretive process, which includes the shifting, ever-unfolding context of previously interpreted events, the necessary and progressive modifications of which contribute to the uncertainty and fallibility of clinical interpretations. Thus, as Tuckett (1994a) observes cogently, "interpretations rest on interpretations, rest on interpretations, rest on interpretations, etc." (p. 869).

With respect to the basic concepts or background assumptions that underlie Freud's interpretive system, what these core concepts have most in common is their generality, as a result of which they do not give rise to single but to alternative interpretive hypotheses (Applegarth 1991). De Groot (1969) points out that broad general background assumptions and concepts of this kind do not force interpretations into preconceived conclusions; new, unique interpretations of the data are possible within the general theoretical framework of a science. By contrast, specific clinical theories tend to generate single rather than alternative interpretive hypotheses. Thus theory-driven clinical interpretations based on specific clinical theories often are not applicable to the individual patient, and may interfere with the discovery or construction of unique personal meanings and determinants. Reconstructions are especially prone to this problem; that is, therapists sometimes use a particular model of early infantile life to guide their understanding of a patient's associations (cf. Lichtenberg 1983). Use of specific pathogenetic theories in clinical interpretations, however, all too easily and unsuspectingly can become indoctrination (Paniagua 1985). Arlow (1991) refers to this type of reconstruction as a form of genetic fallacy, that is, postulating a singular and direct connection between a particular childhood experience, or type of early life experience, and adult behavior.

IS THE SELF-ANALYTIC
PROCESS SPONTANEOUS?

The example of self-analysis reported by Beiser (1984) contains a number of interesting parallels with Maria Kramer's (1959) experiences and report, for example, the spontaneity of the process, the remission of long-standing symptoms that had not been resolved by previous formal analyses or by numerous deliberate attempts at self-analysis, and some similarities in the underlying pathodynamics revealed by the self-analytic activities in both of these experienced psychoanalysts. With the exception of Fleming's (1971) reference to interpretation as integral to the process of self-analysis, however, and Kramer's (1959) reference to resistances limiting one's finding the correct interpretation, Beiser's review of the literature reported little or nothing about the role of clinical interpretive competence in the development of a capacity for self-analysis.

Kramer emphasized the spontaneous, autonomous nature of the self-analytic function in herself; but I submit that it is possible that Kramer's previously active attempts at self-analysis may have initiated a preconscious process of interpretive reflection and working through that led only later to the emergence of previously repressed contents. It is important to note in this connection that much or most interpretive processing goes on outside of awareness, and that the time it takes to solve complex (including interpretive) problems preconsciously may produce an illusion that a later emergence of insight is spontaneous. For example, citing the Zeigarnik (1927) effect—that people tend to be more successful in recalling incomplete tasks than completed ones—Rosner (1973) writes:

> Insight in problem solving often comes about through a restructuring of the problem. This restructuring may occur when the person is not directly in contact with the problem. When contact is re-established with the problem, however, the insights developed during the "restructuring interval" are applied immediately. [p. 563]

Schlessinger and Robbins's (1983) conclusions differ somewhat from Maria Kramer's hypothesis regarding the development and nature of the autoanalytic function. Kramer did not report use of another person, real or imaginary, in her successful autoanalytic activities, whereas Schlessinger and Robbins reported that in some of their follow-up cases a "benign presence" facilitated the former patients' self-analytic efforts; they postulated that the benign presence may represent a residue of the therapeutic alliance that had been such an important part of the formal treatment experience (cf. also Kantrowitz 1990b, 1999).

Still another view is suggested by Paula Heimann (1977), who draws on Gitelson's (1952) concept that the experienced analyst as interpreter acts as his own supervisor; for "no analyst worth his salt fails to scrutinize his own work" (Heimann 1977, pp. 317). A similar type of self-observation and self-evaluation may become part of one's clinical interpretive competence, not only in therapists but in successfully treated patients generally.

Kramer suggested that the learning of the autoanalytic function appeared to result from a process of identification with the therapist's interpretive functions. Klauber (1972) suggested that, just as a child establishes a link with the mother's *functions* (not only with the mother herself) in order to shelter himself from changes in the object relation, the good results of depth psychological treatments may result in part from patients establishing a relation to the therapist's (especially interpretive) function.

Employing the concept of identification as a mechanism of coping with loss—in this case, loss of one's therapist at the end of the treatment—Schlessinger and Robbins concluded that self-analytic activity, which develops during the therapeutic process, appeared to be consolidated by the intensified identification with the therapist during the process of terminating analysis. If we apply Klauber's concept, however, patients may identify also with the therapist and his or her functions in anticipation of termination.

POSSIBLE RELATIONS TO INTERPRETIVE TECHNIQUE

The thesis presented here may have some relevance to the issue of how interpretations are communicated to patients. Contrary to Theodore Reik's (1949) advice to present interpretations in the form of statements without adding one's reasons for their formulation, and Etchegoyen's (1989) insistence that in order to avoid "the mortal sin of intellectualization . . . the analyst must be like Cassandra the slave, offering her prophesies without ever explaining them" (p. 374), I suggest that it may be advantageous in promoting the development of self-interpretive competence in the patient if the therapist provides some relevant information about how his or her interpretations are construed, for example, calling attention to key clues in the clinical material that appeared to suggest possible latent contents, explaining specific psychodynamic heuristics that may have suggested a particular latent meaning or determinant, mentioning how alternative constructions have been considered and assessed in selecting the most plausible interpretation, and other such basic methods and concepts of one's interpretive approach.

I do not mean by this that the therapist should attempt to teach the patient how to interpret clinical data—at least, not didactically, and

I do not mean to imply that the origins of self-interpretive competence consist solely of what patients learn about this process in the course of their treatments (see, e.g., Fonagy and Target 1996, Main 1993, David Stern 1985, for earlier developmental foundations of this capacity). What I have in mind is that, conceivably, the more the therapist shares his or her interpretive reasoning and strategies with the patient, the more opportunity the patient may have to develop clinical interpretive competence. It seems likely also that giving the patient ample opportunity to use and practice his or her own self-interpretive capacity during the therapeutic process may promote more robust development of self-interpretive competence. Reik conceded, for example, that in exceptional cases such as training another analyst, adding one's reasons for arriving at particular interpretations might be warranted, but my suggestion is that such a practice might be useful at times in all analyses.

The hypothesis that patients in well-going analyses and dynamic psychotherapies learn the therapist's interpretive conventions raises a further question whether the therapist's interventions act primarily as suggestions to the patient regarding the clinical interpretive code. If clinical interpretations were presented authoritatively as apodictic statements, they might well have a significant suggestive effect, but if they are conveyed tentatively and collaboratively as possibilities, the likelihood of suggestive influence is reduced. Another important interpretive convention that the patient needs to learn, both for effective collaboration in the therapeutic relationship and for future self-inquiry, is that depth psychological interpretation is difficult and fallible, which calls for an undogmatic, scientifically skeptical attitude on the part of the interpreter. Ideally, therefore, the patient learns our interpretive conventions not under the pressure of suggestions from, or an inner need to please, the therapist, but from repeated experiences of mutual search for the most plausible interpretation at a given time. If suggestive effects appear to occur in connection with interventions, those effects themselves then become a necessary focus of interpretive inquiry (Rubovits-Seitz 1998; see also Chapter 7, and Hoffman's [1998] concept of dialectical or critical constuctivism).

SUMMARY

The principal evidence I have adduced for the gradual development of clinical interpretive competence in patients is the observation that during the course of a well-going therapeutic process patients become increasingly able to interpret their own productions. Another source of evidence is French's finding that the recurrent dynamic cycles of a therapeutic process speed up gradually as the treatment progresses, which appears to suggest that a learning process is occurring in both the patient and the therapist; that is, the therapist becomes increasingly familiar with the patient's recurring patterns of conflicts and defenses, and the patient becomes increasingly confident and effective in associating freely, in observing his or her own productions, and in learning to apply the conventions or code of depth psychological interpretation to his or her own associations and other data.

I have postulated further that the concept of a depth psychological interpretive code or conventions is related to (1) the semiotic aspects of clinical interpretation, that is, the clues in clinical data that serve as signs to inform and guide the therapist's construal of latent meanings and determinants, and (2) the process of recoding, which is an important feature in the psychology of communication.

The principal prerequisite knowledge or conventions of our interpretive approach appear to include (1) the relatively small number of basic general (core) concepts or background assumptions of psychoanalysis, in contrast to specific clinical theories—the general concepts including an unconscious mind, meaning, continuity, determinism, overdetermination, instinctual drives, conflict, defense, repetition, transference, and the importance of childhood experiences; (2) a relatively large number of often useful psychodynamic heuristics; and (3) the previous, progressively modified interpretations employed in the entire therapeutic process.

I have drawn on concepts and clinical examples of various investigators, including Freud, to explicate and illustrate the development of and relations between self-interpretive and self-analytic competences. Maria Kramer emphasized the interesting and original, but controversial, possibility that in some instances effective self-analytic activity may operate spontaneously and autonomously, rather than from consciously active efforts at self-analysis. I have suggested alternatively that the apparent spontaneity of the process described by Kramer might have resulted from previous conscious efforts at self-analysis, which may have initiated a preconscious process of reflection and working through, culminating later and unexpectedly in conscious insight—a phenomenon that may seem spontaneous, but may be a delayed effect of an earlier, underlying, ongoing process.

Whereas Sterba and Maria Kramer attributed the patient's learning of interpretive conventions to an identification with the therapist's analyzing functions—for example, in coping with loss of the analyst at termination—I have argued, in agreement with Michael Basch (1976), that such learning appears to occur bit by bit, that is, very gradually throughout the course of an analytic process—not only through identification with the analyst's interpretive competence, but also from observing, reflecting on, and being helped by the therapist to understand and learn the complex conceptual thinking that is involved in the self-interpretive process.

PART II

The Interpretive Process through an Entire Treatment

INTRODUCTION

This part of the present volume applies two proposed improvements in clinical case reports, namely, more frequent reports of whole treatments, and greater emphasis on the presentation of clinical evidence (Rubovits-Seitz 2000, pp. 391–96). These two suggested improvements are related, because an important source of clinical evidence—the justification of interpretations—draws on the data of the whole treatment.

In an article on "The Case History," Robert Michels (2000, pp. 353–375, 417–420) notes that our clinical literature consists largely of vignettes rather than full-length accounts of the therapeutic process, and he raises the question of why this is so. In one of his writings, Freud (1918, p. 8) asserted that reporting a complete history is "technically impractical," "socially impermissible," and in any event would be "unconvincing." Elsewhere, however, he (1905, p. 18) concluded that an "intelligent, consistent and unbroken case history" is only possible at the end of a treatment; that completed cases offer the advantage of hindsight; that definitive interpretation of any fragment must await completion of the whole analysis—"the whole analysis is needed to explain it" (1911, p. 93; see also Schafer 1986, Goldberg 1997), and thus the preparation of a case report is best postponed until the treatment is over.

In his report of the Wolf Man, Freud (1918) referred to another advantage of waiting until the end of a treatment before writing a report of the case, namely, that the understanding of a patient's neurosis is more possible during the last period of the treatment, when resistances are reduced and the patient's free associations are more lucid (for similar views on the clarification of pathodynamics during later stages of treatment, see French 1954, Leavy 1980, Mahony and Singh 1979, Rubovits-Seitz 1987, 1992, 1998, Seitz 1968, Waelder 1962).

The proposal of more frequent case reports dealing with whole treatments does not imply the elimination of clinical vignettes, however. The latter serve an important function in case reports by illustrating relevant themes in the therapeutic process, and vignettes are consonant with the way treatments actually proceed, that is, by relatively discrete dynamic episodes that coalesce only gradually over months or years into larger configurations.

In his assertion that definitive interpretation of any fragment must await completion of the whole treatment, Freud (1911) hinted at an additional advantage of studying and reporting the entire therapeutic process—namely, the availability of more extensive clinical evidence. Freud's use of the term "definitive" in this context implies issues of completeness and accuracy, which are among the most neglected aspects of our science. Klumpner's (1989) review of sixty frequently cited papers in the clinical literature revealed, for example, that none of those well-known publications offered direct evidence for the claims being made.

For depth psychological therapies to make scientific claims, some model of justifying interpretations is essential. As Sherwood (1969) observed, "The essence of science is not so much the existence of a body of facts as the existence of a method, a procedure by which 'facts' can be systematically ascertained and progressively revised" (p. 260). The accuracy of interpretations depends on the power of evidence, which consists of empirical data and of logical arguments that support or disconfirm specific conclusions. Being the first-level inferences, the lowest level theoretical statements of psychoanalysis and dynamic psychotherapy, interpretations are the only propositions that can be tested by direct empirical evidence, that is, by data of the case being studied. Higher level clinical theories are tested in other ways.

Chapters 10 through 22 present selected therapy sessions, with summaries of intervening case material, from the therapeutic process of a continuous, completed case. The interpretations in this case are considerably more advanced than the clinical illustrations presented in previous chapters. The case is not an example of excellent or ideal interpretive work; for example, I made numerous interpretive errors during the patient's treatment; but posttherapeutic application of the RC approach made it possible to identify at least some of the errors, to review why they occurred, to postulate revised interpretations, and to suggest how they might have been recognized during the therapy itself—all of which are instructive in themselves.

Despite the difficulties of this case (or perhaps partly because of them), I believe it is a useful one to study. In addition, the eventual therapeutic result was so positive that I think clinicians may find it both instructive and encouraging.

The therapy sessions from this case were selected to illustrate the process of construing, formulating, justifying, communicating, and progressively modifying clinical interpretations. Commentary regarding the interpretations includes (1) my formulation of each session, (2) comparisons of interpretations made during the treatment with formulations based on detailed posttherapeutic study of the entire therapeutic process, (3) checking the formulations against all of the clinical data in the interpreted sessions, and (4) additional commentary concerning more specific interpretive problems that occurred in some of the sessions.

Ideally, the material of intervening sessions would have been summarized—like the sessions selected for illustrating interpretations and commentaries—in terms of the empirical data of those sessions. The amount of data involved in multiple intervening sessions is so extensive, however, that it was not feasible to base their summaries solely on empirical content. To deal with that problem, I abstracted the intervening sessions in the more condensed language of psychodynamic formulations. The dynamic trends in the intervening sessions were derived, however, not only from my interpretive impressions and hypotheses during the treatment, but also from my posttherapeutic investigation of the entire therapeutic process, employing the RC approach (Rubovits-Seitz 1987, 1998).

Readers will probably gain most from these chapters if they actively formulate their own interpretations of the case material, and then compare their constructions with the author's formulations and associated commentaries. Comparisons of interpretations will be facilitated if readers employ the following series of questions to organize their formulations:

1. What are the precipitant, the principal current (thematic) conflict of the session, and the sequence of defenses against that conflict?

2. How did you arrive at and justify your formulation?

3. What (if anything) would you interpret to the patient at this time, and why?

CHAPTER TEN

Case History, and Interpretation of Session 8

DIAGNOSTIC INTERVIEWS (SUMMARY OF THE FIRST THREE SESSIONS)

Ms. White was a short, attractive, shy 36-year-old woman. She was referred to me by her internist to whom she confided that she felt there was something wrong with her sexually because she was unresponsive during intercourse. Three months previously her husband had left her without explanation after 11 years of marriage. She assumed all the blame for the breakup of her marriage, feeling that her sexual frigidity must have been responsible. She had finished college, was 25 years old, and worked as a librarian when they met; he was 19 at the time, a high school dropout who had enlisted in the army. She described the marriage as happy at first when they traveled around from one army post to another. They had a child after her husband was discharged from the service, but the child was defective and died a year later. She wanted more children but her husband refused. Their sexual relations became infrequent after the birth of the defective child, her husband eventually becoming impotent. She realized that something was wrong between them and tried to get him to talk about it. He wouldn't, so she let things ride. They had no sexual relations for the last five years of their marriage, which she assumed was her fault. During the past year they were finally able to buy the "dream house" that they had wanted for a long time. Immediately after buying it, her husband left without explanation. She gave him a divorce and a very liberal settlement, asking almost nothing for herself because she felt that her sexual frigidity and inability to give him a normal child fully justified his leaving her.

Asked what kind of a wife she had been in other respects she said that as far as she knew he had no other complaints. She had been devoted to him, almost never found fault with him, was very agreeable about letting him make decisions, was a good cook and housekeeper, and worked and contributed as much as he did to their income—in other words she was a model wife, according to her standards of what a wife should be, except for her feelings of sexual and reproductive failure.

Because the patient's speech and thought stream were slow and halting, the preceding description of her marriage and divorce took her an entire session to tell. She seemed acutely embarrassed and ashamed as she referred to the sexual problem. She was intelligent and related to me with shy warmth. Cognitive functions were intact, and, with the exception of her self-effacing tendency, no other special preoccupations were elicited. Asked about feelings of depression she was stoical in her response, saying that she was trying to keep busy so that she wouldn't think about things too much. On further questioning, however, she acknowledged that she had been sleeping poorly, her appetite was minimal, and she had lost about ten pounds in recent months. She denied symptoms of anxiety or phobias, but blushed and became uncomfortable when asked about obsessions and compulsions. Because of her discomfort I did not pursue the question further at the time. Physical health was good; she had never had a serious illness, operation, or injury. Family history was negative for psychiatric disorders.

The next two diagnostic interviews were devoted to her past personal history, which required considerable questioning on my part. As in her first interview, she spoke haltingly with long pauses, blocking for as long as several minutes. As a result, the amount of information obtained about her life was relatively meager. She was the eldest of three daughters in a poor Appalachian family. Her father was a coal miner, hard working, God-fearing, and honest, but not very accessible to his children.

She could not remember her mother, who died during childbirth with the third daughter (who survived) when the patient was 4 years old. Her father remarried within a year, which she could remember. Asked how she felt about it, she shrugged and said, "It didn't affect me." Her memories of years 4 to 8 were very sketchy. She didn't like or get along with her stepmother. When she was 8 years old, the three daughters of her father's first marriage were sent to live with and be raised by five spinster aunts (her father's sisters). When asked how she felt about being sent to live with her aunts, she denied any particular feeling about it. Her father and stepmother went on to have six children of their own, whom the patient barely knew because she seldom saw her father after she and her sisters left their original family home.

The five aunts lived together in a large house that had ample room for the three little girls. When she spoke of her aunts she lumped them together as a unit rather than referring to them individually. She described the household as a peaceful and stable one in which everything was done according to regular schedules and routines. All five of the aunts were schoolteachers, and "they ran the house like a classroom." She did not volunteer any information about her sisters, and when asked about them she could think of nothing to say. Yes, she got along with them. No, she had no problems with them. She always did well in school, being a favorite of some teachers because she was quiet and studious. She had few friends during early childhood but did have a few fairly close ones during later grade school and high school.

She did not date until college, and then only occasionally. After college she took a teaching position in a small mining town where she had her first sexual experiences. She became pregnant and had an abortion. She choked up suddenly and almost wept as she told about the abortion. "I wish I hadn't gotten the abortion! It would have been better to go ahead and have the child." She left the mining town and took a job as librarian in another city where she met and married her husband. Her work adjustment had always been good; she had continued her career as a children's librarian to the present time. Her social life during marriage had not been very active but included occasional entertainment with other couples, going to movies and sporting events with her husband, and a close relationship with one woman friend in whom she confided. Since her separation and divorce she was even less inclined to socialize, spending most of her spare time alone. No history of alcohol or drug abuse. She had been raised in a fairly strict Southern Baptist congregation but was not religious and did not attend church.

I recommended an exploratory type of psychotherapy, but told her that I would not be able to start her treatment for about two months. She accepted the recommendation and said she would wait. She called three times, however, to request appointments during the waiting period. Summaries of those three appointments follow.

SESSION 4 (SUMMARY)

A week later she called requesting an appointment; I was able to see her a few days later. She talked about being unable to get her former husband off of her mind. She tortured and blamed herself endlessly about the failure of her marriage. This time she acknowledged feeling depressed. [I called attention to how self-accusatory she was being, rather than accusatory toward her husband.] She then expressed some angry feelings toward him for doing this to her. He let the marriage go on for five years without telling her that he didn't love her anymore. She feels hurt and angry about that. If he had told her sooner, she might have remarried and had a chance to have children. She felt better at the end of the session. (The psychological report diagnoses her as schizophrenic, but I don't believe it; I've requested further psychological tests from someone else.)

SESSION 5 (SUMMARY)

Two weeks later she called and requested another appointment. She was clearly less depressed, looked younger and brighter, and dressed in a rather adolescent-looking outfit with a jockey type of hat. She said that she felt better and was working better, but was plagued by questions about what is wrong with her sexually that made her husband reject her. Originally she thought it must be something wrong with her genitalia because she had no vaginal sensations during intercourse. She consulted several doctors about that, but all told her that she was normal physically. Then she began to worry that she must be abnormal psychologically, that she may have some kind of perversion. [I asked what she meant by that?] She wondered if it might be homosexuality or masturbation or some other substitute for pleasure from intercourse. She blocked for several minutes. [I asked if she could elaborate any further regarding homosexual interests or masturbation?] She seemed relieved to be asked, for she rushed on to tell the history of her masturbation. She began masturbating when she was 8 or 9 years old, and has continued it ever since. She has always felt very guilty about it, and has thought that she may have spoiled normal sex for herself by "habituating myself to self-stimulation." [I said with a smile: "That sounds like something you may have read in a book."] She agreed a little sheepishly. She then said in a confessional tone that she has frequent thoughts of her husband's coming back to her; for without him she has nothing to look forward to. [I commented: "If you get some of these problems worked out, how can you be sure you'll want him back?"] More in sadness than anger she then described him, for the first time, as rather immature, unsophisticated, and not very intelligent. (Second Rorschach test supports my strong clinical impression of psychoneurotic pathology, with no indication of overt or latent schizophrenia.)

SESSION 6 (SUMMARY)

She called a month later for another appointment. It was Christmas time and she was afraid that she might do something "silly" over the holidays regarding her ex-husband. [Namely?] She might go to him impulsively, confess to him that she had had an abortion before marriage (which she had never told him), admit that everything was her fault, and "give him anything he wants." She knows that would be stupid, but doesn't know whether she can resist the impulse. She has to get these things settled *right now* to get some peace of mind, or else she will crack up. [I asked whether she thought waiting for treatment might be increasing her tension?] She was surprised, became reflective, then agreed that it was. We set a date for her therapy to begin "officially" soon after the holidays. She seemed considerably relieved at the end of the session. I did not hear from her again until she came for the appointment we had agreed on.

SESSION 7 (SUMMARY)

[I asked her to bring me up to date on how she had been since I last saw her.] She replied that her ex-husband had remarried shortly before Christmas, and that things had gone about as usual for her. [How did she react to her ex-husband's remarriage?] It made her feel that the relationship with him is now definitely over. Her previous hopes that they might get back together were ended by his marrying someone else. She has felt sad and has wept about it, but since crying she has felt less preoccupied with him and with her hopes of reconciliation. (I noted to myself that she said nothing about a possible implication of his remarrying so soon after separation and divorce from her, namely, that he may already have been involved with his second wife before he left Ms. White. I decided against bringing up such a potentially sensitive issue when she was just starting therapy, electing instead to wait for that matter to surface when she was more prepared emotionally to deal with it.) [I asked how she felt about going ahead with her treatment?] She still feels it is the thing to do, but is confused about how it works. [I explained the procedure of free association, and we discussed arrangements for her to start with one appointment a week; then, depending on how she felt about it, we might increase the frequency of her appointments.] She asked abruptly whether other people had benefited from such treatment? [I suggested that we explore why she asked that question], which led directly to some of her doubts about therapy, especially her fear of the unknown and anxiety about discussing problems and memories that are disturbing to her. She also mentioned a fantasy that when the treatment is over she might not be able to make her own decisions as well as before, but might need someone to make decisions for her. [What does she hope to gain from treatment?] She listed several things: One is to have more self-confidence and to be more capable of making decisions. Another is to feel less "held in" with people, that is, to be more natural and spontaneous in relationships with people. She also hopes to have a better understanding of herself about sex; she feels she has been naive about sex.

SESSION 8 (FIRST INTERPRETIVE EXERCISE)

She began her next appointment exactly where she had ended the last session, (which gave me the impression that her therapy must be very much on her mind.) Something else she hopes to accomplish in her treatment is an ability to respond to men sexually, so that if she meets another man and they get interested in each other, she will be responsive. She asked anxiously whether I thought she could change in that way? ["Let's explore what makes you ask that question."] Once again she began to recognize doubts and misgivings about the treatment. "It seems so indefinite! That worries me. If I knew I were going to have my arm cut off, that would be bad and I'd regret it, but at least I'd know what was going to happen. This way I don't know." She has been reading books about therapy including one by Jung, *The Masculine Mind.* She is afraid of becoming overly preoccupied with sex, whereas in the past she was not concerned with it at all. ["You want therapy to make you freer sexually, but are afraid it might make you too free?"] She blushed. Changes have always been difficult for her. Her ex-husband was always excited about changes but she was reluctant to change anything. She went on at length about her dread of change, giving several examples. ["This helps to explain why you asked apprehensively whether treatment will change you sexually."] She thought for a moment, nodded reflectively, and said, "That's right! If I'm so uptight about making even minor changes, no wonder I'm scared of changing something big like sex. That's something I don't like about myself—my fear of change. I hope I can get over that."

COMMENTARY

Author's (Re)interpretation of Session 8 (Based on Posttherapeutic Application of the RC Approach)

The following series of clues in sessions 1 through 8 suggests a formulation that differs somewhat from my interpretive impressions at the time of treating Ms. White:

> *Clue 1:* Starting with the dynamic context of session 8, the patient sought treatment because of an increasingly painful emotional

pressure brought on by her husband leaving her. In session 4, I misconstrued that pressure as "the (repressed) fury of a woman scorned."

Clue 2: A contiguity of associations in session 6 suggests a different source of the emotional pressure: Just before blurting out desperately that she would crack up unless she got these problems settled immediately, she mentioned a fantasy of going to her husband and "confessing" a premarital abortion. The content and juxtaposition of these associations suggest that the intense inner pressure was probably due to guilt.

Clue 3: The latter hypothesis can be checked by looking for other indications of latent guilt feelings. Numerous such clues are present in the clinical data; in fact, a repetitive theme suggesting inner guilt runs through the first eight sessions—for example, blaming herself repeatedly for the failure of her marriage.

Clue 4: In the immediately preceding session (number 7), despite her eagerness for treatment (i.e., for relief of the painful inner pressure), she seemed very apprehensive about starting therapy. She said she dreaded thinking about memories that were disturbing to her. Thus starting therapy may have activated the following conflict: her hope that therapy will relieve her inner guilt, *versus* dread of facing and feeling the pain of her guilt.

Checking This Formulation Against All of the Clinical Data

Does the revised conflict account more-or-less completely and coherently for all of the clinical data in session 8? If the posited thematic conflict is correct, it should be possible to demonstrate that all, or at least most, of the data are related dynamically to that conflict—either as allusions to the conflict itself, or (more commonly) as a series of defenses against it. Review of the patient's associations in session 8 suggests the following possible connections with the revised thematic conflict:

Assn. 1 ("I hope that treatment will help me become able to respond to men sexually"): As she has done in previous appointments, she defensively substitutes and foregrounds an erotic problem in place of the more disturbing latent guilt conflict. (Erotization is a common defense, particularly in hysterical pathology).

Assn. 2 (Doubts about treatment: "It seems so indefinite"): The doubts imply that she is not committing herself very completely to therapy or to hope of relief from inner guilt—a compound defense employing rationalization and avoidance.

Assn. 3 (Arm cut off): A punishment fantasy—a self-punitive, masochistic mechanism that relieves inner guilt through suffering, rather than facing and feeling the guilt—usually associated with depressive pathology. (The fantasy of cutting her arm off may derive also from masturbation guilt, since the arm and hand are used to masturbate.)

Assn. 4 (Reading psychiatric books): An intellectual defense—looking into the subject rather than into herself (cf. her choice of career).

Assn. 5 (Fear of becoming overly preoccupied with sex): Returns to the erotic substitution defense. What she really fears (unconsciously) is being overwhelmed by feelings of guilt. [During her treatment, I mistakenly interpreted a superficial (preconscious) conflict associated with her erotic defense—a technical error (see below)].

Assn. 6 (Blushes in response to my interpretation): Her blush suggests that the erotization defense includes erotic fantasies about me. The erotic fantasies produce secondary (preconscious) conflict with her feminine pride, that is, exposure of the fantasies would arouse shame.

Assn. 7 (Fear of change): A phobic-avoidance defense, that is, avoidance of potentially painful feelings by remaining as she is—another frequent defense in hysterical pathology.

Assn. 8 (Readily agrees with therapist's further [incorrect] interpretation of erotic conflict): The intellectual nature of her response suggests that my overly superficial interpretations have reinforced the erotic defense, making it easier for her to avoid the underlying guilt conflict (cf. Glover 1931).

Interpretive Errors

At the beginning of this patient's treatment I missed the thematic (guilt) conflict, but caught on to it soon afterward. Originally I mistook the repetition of a particular defense (the erotic substitution mechanism) for the underlying conflict of the session—one of the most common interpretive errors that clinicians make.

In retrospect, the following heuristic clues might have helped me to avoid the error: (I) The erotic trend was manifest in the patient's associations, hence too superficial to be the thematic conflict of the session. The principal (or thematic) conflict of a session is never manifest, but runs like an undercurrent through all of the data. (2) Sexual inhibition was one of the patient's symptoms, and dwelling on symptoms is almost always defensive. (3) The persistence of her (conscious) focus on the erotic issue fits the heuristic, "You know a defense by its excessiveness."

Mistakes are inevitable in interpretive work because clinical interpretation is inherently difficult and fallible. Fortunately, due to its duration and cyclical nature the therapeutic process is fairly forgiving of mistakes. Some, but not all, of the mistakes in this case are attributable to the fact that I treated this patient early in my practice of psychoanalysis. Since that time I have studied and restudied my records of the case applying the RC method to check interpretations carefully. It provides opportunities to correct interpretive errors—*if* the therapist accepts his or her fallibility and is alert to the frequent discrepancies between interpretive hypotheses and the actual clinical data. Since both interpreters and our interpretive methods are fallible, we must expect such discrepancies, attempt to recognize them, and use them to improve our depth psychological understanding of and communications to patients.

CHAPTER ELEVEN

Interpretation of Session 10

SESSION 9 (SUMMARY)

The partial success of her erotic defense in session 8 was mixed with underlying disappointment that I had not relieved her abortion (and probably other sources of) guilt. As a result, she remained focused on hope of such relief in session 9, along with the fear that therapy (more specifically, that I) would make her face and feel the pain of her guilt. Among her defenses against that conflict in session 9 was displacement of guilt from the abortion to guilt about her defective child. (The defective child had been carried to term, and Ms. White had cared for her until she died. Her self-blame regarding the defective child was thus considerably less than her guilt about the aborted child. The type of displacement involved in this type of defense is sometimes called a "lesser crime" mechanism, that is, avoiding a larger guilt by confessing a smaller one.) Near the end of session 9, I responded to her agitated insistence on knowing the truth about herself, "even if it hurts" (a counterphobic defense) by asking whether she would like to increase the frequency of her appointments to give her more time to work on the problems. She said she would, so her appointments were increased to twice a week.

SESSION 10 (SECOND INTERPRETIVE EXERCISE)

She started the appointment by saying (in a tone of mock dismay): "This early morning business is *awful!*" She then asked abruptly why I had "suggested" (!) more frequent sessions? [What are your thoughts about that?] She blushed and hurried on to deny that she had any such thoughts. [Just say whatever comes to your mind about it.] She was unable to say anything about it, and blocked for several minutes. [I raised the question about more frequent sessions because you seemed eager to get on with your therapy as rapidly as possible.] "Oh," she said, with a trace of disappointment. After a pause she took a deep breath and started talking (with difficulty) about her fantasies during masturbation. Her masturbation fantasies are that "someone is being beaten." Also when she sees or hears a child punished, and especially if it cries, she has an erotic feeling. She feels confused about and ashamed of these feelings and fantasies. She has never told anyone about it before and finds it very difficult to talk about it now, but she has decided that this is her chance to do something about her problems, so she wants to be as open and honest as possible. Then with even more hesitation she said that she has never been passionate about a man. She shifted suddenly and exclaimed how blind she was to the problems that were causing her marriage to collapse. She can't understand how she could have been so blissfully unaware of the problem that was threatening her marriage. At this point, however, she feels less preoccupied with that loss than formerly. Now that the situation seems hopeless it isn't as hard to give it up. Near the end of the session she recalled mutual masturbation with a girl in grade school. She expressed surprise at the "strange things" she remembers when she lets her mind wander like this.

COMMENTARY

Author's Interpretation of Session 10

My interpretation of this session corresponded closely with the formulation generated by posttherapeutic application of the RC approach. I based my interpretation mainly on the following set of clues in the patient's associations:

Clue 1 (Her initial association, "This early morning business is *awful*," in a tone of mock dismay): I noticed that the words of this opening gambit did not fit the "music" (i.e., tone) of her message. She protested that therapy (coming more often, at an earlier hour) was "awful," but the "music" was more like a love song. I suspected that she was secretly pleased to be coming more often, but for pride reasons was attempting to conceal her pleasure.

Clue 2 (Her question why I had increased the appointments): Her subtle distortion of our agreement to increase the appointments made it sound as though it was I, not she, who wanted the change. I thought to myself that this might be another (in this case a projective) defense against revealing her secret pleasure in seeing me more often.

Clue 3 (Her blush and blocking when I asked for her thoughts about increasing the appointments): These reactions seemed to fit the possibility that she was trying to conceal erotic feelings and fantasies about seeing me more frequently.

Clue 4 (Her tone of disappointment in response to my purely technical explanation of the appointment change): This also suggested the possibility of hidden erotic feelings. So far all of the associations in the session seemed to imply erotic conflict; but it was still too early in the session to decide on that possibility, so I waited to see what followed.

Clue 5 (Masturbation fantasies of someone being beaten, and erotic feelings when she sees or hears a child crying or being punished): I suspected that the someone being beaten and the crying children represented herself (unconsciously), that is, were based on disguised (projected) masochistic-erotic fantasies. Since masochism implies inner guilt and need for punishment, I began to suspect (a) that latent guilt feelings rather than hurt pride and anger were the source of her intense inner pressure; (b) that the conspicuous erotic trend in previous sessions, and early in the present session, was probably a substitution defense against the inner guilt (to paraphrase the defense: "Love me! Make me feel lovable instead of bad and unwanted"); and (c) that in this context her ambiguous remark at the beginning of the present session ("This early morning business is *awful*," in a tone of mock dismay) could indicate disguised pleasure from fantasied submission to a painful ordeal inflicted by the therapist.

My tentative earlier impression that the thematic conflict of this session might be erotic feelings toward me and the shame about exposure of such feelings was no longer tenable. The subsequent material in session 10 suggested the following revised interpretation: her masochistic-erotic desire for the therapist to beat her, *versus* shame about the perverse nature of that desire.

Checking My Hypothesis Against All of the Data

Assn. 1 ("This early morning business is awful," in a tone of mock dismay): Thinly disguised pleasure from fantasied submission to painful punishment inflicted by the therapist.

Assn. 2 (Making it seem that it was I, not she, who wanted to increase the appointments): Projection of her latent masochistic wish to be forced into increasingly painful treatment, that is, telling herself (unconsciously) that it was not she who wished to be punished, but that the therapist felt she deserved and needed to be punished.

Assn. 3 (Blush and blocking when I asked about her reactions to the increase in appointments): Disguised expressions of both the pleasure and shame she felt about the fantasy of therapist forcing her punitively.

Assn. 4 (Her disappointed tone in response to my purely technical explanation of the appointment change): She was disappointed that I did not play the role she had assigned to me (unconsciously) in her latent masochistic fantasy.

Assn. 5 (Telling her masturbation fantasies and her erotic reactions to a child being punished or crying): At least two major defensive mechanisms appeared to be involved here: (a) Her own unconscious wish to be beaten is projected to an image or perception of someone else being beaten. (b) By telling such painfully embarrassing things about herself, she enacts the latent masochistic fantasy in her relationship with me—a defensive transference enactment of the thematic conflict—which is classified as defensive because she acts out the conflict (sometimes called "acting in" when enacted with a therapist), rather than making the conflict conscious and putting it into words.

Assn. 6 (Stressing that she tells these painful secrets to facilitate her treatment): A rationalization to conceal the latent pleasure and avoid feelings of shame from the transference enactment of her masochistic fantasy.

Assn. 7 (Never passionate about a man): The agonized affect accompanying this disclosure suggests a continuation of the defensive transference enactment, combined with substitution of a less shameful sexual symptom (frigidity) for the more conflicted masochistic-erotic fantasies.

Assn. 8 (The sexual problem in her marriage): She now displaces the current conflict concerning the therapist to her husband in the past, and again substitutes sexual inhibition, which is less shameful to her, for the sexually perverse feelings and fantasies toward me.

Assn. 9 (Mutual masturbation with a girlfriend in childhood): Again she displaces the conflict about therapist to a person in the past, and substitutes a less disturbing sexual activity for the masochistic-erotic perversion.

What (If Anything) Should the Therapist Communicate to the Patient at This Point

A question of interpretive technique arises: Should the therapist interpret the current thematic conflict to the patient? The answer depends partly on whether the therapist feels fairly confident that his posited thematic conflict and its associated defenses represent not just *a* plausible, but the *most* plausible, interpretation of the current material. After testing my revised conflict against all of the clinical data, I felt fairly sure of its plausibility, but not yet confident that it was the most plausible interpretation at the time (cf. the technical heuristic that when one is uncertain of an interpretation, it is usually better to wait). I also felt hesitant to communicate the interpretation to the patient for several additional reasons: First, I was concerned that it might produce too much pride injury in the patient. Second, it seemed too early in the patient's treatment to make such an interpretation. Third, in the present context, making the interpretation at this point would tend to gratify her masochistic-erotic wish for me to "beat" her (symbolically) with painful interpretations. I decided to wait, therefore, for a later, dynamically more propitious opportunity to interpret this conflict.

CHAPTER TWELVE

Interpretation of Session 14

SESSIONS 11 TO 13 (SUMMARY)

Ms. White appeared to be disappointed (preconsciously) that confiding her masochistic-erotic fantasies did not elicit more response from me, which led to a temporary defensive withdrawal in session 11. In sessions 12 and 13, however, the masochistic-erotic conflict became thematic again, this time in the form of trying (unconsciously) to get me to push her about lying down on the couch and telling even more painful things about herself.

SESSION 14 (THIRD INTERPRETIVE EXERCISE)

"I had a hard time getting up this morning" (in a tone of dejection and shame). She knows that the therapist will just tell her to go ahead and quit, but she keeps getting disgusted and discouraged because all she does is go in circles. ["What makes you think I will tell you to quit?"] She laughed abruptly, then exclaimed what a failure she has made of her life—the abortion, the baby that died, her failure as a wife. None of those things can be erased, and no matter how much she talks about them they'll still be there, proof of her inadequacy. Yet all she wants are just simple, ordinary things—a husband who loves her and whom she loves, children, and a home. It would be easier to give up hoping for those things; that way she wouldn't go on beating her head against a wall and feeling so disappointed. (Tears came to her eyes as she said that, but she shook off the sadness with an impatient refusal to feel sorry for herself.) She returned to the question of whether to continue therapy or not. (She paused and seemed to wait expectantly, but I remained silent.) What good would it do to go on? Better to forget the whole thing and give up her hopes of happiness. [When I told her it was time to stop], she hurried on to repeat that sooner or later she knows that I will tell her to quit because she isn't getting anywhere. ["There must be some other reason you think that."] She then said forcefully, "Well, if I were you, *I* certainly would!" [I commented softly, "But I'm not you."] "That's *right!*" she said angrily, "which is fortunate for *you!*" She then got up and left quickly.

COMMENTARY

Author's (Re)interpretation of Sesson 14
(Based on Posttherapeutic Application of the RC Approach)

The following clues in Session 14 foretold the (re)interpretation arrived at by applying the RC approach:

> *Clue 1* (Her fantasy early in the session that I will tell her to quit):
> This is an important clue because it is repeated two more times
> during this same therapy session. The conscious fantasy that I
> will tell her to quit may imply an unconscious fantasy that I want
> to get rid of her. Although her current preoccupation with quit-
> ting treatment has the earmarks of yet another masochistic fan-
> tasy, it also seems different from her recent masochistic-erotic
> fantasies in that the new fantasy appears to be self-punitive with-
> out being erotized.
>
> *Clue 2* (In the middle of the session she raised the question whether
> to continue therapy, and then waited expectantly for me to tell
> her whether to go or stay): This appears to be another version
> of the first clue, this time involving a testing, manipulative, par-
> tial enactment of the latent self-riddance fantasy.

Clue 3 (At the end of the session she insists again that I will tell her to quit): The repetitiveness of this fantasy suggests that it is driven dynamically by an intense and pervasive unconscious conflict and/or defense—or by a compromise formation encompassing both.

Clue 4: Some of the most frequent clues to latent meanings in clinical data are similarities (often analogic in type), contrasts, contiguities, and repetitions. The fantasy of my getting rid of her is analogically similar to an important source of guilt in this patient, namely, the child she got rid of by induced abortion. One may conjecture, therefore, that the fantasy of my getting rid of her serves as an atonement defense—to relieve inner guilt about riddance feelings, fantasies, and acts toward others (especially toward a child or children). A self-punitive fantasy of this kind follows the so-called principle of talion—eye for an eye, tooth for a tooth: She got rid of a child, so she should suffer the same fate; she should be gotten rid of, aborted from her treatment.

Taken together, the foregoing clues suggest the following interpretive formulation of session 14:

Precipitant: Frustration of her recent masochistic-erotic wishes for therapist to force, beat, and punish her physically.

Thematic conflict: Getting rid of a child vesus guilt.

Principal defenses: A nonerotized self-punitive fantasy, and attempted therapeutic enactment, of an atoning (talion) punishment in which she would be be gotten rid of, "aborted" from her treatment.

Checking This Interpretation Against All of the Current Data

Assn. 1 (Hard time getting up [to come to her appointment]): Defensive procrastination and avoidance to keep from facing her inner guilt. Her tone of dejection and shame suggests that the guilt is currently closer to the surface, less well defended against, than formerly.

Assn. 2 (Therapist will tell her to quit): A projected, nonerotized, masochistic fantasy of therapist getting rid of her, "aborting" her from her treatment—a talion punishment for the child she aborted (and, psychogenetically, for the younger siblings she may have wished to get rid of). The atonement defense involves a compound mechanism: avoiding the feeling of guilt by turning the riddance feelings against herself.

Assn. 3 (Sudden laughter): My question and tone implied that I would not get rid of her. This frustrated her defensive need for punishment, but it relieved secondary (preconscious) anxiety about losing her relationship with me. The sudden laughter expressed relief of the latter anxiety.

Assn. 4 (What a failure she is): Defensive substitution of less painful inferiority feelings for the more painful and imminent guilt about riddance feelings toward children.

Assn. 5 (All she wants are just simple, ordinary things): A rationalization to justify wanting anything at all for herself—sometimes called "bribing the superego." The inner guilt makes her feel that she is not entitled to anything, including her present treatment.

Assn. 6 (Better to give up hope for love): A compound mechanism that includes defensive pessimism, rationalization, and substitution of fantasied future deprivations in place of her dreaded wish for punishment in the present (by having to give up her treatment and relationship with me).

Assn. 7 (Tears, followed by refusal to feel sorry for herself): She began to feel sorry for herself at the prospect of present and/or future deprivations; but the inner guilt made her feel that she was not entitled to self pity or crying about her situation.

Assn. 8 (Whether to continue therapy, and waiting for me to tell her what to do): Another defensive enactment—an "alloplastic" in contrast to an "autoplastic" mechanism—in which waiting for me to answer involves a manipulative projection (to me) of her underlying masochistic self-riddance fantasy.

Assn. 9 (What good would it do to go on? Better to give up her hopes of happiness): Returns to the defensive pessimism and rationalization of assn. 6.

Assn. 10 (Stays overtime and insists again that I will tell her to quit):
Still another enactment in which, by staying overtime, she attempts to provoke me into making her leave. Attributing her self-
punitive motive to me involves, as before, a projective defense;
that is, she projects her own self-rejecting superego to me in an
attempt to escape the intolerable severity of her guilt for repressed
riddance feelings toward children.

Assn. 11 (Angry response to therapist's comment that he is not she):
Therapist's comment undercut her projective defense by (figu-
ratively) handing her superego back to her. She reacted with
frustration and anger that I did not cooperate and play the role
that she had assigned to me in her transference enactment. (Note
that the type of transference involved here is narcissistic rather
than object related, because what she attributed to me was a self-
image, not an image of some other person in her life.)

The ability of the posited (re)interpretation of session 14 to account consistently and comprehensively for all of the data in the session
lends support to the possibility that this construction is not only *a* plausible but the *most* plausible interpretation at the time. It is important to
remember, however, that justification of this kind (by internal evidence)
is only partial, and that future developments in the therapeutic process
may, and often do, necessitate revisions of earlier interpretive formulations. The interpretation of session 14 presented here, for example, rather
than representing my original formulation of the session while treating
Ms. White, was based on extensive subsequent data and interpretations
in the case (by application of the RC approach).

Review of Major Defenses During the First Fourteen Sessions

In addition to the various defensive shifts that occur in each therapy
session, certain major defense configurations tend to persist over a number of sessions. For example, Ms. White's masochistic-erotic defense(s)
predominated during a series of earlier sessions. Prior to that, an erotization mechanism was the dominant defense for a number of sessions.
Still another major defense emerged in session 14—a nonerotized, self-

punitive, talion atonement mechanism. Paraphrasing these three major defenses:

> *Erotization:* "Love me! Make me feel lovable instead of guilty and unwanted."
>
> *Masochistic-erotic defense* (erotization combined with physical punishment): "Force me, beat me, punish me painfully! It will feel good to be punished for my guilt."
>
> *Nonerotized, talion punishment:* "I am guilty of riddance feelings, fantasies, and acts toward children. Eye for an eye, tooth for a tooth, and riddance for a riddance: My punishment should be for someone to get rid of me. My husband got rid of me, which I reacted to as punishment for my guilt; but that was not punishment enough. There is never enough punishment for crimes such as mine. Now that I have found something else I want—therapy with this doctor—he too should get rid of me. Only then can I feel some relief from my guilt."

A Technical Question

Should the therapist interpret the current thematic conflict and masochistic defense to the patient? Ideally, yes. The thematic conflict is the most accessible to, and also the most in need of, interpretation. Unless there are overriding reasons not to do so (as in session 10), the therapist usually should interpret the thematic conflict, the major defenses against it, and also how the defenses attempt to deal with the thematic conflict. For example, if I had recognized and had felt fairly confident about the thematic conflict and the new nonerotized masochistic defense against it (which I didn't at the time of this session), I might have interpreted something like the following to Ms. White during session 14: "Your conviction that I will get rid of you seems self-punitive, which suggests inner guilt. The guilt may be about someone you got rid of—for example, the abortion you once had. Tormenting yourself with the idea that I will get rid of you is a way of trying to atone for that inner guilt."

Limitations of Understanding Early in the Therapeutic Process

If the reader is surprised at the incompleteness of my understanding of Ms. White during her first fourteen appointments, it is important to realize that in the initial phases of every psychoanalysis and dynamic psychotherapy the therapist does not yet know the patient very well, and certainly does not yet understand the patient in depth. It is largely for that reason that therapists usually withhold definitive interpretations during early phases of the treatment.

As I have emphasized elsewhere (1998) in this connection, unless and until the clinician has assimilated, and organized in retrievable form, extensive and specific details of an individual patient's life history, emotional vulnerabilities, personality patterns, and current psychological functioning, general knowledge of mental functions and familiarity with interpretive methods and their rationale (that is, interpretive competence) are of little help in understanding the patient's highly personal unconscious meanings and determinants at a given time. It is largely the therapist's unique and extended exposure to, and accessible memory of, innumerable details about the patient that produce the competence to interpret insightfully, and detailed depth psychological knowledge of this kind develops only very gradually in the course of the therapeutic process.

CHAPTER THIRTEEN

Interpretation of Session 24

SESSIONS 15 TO 23 (SUMMARY)

The erotic defense-transference returned and escalated (paraphrased previously as, "Love me, so I won't feel so guilty and unlovable"). By session 18 the erotic hopes had become so intense that they activated deeper unconscious triadic fantasies of winning me away from my wife—suggested by associations such as "The most interesting men are already married," and other similar associations. As conflict about the triadic transference to me increased, displacement occurred to her best friend's marriage and current pregnancy; this displacement deflected the triadic conflict (temporarily) away from her relationship with me. In session 19 she became agitated about recent changes in her menses, which she interpreted anxiously as "a tumor or something in my uterus"—another form of the previously described nonerotized masochistic fantasy, serving in this instance to atone for underlying oedipal guilt, which appeared to include a guilt-laden fantasy of a forbidden pregnancy (cf. her preoccupation with her best friend's pregnancy, and her fantasy of "something in my uterus"). In session 21 she guiltily "confessed" to me that she had sexual feelings toward her best friend's husband, and in session 23 she confessed even more guiltily that she was experiencing sexual feelings toward me and the fear that I might betray her to my wife. Bearing out

Freud's (1923a) comment that the meanings of things one hears are for the most part recognized only later, she told me eight sessions later that on the night following session 23 she became so "horny" that she had sex with a stranger, and for the first time in her life experienced orgasm during intercourse.

SESSION 24 (FOURTH INTERPRETIVE EXERCISE)

Discouraged and disgusted with herself; accused herself of being dumb, not knowing clever things to say. Blocking set in. ["Has anything happened to make you feel that way?"] *"Everything"* makes her feel that way! More blocking. ["By saying 'everything' you avoid anything specific that is bothering you."] Wry grimace, followed by recalling a recent incident at work in which she told a story to children (she is a children's librarian). A colleague told her that she had never heard Ms. White do it better. Instead of feeling pleased by the compliment, however, she felt self-critical because she had been copying someone else's style in telling the story. The colleague's praise merely goes to prove that she has nothing herself, is just a poor imitation of other people. She imitates other people a lot— so much so that there is no real person that is herself. Also, she went out of town to be with friends for the weekend. They invited an eligible bachelor to meet her, but she was a "complete washout." The way she acted the man couldn't possibly have become interested in her. Associations then turn to the day last week when her feelings of discouragement began. ["That was the day of your last appointment. Can you remember anything in that session that might have set off your present mood?"] She can't remember what she talked about that day. More associations about imitating others. ["Is there anything about your treatment or about me that you may be imitating?"] She groaned as if hit by the sudden recognition of something. "As you probably already know," she went on, whenever anyone is kind to her nowadays she becomes "attached" to them. She's afraid that is happening to her with me. The day after the reading incident she didn't have an appointment, and for the first time since her treatment began she noticed that she missed seeing me that day. She knows that isn't the purpose of this treatment, and that she shouldn't feel that way, but she can't help it. ["Your self-criticisms today show how much conflict you feel about your attachment to me."]

COMMENTARY

Author's Formulation of Session 24 (Which Corresponds Well with the Posttherapeutically Derived Interpretation)

The following formulation illustrates that sometimes a therapist must wait until a session is almost over before a particularly revealing clue suggests a dynamic theme for the session's otherwise rather obscure associations. Although I recognized and interpreted several separate, transitory defenses during the session (generalization, isolation, avoidance, and substitution), I was unable to understand the latent conflict being defended against until the end of the session. Finally, after a series of interventions that weakened the patient's avoidance of the transference relationship, she confided (against resistance) that she had missed me on a day when she did not have an appointment. That was the first time she had experienced or expressed feelings of "attachment" to me, as she called it. The absence of her more usual blushing and coyness suggested that the feelings were not so much erotic or romantic, but probably dependent in character. On that basis I constructed the following interpretive hypothesis (to myself) at the end of the session:

> *Precipitant:* The recent growing intensity of her guilt-laden triadic-oedipal transference to me had become so disturbing that it precipitated an abrupt defensive regression—the defensive function of the regression being suggested by the suddenness of the change; deeper, drive-related shifts occur more gradually.
> *Thematic conflict:* Dependent defense transference *versus* shame.

Checking This Formulation Against All of the Current Data

Assn. 1 (Self-critical about being "dumb" and socially inept): Substitution of (less disturbing) inferiority feelings about her intelligence and social skills (neither of which is deficient) for more disturbing feelings of shame about her increasing dependence on me. (Note: Defensive substitutions of this kind are very common in depth psychological therapies.)

Assn. 2 ("Everything" makes her feel that way): A defensive generalization, to avoid the specific inner conflict that is disturbing her.

Assn. 3 (Wry grimace): A disguised, ambivalent acknowledgment that my interpretation of the generalization defense was on target.

Assn. 4 (Telling the children's story): Her associations about the children's story pictured herself initially as a competent, professional adult—someone on whom others (e.g., children) depend. Recalling the incident thus served (temporarily) to conceal her own dependence by substituting an overcompensatory (professional adult) image of herself.

Assn. 5 (Self-critical about the story incident, describing herself as imitative and intellectually inferior): She was unable to sustain the defensive, overcompensatory image of herself, possibly because it ran the risk of reactivating triadic conflicts. As in assn. I, she substitutes intellectual inferiority for feelings of shame about dependence—a "lesser shame" defense similar to the "lesser crime" mechanism discussed previously.

Assn. 6 (Refers to herself as a "complete washout" with the eligible bachelor): Displacement from therapist to the bachelor, and substitution of shame about social ineptness for the greater shame of dependence.

Assn. 7 (Recalls the day that depressive symptoms began, but not the specific emotional events that gave rise to them): An isolation mechanism (in which she isolates a factual memory from its associated emotional memory)—seen commonly in obsessional symptoms. Note, for example, that she has obsessed during the present session about her alleged lack of intelligence and social skill. It is important to keep in mind that, like other symptoms, obsessions are "red herrings" that attempt to cover up the real problem (i.e., the thematic conflict). It would be a mistake to assume, however, that obsessions always indicate a certain type of underlying conflict (e.g., "anal" conflicts concerning control, withholding, defiance, cruelty, and destructiveness). Obsessional mechanisms (isolation, intellectualization, circumstantiality, ambivalent alternation, and indecision) can serve as defenses against any and all types of conflicts.

Assn. 8 (After therapist undercut her isolation mechanism by connecting the onset of her depressive mood with the day of her last appointment, she "drew a blank" for that session and returned to self-criticism about imitating others): Defensive amnesia for the content of the previous session was based on repression of disturbing feelings of dependence on me. Note in this connection that all three of her professed, substituted inferiority feelings (her alleged lack of intelligence, social skills, and a personality of her own) have certain similarities with the psychology of infants. Although I did not recognize this parallel at the time of the present session, in retrospect it can be seen as a subtle clue to the content of her current thematic conflict, that is, shame about (defensively) regressive, infantile feelings toward me.

Assn. 9 (When the substitution defense was weakened by connecting the self-critical image of herself with her relationship to me, she groaned): The groan appeared to express disguised acknowledgment of the connection I made.

Assn. 10 (Dependent feelings toward me begin to emerge, but ambiguously and intellectually): She attempts to reduce the pride conflict (shame) by circuitousness and ambiguity (both avoidance mechanisms), and by rationalization that she "can't help it." [I attempted to weaken these defenses and expose the thematic conflict more clearly by interpreting her shame about feelings of dependence on me.]

Oedipal Transferences and Defensive Regressions

In patients with primarily neurotic pathology, oedipal conflicts sometimes become thematic very briefly within the first few months of the therapeutic process (as in the present case). The patient's ego has not yet been strengthened sufficiently by therapy to deal with such intense conflicts, however, so the oedipal conflicts are characteristically re-repressed, accompanied by defensive regression to preoedipal states. Therapeutic work on the preoedipal conflicts and defenses strengthens the ego, so that as oedipal conflicts become thematic again (cyclically) in the therapeutic process, they are more accessible to interpretation, working through, and insight.

Interpreting Defenses

This session also illustrates that the therapeutic value of interpreting defenses to the patient is not based primarily on its immediate insight-producing potential, but rests even more importantly on its heuristic, data-generating capability. For example, by interpreting and thereby weakening the generalization, isolation, and substitution mechanisms in session 24, more thematic and interpretable data could emerge—including the crucial associations about her "attachment" to me.

CHAPTER FOURTEEN

Interpretation of a Dream in Session 85

SESSIONS 25 TO 80 (SUMMARY)

The indications of regression that appeared (against resistance) in session 24 were the harbinger of the first sustained dependent transference in Ms. White's therapeutic process; it continued for over fifty sessions. Conflict about the dependent feelings took the form initially of anxiety that I would become disgusted with her for acting like a "whining baby" (a projection of her inner self-disgust about such feelings). As the regression deepened and intensified she (1) turned to religion for the "comfort and security" that she could not get from me; (2) began to recognize how dependent she had been on her husband, that he had been like a mother to her; (3) developed a marked increase in appetite, especially for sweets; (4) became increasingly anxious about an upsurge of possessive feelings toward me, that is, not wanting to share me with others; (5) developed sibling rivalry transferences to my other patients; (6) experienced moderately severe separation anxiety when I was away for a week; and (7) reacted with depression when her best friend Betty's baby was born. She expressed envy of Betty for having a child, but subtle hints suggested that it was the baby she envied. Frustration of dependent longings in the transference produced bitter complaints that "she wants so much but gets so little from me." Angry demanding feelings toward me escalated—for example, insisting that she needed more help from me, that I answer her questions, give her advice, and other such demands. This phase of dependent aggression continued for approximately twenty sessions, accompanied by increasing guilt and fear of alienating and losing me (as a mother figure).

Sessions 81 to 84 (Summary of Several Appointments Immediately Preceding the Session to be Interpreted)

As the intensity of anxiety and guilt about hostile-dependent feelings toward me peaked, the dependent transference receded and was replaced by a defensive anal regression. Colitis with severe intermittent constipation and diarrhea set in. Concomitantly she became very blocked in her therapy sessions, stubbornly refusing to express whatever came to her mind (cf. the retentive anal phase). In session 83 the regressive anal conflicts were transferred to the issues of lying down and telling her dreams. She reported a transference fantasy of my pressuring her to lie down so that she would "bring out the dark, dirty things" in her dreams. (The anal symbolism of these transferences had transformed the couch into a toilet on which she felt pressured to produce symbolic feces in the form of dreams.) She reacted to the fantasied pressure with anal-expulsive and sadistic feelings toward me versus fear of "losing control" of the feelings and alienating or harming me. Masochistic-erotic fantasies reappeared at this point—now a defense against anal aggression. For example, in session 84 [when I interpreted to her that she seemed to want me to coax her to lie down and tell her dreams], she construed the comment (unconsciously) as a "spanking," to which she responded with transference compliance—dutifully producing several "dream-stools"—the first dreams that she had reported in her therapy:

> 1. A plane was flying along, and there was a body hanging out of the window of the plane.
>
> 2. A cart was rolling backward down a hill. "I put on the brakes as hard as I could, but couldn't stop it."

3. "I was going to some kind of a fair or something with two girls that I plan to go on vacation with. There was a big crowd. The car was there, but I had a desperate sinking feeling that we would be left there. There was a fence, and on the other side were people undergoing some kind of examination. There were a lot of couches there. There was a pregnant woman there who was being examined for something. I seemed to be there, too. The man who rented us our apartment kept coming up to me and asking me for the keys. Again I had that sinking feeling that I might be left there—left alone in the crowd."

After telling the dreams she hastened to protest how silly and dull the dreams were, which only proves how unimaginative she is. She insisted that the dreams made no sense at all. [I told her it was time to stop today, but perhaps we could try to understand the dreams next time.]

SESSION 85 (FIFTH INTERPRETIVE EXERCISE)

Ms. White feels better than last week when she felt "out of control." She has always feared "making a fool of myself in therapy." When she tries to please someone she is curious to know how that person feels about it. Over the weekend she wondered whether she really is the sort of person who wants to be coaxed into things, as the therapist said about her last week (in connection with her ambivalence about lying down and telling her dreams). She resists change of any kind, but if someone becomes displeased with her about resisting, she will go ahead and make the change to keep the person from feeling disgusted with her. She connects all this (spontaneously) with telling the dreams for the first time in the previous session, after the therapist said she seemed to want to be coaxed about it. ["We didn't have time to study the dreams last time, so why don't you tell them again now?"] In retelling the dreams she left out the part about people being examined on couches. [I called attention to the omission and asked what it brought to her mind.] She protested irritably that it didn't bring anything to mind, and then blocked for a while. Finally she blurted out in a spiteful tone that it probably had something to do with the fact that she can't lie down and talk. She is afraid to, for fear of what she might say or do. It would be like someone looking into her head! She feels that she has to lie down, but if she does she won't be able to talk. ["What makes you feel you have to lie down?"] A previous psychiatrist told her to. She knows she doesn't have to here, but she has the feeling, as in the dream, that if she doesn't do so she'll be left all alone.

She then recalled and told a dream from last night: "I leaned back against a man, and had all the feelings you would have from leaning back against a person like that." She did not associate to the dream spontaneously, but appeared to wait for me to tell her what to do. ["What are your thoughts about the man in the dream?"] His name was Larry, but she doesn't know anybody with that name. She blocked. ["What comes to mind about leaning back against him?"] It reminds her of leaning on someone, depending on him, wanting someone to lean on. When she did that in the dream it stimulated a lot of sexual feelings in her, such as she has been experiencing lately but doesn't understand. ["Do you remember what you were talking about when you recalled the dream a minute ago?"] She thought about it for a while, but couldn't remember. ["You were talking about lying down. Does that fit with the dream?"] She blushed and nodded.

COMMENTARY

Author's Interpretation of the Dream in Session 85 (Which Corresponded Well with the Posttherapeutically Derived Formulation)

The most frequent unit of clinical data that therapists interpret is the individual therapy session, but interpreting a smaller unit of clinical data such as a dream is no different in principle than the formulation of an entire session (see, for example, Boyer 1988, French 1958b). Whatever the nature or size of the data sample, the psychoanalyst or dynamic psychotherapist attempts to formulate the precipitant, the principal current (thematic) conflict, and the repertory of defenses against that conflict. Since the dream in session 85 occurred the night before and is a central

feature of that session, one can assume that the dream's dynamics probably correspond closely with the dynamic theme of the session as a whole.
The latter assumption is based on the basic depth psychologic concept
or background assumption of *continuity*, and on the contextual definition
of meaning: "The meaning of an event [in this case, the dream] is the
psychological continuity into which it fits" (Rapaport 1944, p. 216).

I based my interpretation of the dream in session 85 on the following set of clues:

> *Clue 1* (A continuity of associations, that is, her conflict about lying
> down, followed immediately by a dream of erotic feelings toward
> a man on whom she leans back): The juxtaposition of asso-
> ciations suggests a connection between her conflict about lying
> down and erotic feelings toward me.
>
> *Clue 2* (An analogic similarity between lying down during her
> therapy sessions and leaning back against a man): My chair is at
> the head of the couch on which she sits. If she were to lie down
> she would have to turn her back toward me and lean or lie back
> in my direction.
>
> *Clue 3* (In retelling a dream from the previous session she left out
> a part about people, presumably including herself, being exam-
> ined on couches): The omission suggests repression of an in-
> tensely activated fantasy-wish to lie down on the couch.
>
> *Clue 4* (Early in the session she mentioned fear of "making a fool
> of myself in therapy"): That expression could connote "making
> a fool of myself over a man"—that is, romantic-erotic over-
> involvement with me.

Putting these several clues together, I inferred tentatively (to myself) that the dynamic theme of session 85, and of the dream in that session,
dealt with conflict about lying down—not, however, the same anal-
aggressive conflict and toilet symbolism that were transferred to the couch
in session 84. The conflict about lying down in session 85 appeared to
involve multiple sources of fantasied erotic gratification, including dependent ("leaning on the man"), anal (her backside in contact with the

man), and genital (she felt a "lot of sexual stimulation" from physical contact with the man). Based on these clues and interpretive reasoning, I constructed the following interpretive hypothesis: as the *precipitant*, her transference compliance in the previous session resulted in some relief of anal-aggressive conflict, and some reconciliation with the therapist. With that in mind, she was eager to extend her compliance in session 85 by lying down on the couch. Her eagerness to do so aroused a number of erotic fantasies, however, which led to the following *thematic conflict*: fantasies of polymorphous-perverse erotic gratifications from lying down and being physically closer to me, *versus* fear of becoming overstimulated erotically, shame about "making a fool of myself" romantically over me, and guilt about "forbidden" sexual desires toward me.

Checking This Formulation Against All of the Current Data

Assn. 1 (The initial association about feeling better, not "out of control" as previously): Her compliance in the previous session helped her to gain control of the increasingly destabilizing, anal-aggressive transference, and to regain a feeling of reconciliation with me.

Assn. 2 (Fear of "making a fool of myself in therapy"): The expression she used is idiomatic for becoming infatuated with a man who does not return the feelings. The phrase "in therapy" is a euphemistic displacement to avoid specifying the specific man involved (therapist).

Assn. 3 (When she tries to please "someone," she wants feedback about how "the person" feels about it): "Someone" and "the person" are defensive generalizations to avoid specifying that it is therapist from whom she wants a response. Having presented him with dreams in the previous session, she hopes he will return the favor by acknowledging her "gift."

Assn. 4 (Wonders whether she is the sort of person who wants to be coaxed, as therapist said last time): This association suggests the continuity between the present and previous sessions, but she substitutes the issue of wanting to be coaxed for what she really wants unconsciously, which is much more than coaxing.

Assn. 5 (Resists change, but complies if "someone" becomes displeased with her; then connects this with telling a dream when therapist said she wanted to be coaxed): Supports the conclusion in previous session that she reacted to my comment about coaxing as a fantasied punishment, to which she complied by reporting a series of dreams.

Assn. 6 (In retelling the dream she left out a part about people being examined on couches): Her repression of that dream image suggested that lying down was again a key issue and source of conflict.

Assn. 7 (Responds irritably and spitefully to therapist's questions about the omitted dream image): This type of defensiveness represents an aggressive protest—a compound mechanism consisting of disavowal, rationalization, and overcompensatory aggression.

Assn. 8 (The fantasy and feeling that she must lie down or she will be left all alone): Another compound mechanism in which she projects to me her own insistent, disavowed wish to lie down, at the same time projectively rationalizing that it is not something *she* wants to do but that she must do to avoid abandonment by the therapist. The latter fantasy seems related to the earlier, guilt-motivated, masochistic mechanism of expecting me to get rid of her. In the present context, however, the guilt appears to be a reaction to forbidden, polymorphous-perverse, sexual urges.

Assn. 9 (The dream in session 85): She substituted an image of leaning back for the posture of lying down, and she generalized about "a" man and about "all the feelings" to conceal the specifically erotic nature of the feelings toward a specific man, namely, me. A subtle defensive syntactical ambiguity also occurs in the wording of the dream. The phrase "like that" at the end of the dream seems to belong after "leaning back." As she worded it, "a person like that" implies some special quality of the person against whom she leaned—perhaps a disguised reference to sex appeal. If so, this element of the dream suggests further that the thematic conflict included genital as well as pregenital erotic desires (cf. polymorphous-perverse sexual fantasies).

Assn. 10 (The name *Larry,* and not knowing anyone by that name): This association cannot be accounted for by the present formulation.

Assn. 11 (Emphasizes dependence in her associations to "leaning on" the man): A compound regressive and isolation defense against the polymorphous-perverse sexual excitement associated with her fantasy-wish to lie down and be physically closer to me.

Assn. 12 (Leaning back against the man stimulated "a lot of sexual feelings" in her): The phrase "a lot" is defensively ambiguous; it could mean a large amount, a wide variety, or both. A diversity of erotic feelings fits my impression that her wish is for polymorphous-perverse erotic sensations. "Large amount" fits her fear of overstimulation and overinvolvement.

Assn. 13 (Not only did she feel "a lot of sexual feelings" in the dream, but also she has been experiencing the same amount and kind of feelings in the waking state): She adds that she "doesn't understand" the latter feelings, but the implication is that she has become obsessed and perhaps flooded with erotic feelings and fantasies. She does not divulge the exact nature of the sexual feelings, however (suppression).

Assn. 14 (Blushes and agrees when therapist points out the contiguity and implied dynamic connection between her preoccupation with lying down, on the one hand, and erotic feelings, on the other): She had employed an isolation mechanism to avoid recognizing the connection. The blush suggested again that I was the object of her intensely erotized preoccupation with lying down.

Some Process Aspects of the Polymorphous-Perverse Transference in Session 85

Like sessions 25 and 80, session 85 is a transition point in Ms. White's therapeutic process. For the past sixty sessions, she has been preoccupied with regressive dependent, followed by anal-erotic and -aggressive, transferences to me. At this point, genital-erotic urges toward me are added to the continuing mix of pregenital strivings. The latter development, combined with the patient's progress in dealing with anal-aggressive conflicts in session 84, suggests that a process of emergence from pregenital regression is under way, and that she is beginning once again to confront genital urges toward me. At the same time, one senses a reluctance to give up the pregenital gratifications. The result is a very conflicted polymorphous-perverse mixture of erotic feelings and fantasies transferred to me in session 85.

The Technical Problem of How to Deal with the Dreams

I felt that an acknowlegment of her progress in telling her dreams was called for, but that direct praise might overgratify her eagerness for approbation. My suggestion that we "study" the dreams attempted to accomplish several purposes simultaneously: (1) To acknowledge that reporting the dreams was useful—that is, my reference to "studying" the dreams carried the implication that the dreams were valuable information and worthy of additional attention; (2) the risk of overgratifying her was minimized by framing the acknowledgment in clinical-scientific terms; (3) because of her inhibition about and inexperience in analyzing dreams, she needed some education in this aspect of the therapeutic work; and (4) asking a patient to retell a dream is a common interpretive heuristic because changes from the original dream report suggest specific areas of repressed conflict. Interpretive technique often, if not usually, serves multiple purposes, as in this example.

CHAPTER FIFTEEN

Interpretation of Session 123

SESSIONS 86 TO 122 (SUMMARY)

As Ms. White emerged from the relatively prolonged periods of dependent and anal regression, triadic erotic and competitive feelings toward me and my wife (also toward my secretary as an additional female rival; note that her father had two wives) reappeared, and were displaced defensively, as before, to her best friend Betty and her husband. Whereas the earlier phase of oedipal transference had been very brief, lasting for only five sessions (19 to 23), the present triadic (and at times quadruple) transferences continued for twenty-five sessions, suggesting that the oedipal conflicts were somewhat less disturbing at this point and did not need to be re-repressed as quickly. As the oedipal transferences increased, she became obsessed with an anxious fantasy that "someone" would walk in during her session and "catch me in the act" (projection of guilt about her own oedipally-driven primal scene curiosity, transferred currently to my relationships with my wife and secretary). Frustration of her erotic feelings toward me produced intense anger, but anxiety about alienating or losing me activated equally intense resistances both to awareness and expression of the rage. [An opportunity arose to comment on her character pattern of naïveté and innocence.] She felt so humiliated by the interpretation that she stomped out of the session in anger. Despite this violent initial reaction, however, the interpretation appeared to weaken the character defense to some extent. She then became obsessed with a guilty fantasy of people finding out about her abortion, followed by an obsessive fear that she had become pregnant as a result of a recent sexual experience.

SESSION 123 (SIXTH INTERPRETIVE EXERCISE)

She started the session by saying with a tone of irony that she was "Alright, for a change." She then told a dream from the night before: "The dream was about coming to see you. You had changed buildings. Two of my aunts were with me. I felt the way I would if they knew that I come to see you— sort of ashamed and guilty. A little girl came in to see you. She opened a bag and dumped out its contents for you to see. It was a bunch of bones. The bones still had meat on them. My aunts were shocked and disgusted."

Her associations to the dream were that she never felt that she could go to her aunts and talk to them. She felt they wouldn't know the answers, wouldn't understand, or would disapprove. They would never have approved of kissing a boy, for example. Her husband was the only person she could talk to about problems. She laughed uneasily and said it must sound as though she has a "shady past." [A skeleton in the closet?] She looked startled, then nodded. She recalled another dream from a week or so ago: Her husband was holding a little box. (She blocked and tears came to her eyes.) [Yes?] She thought it might be a gift; but the box was rectangular, like a little coffin.

She spoke again of her aunts not understanding. ["Your aunts may have represented your own conscience in the dream."] She looked surprised, then nodded; but she switched abruptly and denied that the dream made any sense to her. She began to cry softly, which continued to the end of the session.

COMMENTARY

Author's Interpretation of the First Dream in Session 123, (Which Corresponded Well with the Posttherapeutically Derived Formulation)

I based my interpretation on the following set of clues in session 123:

Clue 1: The dynamic context at the time of the "bag of bones" dream included (a) her current triadic (or quadruple: see below) transferences to me, my wife, and secretary. (b) increasing guilt about a past pregnancy and abortion, and about the possibility of being pregnant currently (cf. her obsessions at the end of the summary for sessions 86 to 122).

Clue 2: An analogic similarity between her guilty obsessions about pregnancy and abortion, on the one hand, and what appears to be an abortion symbol in the dream (i.e., emptying out the dead contents of a bag [womb]).

Clue 3: Repetition of the dead baby theme in the second dream (her husband showing her a small, coffin-shaped box).

Clue 4: Parallels between the dream image of two aunts being shocked (cf. she had two mothers), and the associations about the mother figures not being understanding, their disapproving of her kissing a boy, and her uneasy laughter about having a "shady past."

Clue 5: Parallels between the two disapproving mother figures in the dream, her current competitive transferences to two women rivals for my favor (my wife and secretary), and the fact that her father had two wives. The images of two disapproving mother figures may suggest that her oedipal conflicts and transferences are quadruple rather than triadic (i.e., involve her father, two mothers, and herself).

Clue 6: An analogic similarity between the dream image of showing me the "shocking" and "disgusting" contents of the bag, and what she does in treatment, namely, exposing shameful feelings, fantasies, and memories to me.

Clue 7: The dream image of a "little girl" (herself as a child) showing me a symbol of pregnancy and abortion. This clue, combined with the image of two disapproving mother figures, and the uneasy reference to her "shady past," gave me the impression that she was beginning to confront some childhood origins of her conflicts.

Putting these various clues together, I constructed (to myself) the following tentative interpretation of the dream:

Precipitant: Recent interpretive weakening of a character pattern in which she presented herself as a naive, innocent young girl. Her initial, very defensive, violently oppositional response to that interpretation was followed by increasingly guilty obsessions about a forbidden past pregnancy and abortion, and the possibility that she may be pregnant currently.

Thematic conflict: Her current triadic (or quadruple) transferences to me, my wife, and secretary include an oedipal wish for a forbidden, "incestuous" child from me, versus guilt about the "incestuous" aspect of her transference wish about pregnancy, and about hostile-competitive feelings toward two women rivals (mother figures) and their pregnancies (therapist's wife and secretary in the present, father's two wives in the past).

Checking This Formulation Against All of the Current Data

Assn. 1 (The content and tone of her initial association) imply that usually she is not alright—thus bribing her conscience to relieve guilt: "See how I suffer! I suffer almost all of the time. Haven't I suffered enough?"

Assn. 2 (The dream):

(a) (Coming to see therapist): Substitutes professional contact with therapist for her transference wishes to have an (oedipal)-erotic relationship with him.

(b) (Therapist had changed "buildings"): Another substitution, this time for the much more radical changes that she wishes therapist would make, namely, leave his wife and secretary, become *her* husband and father of *her* children.

(c) (The two aunts who are shocked and disgusted at what she reveals to therapist): Mother and stepmother figures, who represent both a projection of her own superego, and displacements from her oedipal rivals (mother and stepmother in the past, therapist's wife and secretary in her current transferences).

(d) (She would feel ashamed and guilty if they knew of her treatment): A "lesser crime" mechanism, that is, she substitutes her wish for treatment from me (at most a relatively minor "offense") for the much more guilt-laden wish to have an "incestuous" relationship and child with me.

(e) (A little girl comes in to see therapist): A projected self-image that is both defensive (cf. her character pattern of acting like a naive, innocent little girl), and at the same time a possible allusion to the childhood origins of her current conflict.

(f) (Dumps out a bag of bones for therapist to see): A highly condensed, compound symbolic image of (I) her attempt to "open up" more to therapist in her treatment; (2) a transference fantasy of giving birth to an idealized, "incestuous" child fathered by therapist, which, however, because of oedipal guilt, must be deformed and demented (as her own child was), or dead; (3) multiple, guilt-laden abortion fantasies—not only toward her own forbidden real and fantasied pregnancies, but also toward the pregnancies of her oedipal rivals (mother and stepmother in childhood, transferred to therapist's wife and secretary in the present), and also toward her siblings as a child.

(g) (The bones still had some meat on them): A macabre image implying that the old childhood conflict (oedipal wish for an incestuous child from father and the guilt) is not completely "dead," but is still partially alive and active in her (e.g., is being relived currently in her relationship with me).

Assn. 3 (Her complaints that she could not discuss problems with her aunts, who would disapprove of anything sexual like kissing): In addition to projecting her own superego to memories of her disapproving aunts (as mother and stepmother figures), she also bribes her conscience in the following manner: "I have had to do without a mother's understanding and guidance, so I should not be criticized so severely for my mistakes and bad thoughts." She also substitutes the much "lesser crime" of kissing a boy for the greater guilt of desiring an incestuous child.

Assn. 4 (Her husband was the only person to whom she could tell her troubles)—yet she never told him about her premarital abortion. The defense mechanisms involved here appear to be displacement from therapist to her ex-husband, and substitution of confiding relatively minor, "everyday" problems for revealing her deeper, guilt-laden experiences and transference fantasies.

Assn. 5 (Uneasy laugh, and reference to her "shady past"): The uneasiness of her laugh betrayed anxiety about weakening of defenses against exposure of the current transference fantasies. The remark about her "shady past" suggested that guilt feelings—some perhaps from her early life—were in fact beginning to emerge.

Assn. 6 (Therapist's metaphor of a "skeleton in the closet" reminded her of a recent dream in which her husband showed her a small, coffin-shaped box): She projected an image of her own inner self-accusations about forbidden and destroyed pregnancies to her ex-husband (displaced from therapist), confronting her with evidence of her guilt. A "lesser crime" substitution and bribing her conscience also are involved here, that is, closest to the surface the little coffin image referred to her defective child whom she carried to term and cared for until she died. As a result she felt least guilty about that pregnancy and child, viewing it as a fantasied punishment that she could use to relieve guilt about real, imaginary, forbidden, and destroyed pregnancies.

Assn. 7 (Blocking and tears): As the guilt emerges ever closer to consciousness, associations and speech are shut down (suppressed). The tears serve a defensive function in the present context—still another instance of bribing her conscience by feeling, "Poor me! See how I suffer! Must I be burdened with even more painful guilt?"

Assn. 8 (Returns to her complaints that her aunts were not understanding): See the discussion of assn. 3.

Assn. 9 (Denial that the dream made any sense): See assn. 7. Her insistence that the dream made no sense involved mechanisms of disavowal and rationalization.

What, If Anything, Should the Therapist Interpret to the Patient at This Point?

Interpretive technique allows therapists considerable leeway in what they communicate to patients. Depending on the dynamic circumstances at the time, a therapist may choose to emphasize conflict or defense, content or process, present or past, therapeutic or extratherapeutic transferences. As a rule, however, interpretations to the patient should be brief, focused, and sparing in content; otherwise the patient may be confused rather than enlightened. With these heuristics in mind, I said to the patient at the end of the session: ["Both dreams seem to deal with guilt about pregnancies, babies, and abortion. Picturing yourself as a young girl in last night's dream suggests that your guilt about pregnancy and abortion may have begun long before the abortion you had and the child you had who died. The guilt could have begun during your childhood."] My aim in conveying this interpretation was to reinforce what seemed to be a beginning effort on the patient's part to confront some of the childhood origins of her guilt—to encourage and facilitate further such exploration and understanding. I realized that encouraging such exploration might increase her anxiety about doing so, which turned out to be the case.

Pregnancy Fantasies and Psychopathology

For another example of a childhood pregnancy fantasy in the transferences of an adult patient, see the clinical illustration in Chapter 3.

CHAPTER SIXTEEN

Interpretation of Session 147

SESSIONS 124 TO 146 (SUMMARY)

Soon after the "bag of bones" dream, the patient's second major dependent transference set in. This time, however, it continued only half as long as previously. Conflict increased between her wish for more dependence *versus* anxiety about loss of autonomy. The regression had included narcissistic symbiotic fantasies of expecting me to understand her whether she made herself clear or not. During the regression she dreamed of a monster called a "Hydra" with a large, suction-cup mouth and tentacles—an image of the oral, clinging, dependent part of herself that had characterized her relationship with her husband, and now was transferred to me. Severe blocking developed, with refusal to talk about her feelings toward me—the onset of her second major anal regression. She complained that I was "pushing" her to lie down, but added: "I would never get anywhere if I weren't pushed, however, so I hope you won't stop pushing me even if I complain about it." [I commented that she seemed to want me to force her to lie down, not just for therapeutic reasons but for some hidden erotic pleasure in being forced. At the same time, I added, her wish to be forced was frightening to her—a conflict between wanting and fearing it.] The interpretation startled her; she became anxious, then angry, and threatened repeatedly to quit therapy.

SESSION 147
(SEVENTH INTERPRETIVE EXERCISE)

She started by saying that the children at her school got their report cards today. She noticed a little boy who flunked science but was undaunted by it. After the last session she cried for the first time in quite a while. She felt sad, like she had lost something valuable to her. She was surprised that the crying was a relief to her rather than the uncontrollable crying when her husband left her. She dreamed of a war, and because of the war her husband came back to her. Her associations to the dream were that she wishes those days were back again. During the war she had what she wanted (said sadly, tearfully). Then she wondered about the First World War, and why there was never any discussion of it in her family. She didn't even know whether her father was in that war. ["The dream and your associations about the two World Wars suggest a parallel between those two periods of your life. The First World War was from 1914 to 1918, the first four years of your life, when your mother was alive. You met and married your husband during the Second World War. During both wars, therefore, you had what you wanted and loved; and after each war you lost the person you loved and depended on."]

She responded to the interpretation by recalling a dream from the night before: "I was walking along a highway, pushing a little carriage, like those in Mother Goose books. I had a kitten in the carriage. Someone said the road ahead was difficult and I should turn back, but I went on. There was a curve in the road, and a bunch of men working on the side of the road where it was muddy. I pushed the carriage through the mud, weaving among the men to get by. One man had one of those drills that makes so much noise [jackhammer]. I had to go right by him; the pounding and noise frightened me. I got by somehow and went on along the highway, which seemed familiar to me. It seemed I had been that way before." She was puzzled that she didn't reach a destination in the dream. [Well, your therapy and life aren't over yet, I commented,] adding that it was time to stop today. She seemed happy as she left the session.

COMMENTARY

Author's (Re)interpretation of Session 147
(Based on Posttherapeutic Application of the RC Approach)

The following clues in session 147 foretold the retrospectively-derived interpretation, which differed in some respects from my impressions at the time of the session:

> *Clue 1:* The immediately preceding context of session 147 included a defensive anal regression, highlighted by an ambivalent transference to me focused on the issue of lying down. She insisted and complained that I was "pushing" her, on the one hand, but at the same time urged me to "keep pushing me even if I complained about it." [I interpreted to her that she seemed to want me to force her, not just for therapeutic reasons but for some hidden erotic pleasure of being forced *versus* conflict about the wish to be forced.] She reacted to the interpretation with anxiety, then anger, then with threats of quitting therapy—emergency defenses to ward off the recognition of her masochistic-erotic wishes. Her intensely emotional and defensive reactions to the interpretation suggested that it would probably be the precipitant of the thematic conflict in session 147.
>
> *Clue 2:* Initial associations sometimes "telegraph" important dynamic trends in therapy sessions (see, e.g., Lipton 1958, Seitz 1955). Session 147 began with an association about a child who received a failing grade but was undaunted by it. At the time of the session, I inferred that this initial association was a self-reference that seemed to imply that Ms. White was adapting to and integrating the interpretation of her masochistic-erotic defense—that is, like the schoolboy she viewed it as a failure in herself, but one that she could surmount. Reinterpretation of this initial association in the light of later material suggested, however, that my impression was only partly right (as clinical inferences and interpretations often are). I failed to recognize that being undaunted by a failure might also

indicate a defensive warding off (denial) of a disturbing reality. In retrospect, therefore, the initial association suggested that her reactions to the interpretation included both adaptive and defensive components (cf. the basic concept of overdetermination and its corollary, the principle of multiple function [Waelder 1930]).

Clue 3: Sadness and weeping (but with relief) after the previous session: Originally I considered her weeping with relief to be further evidence of an adaptive response to the interpretation. That is, after an initial reaction of anxiety and defensiveness, patients often respond with relief to the therapeutic exposure of their darkest secrets. What I did not notice at the time of the session, however, was that her associations did not include any indication of the reasons for the sadness and weeping; the affective reactions were defensively isolated from their source. In retrospect, this material suggested again, as in clue 2, that her reaction to the interpretation had both adaptive and defensive meanings.

Clue 4: A parallel between my interpretation of her masochistic-erotic pattern, which startled and frightened her, and the dream image of being frightened by the workman with a jackhammer. Note, for example, the functional analogy between the interpretation of a defense and the function of a jackhammer; both are used to break through resistant surface structures to get at what lies beneath. At the time of this session, however, all I concluded tentatively from the analogy was that she seemed to be adapting to the interpretation satisfactorily (cf. she "got by" the workman with the frightening jackhammer, and proceeded down the highway). Retrospective study suggested that this dream also included a defensive use of my disturbing interpretation—to "get by" (in the sense of evade) rather than to understand and modify the masochistic-erotic pattern.

Putting these several clues together suggested the following (post-therapeutic) interpretive formulation of Session 147:

Precipitant: My interpretation of the secret erotic pleasure she obtained from fantasies of being forced threatened both the guilt-relieving function and also the pleasure-gain of her masochistic-erotic defense (see Explanatory Note, below).

Thematic conflict: Therapeutic aims motivate her to give up or modify the masochistic defense *versus* reluctance to give up a defense that both protects her from guilt and provides erotic pleasure.

Checking This Formulation Against All of the Current Data

Assn. 1 (The schoolboy who was undaunted by a failing grade): Both defensive and adaptive meanings appear to be condensed in this initial association. The more adaptive meaning is represented by the child (patient) facing an emotional crisis courageously. Defensively, in addition to projecting her current problem to the schoolboy, she also employed a substitution mechanism—a defense that she has used in every session formulated thus far. In this instance she substituted feelings of failure (inferiority feelings) for more disturbing feelings of guilt (see session 14 for another distinctive example of the same substitution).

Assn. 2 (Tearful feelings of sadness and loss, but with relief, following the previous session): Once again, both adaptive and defensive meanings seem to be condensed in this material. Weeping with relief is adaptive, but what was relieved following session 146? Possibly the burden of hiding the masochistic-erotic pattern. The defensive aspect of her tearful sadness was isolation of the affect from its ideational content, that is, from the reason for these emotions.

Assn. 3 (Dream of another war and her husband coming back to her): Unlike the previous associations, this material is purely defensive. She reverts to her old love-seeking (erotization) mechanism: "Love me, so I won't feel like a pariah!" A displacement from therapist to her ex-husband presumably also is involved here.

Assn. 4 (Associations about World War I, and lack of discussion about it in her childhood family): The contiguity of these associations with nostalgia for her husband suggests that her longing was for a mother's love and forgiveness, because, as I reminded her, World War I was the period when her mother was alive. Related dynamic reasoning suggests that the guilt for which she attempted to atone by means of the masochistic-erotic mechanism was probably guilt toward her mother. The memory that her family did not discuss World War I may include a defensive projection to her family of her own avoidance (repression) of guilt toward her mother.

Assn. 5 (Dream of the night before): The lack of associations to this dream makes the following formulation speculative:

(a) (Walking along a highway): A possibly condensed symbol of both childhood development and the therapeutic process.

(b) (Pushing a little carriage with a kitten in it): The kitten may represent her fantasied, guilt-laden, incestuous baby from father (therapist in the present). The word "mother" also appears in this material, that is, the carriage was "like those in *Mother* Goose books," which may suggest some ambiguity about whether the baby and carriage were really hers or whether they were her mother's.

(c) ("Someone" said the road ahead was difficult and that she should turn back, but she went on): A warning to herself in the dream, possibly condensing (1) an adaptive component from the protective part of her superego, and (2) a defensive avoidance mechanism (cf. her threats of quitting therapy).

(d) (A curve in the road ahead): A possible symbol of potentially dangerous changes ahead.

(e) (Bunch of men working on the side of the road in the mud): Might refer to putting men (therapist/father) to one side, defensively minimizing their importance. It may also depreciate them by putting them in the mud (cf. therapist deals with dirty things like his recent interpretation, and father was a coal miner). Since the dynamic context at this time involves a defensive anal regression, the mud may also represent her feces—for example, a hostile fantasy of defecating on the men.

(f) (She pushes the carriage through the mud and weaves among the men): She has gone to the side of the road where the men and the mud are. Why? To show off her baby? Moving closer to therapist and "getting my feet wet (muddy)" in the therapeutic process could suggest an adaptive move; but weaving in and out, back and forth, seems more defensively ambivalent, uncommitted, avoidant.

(g) (Passes close to the workman with a jackhammer and is frightened by its pounding and noise): Since the dynamic context at the time of this session is predominantly anal, the more common phallic symbolism of a jackhammer with its powerful up and down motion may not apply here. Functional interpretation of the jackhammer suggests a different meaning, namely, its function of breaking through resistant surface layers to expose what lies beneath (cf. the analogic similarity to interpretations). If the workman with the jackhammer represents me and my "interpretive instrument," what is she afraid of? Perhaps of what she desires, that is, her masochistic-erotic wish for me to "pound" her repeatedly with jarring interpretations like the recent one, both to relieve guilt and also to obtain erotic pleasure.

(h) ("Somehow she got by" the man with the jackhammer): "Got by" him could mean that she evaded the therapist's interpretation and its implications, possibly using it to gratify rather than understand and modify her masochistic-erotic defense.

(i) (The highway seemed familiar; she had been that way before): May indicate that she is repeating her old pathogenic developmental pattern, rather than remembering, understanding, and modifying it through insight. (Posttherapeutic study of this patient's entire therapeutic process revealed that insight into her masochistic-erotic character defense developed very slowly, as one would expect, in association with a very gradual and prolonged working through process.)

Assn. 6 (Puzzled that she didn't reach a destination in the dream): Another possible clue that she may be repeating an old pattern rather than reaching the therapeutic goals of understanding and change.

Assn. 7: (Happy as she left the session): My failure to recognize and interpret her defensive use of the previous interpretation (i.e., her using it to gratify rather than understand and modify her masochistic-erotic pattern) let her off easy, so to speak. Hence she leaves the session relieved and happy that she "got by" the therapist and his interpretation without having to recognize the masochistic-erotic pattern, face her inner guilt, and give up the erotic gratification from masochistic fantasies.

Role of Dynamic Reasoning in the Interpretive Process

Understanding latent conflicts necessitates dynamic reasoning, an example of which follows: If Ms. White had taken the interpretation of her masochism seriously and had begun to recognize that she obtained erotic pleasure from her fantasy of being forced ("pushed"), that beginning insight would have detracted not only from the pleasure but also from the atoning, guilt-relieving capability of her masochistic defense, bringing her closer to facing and feeling the pain of her guilt. Why would it affect the guilt-relieving function of her masochism? Because in order to relieve guilt an atonement mechanism must produce suffering, not just pleasure. For the patient to maintain her masochistic-erotic defense, therefore, an isolation defense must have been operative, preventing her from recognizing that her self-imposed suffering also served as a source of pleasure. In depth psychological treatments, patients struggle with similar such conflicts whenever an interpretation exposes and thus begins to weaken an important defense.

The Problem of Confirmation Bias

At first glance, session 147 seems to provide a number of good clues or leads to a plausible interpretation, but on closer study it illustrates how difficult clinical interpretation can be. At the time of this session I recognized that the patient was still reponding to my interpretation of her masochistic-erotic pattern, but I was overly impressed with what I took to be indications of adaptive, in contrast to defensive, reactions early in the session, and missed the later clues (especially in the second dream) that she might be using the interpretation defensively to gratify or "get by" its implications rather than understand and modify the neurotic pattern. My error in this instance illustrates the ever-present problem of confirmation bias, a universal and apparently ineradicable tendency in human beings to overvalue their own beliefs and to resist giving up a favored viewpoint (see Eagle 1980, Rubovits-Seitz 1998, Tweney et al. 1981).

In clinical interpretation, confirmation bias often takes the form of seeking information that supports a particular construction while ignoring potentially disconfirmatory data. Thus clinicians may focus on what they want and expect to find (Abraham 1986)—as I did in my persistent emphasis on adaptive rather than defensive aspects of her associations. In addition, our communications to patients sometimes foster confirmatory responses (Wilson Dallas and Baron 1985). The ambiguity of clinical data facilitates such hypothesis-confirming responses between therapist and patient.

There are two principal methods of combatting confirmation bias: (1) use of multiple hypotheses to reduce the interpreter's commitment to a single, favored hypothesis (Diesing 1985a, Platt 1964); and (2) testing hypotheses by disconfirmation rather than by confirmatory methods (Popper 1963). In actual practice, however, neither multiple hypotheses nor use of disconfirmation adequately controls confirmation bias (Holt 1988, Mynatt et al. 1977, Tweney et al. 1981).

Since therapists must formulate interpretations fairly rapidly and on the basis of incomplete information (e.g., without knowledge of future developments in the case), there is no known way of preventing errors produced by cognitive limitations and human biases (Turk and Salovey 1988). One way of reducing and correcting such errors, however, is for therapists to recognize, accept, and be on the lookout at all times for the possibility that confirmation bias may be distorting their clinical judgments and interpretive reasoning.

CHAPTER SEVENTEEN

Interpretation of Session 186

SESSIONS 148 TO 185 (SUMMARY)

When the second major dependent and anal regressions had run their course, indications of increasing independence and insight began to appear, for example: (1) Ms. White became able to use automatic elevators, about which she had always been phobic; (2) she took steps to seek a higher degree in her profession; (3) she began to take more initiative in her therapy, attempting to interpret and understand her own free associations, fantasies, and dreams; (4) she had a dream during this period in which she was flying a plane herself, with an instructor merely monitoring her performance; and (5) she recognized spontaneously that her earlier fear of becoming inseparably dependent on me had been based on a hidden wish for permanent dependence.

Session 186 occurred following the Christmas holidays, during which I was away for a week. She did not show up for her first postholiday appointment.

SESSION 186 (EIGHTH INTERPRETIVE EXERCISE)

She apologized for missing the previous session. The weather was bad and she had car trouble. Considerable blocking today, which frustrated her. She blurted out that she had a lot of things she wanted to talk about, but as usual when she gets here she can't relax and say them. [Any idea why?] She answered that it's like a *dream* she had:

> I was here talking to you. I kept saying the same thing over and over, something about "2." You got bored and irritated with me and said: "Can't you at least make it 3?" Your secretary came in at that point and you went out with her. Then I seemed to be out of the room, too. When I came back there was a family here, all talking at once, a man and his wife and two children. The man was holding the youngest child in his arms.

Her associations emphasized that the family in the latter part of the dream were talking very freely and spontaneously, unlike she does here. She wishes she could be that spontaneous in her therapy. [What about the numbers 2 and 3?] "Two's company, three's a crowd," but she doesn't know what that could mean. [The dream started with just the two of us; then my secretary came in, making it 3; and it ended up being a crowd.] She protested quickly that she didn't want me all to herself; she was aware of no such feelings. It would be unreasonable for her to expect an exclusive relationship with me. [If you had such feelings, would you say so?] "Absolutely not! Maybe such feelings are there, but if so I can see no advantage in talking about it." [But isn't therapy a "talking cure"?] She answered angrily: "I don't believe that!" She continued to protest how useless it would be to let herself feel "that way" about me. [Because it would be frustrating?] "Yes, that is *exactly* how I feel! Why should I let myself in for that?" She rushed on about how during the recent Christmas holidays she wouldn't let herself feel it made any difference to her whether I was here or not.

COMMENTARY

Author's Interpretation (to Himself) of Session 186 (Which Corresponded Well with the Posttherapeutically Derived Formulation)

I based my interpretation on the following clues in session 186:

> *Clue 1:* The dynamic context in which session 186 occurred, a postregressive, progressive phase of the therapeutic process in

which the patient showed increasing independence and insight, alerted me to the possibility that unresolved triadic (oedipal) conflicts might become reactivated.

Clue 2: Dream content emphasizing the numbers 2 and 3, followed by my secretary intruding into the session, also suggested that a shift from dyadic to triadic conflicts may have been occurring.

Clue 3: A parallel (similarity) between missing her previous appointment and being blocked in the present session. Both suggested an intensification of resistance against therapeutic contact and communication by an avoidance mechanism.

Clue 4: A parallel between patient missing her previous appointment, and her reference (at the end of this session) to my being away during the Christmas holidays. This parallel raises the question whether she may have missed her previous appointment (unconsciously) as retaliation for my absence at Christmastime.

Clue 5: The contrast between her difficulty talking in the present session, and the spontaneity of the family in the dream: This clue does not necessarily indicate that her main problem (thematic conflict) at this time is that of communicating freely, because she is conscious of that problem, and its motivation is probably defensive. The contrast probably alludes to some other source of envy toward the family—perhaps their loving (including physical) contact and closeness to each other.

Clue 6: Vigorous protest that she does not want me all to herself, the intensity of which suggests the opposite.

Clue 7: The contrast between what she seems to want (an exclusive relationship with me), and how little she allows herself to have in the dream. The contrast suggests not only disguise but also atonement for guilt by a self-abnegating defense.

Putting these various clues together suggested the following interpretive formulation of session 186:

Precipitant: It is often useful to distinguish between a more general precipitating *situation*, such as the dynamic context in which a session occurs, and a more discrete and specific precipitating *event*.

The precipitating situation of session 186 appeared to be her recent progressive changes emotionally, which may have reactivated triadic, romantic-erotic feelings toward me. The precipitating event appeared to be my having canceled some of her sessions during the Christmas holidays.

Thematic conflict: Hostility toward therapist and jealous envy of his wife and family, for frustrating her romantic-erotic (oedipal) feelings toward him, *versus* guilt.

Checking This Formulation Against All of the Current Data

Assn. 1 (Apologizes and makes excuses for missing previous session): The apology is probably a reaction formation, and the excuses rationalizations to relieve guilt about her spiteful, retaliative motive for missing the session.

Assn. 2 (Blocking): Blocking in this session also appears to be a disguised, spiteful retaliation against therapist: "You didn't talk to me during the holidays, so I won't talk to you now!" (Note that the blocking frustrates her—illustrating the tendency for defenses to create problems and conflicts of their own—which results in shifts from one defense to another and produces a sequential *series* of defenses against the thematic conflict in each therapy session.)

Assn. 3 (The dream):

(a) (Talking to therapist): At the beginning of the dream she has me to herself. Talking in this dream is a guilt-free substitute for the romantic-erotic contact with me that she craves (see also [h] below).

(b) (Saying the same thing, something about "2," over and over): Disguised expression of her concealed wish for endlessly continued (cf. her expression "over and over") dyadic (cf. the number "2") contact with me.

(c) (Therapist bored and irritated with her): Projection of her own boredom and anger at therapist for his absence during the holidays. (*Note:* Up to this point in the dream, her frustrated romantic feelings and anger—the posited primary or "disturbing" motive of the thematic conflict—have dominated the dream imagery. Beginning with the next dream image, however, the secondary or "reactive" motive of the thematic conflict—namely, guilt—emerges.)

(d) (Therapist says, "Can't you at least make it 3?"): Projection to me of her own superego chiding her for her unwillingness to share me with others. The number 3 also may symbolize her current triadic transference to therapist and his wife.

(e) (Therapist's secretary comes in): Displacement from my wife to secretary; and projection to secretary of her own wish to intrude on my relationship with my wife. Guilt about the intrusively competitive feelings toward me and my wife gives rise to a self-abnegating defense at this point.

(f) (Therapist "went out with her"): A possible double meaning here: manifestly means "went out of the room with the secretary"; but colloquially could mean "dated her." Thus her own guilt-laden wish to "go out with" me, a married man, is projected to the secretary.

(g) (Patient was then out of the room, too): May imply following therapist and his secretary (wife), possibly to spy on us and see what we do together—a voyeuristic component of her romantic-erotic interest in me and jealous envy of my wife.

(h) (Returns to find family in office, talking freely and spontaneously): At this point not only my wife but my whole family have replaced her in my office, where she usually has me to herself. As in (a) above, the issue of talking is a guilt-free substitute for the loving closeness, including baby-making, which she desires for herself and for which she feels hostile-envy toward me and my family.

(i) (The youngest child was in the man's arms): Possibly a dependent defense, disguising and substituting for her wish to be in my arms romantically and erotically. Since guilt does not allow her even the fantasy of being therapist's lover, she would rather be a child-in-arms to him than nothing.

Assn. 4 (Wishes she could be that spontaneous): Substitutes a wish to be able to talk freely for what she really wants—freedom from the guilt that prevents her from being openly, spontaneously romantic and erotic with me.

Assn. 5 ("Two's company, three's a crowd"): Further indication of her wish to have me all to herself, and her resentment at having to share me with my wife and family.

Assn. 6 (Insists that she doesn't want therapist to herself): A defensive protest and disavowal.

Assn. 7 (Unreasonable to expect an exclusive relationship with me): A rationalization that attempts further to conceal her hidden wish for the very thing she disavows.

Assn. 8 (Sees no advantage in talking about it even if she had such feelings): Another rationalization, which in this case also attempts to justify her ignoring the therapeutic contract.

Assn. 9 (When I remind her indirectly of the therapeutic contract, she blurts out, "I don't believe that!"): An aggressive protest and disavowal, to ward off guilt about both the thematic wish to have me to herself, and also guilt about breaking the therapeutic contract.

Assn. 10 (It would be "useless" to let herself feel "that way" toward me): Another rationalization and also a generalization. (Note the series of rationalizations and their aggressively protesting tone, which suggests that the frustrated romantic-erotic feelings and anger toward me are getting closer to the surface and require increasingly intense defensive efforts to keep them repressed.)

Assn. 11 (Agrees emphatically that it would be too frustrating to admit such feelings to herself): Little by little, my gently confronting series of interventions has shown that she is trying very hard to protect herself from feeling romantic frustration.

Assn. 12 (During the Christmas holidays she "wouldn't let myself feel" that it mattered whether she saw me or not): Her wording comes very close to admitting that the romantic feelings are there but that she wards them off. Her mention for the first time of the Christmas holidays is further evidence that the frustrated romantic-erotic feelings are emerging. (I have been careful not to insist that she experience or admit the romantic-erotic feelings, because if I did she might then project to me that I was "seducing" or "pushing" her to feel romantically toward me.)

A Dynamic Question

The question arises: Will her currently emerging romantic-erotic-triadic feelings toward me and my family continue to increase in the appointments that follow? Or are the oedipal conflicts that underlie these transferences still too intense and thus may precipitate another regressive flight? Is there any way to predict what will happen next?

The answer is, not really. Predicting depth psychological events is not very reliable, due to the complex psychodynamic and psychoeconomic factors that are involved but not yet known to the clinician. Usually all we can do is wait and see what happens.

CHAPTER EIGHTEEN

Reconstruction of a Screen Memory in Session 206

SESSIONS 187 TO 205 (SUMMARY)

Soon after the onset of her third major oedipal transference, a depressive mood set in accompanied by self-recriminations about both her premarital abortion and the defective child she had while married. As in previous dynamic cycles, her persistent guilt about those events was overdetermined by transferences of oedipal guilt based on her wish for an incestuous child from her father (transferred to me in the present). A craving for sweets returned, a harbinger of her third dependent regression.

SESSION 206
(NINTH INTERPRETIVE EXERCISE)

She has begun to notice recently that she tends to think about the future instead of the present. She procrastinates, putting off anything she fears, dreads, or doesn't like. She gives examples from her work and therapy. She has decided that it is too costly to do that—it makes matters worse. [The most recent example is your decision to lie down during the sessions, but then putting it off again.] She exclaimed desperately that she becomes too frightened, which blocks her. [Yes, you postpone it to avoid the anxiety. But what if you would face the anxiety and feel it, rather than fleeing from it?] Instead of answering this question she wondered where the procrastination pattern came from in her life. She recalled a "strangely vivid memory" from childhood:

There were some daffodils at the corner of the house. In the green stuff growing there I found some Easter eggs. My next younger sister opened one of the eggs and found a baby chick inside. It was dead. My sister got a knife and cut up the baby chick, hacked it to pieces. I was horrified but she seemed to enjoy it.

She felt puzzled about the clarity and isolated quality of the memory. It seemed unrelated to anything else that she could recall from chilhood. She must have been four or five years old when that incident occurred. [The age when your baby sister was born and your mother died.] Tears came to her eyes, and she began to cry. She said through her tears that she should be able to remember more about those years, but she can't even remember her mother or the baby. How can it be important if she can't even remember it? [You haven't let yourself remember it *because* it was so important.] Her associations turned to the abortion, and how she has never been able to get over feeling guilty about it. She has tried to tell herself that she paid the price for that mistake by her daughter's death and her husband leaving her; but even that didn't stop the guilt. Every time she sees a baby she feels guilty about the abortion. She even wishes people knew about it and criticized her for it, because then maybe she would feel she had been punished enough and wouldn't have to feel so guilty any more. She keeps looking for ways to relieve the guilt. She is afraid to face the full force of the guilt because she doesn't think she could stand it. [You are facing it gradually. The guilt that you feel about it is accentuated by childhood guilt. (The remainder of my interpretation will be added later in this chapter).]

COMMENTARY

Author's Reconstruction of the Screen Memory in Session 206, (Which Corresponded Closely with the Posttherapeutically Derived Formulation)

I based my reconstruction of the screen memory on the following clues in session 206:

Clue 1: The dynamic context in which session 206 occurred was another dependent regression, which developed suddenly (hence defensively) as a regressive flight from oedipal conflict.

Clue 2: The dependent regression did not appear to be quite as deep this time; for example, the imagery of her screen memory was triadic rather than dyadic (i.e., included her sisters). During this dynamic cycle she regressed defensively from a triadic oedipal conflict to a triadic pregenital dependency.

Clue 3: The parallel between her age at the time of the screen memory, and her age at the time of her mother's death, when her youngest sister was born.

Clue 4: Her tearful response to my interpretation (of clue 3) suggests that the posited parallel was probably correct (cf. Bucci's [1985, 1988] proposal that verbal and nonverbal information is encoded in different symbolic forms and in separate systems. She postulates further that the directness and strength of interpretive linkages with nonverbal representations, such as expressing or reporting emotions in the therapy session, are indicators that an interpretation has made connection with the nonverbal system and therefore is probably accurate).

Clue 5: A contiguity of associations: Tearfulness about the death of her mother when her youngest sister was born, juxtaposed with associations about painfully persistent guilt feelings related to her abortion. The contiguity suggests that guilt feelings associated originally with ambivalence toward her mother (for her pregnancy with her baby sister) were reactivated by and transferred to Ms. White's later abortion experience.

Putting these clues together led to the following tentative reconstruction of the screen memory in session 206:

Precipitant (of the screen memory): Her mother's pregnancy with her youngest sibling during the patient's oedipal period of development.

Genetic conflict: Both oral and phallic sources of sadistic feelings toward her mother and mother's pregnancy *versus* guilt.

Checking This Formulation Against All of the Current Data

Assn. 1 (Daffodils and "green stuff" at the corner of the house): It is not entirely clear whether the daffodils were blooming or consisted only of "green stuff," that is, the leaves of the plants. Although daffodils bloom at around Easter other contents of the screen memory (e.g., the theme of death) might suggest that they were not in bloom. Since both house and earth often symbolize mother (a house because it shelters, and earth because of its fertility), the "green stuff at the corner of the house" may represent a part of her mother's body. The nest-like character of the plants in which the eggs were found suggest either womb or genital symbolism, or both.

Assn. 2 (Easter eggs): Womb and pregnancy symbols, that is, her mother's pregnancy with patient's youngest sister (the latter suggested by patient's age at the time of the screen memory, and by the fact that her next younger sister was with her during the event). Often Easter eggs are eaten by children, which suggests an oral-aggressive, cannibalistic fantasy toward her mother's pregnancy. Recalling and reporting the screen memory during a phase of triadic dependent regression supports the oral-aggressive implication of Easter eggs. Easter also connotes a return from the grave, resurrection, or rebirth—possibly a guilt- and dependency-motivated restitutive fantasy of undoing her mother's death.

Assn. 3 (Next younger sister opens an egg and finds a dead baby chick inside): To avoid guilt, her own sadistic fantasy of breaking into her mother's body and killing the unborn child is projected to her next younger sister.

Assn. 4 (Sister hacks the baby chick to pieces with a knife): Despite the frequent phallic symbolism of a knife, the present dynamic context of frustrated dependence suggests that the knife may symbolize a tooth (cf. Kipling's *Jungle Books* in which Mowgli called his knife his "tooth"). It is also possible, however, that the sadistic feelings toward her mother included phallic-oedipal as well as oral components—suggested, for example, by (a) her developmental stage at the time of the screen memory, (b) her repeated therapeutic transferences of a guilt-laden wish for an oedipal child from her father, and (c) the phallic features of the knife. Thus I concluded tentatively that the fantasied sadistic attack on her mother and her mother's pregnancy probably included both oral- and phallic-oedipal elements.

Assn. 5 (Patient was horrified, but sister enjoyed it): Again she avoids guilt about her fantasied oral- and phallic-oedipal sadistic attack on her mother's pregnancy by projecting the hostile-destructive feelings to her next younger sister. Patient's saying that she was "horrified by what sister did" can be understood as a projection of feeling horrified at herself for having such fantasies.

Communication of My Interpretive Reconstruction to the Patient

[Your memories of the Easter egg incident provide clues to an important source of childhood guilt that, years later, intensified your guilt about the abortion. Vivid, often isolated childhood memories of that kind can be interpreted somewhat like dreams. The Easter egg memories probably symbolize your mother's pregnancy with your baby sister, your resentment of her pregnancy, and an angry wish to break into her body and destroy the child. Feelings and fantasies of that kind toward parents and siblings make children feel very guilty. Your mother's death at a time when you were having such angry feelings toward her would produce an unbearable amount of guilt that would have to be repressed, where it would remain hidden until an experience such as your abortion or the death of your daughter, could stir it all up again.]

As indicated previously, one usually tries to keep interpretations brief and to the point. But there is a type of interpretive reconstruction, sometimes called a "total interpretation," in which the therapist attempts to bring together and explain a number of related childhood events, conflicts, defenses, and subsequent transferences to adult relationships and experiences, including transferences to the therapist. The preceding interpretive reconstruction is an example of a total interpretation. Reconstructions of this kind are usually not possible until later phases of the therapeutic process, when repeated and extensive working through of conflicts and defenses on the level of transferences results in increasing recall by patients of previously repressed childhood experiences. Freud (1937b) described an example of a similar reconstruction in his "Constructions in Analysis."

CHAPTER NINETEEN

A Prediction Based on Session 220

SESSIONS 207 TO 219 (SUMMARY)

Following the Easter eggs screen memory, Ms. White developed (for the first time) an aunt transference to me. She felt unable to talk freely for fear I would be critical, shocked, judging, and displeased (cf. the earlier "bag of bones" dream in which her aunts were shocked at what she disclosed to me). Eventually she began to recognize that, like her aunts, she herself attempted to conceal disturbing thoughts, especially feelings of shame. In this context her conflict about lying down surfaced again. A dream expressed fear that if she lay down she would humiliate herself by exposing her desires for erotic contact with me. She became increasingly resistant to free association, exclaiming angrily, "I'm not going to tell anybody everything I think or everything I feel!" Colitis with severe constipation set in again, marking the onset of her third major anal regression. As before she tried to provoke me into pushing and forcing her to lie down and tell her most painfully humiliating fantasies and feelings. When that failed she overcontrolled her violent, angry feelings toward me.

SESSION 220 (TENTH INTERPRETIVE EXERCISE)

She started cheerfully, saying that she had decided to stop complaining and forget her worries. Very soon, however, her tone became gloomy and she began obsessing about whether to continue her treatment. She recalled a dream from the night before:

> You were teaching a class, demonstrating patients to students. You pointed to a potentially violent, out-of-control man and said: "This person is insane, but can be helped." Then you pointed to me and said: "Nothing can be done with this person; there is nothing in her to work with."

Her spontaneous associations emphasized how true the dream was; the core of her personality is empty. That is the main reason she can't lie down, because she knows that is what I would find. If she were to lie down, I would expect her to be more spontaneous and to remember more about her childhood, but she would be unable to do so. As long as she doesn't lie down, she doesn't risk that happening. [The dream suggests the opposite, that what you fear is insanity—losing control of too much inner feeling, including violent feelings.] She looked startled, but nodded quickly. Then she choked up and began to cry. She believes she must have transmitted some kind of mental defect to her daughter that made her the way she was. [No, childhood guilt makes you punish yourself with thoughts like that.] She asked abruptly whether there was danger of insanity from this kind of therapy? [It is a common fear in patients, especially when very early and disturbing childhood feelings begin to emerge. Her past history suggests, however, that she has been through some very disturbing experiences in her life and didn't break down from it.] She began to lighten up at that point. Recently she has had the thought that maybe her aunts weren't just burdened by having three little girls to raise; maybe it even added something to their lives. Her feeling that her aunts didn't want them was probably because she didn't really want them. [Good insight!, I commented.]

COMMENTARY

Author's Prediction (Which Corresponded with What Occurred in Session 221)

I based my prediction on the following set of clues in session 220:

Clue 1: The dynamic context in which session 220 occurred involved a defensive anal regression, with emphasis on conflicts about control and masochism. As before, these conflicts were transferred to the issue of lying down during her sessions.

Clue 2: A parallel: at the time of session 220 she was overcontrolling her violent, angry feelings toward me. Her dream in session 220 included a patient with potentially violent, out-of-control feelings. The parallel suggested that the potentially violent, insane person in the dream was herself.

Clue 3: Her response to my intervention (that she feared loss of control and insanity) appeared to support the interpretation, and was followed by relief of anxiety about losing control of her emotions.

Clue 4: The most suggestive clue was the dream image of my saying that the potentially insane patient could be helped. With that statement she seemed to be telling herself (projected to me in the dream) that in order to be helped psychologically she must give up some of her rigid controls, even if she risked acting crazy in the process. That struck me as a distinct turning point in her therapy, and the fact that it occurred in a dream made it seem all the more cogent (i.e., a deeper and emotionally more committed insight, in contrast to a more superficial, intellectual decision).

Putting these several clues together, I made the following tentative prediction (to myself, not to the patient): very soon, possibly in the next session, Ms. White will give up some of her rigid controls during therapy by lying down, associating more freely, and participating more spontaneously in the therapeutic process.

SESSION 221 (OUTCOME OF THE PREDICTION)

She started session 221 by saying, "I'm going to make the effort today," and then she lay down on the couch. She was moderately tense and anxious at first, but by the end of the session appeared to have relaxed considerably. She was able to be spontaneously reflective about the reasons for her anxiety and tension. Her therapy moved along more rapidly after this, and was completed within seventy-five more sessions.

There is a saying in psychoanalysis and dynamic psychotherapy that when a patient becomes able to free associate really well, the treatment is over. In Ms. White's case, when she was finally able to relax her rigid controls, lie down to free associate, and participate spontaneously in the therapeutic process, the end of her therapy was in sight (pun intended).

CHAPTER TWENTY

Interpretation of Session 250

SESSIONS 222 TO 244 (SUMMARY)

Her first dream after lying down was about searching for something from her childhood, something frightening, but in spite of being afraid she went on searching and found what she was looking for. The fourth major oedipal transference set in at this point. She described becoming very upset about dropping an egg and breaking its shell. [I commented that she might be afraid that her own protective shell would be broken.] She became panicky and started to leave in the middle of the session, but changed her mind and stayed. What surfaced following this incident was increasing anxiety about erotic feelings toward me. She was afraid the feelings might become so intense that she would do something impulsive that would lead to serious trouble with my wife. Frustration of the erotic feelings produced anger at me, which led to recall of bitterness toward her father for remarrying, for taking her stepmother's side in altercations between her stepmother and herself, and for sending the children to live with their aunts. She expressed painful feelings of humiliation that her father seemed not to love or even to want her. As the anger and humiliation subsided, tearful sadness welled up in her. She recalled feelings of loss when her father remarried, and when she left her childhood home to live with her aunts. Following these developments, she began a session with the initial association: "I can almost see the beginning of the end of a big project that I've been working on in grad school" (cf. the possible allusion to therapy). She dreamed: "My father died. I didn't want to go to his funeral. But then I thought you would ask me why I didn't want to go, so I went." Associations to the dream included still more sadness and tears about how much she missed her father after leaving her family home to live with her aunts.

SESSIONS 245 TO 249 (SUMMARY)

The fourth major dependent transference set in. This was a brief recurrence of feeling overly dependent on me, during which she dreamed that a man told her she had always been "too fat." (In reality she was slender; latent oral-dependent wishes appeared to have distorted her self-image during the dependent transference.)

SESSION 250
(ELEVENTH INTERPRETIVE EXERCISE)

She started by saying accusingly, "I thought this kind of treatment was supposed to make you happier. Well, it doesn't work that way with me!" Colitis symptoms had returned. She had a terrible day yesterday, felt she was going to pieces; she was afraid she might burst out crying and not be able to stop for a week. "If therapy does that to you, I can't take it—it's too much for me!" [We must have opened up some unusually strong and important feelings last time.] She started to weep, then checked herself, saying that she doesn't let herself cry even though she would probably feel better if she went ahead and cried. Her husband was the only person with whom she could allow herself to cry. He would "put up with it." [You feel that your crying is hard on whomever you're with?] "Of course! Isn't it?" [I think it's hardest on you.] She let out a long sigh, paused, then spoke in a different, more reflective tone: "There is something about my daughter, or about children and babies, that stays on my mind. I had a series of dreams about babies":

Dream 1: "The first dream was about my mother. I couldn't see her very clearly. She was sort of vague. But she seemed to be putting something around my neck. She said it was very important, that she had something she wanted to give me."

Dream 2: "Then I had another dream of going down the street where I saw a crowd of people gathered, the way they do when something has happened. A little child was lying in the street, dressed in a blue coat and bonnet. Whoever had run over her seemed to have left."

Dream 3: "Then I dreamed about a place that was littered with trash and garbage. It was very messy and dirty. There was a baby girl there who had gash marks in her neck."

Dream 4: "The last dream was about going to a telephone booth to call someone—I don't know who. I told the person on the phone that I was going to the cemetery to put some flowers on the grave—I guess my daughter's grave."

Spontaneous associations to the dreams were about what her mother had put around her neck. It was a bib or something that her mother had picked out especially for her and wanted her to have. "It didn't seem so important to me in the dream, but it was to my mother." The child who was run over reminded her of three things: her abortion, her daughter who died, and the first child of her father's second marriage. The latter child was a boy. It was a girl in the dream, but the blue color of the coat suggested a boy to her. She was unable to remember her stepbrother's birth, and doesn't know whether she was bothered by it or not. "But nowadays I can't believe I was as unconcerned about such things as I always thought I was." [The content of the dream suggests one of the feelings you may have had about it.] She was surprised: "You mean the fact that he was dead? Well, uh, I suppose I could have resented him. My father was very proud of finally getting a son." She shifted abruptly and spoke sharply about how much she resented her father's new wife. Her stepmother had outbursts of temper: "She was like a *volcano!* She would *erupt* with anger!" [My interpretation to the patient will be added later.]

COMMENTARY

Author's Formulation of Session 250 (Which Corresponded Well with the Posttherapeutically Derived Interpretation)

I based my interpretation on the following set of clues in session 250:

> *Clue 1:* The dynamic context in which session 250 occurred was the beginning of another defensive anal regression (the return of her colitis). In her several previous phases of anal regression, destructive aggression, masochistic defenses, and fear of losing control of her feelings had predominated. I noted regarding the latter feature that early in session 250 she mentioned fear of being unable to stop crying; and soon after that she started to cry but quickly controlled it.
>
> *Clue 2:* A parallel between the dynamic anal context and dream 3 about a messy, dirty place littered with trash and garbage—all anal symbols.
>
> *Clue 3:* A parallel between the regressive anal context and the functional symbolism of a child's bib (in dream I), that is, protection (cf. defense) against an infant's messiness.
>
> *Clue 4:* A parallel between her association about the bib being important to her mother but not to herself, and material from previous anal regressions, namely, her aunts had told her that her mother was fastidious and kept the house and children very neat and clean.
>
> *Clue 5:* Parallels in dreams 2, 3, and 4 about children who were severely injured, dead, or gotten rid of (the latter suggested in dream 3 by the "place littered with trash and garbage"—perhaps symbolically a garbage dump or toilet).
>
> *Clue 6:* Her reference to an "erupting volcano": a possible symbol of expulsively destructive anal aggression.

Putting these various clues together, I arrived at the following tentative construction:

Precipitant: The preceding phase of oral regression was cut short by the development of secondary conflict about feeling overly dependent on me (cf. the dream of being told that she was "too fat"). The secondary conflict regarding dependent wishes produced a defensive shift to anal regression.

Thematic conflict: Anal sadistic feelings, primarily toward (a) her mother (for having more children, and possibly also for over-zealous cleanliness training—demands for which may have increased after her next younger sibling was born); (b) toward her younger siblings, including step-siblings; and (c) toward her defective daughter; *versus* guilt.

Checking This Formulation Against All of the Current Data

Assn. 1 (Accusatory initial association that treatment was making her feel worse instead of better): Projection of guilt to me from her own sadistic feelings of wanting to make her mother and siblings suffer.

Assn. 2 (Afraid she would not be able to stop crying): Substitution of uncontrolled weeping for fear that she might not be able to control the burgeoning sadistic feelings.

Assn. 3 (Starts to weep, but quickly controls it): A "testing enactment" of her control mechanism. Here she is testing herself. In the next two associations she tests my reactions and attitude.

Assn. 4 (No one but her husband would "put up with" her crying): She implied, [and I interpreted], that she considered her crying and other intense emotions difficult for people to take. A compound mechanism appears to be involved here: (a) a substitution of weeping for sadistic aggression; (b) a rationalization to bolster her control of aggression; and (c) a testing enactment, this time to test my reaction.

Assn. 5 (Change in her tone following my comment that the crying is hardest on her): I seem to have passed her test; that is, she has satisfied herself that I will understand rather than criticize and thus intensify her guilt. (See Weiss and Sampson [1986], who theorize that much of the therapeutic process consists of the patient's unconscious attempts to disconfirm inner pathogenic beliefs by testing them in relation to the therapist.)

Assn. 6 (The series of dreams): There are two notable features of these dreams: (a) Although still thinly disguised, the patient's anal aggression now emerges more directly than it did during previous such regressive phases. Sadistic feelings were defended against formerly by her masochistic mechanisms. At this point in her treatment, guilt about the anal sadism appears to have been reduced sufficiently that self-punitive defenses are less necessary. (b) Much of the sadistic aggression is directed toward her mother, whom she blamed for the birth of her hated siblings. But in the present dreams, to protect her relationship with her mother, sadistic feelings are displaced from mother to her much-less-valued siblings. (Displacements of this kind are common: siblings are often the scapegoats for children's ambivalence toward parents.)

Dream 1 (Mother and the bib): Employing the heuristic of functional symbolism, the purpose of a bib is to protect against infantile messiness; thus the bib may represent her defenses against anal (and oral?) erotic and sadistic impulses—defenses that were probably learned by internalizing her mother's fastidiousness. In the context of her current anal regression it would not be surprising for her dream series to begin with defenses against anal fantasies. As a dream series proceeds, however, the warded off impulses tend to emerge more clearly in later dreams of the series. Dream series, individual therapy sessions, and the therapeutic process as a whole have in common a tendency for underlying conflicts to become more evident (less disguised) in later material. For that reason it is sometimes easier to "read" clinical material backward, as in the RC approach.

It should be mentioned also that the heuristic of functional symbolism is not the only possible approach to understanding the ambiguous imagery of the mother and bib. Other forms of symbolism may be involved: for example, putting something around the neck is sometimes a symbol of guilt (cf. the ancient mariner), and the word "bib" might disguise the somewhat similar sounding word, "babe." Putting these two possibilities together might allude to her guilt about destructive feelings toward babies (younger siblings, cf. the later dreams in this series).

Dream 2 (The child run over in the street): Her associations suggest that this image in the dream condenses children from both her original family and step-family. Sadistic aggression toward siblings is beginning to emerge more clearly at this point, despite her defensive projection of the aggression to "whoever had run over the child."

Dream 3 (Baby girl with gashes in her neck, in a place littered with trash and garbage): The anal quality of the sadism becomes even more evident in this imagery. The placement of the baby girl in such a "messy, dirty place" suggests an anal riddance fantasy toward a younger sibling—possibly dumping her in the toilet or garbage can. The suggestive parallel between the image in dream 1 of a bib around patient's neck and the gashes in the baby girl's neck in dream 3 is not explained by the present formulation, and hence must be considered a partial discrepancy.

Dream 4 (Talking to someone on the telephone, and putting flowers on the child's grave): To conceal her sadistic satisfaction and guilt about the child's death, she pictures herself as grieving and caring—a reaction formation. The image of talking on the phone to someone often represents talking to the analyst—the similarity often being that in both cases the person talked to is not seen.

The preceding interpretations of defenses also account for the associations following the dreams, with the exception of:

Assn. 7 (Resentment toward stepmother): Hostility toward her mother finally begins to emerge, but is displaced (as in fairy tales) to the "wicked stepmother."

Assn. 8 (Stepmother's temper): Displaced again from mother to stepmother, but also a projection of what she secretly wished but feared to do, namely, to let her own sadistic anal aggression erupt like a volcano, burying her mother and siblings in a pile of feces.

My Interpretation to the Patient

When Ms. White said that her stepmother had intense outbursts of temper—that she was "like a volcano," and would "erupt with anger"— I commented: ["Which is what you would like to have done to your mother for having all those babies, and for making you stay so neat and clean.]

At first glance this interpretation may seem to bypass the patient's defensive projection to her stepmother and to aim directly, like an id interpretation, at her own underlying sadistic impulses. Looked at more closely, however, it will be seen that the defensive projection is included *implicitly* in the interpretation. My comment to the patient implied: "What you are saying about your stepmother's anger also applies to you—what you wish you could do." Sometimes interpretations to patients are best made obliquely rather than spelled out pedantically. For example, in their interpretations to patients therapists often employ metaphors and other figures of speech—using especially the patient's own metaphors, as in the present example of a volcano erupting.

CHAPTER TWENTY-ONE

Interpretation of Session 279

SESSIONS 251 TO 265 (SUMMARY)

The fourth (and final) anal regression extended for fifteen sessions, during which guilt-laden riddance feelings toward her defective daughter emerged against intense resistance, followed by recovery of further such feelings toward her siblings and step-siblings in childhood.

SESSIONS 266 TO 278 (SUMMARY)

The fifth (and final) oedipal transference included several weeks of struggling with humiliation and fear of being hurt by my increasing importance to her. She became very angry at me for encouraging her to talk about such feelings, and then leaving her high and dry by doing nothing to relieve or satisfy her feelings. She complained bitterly of repeated frustrations and humiliations of this kind throughout her relationship with me. In session 277 her fury peaked: She exclaimed angrily that I was "just like my husband"—leading her on to think that her love for him was safe, and then pulling the rug out from under her without even explaining what was wrong with her that made him prefer another woman. She then recalled with intense shame how she humiliated herself with her ex-husband by suggesting that he could keep the other woman if only he would stay with her. This led to memories of similar feelings when her father remarried, and to a persistent fantasy that she lacked sex appeal. (The kernel of genetic truth in the latter fantasy, of course, was that as a child she did not yet possess such appeal to grown men, especially to her own father.) In session 278 she blamed her problems and the failure of her marriage on masturbation, which she characterized self-critically as "a childish form of self-love."

SESSION 279
(TWELFTH INTERPRETIVE EXERCISE)

She began by asking, "Isn't your girl (secretary) here any more? I haven't seen her for some time." [I didn't answer.] She became sullen, then told a dream:

> I was at this place where there was to be a party. I was putting little flags in the ice cream servings, like a Fourth of July celebration. I wasn't doing it very well; the ice cream was melting before I could get it done. Then I was coming to see you. Your office was different, had big show windows on the front so people could see in, and people kept coming through the office. I had taken my clothes off and was just wrapped in a towel. I didn't think it was a good idea for the office to be the way it was. You held up a picture of me in a green bathing suit. I was furious that such a picture had been taken, especially without my knowing it. I left and went back to the party. It seemed I had to give the people there an explanation for having been to see you.

Her spontaneous associations to the dream were about envying a woman she knew who was independent and had many men friends and lots of fun. Green suggested jealousy to her. [Toward whom?] She beat around the bush, but eventually said she envied my secretary because she got to spend so much more time with me than she did. She then added with a tone of irritation that she suspected that my secretary probably peeked at her record. [My interpretation to the patient will be added later.]

COMMENTARY

Author's Interpretation of Session 279
(Which Corresponded Closely with
the Posttherapeutically Derived Formulation)

I based my interpretation on the following set of clues in session 279:

Clue 1: The dynamic context in which session 279 occurred was the final phase of oedipal transference in this patient's therapeutic process. During the several sessions immediately preceding session 279, Ms. White had expressed intense anger at me for the frustration and humiliation she experienced from feeling so strongly about me when I did not return her feelings.

Clue 2: Her initial association regarding the fantasy that my secretary (a stepmother figure) no longer worked for me. This suggests a riddance fantasy toward one of her two main oedipal rivals, the other being my wife, to whom she had a mother transference.

Clue 3: The dream and its associations: Her vacillation between going to a party versus seeing me suggests that she may be considering alternatives to the discipline and frustrations of therapy. Her envy of the independent woman, and the Independence Day theme of the party may imply that she herself would like to be more independent, have other loves than her frustrating, platonic relationship with me, so that she too could have "lots of fun." She could not give up her oedipal attachment to me, however, without one last exhibitionistic attempt to seduce me by taking off her clothes and showing off her body. Instead of succumbing to her physical charms in the dream, I made an interpretation (symbolically, in the form of showing her a picture of herself in a green bathing suit)—the interpretation suggesting that her attempt to seduce me was not out of love but jealousy, that is, wanting to get me away from another woman. Her initial reaction to the interpretation was defensive anger, but her associations to the dream suggested that she was jealous of my secretary, that she was intensely, voyeuristically curious about what went on between my secretary and me, as she had been as a child toward her father and stepmother, and that she defensively projected her voyeuristic curiosity to my secretary in her fantasy that the secretary peeked at her record.

Putting these several clues together, I formulated the following interpretation:

> *Precipitant:* Her recent ability to express negative oedipal transference feelings to me appears to have had a liberating effect, helping her to realize that she had alternatives to her frustrating attachment to me.
>
> *Thematic conflict:* Wish to become more independent of me, to have a man (or men) of her own, *versus* reluctance to give up her (oedipally based) fantasy of having me to herself.

Checking This Formulation Against All of the Current Data

Most of the data have been accounted for in the preceding discussion of clues, with the exception of the following:

1. (The association about not doing well at putting the flags in the servings of ice cream): This image may indicate some ambivalence about her readiness for independence. Her doubts may be based on continuing insecurity about sex—suggested, for example, by the image of a party, which often alludes to sexual relations, and possibly also by her difficulty in inserting the (phallic) flags into the soft, yielding dessert.

2. (The dream image of show windows and people coming through my office while she was there): This may suggest a further dimension of her exhibitionistic fantasies, that is, wanting to show off her seduction of me to the world.

3. (The dream image of having to explain to people that she sees me): This may be a rationalization to conceal her erotic, seductive, exhibitionistic motives toward me.

My Interpretation to the Patient

When Ms. White said with a tone of irritation that she suspected that my secretary probably peeked at her record, I commented: ["It seems more likely that your curiosity about me and my secretary makes you want to spy on us, which you probably also wanted to do, or perhaps did do as a child, to find out what your father and stepmother did in private."]

This interpretation to the patient and the interpretation at the end of session 250 have in common an attempt to combine the patient's current transference dynamics with related genetic dynamics in a single interpretive statement. In well-going analyses and dynamic psychotherapies, interpretations of this kind are more possible and thus more frequent toward the end of the therapeutic process. The patient's increasing ability to understand and integrate such insights is an indication that termination of the treatment is approaching.

CHAPTER TWENTY-TWO

Follow-Up Session
Six Months after Termination

SESSIONS 280 TO 310 (SUMMARY)

Ms. White became involved romantically with a man who was attentive and loving toward her. At first she used the new relationship coyly and teasingly in an attempt to make me jealous, [which I interpreted to her]. She reacted with fury at what she called my "indifference" toward her. As her relationship with the man continued she complained of his attentiveness, which she considered a sign of weakness. She preferred the strong, silent, very confident type of man who would dominate her and whom she could look up to. She recognized gradually, however, that the man was someone with whom she could feel equal. Over a period of several months she fell in love with him. We agreed to terminate her treatment shortly before their marriage.

FOLLOW-UP

She came to see me for a follow-up session, as we had agreed, six months after her marriage and honeymoon. Her marriage was going well—even better than she and her new husband had anticipated. They were close, seemed compatible, enjoyed living together, and had good sexual relations in which she was fully responsive. She looked well, seemed confident, and was relaxed and natural with me. She expressed appreciation for my patience with her and for my help. She said if problems arose she would call me. I never heard from her again, however, so I assume and hope that all is well with her.

CONCLUDING COMMENTARY

The review of Ms. White's analysis has illustrated numerous applications of basic concepts and strategies in the construal, formulation, justification, and communication of latent meanings and determinants in the therapeutic process. Before concluding the discussion of this case, a few additional relations between interpretive strategies and the interpretive process will be mentioned.

First, continuous cases are particularly well suited to illustrate Freud's concept that the whole analysis is needed for the definitive interpretation of any fragment. The progressive revisions of constructions and reconstructions throughout the therapeutic process is a characteristic feature of the interpretive process. As Keynes (1962) and Hirsch (1967) have emphasized in related connections, a construction made earlier in the interpretive process may be justified insofar as it represents the most plausible and probable interpretation that could be formulated at the time, but later in the process the earlier construction may have to be reassessed as unjustified, or only partially justified, in the light of further evidence. Constructions and reconstructions always involve a selection and progressive modification of an initially plausible formulation, the justification of which is relative at every stage of the interpretive process.

In the same vein, continuous cases illustrate the gradualness with which depth psychological understanding is achieved (cf. Freud's [1923a] comment that the meanings of what one hears in analysis are for the most part understood only later). Cognitive scientists have found that expertise in solving complex problems (a category of problems for which clinical interpretations of latent meanings and determinants appear to qualify) is not based primarily on special methods or unusual speed of data processing, but depends mainly on an extensive, organized, and retrievable knowledge base, which in the case of depth psychological interpretation involves extensive and specific details of the individual patient's life history, emotional vulnerabilities, personality patterns, and current psychological functioning. It is largely the therapist's unique and extended exposure to, and accessible memory of, innumerable details about the patient that produce the competence to interpret insightfully.

There is some place in the expert's approach for sudden dramatic insights, but they are rare. Most clinical problems are solved by relatively routine and deliberate methods of data processing (see, e.g., Rubovits-Seitz 1998). Freud (1910c) referred to this feature of the interpretive process in his caution "not to rush," and also in a letter to Fliess regarding some parallels between clinical interpretation and Jakob Burkhardt's (1898–1902) *History of Greek Culture*: "For the way in which one should comport oneself in the work of interpretation: The result is not at all to be forced; a gentle attentiveness with regular diligence leads further" (Freud 1985, p. 342).

The continuous case has illustrated also that, as in other forms of scientific inquiry, clinical interpretations rely extensively on recognizing clues that have a bearing on something they seem to indicate (Polanyi 1966). The historiographer Carlo Ginzburg (1989) classifies Freud's approach as a method in which minor details serve as clues that are integrated as signs of crucial, concealed aspects of the mind. The importance of identifying clues in the interpretive process has led to comparisons between clinical interpretation and detective work (see, e.g., Waelder 1939). Individual clues are fragmentary, however, so both clinical interpreters and detectives must fit diverse clues together to form a complete and coherent picture. The latter process has been studied experimentally by Gestalt psychologists. One such experiment, for example, included the following clues: stove, cupboard, glass bottles, chemicals, drawing board, ink, money, and arrest. Fitting these clues together suggests the solution of a workshop for making counterfeit money (Waelder 1960). Detectives' conclusions and Gestalt experiments of this kind usually have only one plausible solution. The clinical interpretive process, by contrast, generates alternative constructions, which necessitate the additional interpretive task of determining which among alternative possibilities is the most plausible hypothesis.

Relationship Between Recurrent Cycles
and Clinical Context in the Interpretive Process

Clinicians rely on context more than on any other heuristic in the interpretive process. Freud (1900) recognized early in the development of psychoanalysis that a correct interpretation can be arrived at only from the clinical context at the time (see also Brook 1992, Bruner 1986, Cavell 1988, Glymour 1993). Arlow (1979) places context first in his list of heuristics employed in interpretive inquiry. In fact, there is no satisfactory way of interpreting a segment of clinical data in isolation from the contexts that accompany, precede, and follow it (Edelson 1988). Furthermore, adjacent contexts themselves must be interpreted. Consequently, to understand and justify a specific latent content, one must interpret an ever-widening context of interpreted events. The latter problem is the basis and rationale of Freud's (1937b) insistence that full interpretation of any clinical fragment must await completion of the whole analysis.

Spence (1991; citing Greenwald et al. 1986) stresses the interpretive advantage of focusing on the conditions under which a given phenomenon makes its appearance—for example, a male patient who provokes arguments with his father only when his mother is present. Such an approach takes both the clinical episode and its context into account, focusing on a series of (contextual) patterns rather than on a series of discrete events. The latter form of interpretive inquiry, according to Spence, is "native to the consulting room" because by investigating under what conditions a phenomenon (such as a symptom, conflict, or defense) appears, we take the recurrent pattern as our basic unit of clinical significance and make pattern matching "the essential clinical activity" (p. 283).

The importance of recurrent observable patterns in the therapeutic process can be extended to include the contextual significance of microstructural relations such as the sequences and cycles identified by the RC approach. That is, recurrent cycles are part of the context (or conditions) under which a given phenomenon makes its appearance. Although such microstructures are not recognizable during the actual treatment of patients, and thus do not contribute to the initial discovery phase of the interpretive process, they can be identified posttherapeutically by studying records of the therapeutic process, and thus can be used retrospectively in the more definitive discovery and justification of interpretations.

"A Child Is Being Beaten": Comparison of the Present Case with Freud's Classic Essay

Both descriptively and dynamically, Ms. White's beating fantasies corresponded closely with those that Freud (1919) reported in his classic paper on the subject (see also Joseph 1965, Person 1997). Freud concluded:

1. Beating fantasies are a variety of masochistic fantasies in general.

2. The presence or absence of physical punishment in childhood plays no part in the development of such fantasies.

3. Like dreams, beating fantasies have both manifest and latent contents.

4. The beating fantasies are associated with masturbation.

5. The beating fantasies have to do with sibling rivalry, gratifying sadistic desires to see the sibling punished by and debased in the eyes of the parent.

6. The fantasy can be analyzed back through its stages of development, one phase of which is an unconscious fantasy in which the patient herself is being beaten.

7. The latent content of the fantasy is overdetermined; it includes oedipal, preoedipal, voyeuristic, bisexual, and primal scene fantasies in addition to sadomasochistic elements.

8. The fantasy has origins in an incestuous attachment to the father. Kris (in Joseph 1965) also emphasized the common pattern of a strong attachment to the father. Much of the fantasy's sadomasochistic component, which includes strong anally fixated elements (e.g., a sadistic concept of intercourse), is in relation to the father.

The principal difference between Ms. White's beating fantasies and those reported by Freud concerned her readiness to discuss such fantasies early in her analysis, in contrast to Freud's observation that patients do not reveal beating fantasies for a long time in analysis due to shame.

Although I was well aware of Freud's theory of beating fantasies at the time of treating Ms. White, I deliberately refrained from applying those theories in my interpretive work with her. Rather, I employed a heuristic interpretive strategy that Michael Parsons (1992) perceptively refers to as the "refinding of theory" in clinical practice (cf. also Rubovits-Seitz 1998, for use of interpretive heuristics rather than specific clinical theories in interpretive work, and for the interpretive attitude).

PART III

Summary and Conclusions

CHAPTER TWENTY-THREE

Integrating Interpretive Inquiry

ALL SCIENCES, even the most exact, employ interpretation to some extent. The human and social sciences need and use it most, because of the extreme variability of personality and behavior, both within and between individuals. Psychoanalysis and dynamic psychotherapy are pluralistic or mixed sciences. To the extent that they deal with biological factors, as in their concern with innate drives and innate ego structures, they are partly natural sciences and employ the scientific method: they search for causes, attempt to establish general laws, explain phenomena by reference to causes and general theories, and they attempt to validate concepts and theories by experimental and controlled manipulation of variables.

To the extent that psychoanalysis and dynamic psychotherapy deal with psychosocial variables, however, they are related more to the human and social sciences, which employ both qualitative and quantitative methodologies. Individual case studies, for example, which rely extensively on interpretation, are qualitative approaches, but quantitative methodologies such as population samples and statistical analyses are used as well. Psychoanalysis and dynamic psychotherapy search for both meanings and causes; are characterized by limited generalization of findings, concepts, and theories; attempt to understand as well as to explain phenomena; and employ both qualitative and quantitative methods of justification.

The fact that psychoanalysis and dynamic psychotherapy are both natural and human/social sciences makes them a complex mixture of methods and concepts. Interpretation, however, belongs mainly to the more humanistic rather than to the methods of natural scientific disciplines. That is, our reliance on interpretive inquiry is based primarily on hermeneutic rather than on natural scientific methods and traditions, but psychoanalysis and dynamic psychiatry are relative newcomers to the art and science of interpreting meanings, which began with Aristotle. Ever since Aristotle's studies of the multiple meanings of certain words, one of the most generic definitions of interpretation has been, "to find double or multiple meanings"—a definition that applies also to clinical interpretation, for example:

> A patient begins a therapy session by saying that the weather is dark and ominous today; a storm seems to be brewing. The psychoanalyst or dynamic psychotherapist wonders silently what other meanings that statement might imply: for example, does it convey something about the patient's inner "climate" or mood? Is a "storm" of intense emotion brewing in the patient and about to be unleashed?

The term *hermeneutics* originated with an early sect of biblical exegetes who called themselves "hermeneuts." Hermeneutic scholars and investigators have been studying the problems, methods, and principles of interpretation for centuries. Originally hermeneutics dealt with the principles that govern the exegesis of texts; but during the seventeenth century Spinoza broadened the concept of "text" to include much more than written documents and scripture. Eventually, the term *hermeneutics* was applied to the art and science of interpreting meanings in texts of all kinds, for example, in literary analysis, legal commentary, and even in spoken communications (including talk therapies).

During the nineteenth and twentieth centuries hermeneutics evolved and expanded into a number of identifiable theories, methods, and schools— clinical interpretation being a relatively recent form of hermeneutics, based largely on Freud's system of demystifying symbols, dreams, fantasies, and myths. In recent years a controversy has arisen in psychoanalysis and dynamic psychiatry about whether these fields should be considered hermeneutic disciplines or whether they are primarily natural sciences—a futile, academic dichotomy. These are very complex fields that cut across several disciplines including biology, psychology, medicine, sociology, linguistics, anthropology, history, and others. Our most prevalent contemporary model, for example, is the pluralistic biopsychosocial model.

THE IMPORTANCE
OF CLINICAL INTERPRETATION

Everything we do in clinical work requires interpretive inquiry. Psychoanalysis and dynamic psychotherapy are depth psychologies, that is, we assume that the problems underlying psychoneurotic pathology are hidden, unconscious. The primary data of these fields consist, however, of what the patient actually says and does during sessions; but these data do not speak for themselves about underlying meanings and determinants. The latter must be construed, surmised, and interpreted from the primary data. We, the clinical interpreters, in collaboration with our patients, are the ones who must attempt to understand and give voice to hidden meanings and determinants.

Interpretive inquiry is our principal method of identifying and understanding latent meanings and determinants. What the scalpel is to the surgeon, interpretive inquiry is to the psychoanalyst and dynamic psychotherapist; it is our stock in trade. As Ricoeur (1970, p. 66) observes, these fields are "interpretation from beginning to end." It starts when the clinician first sees the patient and continues until his or her final session with the patient has ended.

Another reason that interpretive inquiry is so important to both the patient and therapist is because the more completely and accurately the patient is understood, and also understands him- or herself, the greater the therapeutic effect of the treatment. This applies to both supportive and exploratory therapies. In supportive therapy, for example, the therapist's understanding of the patient in depth helps him or her to know when, how, to what extent, and why the patient needs emotional support in specific ways at particular times, and also which of the patient's coping patterns were successful in the past and therefore might be reactivated usefully again. In exploratory therapies interpretive inquiry mobilizes and weakens repressions, promotes insight, and also facilitates the patient's ability to employ self-interpretation to extend his or her capacity for self-understanding (insight)—the latter being among the most important factors in producing and maintaining cure.

Still another reason that interpretive inquiry is so important in our work is because all of our higher level clinical formulations, concepts, and theories are based ultimately on observations and interpretations in the clinical situation. If observation and interpretive understanding are faulty, psychoanalytic and psychodynamic theories themselves must be questioned. Thus interpretive inquiry is important not only to therapeutic technique and results, but also to the science of our fields.

THE ART AND SCIENCE
OF CLINICAL INTERPRETATION

Interpretation is often referred to as a clincial art rather than a science. There certainly is an art of interpretation, particularly in its data processing phase, when creative imagination is needed to generate plausible alternative construals and explanations of the extensive, often confusing clinical material. The art of interpretation does not lend itself to didactic instruction, however. It is learned mainly by experience as a patient in depth psychological therapy, clinical supervision, and clinical experience in the treatment of patients.

In addition, there is some degree of science involved in clinical interpretation, because clinicians are concerned also with the correctness of their interpretations, and have developed a number of methods of justifying them—one of the hallmarks of a science. The science of clinical interpretation deals also with issues such as the effectiveness and rationale of strategies for identifying and formulating unconscious meanings and determinants. The clinical methods and rationale as opposed to the technique of interpretation can be taught didactically to some extent, although experience, supervision, and a scientifically critical attitude toward one's own interpretations are important factors, too.

The best clinical interpreters achieve an effective balance between the art and science of interpretive inquiry. They are able to give free rein to their creative imaginations in order to generate fruitful interpretive hypotheses, but they also systematically check their interpretive hypotheses rather than assuming that their intuitive hunches are correct. Interpretive inquiry is far too difficult and uncertain for clinical complacency or conceit. Scientific tentativeness, humility, and restraint are basic attributes of the best interpreters; thus "the only feeling of certainty and conviction that a therapist may legitimately have is that there is something to be suspected about every feeling of certainty and conviction" (Ellis 1950).

INTERPRETIVE INQUIRY
IN NONCLINICAL FIELDS

One of the reasons I have reviewed some of the history of interpretive inquiry is to emphasize that we have much to learn from other fields about the art and science of interpretation. After all, hermeneutic scholars have studied these problems for centuries, even millennia. If dynamic psychotherapists and psychoanalysts take interpretive inquiry seriously as an important part of their professional and scientific work, rather than taking it for granted as many or perhaps most clinicians (including Freud) have done, they will find it useful to go beyond the literature on clinical interpretation and study the writings of investigators and scholars in other fields who have grappled with these difficult problems—in many cases much longer and more fruitfully than we have.

To illustrate, investigators in the fields of psycho- and sociolinguistics, communication, and human discourse have determined that even ordinary conversation entails constant interpretation on the part of both listeners and speakers. Listening to another person speak, for example, involves more than just the perception of what a speaker is saying; it also necessitates continual *interpretation* of what the speaker means by his or her communications. Studies of this kind have determined also that human speech is highly redundant—presumably to reduce misinterpretations and misunderstandings of each other's meanings. Some experiments have demonstrated, for example, that a speaker's meanings can be grasped when the listener receives only every fourth word of the message.

By contrast, due to repression and the mechanisms of defense, redundancy in the clinical material of patients with psychoneurotic pathology is significantly reduced. As a result, clinicians must employ special interpretive methods to increase the redundancy of patients' communications. One of the methods that therapists use for that purpose is to associate along with patients, using redundancies from their own associations to supplement patients' material. Another method is to ask the patient to associate further to individual elements in dreams and fantasies. These examples illustrate that the problems, methods, and principles of clinical interpretive inquiry have much in common with studies of interpretation in other fields, and that it will repay us to learn all we can from their investigations, experiences, and knowledge.

EPISTEMOLOGIC ASPECTS
OF CLINICAL INTERPRETIVE INQUIRY

The epistemologist Gregorio Klimovsky (1991) points out cogently that clinical interpretation is "an act of knowledge"; that is, we attempt to obtain knowledge through it, with the aim of reading, describing, and explaining such knowledge. Many or most interpretations are propositions, declarative statements, which can be right or wrong. They are hypothetical because their truth or falsity is not known with certainty either by the patient or therapist. In fact, an "interpretation is characterized to a considerable extent by conjecture" (p. 473).

The type of discourse on which clinical interpretations are based involves two kinds of material—direct and indirect. Direct material is observable, empirical, what the patient actually says and does during therapy sessions—the so-called manifest content. The indirect or theoretical material, on the other hand, which consists of unconscious or latent mental phenomena, cannot be observed directly but must be reached indirectly.

The difference between empirical and theoretical material is not peculiar to depth psychologies, but occurs also in certain other disciplines. Some very grand theories have been based entirely on observable material alone, and consequently are called empirical theories—an example being Darwin's (1859) theory of evolution. Such a theory does not refer to theoretical material, but is thoroughly grounded in observations; it is highly explanatory because it accounts for such a large number of facts, permits predictions, and in addition is explained by genetics. That is not the case, however, with genetics itself, chemistry, or depth psychologies (Klimovsky 1991).

In some sense, one could say also that unconscious phenomena can be observed and described, but to speak of the Unconscious, that is, a patient's latent psychic structure and fantasies, is very different than referring to manifest content—what he or she actually says and does. The former involves a nosological leap comparable with the one a chemist makes when he or she no longer refers to the color of litmus paper but to orbiting electrons in the atomic structure of a substance, and the displacement of electrons in the orbits.

Similarly, what happens within a patient's psychic structure and what the depth psychological therapist attempts to understand, "is quite analogous to what interests the chemist as to the internal structure of molecules, atoms, and electrons" (Klimovsky 1991, p. 474). Psychoanalysis and dynamic therapies share a similar problem with all such theories of the natural sciences—"how to ground our knowledge, how to order, to systematize that part of the science which is not directly accessible, directly operable, empirically tangible" (p. 474). The problem of interpretive inquiry is directly related to this question:

> An interpretation always goes beyond the patient's conduct, the empirical datum, and bears much more deeply on primitive structures that are in the Unconscious, on repressed events, on instinctive impulses, and many other elements that are in no way comparable nosologically to what the verbal material and the patient's conduct itself manifest. [p. 474]

How can interpretive inquiry reach the relevant material; what is the procedure? Klimovsky states, "The laws that correlate one type of variable with another, the empirical with the non-empirical, are usually called in epistemoligcal jargon the *rules of correspondence*." They are also hypotheses, laws provided by some scientific theory, which "correlate the visible with what is not visible, manifest material with latent content" (p. 475).

The problem is to provide support for what is conjectural by means of directly observable behavior. The model for this can be expressed as, "If A, then B." If we call observable-type material A and nonobservable, conjectural content B, we can say that our interpretations try to link A to B; thus if we are confronted with A, it is as if we were seeing B. Some epistemologists would object that the only thing that we know, or can know, is A. As Klimovsky argues, however, "the act of knowing, as also the act of perceiving, implies an inextricable and 'gestaltic' mix of empirical and conceptual aspects" (p. 476).

The preceding parts of Klimovsky's essay deal mainly with the type of interpretation that he refers to as a "reading" of latent material from "indicators" [cf. clues] in the manifest content, in contrast to "explanatory" interpretations. When he goes on to discuss the latter type of interpretations his description of the interpretive process becomes much more doctrinal. To illustrate: referring to the "classical Oedipal configuration" (pp. 479–480), he writes:

> In this type of interpretation first a hypothesis is proposed; then, on seeing from the hypothesis, with the help of a law, what is already known (the manifest material) can be deduced, we can say that we have explained it. . . . This is the most usual way of interpreting, because psychoanalysis is rather a modelistic theory: it offers a model of functioning of the psychic apparatus, from which certain consequences arise in relation to the manifest conduct of human beings. . . . In this sense, it seems that laws of the type we are studying operate more frequently, although not in an obligatory fashion, in psychoanalysis: if internally something of type B occurs, something of type A will be seen. In the cases that concern us, therefore, to interpret will be to propose a hypothesis and see how from it is deduced, with the help of laws, what we wanted to explain. [p. 480]

Soon after the above quotation, Klimovsky (1991) mentions that "psychoanalysis has a more deterministic than probabilistic model" (p. 481); and on the following pages he asserts that in addition to the "reading" and explanatory types of interpretations, another possibility is "simultaneous reading and explanation" (pp. 482–483).

My own view, enunciated in my 1998 volume, emphasizes an ad hoc, ex post facto model of clinical interpretive inquiry (cf. Mahony and

Singh 1979). Ad hoc in this context implies a construal of meanings and determinants applicable only to the data studied, rather than representing a more general meaning or determinant derived from a theory. Ex post facto implies that such a meaning or determinant is construed only after the data have been produced, rather than originating in a preexisting theory prior to data production.

Unlike Klimovsky, who speaks of rules of interpretation based on laws, I argue (with Rapaport 1944) that the background assumptions underlying Freud's interpretive system comprise a small number of basic, very general concepts that, because of their generality, tend to generate *alternative* rather than single interpretive hypotheses. These general, core concepts are not laws but background assumptions; they include the unconscious mind, continuity, meaning, determinism, overdetermination, instinctual drives, conflict, defense, repetition, transference, and the importance of childhood experiences.

FUNCTIONAL PHASES
OF INTERPRETIVE INQUIRY

For purposes of exposition and discussion, I find it useful to divide interpretive inquiry into the following overlapping phases or stages:

1. Prerequisite knowledge and "competencies."

2. General methodologic concepts and strategies.

3. Data generating strategies and methods.

4. Data gathering methods.

5. Data selection methods and criteria.

6. Data processing strategies and operations.

7. Construction (and reconstruction) of hypotheses.

8. Checking, revising, and rechecking hypotheses.

9. Selecting the most plausible hypothesis.

10. Justifying the most plausible hypothesis.

11. Verbal reformulation of the hypothesis.

12. Communication of the reformulated hypothesis.

13. Progressive modification of the hypothesis.

14. Reflection on one's interpretive understanding.

To elaborate on the preceding categories: (1) *Prerequisite knowledge* and competencies are preliminary to but necessary for interpretive work—what Gombrich (1969, p. 71) calls the interpreter's need for "a very well-stocked mind." (2) The *basic (core) concepts* are general background assumptions (in contrast to specific clinical theories) of psychoanalysis, dynamic psychotherapy, and clinical interpretation, which orient, guide, and inform interpretive inquiry. The *general strategies* of the interpretive process refer to approaches that facilitate the therapeutic and interpretive processes as a whole, in contrast to particular strategies that deal with specific aspects of interpretation and treatment. (3) *Data generating methods,* some of which are applicable to the patient and others to the therapist; the goal of both is to produce as extensive, diverse, and relevant a database as possible for interpretive inquiry.

(4) *Data gathering methods* have the purpose of observing and collecting as large a number and as wide a variety of clinical data as possible from both patient and therapist. (5) *Data selection methods* and criteria reduce the voluminous clinical data to a workable but adequate sample of highly relevant information. (6) *Data processing* strategies and methods are the pivotal phase of interpretive inquiry, cognitively transforming the selected clinical data and information into unique personal meanings and determinants that are specific to the individual patient.

(7) *Construction* (and *reconstruction*) attempt to construe (i.e., infer) alternative interpretive hypotheses that can explain the clinical data in depth. (8) The alternative hypotheses are then *checked, revised,* and *rechecked* to determine (9) *the most plausible hypothesis*—that is, the one that explains the clinical data most comprehensively and coherently. (10) If posttherapeutic investigation of the therapeutic process is employed, the most plausible hypothesis can be subjected to *diverse methods of justification,* employing multiple, increasingly exacting criteria of evidence and truth.

(11) Before communicating an interpretation to the patient (interpretive technique), the most plausible hypothesis must be *reformulated verbally*, in terms that can be (12) *conveyed to* and *understood by* the patient. As I have indicated in Chapter 8, however, the therapist need not, and perhaps should not, rely mainly on formal interpretations to the patient. As much as possible, it may be useful to encourage the patient to find such understanding himself.

(13) *Progressive modification* of interpretations occurs in response to feedback from and negotiation with the patient, as well as from further information as it accrues during the course of the therapeutic process. (14) *Reflection* on one's interpretive understanding of individual patients occurs both during and outside of therapy sessions, and may lead to the formulation of tentative working orientations and "grounded hypotheses" concerning the patient and the patient-therapist dyad.

LIMITATIONS OF INTERPRETIVE INQUIRY

Numerous problems and limitations beset the process of interpretive inquiry and its methodology—among other reasons because, unlike natural science approaches, interpretive inquiry does not derive from or depend upon scientific laws, nomic universals, or even a formal theoretical structure. Rather, the only solid referent to interpretive statements is their *empirical* bearing. The grounding of interpretations, however, is never purely empirical but relies also on a network of additional interdependent *interpretations* that are (1) inferential low-level theories and thus not strictly empirical, and (2) undergo continuous progressive modification. (The same holds true of inferences generally: we make most inferences not in isolation, but within a network of inductions which are modified as needed when further information requires it.)

Thus to understand a particular meaning one must turn to wider contexts which precede and follow the data in question. In addition to interpretations being based neither on scientific law, nomic universal, or formal theoretical structure, since the adjacent contexts must themselves be interpreted, the grounding of individual interpretations is also not purely observed fact, but is largely a shifting, ever-unfolding context of *interpreted* events: thus interpretations rest on interpretations, rest on interpretations, rest on interpretations, etc. As a result, there is always an element of uncertainty in every possible sphere of interpretation—a gap that must be considered a defining feature of interpretive inquiry, process, and methodology.

The limitations and uncertainties of interpretive inquiry make errors inevitable and frequent in our interpretive work. Liabilities inhere in every phase and aspect of the interpretive process. The principal problems and limitations of interpretive inquiry may be classified according to the following categories: (1) limitations of interpretive *methods*, especially the consensus problem, which concerns the reliability of interpretations; (2) limitations of *interpreters*, particularly the problem of confirmation bias; (3) inherent constraints on *construction* in the interpretive process, including the problem of doctrinal interpretation; (4) *empirical* problems, especially reductive selection of data and methods.

With respect to the limitations of interpretive methods, it is important to distinguish between reliability and justification. Reliability is concerned with the consistency of investigative (including interpretive) *methods*, rather than with the probity of results obtained by such methods. Unlike justification, reliability never refers to hypotheses or to theories, but only to methods. The more complex the phenomena, the less reliability can be expected, but even highly reliable methods do not guarantee—although they may increase the chances of—probative results.

Justification, by contrast, is directed to hypotheses and theories, attempting to determine their probity. In interpretive work it is better to speak of justifying an interpretation rather than proving its validity, for justifying implies only a process of identifying, among alternative constructions, which is the most plausible hypothesis at a given time. The ubiquity and persistence of the consensus problem make it necessary that we employ whatever justifying measures are available—to check, cross-check, and double check the plausibility of our inherently uncertain constructions.

Not only interpretive methods, but interpreters themselves are fallible; for example, they are susceptible to countertransference distortions and to confirmation bias. Because of the latter problem, clinicians often tend to become overcommitted to their original constructions, fail to question their correctness, become intent upon confirming them, and in the process ignore disconfirming data. Numerous investigations suggest that confirmation bias is a universal and probably ineradicable human trait.

Confirmation bias also contributes to an overemphasis on constructions in clinical interpretation. Construction, however, is only a relatively early, tentative, and uncertain step in the interpretive process. The uncertainty of constructions makes it necessary to check, revise, compare, and justify alternative hypotheses. As Freud (1937a) concluded eventually, however, constructions and the working through process of analysis do not resolve conflicts completely. Spitz (1994) notes in this connection, on the other hand, that although "extending the range of consciousness does not interpret away discordance . . . , [rather,] converting unconscious conflict into conscious contradiction actually expands the individual's capacity for experiencing the absurd" (p. 67; cited by Rand 2000, p. 959).

The combination of confirmation bias and overvaluing of constructions contributes, in turn, to reductive selection of clinical data and interpretive methods. Interpretive work, however, requires multiple methods, employing wide varieties of clinical data, to compensate for the limitations of individual data and methods.

Use of specific clinical theories in constructing initial hypotheses exacerbates all of the preceding problems. Interpretations necessarily draw on general concepts or background assumptions, but to impose specific clinical theories on the patient's associations interferes with the discovery of multiple unknown meanings that are unique to the individual patient. Since the limitations and uncertainties of the interpretive process make errors inevitable and frequent in interpretive work, "damage control" becomes a necessary part of interpretive methodology and the interpretive process.

SOME REMEDIAL STRATEGIES

Remedial stategies for the problems and limitations of interpretive inquiry include systematic error-detecting, error-correcting, and justifying procedures, combined with the general strategy of learning from error.

Since mistakes are unavoidable, the clinician employs systematic checking procedures to recognize errors when they occur, attempts to learn from the mistakes, and, if possible, puts such information to use in the interpretive process—as depth psychological therapists have learned to do with countertransference distortions.

Psychoanalysts and dynamic psychotherapists have relied extensively on patients' responses to interpretations as a guide to interpretive relevance and correctness, but patients' responses are one of the less reliable criteria of interpretive justification, because understanding of responses to interpretations also requires interpretation of the responses, and testing one interpretation by another (untested) interpretation is scientifically untenable.

To deal with errors realistically, one must attempt to recognize mistakes when they occur. The strategy of recognizing, correcting, and learning from errors starts with the expectation that the interpreter will make mistakes. That mind-set increases the clinician's alertness to discrepancies between his or her constructions, on the one hand, and all of the clinical data (rather than selected data that support one's hypothesis), on the other. The clinician who accepts the inevitability of errors systematically doubts everything that goes into his proof: his facts, his hypotheses, and how the two fit together.

Because constructions are essentially conjectures about the whole (thematic) meaning of the data being interpreted, it is necessary to employ a series of error-detecting and error-correcting procedures in which the interpreter (1) *checks* how much of the data a particular construction accounts for, (2) *modifies* the construction to account for more of the data, and then (3) *rechecks* the revised construction to determine whether it now covers most of the data. If not, the interpreter may have to discard the original construction and replace it with an alternative hypothesis. The process of checking, revising, and rechecking constructions continues until one is found that accounts comprehensively and consistently for all (or at least most) of the data.

At this point the clinician has selected what appears to be the most plausible interpretive hypothesis from among various competing constructions. In actual therapeutic work with patients, this is essentially as far as the justifying process can go. More definitive justification of clinical interpretations requires additional, posttherapeutic study based on a record of the entire therapeutic process. The record of a completed treatment makes it possible to employ multiple justifying procedures, including microanalytic methods.

Definitive justification of interpretations is the final, most difficult, and, unfortunately, the least utilized step in the error-correction process, in spite of Freud's scientific interest in methods of justifying interpretations. His concepts of interpretive justification included or anticipated a number of justifying strategies employed in contemporary human and social sciences. To illustrate: Freud's jigsaw puzzle model of interpretive justification suggested a *coherence* rather than a "correspondence" theory of truth and justification. It also anticipated the importance of small-scale, microstructural evidence in the justification of interpretations, that is, the complex interrelations of part meanings associated with individual elements of the clinical data. Freud insisted that our results become conclusive only with the intimate detail.

Another prescient aspect of Freud's justifying approach was its pluralism. Postpositivist human science approaches build redundancy into their validity checks as a substitute for infallibility of individual methods; for two proofs are better than one, and multiple checks reduce errors. Freud's pluralistic justifying strategies included (1) use of internal evidence, mainly coherence, encompassing the vast network of observations and interpretations generated by the entire therapeutic process; (2) all of the various (mainly indirect) responses to interpretations; (3) prediction and postdiction, the latter being both the most possible and also useful; and (4) external justification. In addition, the pluralistic nature of Freud's approach included the potential for (5) *cross-validation* of interpretations, based on multiple samples and varieties of clinical data drawn from many episodes and phases of the therapeutic process; and (6) *convergence* of evidence from diverse justifying methods.

To sum up, remedial strategies involve increasingly exacting evaluations of clinical interpretations, the final phases of which include justifying procedures, some of which can be employed during the course of a treatment; but more definitive methods of justification must await a record of the entire completed treatment. The association between interpretive accuracy and therapeutic effectiveness is closer than is generally recognized.

THE INTERPRETIVE ATTITUDE

The clinician's attitude toward the interpretive task, that is, the intellectual and emotional mind-set of the therapist engaged in interpretive work, can both alleviate and aggravate the problems of interpretive inquiry. The problems, limitations, and fallibility of interpretive inquiry necessitate a well-developed tolerance of uncertainty, with flexibility, open-mindedness, and readiness to recognize errors, on the one hand; but, on the other hand, the interpreter also needs a quietly confident attitude regarding the investigative possibilities and potential therapeutic value of interpretive work. The clinician is entitled, therefore, to a modest degree of confidence in interpretations, because their uncertainties are counterbalanced by their riches.

An attitude of compromise is needed also to deal with the contradictory aspects of seeking the most plausible interpretation, on the one hand, as opposed to the realities of interpretive relativism and uncertainty, on the other. Such an attitude necessitates the adoption of (1) a more realistic level of expectation regarding the accuracy versus the fallibility of interpretations; and (2) the realization that, since we cannot escape our contexts, the limits of knowledge are contained within individual schools of thought, and what each school accepts as knowledge is what agrees with the standards and practices of that school. Thus there is not just one truth that corresponds with reality; there are *some* truths that hold within various reference frames. Reality is our views, not something that lies behind and causes our views. Each conceptual framework is only a way of knowing—a specific and limited context. Thus the true test of the therapist as interpreting instrument, according to Schafer (1983), is the capacity to be multiply aware on multiple levels of multiple meanings.

Concerning a modest degree of confidence on the part of interpreters, a viewpoint by the social scientist Paul Diesing (1985b) suggests a cogent justification for such an attitude. In response to the criticism that Freud's research method was unscientific, Diesing points out that every method that science develops has its own characteristic weaknesses and sources of error—weaknesses that are only gradually but never fully recognized or overcome. The methods of science, therefore, are never completely scientific or reliable, but they are improvable. This book has illustrated that at least some progress is being made in improving our methods of interpretive inquiry.

A more specific justification for some degree of confidence in our interpretations is the concept of "meaning types." A type is a simple, low-level variety of theory, a shareable determinate class of meanings that can subsume and represent more than one experience. Types are thus unifying concepts that integrate individual observations—a capability that accounts for a type's indispensable heuristic function; for, paradoxically, an entity's individual characteristics can be known only through a type. Thus at every stage of coming to know anything in particular, we are brought to our knowledge by the heuristic of *type* ideas.

In the clinical situation, for example, when an interpreter gains an impression about the type of latent disturbance being expressed (and disguised) in the patient's associations, the type conception is used as a whole meaning to provide a basis for understanding specific details. If the individual associations (part meanings) do not fit the originally posited type of latent disturbance fairly completely and coherently, the type conception is modified and checking-revising-rechecking operations are initiated and continued until a satisfactory fit is found.

Since we are never able to revise and refine type conceptions precisely enough to achieve a perfect fit, the ideal of a completely correct interpretation is not attainable. We are able, however, to construct and often to justify the most plausible interpretation among alternative hypotheses at a particular time—that is, the interpretation that resonates with what is dynamically most relevant, hierarchically dominant, affectively most highly charged, evidentially supportable, readily communicable, and therefore optimally meaningful to the patient at a given time.

We are able to do that, and to achieve therapeutic effects by doing so, even though our interpretations are never absolutely accurate; for the concept of type conceptions implies that clinical interpretations may not need to be completely accurate. That is, as a type conception, an interpretation applies to a certain class of phenomena, and even such a limited, class-bound degree of specificity and veridicality may be sufficient to resonate with whatever type of latent disturbance is most emergent in the patient's mind at the time. Since type conceptions are such an important, ubiquitous, and shareable means of communication, the interpretive type conception that the therapist conveys to a patient may be good enough, therefore, both dynamically and therapeutically, by being in what Freud called "the neighborhood" of the patient's currently thematic latent disturbance.

The concept of type conceptions is congruent also with Hartmann's (1951) suggestion regarding the "multiple appeal" of interpretations (which affect multiple aspects of a dynamic system), as well as Rubinstein's (1980) proposal of "indirect" prediction and postdiction, that is, the possibility of predicting or postdicting classes of, in contrast to specific, events.

The concept of good-enough (sufficiently accurate) interpretations differs, on the other hand, from Freud's view that our constructions often do not lead to the patient remembering what has been repressed. Instead, Freud (1937b) proposed, "we produce in him an assured conviction of the truth of the construction which achieves the same result as a recaptured memory"(p. 265)—a conclusion, however, that makes interpretively facilitated therapeutic change seem suspiciously like a faith cure. The concept of good-enough interpretations differs also from the narrational project of Schafer, Spence, and others, which de-emphasizes the criterion of interpretive accuracy and views psychoanalytic narratives as constructed psychoanalytic fictions. By contrast, the concept of clinical interpretations as type conceptions—the multiple appeal of which may be good enough to facilitate therapeutic effects—provides a scientifically grounded basis for a modest degree of confidence that the clinical construal of latent disturbances "is not a mere chimera but involves the identification of real entities" (Eagle 1980, p. 423).

References

Abend, S. (1989). Countertransference and psychoanalysis. *Psychoanalytic Quarterly*, 58:374–395.

Abraham, I. (1986). Diagnostic discrepancy and clinical inference. *General Social Psychology Monograph*, 112:41–102.

Akhtar, S. (2000). From schisms through synthesis to informed oscillation: an attempt at integrating some diverse aspects of psychoanalytic technique. *Psychoanalytic Quarterly*, 59:265–288.

Alpert, M., Cohen, N. Martz, M., and Robinson, C. (1980). Electroencephalographic analysis: A methodology for evaluating psychotherapeutic process. *Psychiatry Research*, 2:323–329.

Andresen, J. (1983). Guided tours or lonely searches. Review of *Dire Mastery: Discipleship from Freud to Lacan*, by F. Roustang (1982). *Contemporary Psychiatry*, 2:141–142.

Anzieu, D. (1970). Eléments d'une théorie de l'interpretation. *Revue Francais Psychoanalyse*, 36:755–820.

———. (1975). *Freud's Self-Analysis*, trans. P. Graham. London: The Hogarth Press, 1986.

Applegarth, A. (1991). Review of *Psychoanalysis: A Theory in Crisis*, by M. Edelson (1988). *International Journal of Psychoanalysis*, 72:742–745.

Argelander, H. (1984). A comparative study of verbatim and recollected protocols. *Psyche*, 38:385–419.

Arlow, J. (1969). Fantasy, memory, and reality testing. *Psychoanalytic Quarterly*, 38:28–51.

————. (1979). The genesis of interpretation. *Journal of the American Psychoanalytic Association*, (Suppl.) 27:193–206.

————. (1987). The dynamics of interpretation. *Psychoanalytic Quarterly*, 56: 68–87.

————. (1991). Methodology and reconstruction. *Psychoanalytic Quarterly*, 60: 539–563.

————. (1992). Foreword. In *Psychotherapy: The Analytic Approach*, ed. M. Aronson, M. Scharfman, pp. xv–xix. Northvale, NJ: Jason Aronson Inc.

————. (1995). Stilted listening. *Psychoanalytic Quarterly*, 64:215–233.

Arnheim, R. (1969). *Visual Thinking*. Berkeley,CA: University of California Press.

Arnoult, C., and Anderson, G. (1988). Identifying and reducing causal reasoning biases in clinical practice. In *Reasoning, Inference, and Judgment in Clinical Psychology*, ed. D. Turk, P. Salovey, pp. 209–231. New York: Free Press.

Atkinson, R. (1978). *Knowledge and Explanation in History*. Ithaca, NY: Cornell University Press.

Bachrach, (1993). The Columbia Records project and the evolution of psychoanalytic outcome research. In *Research in Psychoanalysis: Process, Development, Outcome*, ed. T. Shapiro, R. Emde. *Journal of the American Psychoanalytic Association*, (Suppl.) 41:279–297.

Balint, M. (1965). *Primary Love and Psychoanalytic Technique*. New York: Liveright.

————, et al. (1972). *Focal Psychotherapy: An Example of Applied Psychoanalysis*. London: Tavistock.

Balter, L., Lothane, Z., and Spencer, J. (1980). On the analyzing instrument. *Psychoanalytic Quarterly*, 49:474–504.

Baranger, M. (1993). The mind of the analyst: from listening to interpretation. *International Journal of Psychoanalysis*, 74:1–10.

Barglow, P., and Sadow, L. (1971). Visual perception: development and maturation from birth to adulthood. *Journal of the American Psychoanalytic Association*, 19:433–450.

Barratt, B. (1984). *Psychic Reality and Psychoanalytic Knowing*. Hillsdale, NJ: The Analytic Press.

————. (1990). Reawakening the revolution of psychoanalytic Method. *Psychoanalysis and Contemporary Thought*, 13:139–163.

Barron, J. (Ed.) (1993). *Self-Analysis.* Hillsdale, NJ: The Analytic Press.

Barthes, R. (1977). *Image, Music, Text.* New York: Hill and Wang.

Barzun, J. (1956). Cultural history: a synthesis. In *The Varieties of History,* ed. F. Stern, pp. 387–402. New York: Meridian Books.

Basch, M. (1976). Psychoanaltyic interpretation and cognitive transformation. *International Journal of Psychoanalysis,* 62:151–175.

———. (1983). Empathic understanding: A review of the concept and some theoretical considerations. *Journal of the American Psychoanalytic Association,* 31:101–126.

———. (1984a). The selfobject theory of motivation and the history of psychoanalysis. In *Kohut's Legacy: Contributions to Self Psychology,* ed. P. Stepansky, A. Goldberg, pp. 3–17. Hillsdale, NJ: The Analytic Press.

———. (1984b). Selfobjects and selfobject transference: theoretical implications. In *Kohut's Legacy: Contributions to Self Psychology,* ed. P. Stepansky, A. Goldberg, pp. 21–41. Hillsdale, NJ: The Analytic Press.

Bastick, T. (1982). *Intuition: How We Think and Act.* New York: Wiley.

Baum, O. (1977). Countertransference and vicissitudes in an analyst's development. *Psychoanalytic Review,* 64:539–550.

Beiser, H. (1984). Example of self-analysis. *Journal of the American Psychoanalytic Association,* 32:3–12.

Bem, D., and Allen, A. (1974). On predicting some of the people some of the time: The search for cross-situational consistencies in behavior. *Psychological Review,* 8:506–520.

Beres, D. (1968). The role of empathy in psychotherapy and psychoanalysis. *Journal of the Hillside Hospital,* 17:362–369.

———, and Arlow, J. (1974). Fantasy and identification in empathy. *Psychoanalytic Quarterly,* 43:26–50.

Berg M. (Rep.) (2000). Subjectivity and objectivity. *Journal of the American Psychoanalytic Association,* 48:539–548.

Bergson, H. (1946). *The Creative Mind.* New York: Philsophical Library.

Berkson, W., and Wettersten, J. (1984). *Learning from Error.* La Salle, IL: Open Court.

Bernardi, R. (1989). The role of paradigmatic determinants in psychoanalytic understanding. *International Journal of Psychoanalysis,* 70:341–357.

Bernfeld, S. (1941). The facts of observation in psychoanalysis. *Journal of Psychology,* 112:289–305. Also in *International Review of Psychoanalysis,* 1985. 12:341–351.

Bernstein, R. (1988a). Interpretation and its discontents. In *Hermeneutics and Psychological Theory*, ed. S. Messer, L. Sass and R. Woolfolk, pp. 87–108. New Brunswick, NJ: Rutgers University Press.

Bhaskar, R. (1975). *A Realist Theory of Science*. Leeds, UK: Leeds Books.

Bion, W. (1970). *Attention and Interpretation*. London: Tavistock.

Birdwhistell, R. (1970). *Kinesics and Context*. Philadelphia: University of Pennsylvania Press.

Blum, H. (1976). The changing use of dreams in psychoanalytic practice: dreams and free association. *International Journal of Psychoanalysis*, 57:315–324.

———. (1980). The value of reconstruction in adult psychoanalysis. *International Journal of Psychoanalysis*, 61:39–52.

———. (1986). Countertransference and the theory of technique discussion. *Journal of the American Psychoanalytic Association*, 34:309–329.

Bollas, C. (1987). *The Shadow of the Object. Psychoanalysis of the Unthought Known*. New York: Columbia University Press.

Böhn, T. (1999). The difficult freedom from a plan. *International Journal of Psychoanalysis*, 80:493–506.

Bouchard, M. (1995). The specificity of hermeneutics in psychoanalysis. *International Journal of Psychoanalysis*, 76:533–546.

Boyer, L. (1988). Thinking of the interview as if it were a dream. *Contemporary Psychoanalysis*, 24:275–281.

Bransford, J., and Franks, J. (1971). The abstraction of linguistic ideas. *Cognitive Psychology*, 2:331–350.

———, and Johnson, M. (1973). Considerations of some problems of comprehension. In *Visual Information Processing*, ed. W. Chase, pp. 383–438. New York: Academic Press.

Brenman, E. (1980). The value of reconstruction in psychoanalysis. *International Journal of Psychoanalysis*, 61:53–60.

———. (1984). Discussion of Van Spruiell's paper "The Analyst at Work." *International Journal of Psychoanalysis*, 65:31–37.

Brenneis, C. (1994). Observations on psychoanalytic listening. *Psychoanalytic Quarterly*, 63:29–53.

———. (1999). What the analyst does not hear. *Psychoanalytic Quarterly*, 68:84–98.

Brent, J. (1960). *Charles Sanders Peirce: A Life*. Revised and enlarged edition. Bloomington, IN: Indiana University Press.

Breuer, J., and Freud, S. (1895). Studies on hysteria. *Standard Edition*, 2:1–335. London: Hogarth, 1955.

Brice, C. (Rep.) (2000b). Spontaneity versus constraint: dilemmas in the analyst's decision making. *Journal of the American Psychoanalytical Association*, 48:549–560.

Brockman, R. (1998). *A Map of the Mind: Toward a Science of Psychotherapy*. Madison, CT: Psychosocial Press.

Brody, E. (1990). *Psychoanalytic Knowledge*. Madison, CT: International Universities Press.

Bronowski, J. (1978). *The Origin of Knowledge and Imagination*. New Haven, CT: Yale Universiy Press.

Brook, A. (1992). Psychoanalysis and common sense psychology. *The Annual of Psychoanalysis*, 20:273–303.

Brooks, P. (1994). *Psychoanalysis and Storytelling*. Oxford, UK: Basil Backwell.

Bruner, J. (1986). *Actual Minds, Possible Worlds*. Cambridge, MA: Harvard University Press.

Bucci, W. (1985). Dual coding: a cognitive model for psychoanalytic research. *Journal of the American Psychoanalytic Association*, 33:571–607.

———. (1988). Converging evidence for emotional structures. In *Psychoanalytic Process Research Strategies*, ed. H. Dahl, H. Kächele, H. Thomä, pp. 29–49. Berlin: Springer.

Buckley, P. (Ed.) (1986). *Essential Papers on Object Relations*. New York: New York University Press.

Busch, F. (1999). *Rethinking Clinical Technique*. Northvale, NJ: Jason Aronson Inc.

Calder, K. (1979). An analyst's self-analysis. *Journal of the American Psychoanalytic Association*, 28:5–20.

Campbell, D. (1966). Pattern matching as an essential to distal knowing. In *The Psychology of Egon Brunswik*, ed. K. Hammond, pp. 81–166. New York: Holt, Rinehart and Winston.

Caston, J. (2000). Review of *A Map of the Mind*, by R. Brockman (1998). *International Journal of Psychoanalysis*, 81:181–185.

Cavell, M. (1988). Interpretation, psychoanalysis and the philosophy of science. *Journal of the American Psychoanalytic Association*, 36:859–879.

Chassan, J. (1956). On probability theory and psychoanalytic research. *Psychiatry*, 19:55–61.

———. (1957). On the unreliability of reliability and some other consequences of the assumption of probabilistic patient–states. *Psychiatry*, 20:163–171.

Cherry, C. (1957). *On Human Communication*. New York: Science Editions, 1961.

Cheshire, N. (1975). *The Nature of Psychodynamic Interpretation*, London: Wiley.

Chessick, R. (1989). *The Technique and Practice of Listening in Intensive Psychotherapy*. Northvale, NJ: Jason Aronson Inc.

———. (1992). *What Constitutes the Patient in Psychotherapy: Alternative Approaches to Understanding Humans*. Northvale, NJ: Jason Aronson Inc.

Clippinger, J. (1977). *Meaning and Discourse: A Computer Model of Psychoanalytic Speech and Cognition*. Baltimore, MD: The Johns Hopkins University Press.

Cohen, N., and Alpert, M. (1981). Styles of listening and clinical sensitivity. *Archives of General Psychiatry*, 33:854–857.

Colby, K., and Parkinson, R. (1974). Pattern-matching rules for the regulation of natural language dialog expressions. *American Journal of Computational Linguistics*, 1:1–70.

———, and Stoller, R. (1988). *Cognitive Science and Psychoanalysis*. Hillsdale, NJ: Lawrence Erlbaum.

Collins, A., and Loftus, E. (1975). A spreading activation theory of human memory. *Psychological Review*, 82:407–428.

Coltrera, J. (1981). On the nature of interpretation: epistemology as practice. In *Clinical Psychoanalysis, Vol. 3*. pp. 83–127. New York: Jason Aronson Inc.

———. (1983). Review of *Explorations in Psychoanalysis*, by R. Greenson, 1978. *Journal of the American Psychoanalytic Association*, 31:715–730.

Conigliaro, V. (1997). *Dreams as a Tool in Psychoanalytic Psychotherapy*. Madison CT: International University Press.

Cremerius, J. (1982). Kohut's Behandlungstechnik. Eine Analyse. *Psyche*, 36: 17–46.

———. (1984). *Vom Handwerk des Psychoanalytikers: Das Werkzeug der Psychoanalytischen Technik*. Stuttgart- Cannstadt: Frommann-Holzborg.

Crits-Christoph, P., Cooper, A., and Luborsky, L. (1988). The accuracy of therapists' interpretations and the outcome of dynamic psychotherapy. *Journal of Consulting and Clinical Psychology*, 56:490–495.

Culler, J. (1982). *On Deconstruction*. Ithaca, NY: Cornell University Press.

Dahl, H. (1988). Frames of mind. In *Psychoanalytic Research Strategies*, ed. H. Dahl, H. Kächele, H. Thomä, pp. 51–66. Berlin: Springer.

Dalbiez, R. (1941). *Psychoanalytical Method and the Doctrine of Freud, Vols. I and II*, trans. T. Lindsay. New York: Longmans, Green.

Darwin, C. (1859). *The Origin of Species by Means of Natural Selection*. New York: The Modern Library.

———. (1888). *The Life and Letters of Charles Darwin*. New York: Basic Books.

Davidson, D. (1986). A coherence theory of truth and knowledge. In *Truth and Interpretation*, ed. E. LePore, pp. 307–319. Oxford, UK: Basil Blackwell.

Davis, W. (1978). *The Act of Interpretation: A Critique of Literary Reason*. Chicago: University of Chicago Press.

De Bea, E., and Romero, J. (1986). Past and present in interpretation. *International Review of Psychoanalysis* 13:309–321.

De Beaugrande, R. (1980). *Text, Discourse, and Process: A Multidisciplinary Science of Texts*. Norwood, NJ: Ablex.

———. (1984). Freudian psychoanalysis and information processing: notes on a future synthesis. *Psychoanalysis and Contemporary Thought*, 7:147–194.

De Groot, A. (1969). *Methodology: Foundations of Inference and Research in the Behavioral Sciences*. The Hague: Mouton.

———. (1983). Heuristics, mental programs, and intelligence. In *Methods of Heuristics*, ed. R. Groner, M. Groner, and W. Bischof, pp. 109–129. Hillsdale, NJ: Lawrence Erlbaum.

Dennett, D. (1991). *Consciousness Explained*. Boston, MA: Little Brown.

Diamond, D. (1983). The Anatomy of the Third Ear: Clinical Experience and the Inference Process in Psychotherapy. Unpublished doctoral dissertation, Department of Psychology, University of Michigan, Ann Arbor.

Diesing, P. (1971). *Patterns of Discovery in the Social Sciences*. Chicago: Aldine.

———. (1985a). Hypothesis testing and data interpretation: the case of Milton Friedman. *Research in the History of Economic Thought and Methodology*, 3:61–89.

———. (1985b). Comments on "Why Freud's research methodology was unscientific" by von Eckhardt. *Psychoanalysis and Contemporary Thought*, 8:551–566.

Dittman, A., and Wynn, L. (1961). Linguistic techniques and the analysis of emotionality in interviews. *Journal of Abnormal and Social Psychology*, 63:201–204.

Dorpat, T. (Rep.) (1973). Research on the therapeutic process in psychoanalysis—panel report. *Journal of the American Psychoanalytic Association,* 21:168–181.

Dowling, S. (1987). The Interpretation of dreams in the reconstruction of trauma. In the *Interpretation of Dreams in Clinical Work,* ed. A. Rothstein, pp. 47–56. Madison, CT. International Universities Press, 1987.

Duncan, D. (1989). The flow of interpretation: the collateral interpretation, force and flow. *International Journal of Psychoanalysis,* 70:693–700.

———. (1990). The feel of the session. *Psychoanalysis and Contemporary Thought,* 13:3–22.

Eagle, M. (1980). Psychoanalytic interpretations: veridicality and therapeutic effectiveness. *Noûs,* 4:405–425.

———. (1984a). *Recent Developments in Psychoanalysis.* New York: McGraw-Hill.

Eccles, J. (1974). The world of objective knowledge. In *The Philosophy of Karl Popper,* ed. P. Schilpp, pp. 349–350. La Salle, IL: Open Court.

Eco, U. (1985). Producing signs. In *On Signs,* ed. M. Blonsky. Baltimore: Johns Hopkins University Press.

Edelheit, H. (1969). Speech and psychic structure: the verbal-auditory organization of the ego. *Journal of the American Psychoanalytic Association,* 17:381–412.

Edelson, M. (1975). *Language and Interpretation in Psychoanalysis.* Chicago: University of Chicago Press.

———. (1978). What is the psychoanalyst talking about? In *Psychoanalysis and Language,* ed. J. Smith, pp. 99–170. *Psychiatry and the Humanities, Vol. 3.* New Haven, CT: Yale University Press.

———. (1980). Language and medicine. In *Applied Psycholinguistics and Mental Health,* ed. R. Rieber, pp. 177–204. New York: Plenum.

———. (1984). *Hypothesis and Evidence in Psychoanalysis.* Chicago: University of Chicago Press.

———. (1988). *Psychoanalysis: A Theory in Crisis.* Chicago: University of Chicago Press.

———. (1992a). Can psychotherapy research answer the psychotherapist's questions? *Contemporary Psychoanalysis,* 28:118–151.

Efird, J. (1984). *How to Interpret the Bible.* Atlanta: John Knox Press.

Ehrenberg, D. (1992). *The Intimate Edge: Extending the Reach of Psychoanalytic Interaction.* New York: Norton.

Ehrlich, L., and Wisser, R. (ed.) (1988). *Karl Jaspers Today*. Washington, DC: University Press of America.

Einhorn, H. (1988). Diagnosis and causality in clinical and statistical prediction. In *Reasoning, Inference, and Judgment in Clinical Psychology*, ed. D. Turk and P. Salovey, pp. 51–70. New York: The Free Press.

———, and Hogarth, R. (1986). Judging probable cause. *Psychological Bulletin*, 99:3–19,

Einstein, A. (1934). *Essays in Science*. New York: Philosophical Library.

Eissler, K. (1950). The Chicago Institute of Psychoanalysis and the sixth period of the development of psychoanalytic technique. *Journal of General Psychology*, 42:103–157.

———. (1951). Remarks on the psychoanalysis of schizophrenia. *International Journal of Psychoanalysis*, 32:139–156.

———. (1953). Notes on the emotionality of a schizophrenic patient and its relation to technique. *Psychoanalytic Study of the Child*, 8:199–251.

———. (1958). Remarks on some variations in psychoanalytic technique. *International Journal of Psychoanalysis*, 39:222–229.

———. (1959). The function of details in the interpretation of works of literature. *Psychoanalytic Quarterly*, 28:1–20.

———. (1963). Freud and the psychoanalysis of history. *Journal of the American Psychoanalytic Association*, 11:675–703.

———. (1968). The relation of explaining and understanding in psychoanalysis: demonstrated by one aspect of Freud's approach to literature. *Psychoanalytic Study of the Child*, 23:141–177.

Ekman, P. (1965). Communication through nonverbal behavior: a source of information about an interpersonal relationship. In *Affect, Cognition and Personality*, ed. S. Tomkins and C. Izard, pp. 390–442. New York: Springer.

Ellis, A. (1950). An introduction to the principles of scientific psychoanalysis. *Genetic Psychology Monographs*, 41:147–212.

Engle, G. (1975). Ten years of self-analysis—reaction to the death of a twin. *International Journal of Psychoanalysis*, 56:23–40.

Erdelyi, M. (1999). The unconscious, art, and psychoanalysis. *Psychoanalysis and Contemporary Thought*, 22:609–626.

Etchegoyen, R. (1989). *The Fundamentals of Psychoanalytic Technique*. London: Karnac Books.

Faimberg, H. (1997). Misunderstanding and psychic truths. *International Journal of Psychoanalysis,* 78:439–457.

Faust, D., and Meehl, P. (1992). Using scientific methods to resolve questions in the history and philosophy of science: some illustrations. *Behavioral Therapy.,* 23:195–211.

Felman, S. (1987). *Jacques Lacan and the Adventure of Insight.* Cambridge, MA: Harvard University Press.

Fenichel, O. (1941). *Problems of Psychoanalytic Technique.* New York: Psychoanalytic Quarterly.

———. (1945). *The Psychoanalytic Theory of Neurosis.* New York: Norton.

Ferenczi, S. (1925). *Further Contributions to the Theory and Technique of Psychoanalysis.* London: Hogarth, 1950.

Fischer, R. (1986). Toward a neuroscience of self-experience and states of self-awareness and interpreting interpretations . In *Handbook of States of Consciousness,* ed. B. Wolman and M. Ullman, pp. 3–30. New York: Van Nostrand Reinhold.

Fish, S. (1989). Withholding the missing portion: psychoanalysis and rhetoric. In *Doing What Comes Naturally,* by S. Fish, pp. 525–554. Durham, NC: Duke University Press,

Fisher, C. (1954). Dreams and perception. *Journal of the American Psychoanalytic Association,* 3:380–445.

———. (1956). Dreams, images, and perception: a study of unconscious-preconscious relationships. *Journal of the American Psychoanalytic Association,* 4:5–48.

———. (1959). Further observations on the Poetzl phenomenon—a study of day residues. *Psychoanalytic Quarterly,* 28:441–443.

Fisher, S., and Greenberg, R. (1977). *The Scientific Credibility of Freud's Theory and Therapy.* New York: Basic Books. (Columbia Univ. Press, 1985, pbk.)

Fiske, D., and Shweder, R. (1986). *Metatheory in Social Science.* Chicago: University of Chicago Press.

Fiumara, G. (1990). *The Other Side of Language: A Philosophy of Listening,* trans. C. Lambert. London: Routledge.

Fleming, J. (1971). Freud's concept of self-analysis. In *Currents in Psychoanalysis,* ed. T. Marcus, pp. 14–17. New York: International Universities Press.

Fonagy, P., and Target, M. (1996). Playing with reality; I. theory of mind and normal development of psychic reality. *International Journal of Psychoanalysis*, 77:217–233.

———. (2000). Playing with reality; III. the persistence of dual psychic reality in borderline patients. *International Journal of Psychoanalysis*, 81:853–874.

Forrester, J. (1980). *Language and the Origins of Psychoanalysis*. New York: Columbia University Press.

Fosshage, J., and Loew, C., eds. (1987). *Dream Interpretation: A Comparative Study*, rev. ed. New York: PMA.

Franklin, G. (1990). The multiple meanings of neutrality. *Journal of the American Psychoanalytic Association*, 38:195–220.

Frederickson, J. (1998). *Psychodynamic Psychotherapy: Learning to Listen from Multiple Perspectives*. Philadelphia: Brunner-Mazel.

Freedman, N. (1983). On psychoanalytic listening: the construction, partial paralysis, and reconstruction of meaning. *Psychoanalysis and Contemporary Thought*, 6:405–434.

Freeman, T. (1998). *But Facts Exist: An Enquiry into Psychoanalytic Theorizing*. London: Karnac Books.

French, T. (1952). *The Integration of Behavior, Vol. I: Basic Postulates*. Chicago: University of Chicago Press.

———. (1954). *The Integration of Behavior, Vol. II: The Integrative Process in Dreams*. Chicago: University of Chicago Press.

———. (1955a). Discussion of "Relation of Initial Associations to Focal Conflict in Analytic Interviews" by P. Seitz. Presented to the Chicago Psychoanalytic Society, Feb. 22.

———. (1955b). The problem of consensus. Presented to the Panel on "Validation of Psychoanalytic Techniques," rep. J. Marmor. *Journal of the American Psychoanalytic Association*, 5:496–505.

———. (1958a). *The Integration of Behavior, Vol. III: The Reintegrative Process in a Psychoanalytic Treatment*. Chicago: University of Chicago Press.

———. (1958b). The art and science of psychoanalysis. *Journal of the American Psychoanalytic Association*, 6:197–214. Also in *Psychoanalytic Clinical Interpretation*, ed. L. Paul, pp. 200–219. London: Free Press of Glencoe (Macmillan), 1963; and in *Psychoanalytic Interpretations: The Selected Papers of Thomas M. French, M.D.*, pp. 408–425. Chicago: Quadrangle, 1970.

————, and Wheeler, D. (1963). Hope and repudiation of hope in psychoanalytic therapy. *International Journal of Psychoanalysis*, 44:304–316.

————, and Fromm, E. (1964). *Dream Interpretation: A New Approach*. New York:
Basic Books.

Freud, A. (1936). *The Ego and the Mechanisms of Defense*. New York: International
Universities Press, 1946.

————. (1954). The widening scope of indications for psychoanalysis. *Journal
of the American Psychoanalytic Association*, 2:607–620.

————. (1968). Acting out. *International Journal of Psychoanalysis*, 49:165–170.

Freud, S. (1887–1902). *The Origins of Psychoanalysis: Letters to Wilhelm Fliess*. New
York: Basic Books.

————. (1893–95; with Breuer, J.). Studies on hysteria. *Standard Edition*, 2:3–
335. London: Hogarth, 1955.

————. (1900). The interpretation of dreams. *Standard Edition*, 4 and 5. London: Hogarth, 1953.

————. (1901). The psychopathology of everyday life. *Standard Edition*, 6:1–310.
London: Hogarth, 1960.

————. (1905a). Fragment of an analysis of a case of hysteria. *Standard Edition*,
7:3–124. London: Hogarth, 1956.

————. (1905b). Jokes and their relation to the unconscious. *Standard Edition*,
8:3–258. London: Hogarth, 1960.

————. (1908). Creative writers and daydreaming. *Standard Edition*, 9:141–154.
London: Hogarth, 1958.

————. (1909a). Analysis of a phobia in a five-year-old boy. *Standard Edition*,
10:3–152. London: Hogarth, 1953.

————. (1909b). Notes upon a case of obsessional neurosis. *Standard Edition*,
10:153–318. London: Hogarth, 1955.

————. (1910a). Five lectures on psychoanalysis. *Standard Edition*, 11:9–55.
London: Hogarth, 1957.

————. (1910b). The antithetical meaning of primal words. *Standard Edition*,
11:153–162. London: Hogarth, 1957.

————. (1910c). "Wild" psychoanalysis. *Standard Edition*, 11:219–230. London:
Hogarth, 1957.

————. (1911a). Psychoanalytic notes on an autobiographical account of a case
of paranoia (dementia paranoides). *Standard Edition*. 12:3–84. London:
Hogarth, 1958.

———. (1911b). The handling of dream-interpretation in psychoanalysis. *Standard Edition*, 12:89–96. London: Hogarth, 1958.

———. (1912a). The dynamics of transference. *Standard Edition*, 12:97–108. London: Hogarth, 1958.

———. (1912b). Recommendations to physicians practising psychoanalysis. *Standard Edition*, 12:109–120. London: Hogarth, 1958.

———. (1913a). On beginning the treatment (Further recommendations on the technique of psychoanalysis, I). *Standard Edition*, 12:121–144. London: Hogarth, 1958.

———. (1913b). On psychoanalysis. *Standard Edition*, 12:205–212. London: Hogarth, 1958.

———. (1914b). On narcissism: an introduction. *Standard Edition*, 14:67–104. London: Hogarth, 1957.

———. (1914d). The Moses of Michelangelo. *Standard Edition*, 13:211–236. London: Hogarth, 1955.

———. (1915a). Observations on transference love (Further recommendations on the technique of psychoanalysis III). *Standard Edition*, 12:157–171. London: Hogarth, 1958.

———. (1915b). Instincts and their vicissitudes. *Standard Edition*, 14:109–140. London: Hogarth, 1957.

———. (1915d). The unconscious. *Standard Edition*, 14:159–216. London: Hogarth, 1957.

———. (1915–16). Introductory lectures on psychoanalysis, Parts 1 and 2. *Standard Edition*, 15:9–239. London: Hogarth, 1963.

———. (1916–17). Introductory lectures on psychoanalysis, Part 3. *Standard Edition*, 15:243–296. London: Hogarth, 1963.

———. (1916). Some character types met with in psychoanalytic work, II. Those wrecked by success. *Standard Edition*, 14:309–337. London: Hogarth, 1957.

———. (1918). From the history of an infantile neurosis. *Standard Edition*, 17:3–122. London: Hogarth, 1957.

———. (1919). "A child is being beaten." A contribution to the study of the origin of sexual perversions. *Standard Edition*, 17:179–204. London: Hogarth, 1957.

———. (1920). Beyond the pleasure principle. *Standard Edition*, 18:3–144. London: Hogarth, 1955.

———. (1922). Postscript to the "Analysis of a phobia in a five-year-old boy." *Standard Edition*, 10:148–149. London: Hogarth, 1953.

———. (1923a). Two encyclopaedia articles. *Standard Edition*, 18:235–262. London: Hogarth, 1955.

———. (1923b). Remarks on the theory and practice of dream interpretation. *Standard Edition*, 19:109–124. London: Hogarth, 1961.

———. (1924). A short account of psychoanalysis. *Standard Edition*, 19:191–212. London: Hogarth, 1961.

———. (1925a). Some additional notes on dream-interpretation as a whole. *Standard Edition*, 19:125–140. London: Hogarth, 1961.

———. (1925c). An autobiographical study. *Standard Edition*, 20:3–76. London: Hogarth, 1959.

———. (1926a). Inhibitions, symptoms, and anxiety. *Standard Edition*, 20:87–174. London: Hogarth, 1959.

———. (1926b). Psychoanalysis. *Standard Edition*, 20:259–270. London: Hogarth, 1959.

———. (1931). Letter to Georg Fuchs. *Standard Edition*, 22:251–252. London: Hogarth, 1964.

———. (1933). New introductory lectures on psychoanalysis. *Standard Edition*, 22:3–184. London: Hogarth, 1964.

———. (1935). Postscript (1935) to *An Autobiographical Study*. *Standard Edition*, 20:71–74. London: Hogarth, 1959.

———. (1936). A disturbance of memory on the Acropolis. *Standard Edition*, 22:239–248. London: Hogarth, 1964.

———. (1940a). An outline of psychoanalysis. *Standard Edition*, 23:144–207. London: Hogarth, 1964.

———. (1940b). Some elementary lessons in psychoanalysis. *Standard Edition*, 23:279–286. London: Hogarth, 1964.

———. (1985). *The Complete Letters of Sigmund Freud to Wilhelm Fliess*, ed. J. Masson. Cambridge, MA: Harvard University Press.

———, and Silberstein, E. (1872–1875). Correspondence. Freud Collection, D-2. Library of Congress, Washington, DC.

Friedman, L. (1969). The therapeutic alliance. *International Journal of Psychoanalysis*, 50:139–153

———. (1975). Clinical implications of current object relations theory. *International Journal of Psychoanalysis*, 56:137–145.

———. (1978). Trends in the psychoanalytic theory of treatment. *Psychoanalytic Quarterly*, 47:524–535.

———. (1988). *The Anatomy of Psychotherapy*. Hillsdale, NJ: The Analytic Press.

———. (2000). Modern hermeneutics and psychoanalysis. *Psychoanalytic Quarterly*, 69:225–264.

Fromm, E. (1951). *The Forgotten Language*. New York: Rinehart.

Gabbard, G. (2000). Disguise or consent: problems and recommendations concerning the publication and presentation of clinical material. *International Journal of Psychoanalysis*, 81:1071–1086.

Gadamer, H. G. (1975). *Truth and Method*. New York: Seabury.

———. (1976). *Philosophical Hermeneutics*, trans. D. Linge. Berkeley, CA: The University of California Press.

Galatzer-Levy, R. (1991). Introduction: Self psychology searches for its self. In *The Evolution of Self Psychology: Progress in Self Psychology, Vol. 7*, ed. A. Goldberg, pp. xi-xvii. Hillsdale NJ: The Analytic Press.

Galton , F. (1879–1880). Psychometric experiments. *Brain*, 2:149–162.

Gardner, M. (1983). *Self Inquiry*. Boston: Little Brown.

———. (1991). The art of psychoanalysis: on oscillation and other matters. *Journal of the American Psychoanalytic Association*, 39:851–870.

Garduk, E., and Haggard, E. (1972). *Immediate Effects on Patients of Psychoanalytic Interpretations*. New York: International Universities Press.

Gassner, S., Sampson, H., Brumer, S., and Weiss, J. (1986). The emergence of warded-off contents. In *The Psychoanalytic Process*, by J. Weiss and H. Sampson, pp. 171–186. New York: Guilford.

Gedo, J. (1979). *Beyond Interpretation*, rev. ed. Hillsdale, NJ: The Analytic Press.

———. (1980). Reflections on some current controversies in psychoanalysis. *Journal of the American Psychoanalytic Association*, 28:363–383.

———. (1981). *Advances in Clinical Psychoanalysis*. New York: International Universities Press.

———. (1984). Letter to the editor. *Review of Psychoanalytic Books*, 3:511–515.

———. (1986). Relevance or reductionism in interpretation: a reprise of the psychoanalysis of Kleist's puppet theater. In *Conceptual Issues in Psychoanalysis*, pp. 186–199. Hillsdale, NJ: The Analytic Press.

Gergely, G. (1992). Developmental reconstructions: infancy from the point of view of psychoanalysis and developmental psychology. *Psychoanalysis and Contemporary Thought*, 15:3–56.

Gettys, C., and Fisher, S. (1979). Hypothesis plausibility and hypothesis genera-
tion. *Organization of Behavior and Human Performance*, 24:93–110.

Gill, M. (1984). Transference: a change in conception or only in emphasis? *Psychoanalytic Inquiry*, 4:489–524.

————. (1991a). Indirect suggestion: a response to Oremland's *Interpretation
and Interaction*. In *Interpretation and Interaction*, by J. Oremland, 1991, pp. 137–
163.

————. (1991b). Merton Gill speaks his mind. *American Psychoanalysis*, 25:395–
413.

————. (1994). *Psychoanalysis in Transition*. Hillsdale, NJ: The Analytic Press.

————. and Hoffman, I. (1982). *Analysis of Transference: Vol. II, Studies of Nine
Audio-recorded Psychoanalytic Sessions*. New York: International Universities
Press.

Gillett, E. (1999). Review of *But Facts Exist*, by T. Freeman (1998). *Psychoanalytic
Books*, 10:303–307.

Ginzburg, C. (1989). *Clues, Myths, and the Historical Method*, trans. J.and A. Tedeschi.
Baltimore, MD: Johns Hopkins University Press.

Giovacchini, P. (1989). *Countertransference Triumphs and Catastrophes*. Northvale, NJ:
Jason Aronson Inc.

Gitelson, M. (1962). The curative factors in psychoanalysis: I. The first phase
of psychoanalysis. *International Journal of Psychoanalysis*, 43:194–205.

Glaser, B., and Strauss, A. (1967). *The Discovery of Grounded Theory: Strategies for
Qualitative Research*. Chicago: Aldine.

Glover, E. (1931). The therapeutic effect of inexact interpretation: a contribution to the theory of suggestion. *International Journal of Psychoanalysis*, 33:403–
409.

————. (1952). Research methods in psychoanalysis. *International Journal of Psychoanalysis*, 33:403–409.

Glymour, C. (1993). How Freud Left Science. In *Philosophical Problems of the Internal and External Worlds*, ed. J. Earman, A. Janis, G. Massey, R. Rescher,
pp. 461–487. Pittsburgh, PA: University of Pittsburgh Press.

Goldberg, A. (1978). *The Psychology of the Self: A Casebook*. New York: International
Universities Press.

————. (1988). *A Fresh Look at Psychoanalysis: The View from Self Psychology*. Hillsdale,
NJ: The Analytic Press.

————. (1997). Writing case histories (guest editorial). *International Journal of Psychoanalysis*, 78:435–438.

Golland, J. (1991). Review of *The Technique and Practice of Listening in Intensive Psycho-therapy*, by R. Chessick (1989). *Psychoanalytic Books*, 2:401–404.

Gombrich, E. (1969). The evidence of images. In *Interpretation Theory and Practice*, ed. C. Singleton, pp. 35–104. Baltimore. MD: Johns Hopkins University Press.

————. (1972). *Symbolic Images*. London: Phaidon Press, Ltd.

Gordon, C. (1982). *Forgotten Scripts*. New York: Basic Books.

Gottschalk, L., and Auerbach, A. (1966). *Methods of Research in Psychotherapy*. New York: Appleton-Century-Crofts.

Gould, S. (1983). For want of a metaphor. *Natural History*, 2:14–19.

Gray, P. (1973). Psychoanalytic technique and the ego's capacity for viewing intrapsychic activity. *Journal of the American Psychoanalytic Association*, 21:474–494.

————. (1982). "Developmental lag" in the evolution of technique for psycho-analysis of neurotic conflict. *Journal of the American Psychoanalytic Association*, 30:621–655.

————. (1986). On helping analysands observe intrapsychic activity. In *Psycho-analysis: The Science of Mental Conflict*, ed. A. Richards and M. Willick, pp. 245–262. Hillsdale, NJ: The Analytic Press.

————. (1994). *The Ego and Analysis of Defense*. Northvale, NJ: Jason Aronson Inc.

Green, A. (2000). Commentary on "The Analyst's Witnessing and Otherness," by W. Poland (2000). *Journal of the American Psychoanalytic Association*, 48:57–66.

Greenacre, P. (1975). On reconstruction. *Journal of the American Psychoanalytic Asso-ciation*, 23:693–712.

Greenberg, J., and Mitchell, S. (1983). *Object Relations in Psychoanalytic Theory*, Cam-bridge, MA: Harvard University Press.

Greenson, R. (1960). Empathy and its viscissitudes. *International Journal of Psycho-analysis*, 41:418–424.

————. (1967). *The Technique and Practice of Psychoanalysis*. New York: International Universities Press.

————. (2000). On the receiving end: facilitating the analysis of conflicted drive derivatives of aggression. *Journal of the American Psychoanalytic Association*, 48:219–236.

Greenwald, A., Pratkanis, A., Leippe, M, and Baumgardner, M. (1986). Under what conditions does theory obstruct research progress? *Psychological Review,* 93:216–229.

Gribinski, M. (1994). The stranger in the house. *International Journal of Psychoanalysis,* 75:1011–1021.

Grice, H. (1975). Logic and conversation. In *Syntax and Semantics, Vol. 3: Speech Acts,* ed. P. Cole and J. Morgan, pp. 41–58. New York: Academic Press.

Grinstein, A. (1983). *Freud's Rules of Dream Interpretation.* New York: International Universities Press.

Groner, R., Groner, M., and Bischoff, W. (Eds.) (1983). *Methods of Heuristics.* Hillsdale, NJ: Lawrence Erlbaum.

Grossman, W. (1967). Reflections on the relationship of interpretation and psychoanalysis. *International Journal of Psychoanalysis,* 48:16–31.

Grünbaum, A. (1984). *The Foundations of Psychoanalysis: A Philosophical Critique.* Berkeley, CA: University of California Press.

———. (1986). Précis of *The Foundations of Psychoanalysis: A Philosophical Critique,* with open peer commentary. *Behavior and Brain Science,* 9:217–228.

———. (1990). Meaning connections and causal connections in the human sciences: the poverty of hermeneutic philosophy. *Journal of the American Psychoanalytic Association,* 38:559–577.

———. (1993). *Validation in the Clinical Theory of Psychoanalysis.* Madison, CT: International Universities Press.

Grubrich-Simitis, I. (1995). *Studien über Hysterie, vom Jos. Breuer und Sigm, Freud in Wien,* accompanied by *Urbuch der Psychoanalyse; Hundert Yahre Studien über Hysterie von Josef Breuer und Sigmund Freud.* Frankfurt-am-Main: S. Fischer.

Guttman, S., and Guttman, I., eds. (1987). Robert Waelder on psychoanalytic technique: five lectures. *Psychoanalytic Quarterly,* 56:1–67.

Hall, J. (1998). *Deepening the Treatment.* Northvale, NJ: Jason Aronson Inc.

Hamilton, V. (1993). Truth and reality in psychoanalytic discourse. *International Journal of Psychoanalysis,* 74:63–79.

Hanly, C. (1990). The concept of truth in psychoanalysis. *International Journal of Psychoanalysis,* 71:375–383.

Harbort, B. (1977). Application of Hermeneutics to Models of Medical Information. Unpublished doctoral dissertation, Ann Arbor, MI: Dissertation Abstracts International, 1987.

———. (1997). Thought, action, and intuition in practice-oriented disciplines. In *Intuition: The Inside Story—Interdisciplinary Perspectives*, pp. 129–144. New York: Routledge.

Harman, G. (1965). The inference to the best explanation. *Philosophical Review*, 74: 88–95.

Harré, R. (1972). *Philosophies of Science*. Oxford, UK: Oxford University Press.

Hartmann, H. (1939). *Ego Psychology and the Problem of Adaptation*, ed. D. Rapaport. New York: International Universities Press.

———. (1951). Technical implications of ego psychology. *Psychoanalytic Quarterly*, 20:31–43.

Hatcher, R. (1973). Insight and self-observation. *Journal of the American Psychoanalytic Association*, 21:377–398.

Havens, L. (1974). The essential use of the self. *American Journal of Psychiatry*, 131:1–10.

Heaton, K., Hill, C., Petersen, D., Rochlen, A. and Zack, J. (1998). A comparison of therapist-facilitated and self-guided dream interpretation sessions. *Journal of Consulting Psychology*, 45:115–122.

Hedges, L. (1991). *Listening Perspectives in Psychotherapy*. Northvale, NJ: Jason Aronson Inc.

Heimann, P. (1950). On countertransference. *International Journal of Psychoanalysis*, 31:81–84.

———. (1977). Further observations on the analyst's cognitive process. *Journal of the American Psychoanalytic Association*, 25:313–323.

Helmholtz, H. (1867). *Helmholtz's Treatise on Physiological Optics*, trans. J. Southall. New York: Dover, 1962.

Henle, M. (Ed.) (1961). *Documents of Gestalt Psychology*. Berkeley, CA: University of California Press.

Herzog, J. (1984). Fathers and young children: fathering daughters and fathering sons. In *Foundations of Infant Psychiatry, Vol. 2*, ed. J. Call, E. Galenson and R. Tyson, pp. 335–343. New York: Basic Books.

Hirsch, E. (1967). *Validity in Interpretation*. New Haven, CT: Yale University Press.

Höffding, H. (1901). *Psychologie*. Leipzig.

Hoffman, I. (1983). The patient as interpreter of the analyst's experience. *Contemporary Psychoanalysis* 19:389–422.

———. (1991). Discussion: toward a social-constructivist view of the psychoanalytic situation. *Psychoanalytic Dialogues*, 1:74–105.

———. (1994). Dialectical thinking and the therapeutic action in the psychoanalytic process. *Psychoanalytic Quarterly*, 63:187–218.

———. (1998). *Ritual and Spontaneity in the Psychoanalytic Process*. Hillsdale, NJ: The Analytic Press.

Hofstadter, D. (1982). Variations on a theme as the essence of imagination. *Scientific American*, Oct., 1982, pp. 20–28.

Hoit, M. (1995). The influence of hermeneutic philosophy on psychoanalysis. *Annual of Psychoanalysis*, 23:13–32.

Holland, N. (1975). *Poems in Persons: An Introduction to the Psychoanalysis of Literature*. New York: Norton.

———. (1978). What can a concept of identity add to psycholinguistics? In *Psychoanalysis and Language*, ed. J. Smith. New Haven, CT: Yale University Press.

Holt, R. (1964). The emergence of cognitive psychology. *Journal of the American Psychoanalytic Association*, 12:650–665.

———. (1978). *Methods in Clinical Psychology* (2 vols.). New York: Plenum.

———. (1988). Judgment, inference, and reasoning in clinical perspective. In *Reasoning, Inference, and Judgment in Clinical Psychology*, ed. D. Turk and P. Salovey, pp. 233–249. New York: Free Press.

Holyoak, L., and Thagard, P. (1996). *Mental Leaps: Analogy in Creative Thought*. Cambridge, MA: MIT Press (Bradford).

Horney, K. (1942). *Self-Analysis*. New York: Norton.

Horowitz, M. (1970). *Image Formation and Cognition*. New York: Appleton-Century-Crofts.

Hunter, K. (1991). *Doctors' Stories: The Narrative Structure of Medical Knowledge*. Princeton, NJ: Princeton University Press.

Isaacs, S. (1939). Criteria for interpretation. *International Journal of Psychoanalysis*, 20:148–160.

Isakower, O. (1939). On the exceptional position of the auditory sphere. *International Journal of Psychoanalysis*, 20:340–345.

————. (1992). The analyzing instrument in the teaching and conduct of the analytic process, ed. H. Wymann, S. Rittenberg. *Journal of Clinical Psychoanalysis*, 1:181–222.

Jacobs, T. (1986). On countertransference enactment. *Journal of the American Psychoanalytic Association*, 34:298–308.

————. (1991). *The Use of the Self: Countertransference and Communication in the Analytic Situation*. Madison, CT: International Universities Press.

————. (1994). Nonverbal communication: some reflections on their role in the psychoanalytic process and psychoanalytic education. *Journal of the American Psychoanalytic Association*, 42:741–762.

————. (1999). On the question of self-disclosure: error or advance in technique. *Psychoanalytic Quarterly*, 68:159–183.

Jacobsen, P., and Steele, R. (1979). From present to past: Freudian archaeology. *International Review of Psychoanalysis*, 6:349–362.

Jacobson, J. (2000). Review of *Tradition and Change in Psychoanalysis*, by R. Schafer (1997). *Journal of the American Psychoanalytic Association*, 48:311–315.

Jaspers, K. (1972). *General Psychopathology*, trans. J. Hoenig, M. Hamilton. Chicago: University of Chicago Press.

Johansen, J. (1986). Strategies of understanding. *Psychoanalysis and Contemporary Thought*, 9:497–561.

Johnson-Laird, P. (1983). *Mental Models*. Cambridge, UK: Cambridge University Press.

Jones, Edward. (1986). Interpreting interpersonal behavior: the effects of expectancies. *Science*, 234:41–46.

Jones, E. (1938). The significance of the grandfather for the fate of the individual. *Papers on Psychoanalysis*, 4th ed., pp. 519–524. Baltimore, MD: Williams, Wood and Co.

Joseph, E. (1965). Beating Fantasies. Kris Study Group, Monograph I. New York: International Universities Press, pp. 30–67.

Kahneman, D., Slovic, P., and Tversky, A. (1982). *Judgment Under Uncertainty: Heuristics and Biases*. New York: Cambridge University Press.

Kainer, R. (1984). From "evenly hovering attention" to "vicarious introspection:" issues of listening in Freud and Kohut. *American Journal of Psychoanalysis*, 44:103–114.

Kantrowitz, J., Katz, A., and Paolitto, F. (1990a). Follow-up of psychoanalysis five to ten years after termination: I. Stability of change. *Journal of the American Psychoanalytic Association*, 38:471–496.

———. (1990b). Follow-up of psychoanalysis five to ten years after termination: II. Development of the self-analytic function. *Journal of the American Psychoanalytic Association*, 38:637–654.

———. (1990c). Follow-up of psychoanalysis five to ten years after termination: III. The relation between the resolution of the transference and the patient-analyst match. *Journal of the American Psychoanalytic Association*, 38:655–678.

———. (1999). The role of the preconscious in psychoanalysis, *Journal of the American Psychoanalytic Association*, 47:65–89.

Kanzer, M. (1961). Verbal and nonverbal aspects of free associations. *Psychoanalytic Quarterly*, 30:327–350.

———. (1972). Superego aspects of free association and the fundamental rule. *Journal of the American Psychoanalytic Association*, 20:246–266.

Kaplan, A. (1964). *The Conduct of Inquiry*. New York: Crowell.

Kartiganer, D. (1985). Freud's reading process: the divided protagonist-narrative and the case of the Wolf Man. In *The Psychoanalytic Study of Literature*, ed. J. Reppen and M. Charney, pp. 3–36. Hillsdale, NJ: The Analytic Press.

Kay, H. (1955). Learning and retaining verbal material. *British Journal of Medical Psychology*, 46:81–100.

Kelly, G. (1955). *The Psychology of Personal Constructs*. New York: Norton.

Kermode, F. (1979). *The Genesis of Secrecy: On the Interpretation of Narrative*. Cambridge, MA: Harvard University Press.

———. (1985). Freud and interpretation. *International Review of Psychoanalysis*, 12:3–12.

Kern, J. (1978). Countertransference and spontaneous screens: an analyst studies his own visual images. *Journal of the American Psychoanalytic Association*, 26:21–47.

Kernberg, O. (1976). *Object Relations Theory and Clinical Psychoanalysis*. New York: Jason Aronson Inc.

———. (1987). An ego psychology-object relations theory approach to the transference. *Psychoanalytic Quarterly*, 56:197–221.

———. (1988a). Psychic structure and structural change: an ego-psychological-object relational theory viewpoint. *Journal of the American Psychoanalytic Association*, (Suppl.) 36:315–337.

————. (1988b). Object relations theory in clinical practice. *Psychoanalytic Quarterly*, 57:481–504.

————. (2001). Recent developments in the technical approaches of English-language psychoanalytic schools. *Psychoanalytic Quarterly*, 70:519–548.

Kettner, M. (1991). Peirce's notion of abduction and psychoanalytic interpretation. In *Semiotic Perspectives on Clinical Theory and Practice*, ed. B. Litowitz and P. Epstein, pp. 163–179. Berlin: Mouton.

Keynes, J. (1962). *A Treatise on Probability*. New York: Torchback.

Killingmo, B. (1990). Beyond semantics: a clinical and theoretical study of isolation. *International Journal of Psychoanalysis*, 71:113–126.

Klauber, J. (1968). On the dual use of the historical and scientific method in psychoanalysis. *International Journal of Psychoanalysis*, 49:80–88.

————. (1972). On the relationship of transference and interpretation in psychoanalytic therapy. *International Journal of Psychoanalysis*, 385–391. Also in *Difficulties in the Analytic Encounter*, 1981, Chapter 2.

————. (1980). Formulating clinical interpretations in clinical psychoanalysis. *International Journal of Psychoanalysis*, 61:195–201.

Klein, D. (1970). *A History of Scientific Psychology: Its Origins and Philosophical Backgrounds*. New York: Basic Books.

Klein, G. (1973). Two theories or one? *Bulletin of the Menninger Clinic*, 37:102–132.

Klein, M. (1975, 1989, 1992, 1997). *The Writings of Melanie Klein*, ed. R. Money-Kyrle. London: Karnac Books.

Klimovsky, G. (1991). Epistemological aspects of psychoanalytic interpretations. In *The Fundamentals of Psychoanalytic Technique*, by H. Etchegoyen, pp. 471–493. London: Karnac Books.

Klumpner, G. (1989). Interview with chairman, Committee on Scientific Activities, American Psychoanalytic Association. *The American Psychoanalyst*, 22:13.

Kohut, H. (1959). Introspection, empathy, and psychoanalysis: an examination of the relationship between mode of observation and theory. *Journal of the American Psychoanalytic Association*, 7:459–483.

————. (1971). *The Analysis of the Self*. New York: International Universities Press.

————. (1972–76). *Heinz Kohut: The Chicago Institute Lectures*, ed. P. and M. Tolpin. Hillsdale, NJ: The Analytic Press.

————. (1977). *The Restoration of the Self*. New York: International Universities Press.

———. (1984). *How Does Ananlysis Cure?* ed. A. Goldberg and P. Stepansky. Chicago: University of Chicago Press.

Kramer, M. (1959). On the continuation of the analytic process after psychoanalysis (a self observation). *International Journal of Psychoanalysis,* 40:17–25.

Kramer, Y. (1989). Discussion of S. Abend, "The Relationship of Unconscious Fantasies to Issues of Termination." Presented to the New York Psychoanalytic Society, Feb. 24, 1987. Abstract: *Psychoanalytic Quarterly,* 58:337–338.

Kris, A. (1982). *Free Association.* New Haven, CT: Yale University Press.

———. (1983). The analyst's conceptual freedom in the method of free association. *International Journal of Psychoanalysis,* 64:407– 412.

———. (1990). The analyst's stance and the method of free association. *Psychoanalytic Study of the Child,* 45:25–41.

Kris, E. (1950). On preconscious mental processes. *Psychoanalytic Quarterly,* 19:540–560. Also in *Selected Papers of Ernst Kris,* pp. 217–236. New Haven, CT: Yale University Press.

———. (1956). On some vicissitudes of insight in psychoanalysis. *International Journal of Psychoanalysis,* 37:445–455.

Kuspit, D. (1999). Psychoanalysis on the cultural barricades. *Psychoanalysis and Contemporary Thought,* 22:531–574.

Labov, W., and Fanshel, D. (1977). *Therapeutic Discourse: Psychotherapy as Conversation.* New York: Academic.

Lacan, J. (1968). *The Language of the Self: The Function of Language in Psychoanalysis.* Baltimore: Johns Hopkins University Press.

Lafarge, L. (2000). Interpretation and containment. *International Journal of Psychoanalysis,* 81:67–84.

Laffal, J. (1965). *Pathological and Normal Language.* New York: Atherton.

Langer, S. (1948). *Philosophy in a New Key: A Study in the Symbolism of Reason, Rite, and Art.* New York: Mentor.

Langs, R. (1978). *The Listening Process.* New York: Jason Aronson Inc.

Larrabee, H. (1964). *Reliable Knowledge.* Boston: Houghton Mifflin.

Laughlin, C. (1997). The nature of intuition. In *Intuition: The Inside Story,* pp. 19–37. New York: Routledge.

Leavy, S. (1973). Psychoanalytic interpretation. *Psychoanalytic Study of the Child,* 28:305–330.

————. (1980). *The Psychoanalytic Dialogue.* New Haven, CT: Yale University Press.

Leider, R. (Rep.) (1984). The neutrality of the analyst in the analytic situation—panel report. *Journal of the American Psychoanalytic Association,* 32:573–85.

————. (1989). Introduction. In *Dimensions of Self Experience: Progress in Self Psychology, Vol. 5,* ed. A. Goldberg, pp. xi–xxvii. Hillsdale, NJ: The Analytic Press.

Leites, N. (1971). *The New Ego: Pitfalls in Current Thinking about Patients in Psychoanalysis.* New York: Science House.

Levenson, E. (1981). Facts or fantasies: on the nature of psychoanalytic data. *Contemporary Psychoanalysis,* 17:486–500.

————. (1983). *The Ambiguity of Change.* New York: Basic Books.

————. (1988). The pursuit of the particular: on the psychoanalytic inquiry. *Contemporary Psychoanalysis,* 24:1–16.

————. (2000). Commentary on "The Analyst's Witnessing and Otherness," by W. Poland (2000). *Journal of the American Psychoanalytic Association,* 48:66–71.

Levine, F., and Luborsky, L. (1981). The core conflictual relationship theme—a demonstration of reliable clinical inference by the method of mismatched cases. In *Object and Self: A Developmental Approach,* ed. S. Tuttman, C. Kaye, and M. Zimmerman, pp. 501–526. New York: International Universities Press.

Lichtenberg, J., and Slap, J. (1977). Comments on the general functioning of the analyst in the psychoanalytic situation. *Annual of Psychoanalysis,* 5:295–312.

————. (1981). The empathic mode of perception and alternative vantage points for psychoanalytic work. *Psychoanalytic Inquiry,* 1:329–355.

———— et al. (1984). *Empathy, I and II.* Psychoanalytic Book Series, Volume 3. Hillsdale, NJ: Analytic Press.

Lilleskov, R. (Rep.) (1977). Nonverbal aspects of child and adult psychoanalysis—panel report. *Journal of the American Psychoanalytic Association.* 25:693–706.

Lipton , S. (1958). A note on the connection between preliminary communications and subsequently reported dreams. *Journal of the American Psychoanalytic Association,* 6:237–241.

————. (1977). The advantages of Freud's technique as shown in his analysis of the Rat Man. *International Journal of Psychoanalysis,* 58:255–73.

————. (1988). Further observations on the advantages of Freud's technique. *Annual of Psychoanalysis,* 16:19–32.

Litowitz, B. (1978). On overdetermination. In *Psychoanalysis and Language,* ed. J. Smith, pp. 355–394. New Haven, CT: Yale University Press.

Little, M. (1951). Countertransference and the patient's response to it. *International Journal of Psychoanalytis,* 32:32–40.

———. (1981). *Transference and Countertransference.* New York: Jason Aronson.

Loch, W. (1977). Some comments on the subject of psychoanalysis and truth. In *Thought, Consciousness, and Reality,* ed. J. Smith, pp. 217–256. New Haven, CT: Yale University Press.

———. (1989). Reconstruktionionen, Konstruktionen, Interpretationen: vom "Selbst-ich" zum "Ich-selbst." *Jahrbuch der Psychoanalyse,* 23:37–81.

Loewald, H. (1970). Psychoanalytic theory and the psychoanalytic process. *Psychoanalytic Study of the Child,* 25:45–68. Also in *Papers in Psychoanalysis,* by H. Loewald, pp. 277–301. New Haven, CT: Yale University Press, 1980.

Loewenstein, R. (1957). Some thoughts on interpretation in the theory and practice of psychoanalysis. *Psychoanalytic Study of the Child,* 12:127–150. Also in *Psychoanalytic Clinical Interpretation,* ed. L. Paul, pp. 162–188. London: Free Press of Glencoe (Macmillan), 1963.

———. (1958). Remarks on some variations in psychoanalytic technique. *International Journal of Psychoanalysis,* 30:202–210.

Lord, C., Ross, L., and Lepper, M. (1979). Biased assimilation and attitude polarization: the effects of prior theories on subsequently considered evidence. *Journal of Personality and Social Psychology,* 37:2098–2109.

Lothane, Z. (1981). Listening with the third ear as an instrument in psychoanalysis: the contributions of Reik and Isakower. *Psychoanalytic Review,* 68:487–503.

Luborsky, L. (1984). *Principles of Psychoanalytic Psychotherapy: A Manual for Supportive-Expressive Treatment.* New York: Basic Books.

Mackay, D. (1982). The problems of flexibility, fluency, and speed-accuracy trade-off in skilled behavior. *Psychological Review,* 5:483–506.

Mahony, P. (1979). The boundaries of free association. *Psychoanalysis and Contemporary Thought,* 2:151–198.

———. (1986). *Freud and the Rat Man.* New Haven, CT: Yale University Press.

———. (1989). *On Defining Freud's Discourse.* New Haven, CT: Yale University Press.

———, and Singh, R. (1975). The interpretation of dreams, semiology, and Chomskian linguistics: a radical critique. *Psychoanalytic Study of the Child,* 30:221–241.

———. (1979). Some issues in linguistics and psychoanalysis: reflections on

Marshall Edelson's *language and interpretation in psychoanalysis. Psychoanalysis and Contemporary Thought,* 2:437–446.

Main, M. (1993). Discourse, prediction and recent studies in atachment: implications for psychoanalysis. *Journal of the American Psychoanalytic Association,* (Suppl.) 41:209–244.

Mahl, G. (1987). *Explorations in Nonverbal and Vocal Behavior.* Hillsdale, NJ: Lawrence Erlbaum Associates.

———, and Schulze, G. (1964). Psychological research in the extralinguistic area. In *Approaches to Semiotics,* ed. T. Sebeok, A. Hayes, and M. Bateson, pp. 51–124. The Hague: Mouton.

Malan, D. (1963). *A Study of Brief Psychotherapy.* London: Tavistock.

Malcolm, R. (1986). Interpretation: the past in the present. *International Review of Psychoanalysis,* 13:433–445.

Malin, A. (Rep.) (1982). Construction and reconstruction: clinical aspects. *Journal of the American Psychoanalytic Association,* 30:213–233.

Manicas, P., and Secord, P. (1983). Implications for psychology of the new philosophy of science. *American Psychologist,* 38:399–413

Margolis, H. (1987). *Patterns, Thinking, and Cognition.* Chicago: University of Chicago Press.

Margulies, A. (1989). *The Empathic Imagination.* New York: Norton.

———. (2000). Commentary on "The Analyst's Witnessing and Otherness," by W. Poland (2000). *Journal of the American Psychoanalytic Association,* 48:72–79.

Marmor, J. (1962). Psychoanalytic therapy as an educational device. In *Psychoanalytic Education,* ed. J. Masserman, pp. 286–299. New York: Grune and Stratton.

Massaro, D. (1998). *Perceiving Talking Faces: From Speech Perception to a Behavioral Principle.* Cambridge, MA: MIT Press.

———, and Storch, D. (1998). Speech recognition and sensory integration. *American Scientist,* 86:236–244.

McDougal, J. (1979). Primitive communication and the use of countertransference. In *Countertransference,* ed. L. Epstein & A. Feiner, pp. 267–303. New York: Jason Aronson Inc.

———. (1980). *A Plea for a Measure of Abnormality.* New York: International Universities Press.

McGuire, W. (1974). The Freud/Jung letters. *Psychology Today,* Feb. 1974, pp. 37–

93; abstracted from *The Freud/Jung Letters: The Correspondence Between Sigmund Freud and C.G. Jung*, ed. W. Mcguire, trans. R. Manheim, R. Hull. Bollingen Series 94. Princton University Press, 1974.

McIntosh, D. (1979). The empirical bearing of psychoanalytic theory. *International Journal of Psychoanalysis*, 60:405–431.

McLaughlin, J. (1988). The analyst's insights. *Psychoanalytic Quarterly*, 57:370–389.

Meehl, P. (1954). *Clinical vs. Statistical Prediction*. Minneapolis, MN: University of Minnesota Press.

———. (1960). The cognitive activity of the clinician. *American Psychologist*, 15:19–27.

———. (1973). Why I do not attend case conferences. In *Psychodiagnosis: Selected Papers*, P. Meehl. Minneapolis, MN: University of Minnesota Press.

———. (1983). Subjectivity in Psychoanalytic Inference: the nagging persistence of Wilhelm Fliess's *Achensee* question In *Testing Scientific Theories*, ed. J. Earman, Minneapolis: University of Minnesota Press, pp. 346–411.

———. (1987). Theory and practice: reflections of an academic clinician. In *Standards and Evaluation in the Education and Training of Professional Psychologists*, ed. E. Bourg, R. Bent, J. Callan, et al., pp. 7–23. Norman, OK: Transcript Press.

———. (1992). Cliometric metatheory: The actuarial approach to empirical, history-based philosophy of science. *Psychological Reports*, 71:339–467. Monograph Supplement 1–V71.

———. (1995). Bootstraps taxometrics: solving the classification problem in psychopathology. *American Psychologist*, 50:266–275.

Meissner, W. (1971). Freud's methodology. *Journal of the American Psychoanalytic Association*, 19:265–309.

———. (1984). Models in the mind: the role of theory in the psychoanalytic process. *Psychoanalytic Inquiry*, 4:5–32.

———. (1991). *What Is Effective in Psychoanalytic Therapy: The Move from Interpretation to Relation*. Northvale, NJ: Jason Aronson Inc.

———. (1998). Review of *Influence and Autonomy in Psychoanalysis*, by S. Mitchell. *Psychoanalytic Books*, 9:419–423.

———. (2000a). The self as relational in psychoanalysis. I. Relational aspects of the self. *Psychoanalysis and Contemporary Thought*, 23:177–204.

————. (2000b). Reflections on psychic reality. *International Journal of Psychoanalysis*, 81:1117–1138.

Merendino, R. (1985). On epistemological functions of clinical reports. *International Review of Psychoanalysis*, 12:327–335.

Mergenthaler, E. (1985). *Textbank Systems: Computer Science Applied in the Field of Psychoanalysis*. New York: Basic Books.

Michels, R. (1983). Contemporary psychoanalytic views of interpretation. In *Psychiatry Update, Vol. 2*, ed. L. Greenspoon, pp. 61–70. Washington, DC: American Psychiatric Press,

————. (1986). Oedipus and insight. *Psychoanalytic Quarterly*, 55:599–617.

————. (2000). The case history. *Journal of the American Psychoanalytic Association*, 48:355–375.

Miller, A., Isaacs, K., and Haggard, E. (1965). On the nature of the observing function of the ego. *British Journal of Medical Psychology*, 38:161–169.

Miller, D. (1999). Review of *Deepening the Treatment*, by Jane Hall (1998). *Psychoanalytic Books*, 10:498–502.

Miller, G. (1967). *The Psychology of Communication*. New York: Basic Books.

Miller, R. (1987). *Fact and Method*. Princeton, NJ: Princeton University Press.

Mills, J. (2000). Dialectical psychoanalysis: toward process psychology. *Contemporary Psychoanalysis*, 23:417–450.

Mitchell, S. (1988). *Relational Concepts in Psychoanalysis: An Integration*. Cambridge, MA: Harvard University Press.

————. (1997). *Influence and Autonomy in Psychoanalysis*. Hillsdale, NJ: The Analytic Press.

Moore, B., and Fine, B. ed. (1990). *Psychoanalytic Terms and Concepts*. New Haven, CT: Yale University Press.

Moss, D. (1985). What you see is what you get: empiricism, psychoanalytic theory, and brief therapy. *Psych-Critique*, 1:21–34.

Moustakas, C. (1990). *Heuristic Research: Design, Methodology, and Applications*. London: Sage.

Myerson, P. (1965). Modes of insight. *Journal of the American Psychoanalytic Association*, 13:771–792.

Mynatt, C., Doherty, M., and Tweney, R. (1977). Confirmation bias in a simulated research environment: an experimental study of scientific inference. *Quantitative Journal of Experimental Psychology*, 29:85–95.

Natterson, J. (1991). *Beyond Countertransference.* Northvale, NJ: Jason Aronson Inc.

Neisser, U. (1967). *Cognitive Psychology.* Englewood Cliffs, NJ: Prentice-Hall.

Newell, A. (1973). Production systems: models of control structures. In *Visual Information Processing,* ed. W. Chase, pp. 463–546. New York: Academic Press.

———, Shaw, J., and Simon, H. (1962). The processes of creative thinking. In *Contemporary Approaches to Creative Thinking,* ed. H. Gruber, G. Turrell, and M. Wertheimer, pp. 63–110. New York: Atherton.

Nisbett, R., and Ross, L. (1980). *Human Inference: Strategies and Shortcomings of Social Judgment.* Rnglewood Cliffs, NJ: Prentice-Hall.

Norman, D. (1969). *Memory and Attention: An Introducion to Human Information Processing.* New York: Wiley.

Norman, H., Blacker, K., Oremland, J., and Barrett, W. (1976). The fate of the transference neurosis after termination of a satisfactory analysis. *Journal of the American Psychoanalytic Association,* 24:471–498.

Nunberg, H. and Federn, E. (Ed). (1962). *Minutes of the Vienna Psychoanalytic Society, Vol. 1.* New York: International Universities Press.

Ogden, T. (1986). *The Matrix of the Mind: Object Relations and the Psychoanalytic Dialogue.* Northvale, NJ: Jason Aronson Inc.

———. (1997). Reverie and interpretation. *Psychoanalytic Quarterly,* 66:567–595.

Olinick, S. (1980). *The Psychotherapeutic Instrument.* New York: Jason Aronson Inc.

———. (1984). Psychoanalysis and language. *Journal of the American Psychoanalytic Association,* 32:617–653.

Orlinsky, D., and Howard, K. (1967). The good therapy hour: experiential correlates of patients' and therapists' evaluation of therapy sessions. *Archives of General Psychiatry,* 16:621–632.

Oskamp, S. (1965). Overconfidence in case study judgments. *Journal of Consulting Psychology,* 29:261–265.

Packer, M. (1985). Hermeneutic inquiry in the study of human conduct. *American Psychologist,* 40:1081–1093.

Paivio, A. (1986). *Mental Representations: A Dual Coding Approach.* New York: Oxford University Press.

Palmer, R. (1969). *Hermeneutics: Interpretation Theory in Schleiermacher, Dilthey, Heidegger, and Gadamer.* Evanston, IL: Northwestern University Press.

Pelikan, J. (1968). Exegesis and hermeneutics, biblical. *Encyclopaedia Britannica*, 8:949–954.

Paniagua, C. (1982). Metaphors and isomorphisms: analogic reasoning in "Beyond the Pleasure Principle." *Journal of the American Psychoanalytic Association*, 30:509–523.

———. (1985). A methodological approach to surface material. *International Review of Psychoanalysis*, 12:311–325.

———. (1991). Patient's surface, clinical surface, and workable surface. *Journal of the American Psychoanalytic Association*, 39:669– 685.

Paris, B. (1997). *Imagined Human Beings: A Psychological Approach to Character and Conflict in Literature*. New York: New York University Press.

Parsons, M. (1992). The refinding of theory in clinical practice. *International Journal of Psychoanalysis*, 73:103–115.

Pavlidis, T. (1977). *Structural Pattern Recognition*. Berlin: Springer.

Peirce, C. (1901). *Abduction and Induction in Philosophical Writings of Peirce*, ed. J. Buchler, pp. 150–156. New York: Dover.

———. (1931–35). *Collected Papers of Charles Sanders Peirce*, ed. C. Hartshorne and P. Weiss. Vols. I-VI. Cambridge, MA: Harvard University Press.

Person, E. (1997). *Freud's paper "A Child Is Being Beaten."* New Haven, CT: Yale University Press.

Peterfreund, E. (1971). *Information, Systems, and Psychoanalysis*. New York: International Universities Press.

———. (1975). How does the psychoanalyst listen? On models and strategies in the psychoanalytic process. *Psychoanalysis and Contemporary Science*, 4:59–101.

———. (1983). *The Process of Psychoanalytic Therapy*. Hillsdale, NJ: The Analytic Press.

Pfeffer, A. (1959). A procedure for evaluating the results of psychoanalysis. *Journal of the American Psychoanalytic Association*, 7:418–444.

———. (1961). Follow-up study of a successful analysis. *Journal of the American Psychoanalytic Association*, 9:562–571.

———. (1963). The meaning of the analyst after analysis—a contribution to the theory of therapeutic results. *Journal of the American Psychoanalytic Association*, 11:229–244.

Phillips, J. (1991). Hermeneutics in psychoanalysis: review and reconsideraion. *Psychoanalysis and Contemporary Thought*, 14:371–424.

Pine, F. (1985). The interpretive moment. In *Developmental Theory and Clinical Process*, pp. 148–159. New Haven, CT: Yale University Press.

———. (1988). The four psychologies and their place in clinical work. *Journal of the American Psychoanalytic Association*, 36:339–357.

———. (1990). *Drive, Ego, Object, Self.* New York: Basic Books.

Platt, J. (1984). Strong inference. *Science*, 146:347–353.

Poland, W. (1984). The analyst's words: empathy and countertransference. *Psychoanalytic Quarterly*, 53:421–424.

———. (2000). The analyst's witnessing and otherness. *Journal of the American Psychoanalytic Association*, 48:17–48.

Polanyi, M. (1966). *The Tacit Dimension.* Garden City, NY: Doubleday.

Polkinghorne, D. (1983). *Methodology for the Human Sciences.* Albany, NY: State University of New York Press.

Pollack, G. (1999). Review of *Consilience: The Unity of Knowledge*, by E.O. Wilson. *Psychoanalytic Books*, 10:479–489.

Polya, G. (1945). *How to Solve It.* Princeton, NJ: Princeton University Press.

Popper, K. (1959). *The Logic of Discovery.* New York: Basic Books.

———. (1963). *Conjectures and Refutations.* New York: Harper.

Posner, M. (1973). Coordination of internal codes. In *Visual Information Processing*, ed. W. Chase, pp. 35–73. New York: Academic Press.

Pötzl, O. (1917). The relationship between experimentally induced dream images and indirect vision. *Psychological Issues*, Monogr. 7, ed. and tr. J. Wolff, D. Rapaport, and S. Annin, pp. 41–120. New York: International Universities Press.

Prideaux, G. (1985). *Psycholinguistics: The Experimental Study of Language.* New York: Guilford.

Racker, H. (1953). A contribution to the problem of countertransference. *International Journal of Psychoanalysis*, 34:313–324.

———. (1958). Countertransference and interpretation. *Journal of the American Psychoanalytic Association*, 6:197–214. Also in *Psychoanalytic Clinical Interpretation*, ed. L. Paul, pp. 220–227. New York: Free Press, 1963.

———. (1968). *Transference and Countertransference.* New York: International Universities Press.

Rand, H. (2000). Who was Rumpelstiltskin? *International Journal of Psychoanalysis*, 81:943–962.

Ramzy, I. (1963). Research aspects of psychoanalysis. *Psychoanalytic Quarterly,* 342:58–76.

———. (1974). How the mind of the psychoanalyst works: an essay on psychoanalytic inference. *International Journal of Psychoanalysis,* 55:543–550.

Rangell, L. (1985). On the theory of theory in psychoanalysis and the relation of theory to psychoanalytic therapy. *Journal of the American Psychoanalytic Association,* 33:59–92.

———. (1987). Historical perspectives and current status of the interpretation of dreams in clinical work. In *Interpretation of Dreams in Clinical Work,* ed. A. Rothstein, pp. 3–24. Madison, CT: International Universities Press.

Rapaport, D. (1944). The scientific methodology of psychoanalysis. In *Collected Papers of David Rapaport,* ed. M. Gill, pp. 165–220. New York: Basic Books, 1967.

Ray, W. (1984). *Literary Meaning.* Oxford, UK: Basil Blackwell.

Raymond, L., and Rosbrow-Reich, S. (1997). *The Inward Eye: Psychoanalysts Reflect on Their Life and Work.* Hillsdale, NJ: The Analytic Press.

Reed, G. (1995). Clinical truth and contemporary relativism: meaning and narration in the psychoanalytic situation. *Journal of the American Psychoanalytic Association,* 43:713–739.

Reichenbach, H. (1951). *The Rise of Scientific Philosohy.* Berkeley, CA: University of California Press.

Reiger, C. (1975). Conceptual memory and inference. In *Theoretical Issues in Natural Language Processing: An Interdisciplinary Workshop,* ed. R. Schenk and B. Nash-Webber, pp. 157–288. Cambridge, UK: Bolt, Berenek, and Newman.

Reik, T. (1933). New ways in psycho-analytic technique. *International Journal of Psychoanalysis,* 5:141–154.

———. (1937). *Surprise and the Psycho-analyst.* New York: Dutton.

———. (1949). *The Inner Experience of a Psychoanalyst.* London: Allen and Unwin.

———. (1968). The psychological meaning of silence. *Psychoanalytic Review,* 55:172–186.

Reis, W. (1951). A Comparison of the Interpretation of Dream Series with and without Free Association. Unpublished Doctoral Dissertation, Western Reserve University.

Renik, O. (1998). The analyst's subjectivity and the analyst's objectivity. *International Journal of Psychoanalysis,* 79:487–497.

Renneker, R. (1960). Microscopic analysis of sound tape: a method of studying preconscious communication in the therapeutic process. *Psychiatry,* 23:347–355.

Reppen, J. (1995). Review of *Psychoanalyst's Talk,* by Hunter (1994). *Journal of the American Psychoanalytic Association,* 43:1197–1201.

Ricoeur, P. (1970). *Freud and Philosophy: An Essay on Interpretation,* trans. D. Savage. New Haven, CT: Yale University Press.

———. (1974). *The Conflict of Interpretations,* ed. D Ihde. Evanston, IL: Northwestern University Press.

———. (1976). *Interpretation Theory: Discourse and the Surplus of Meaning.* Fort Worth, TX: Texas Christian University Press.

———. (1977). The question of proof in Freud's psychoanalytical writings. *Journal of the American Psychoanalytic Association,* 24:835–871.

Rieff, P. (1959). *Freud: The Mind of the Moralist.* Chicago: University of Chicago Press.

———. (1963). *Sigmund Freud: Therapy and Technique.* New York: Collier.

Roche, R. (1989). Notes for an epistemology of psychoanalysis. *International Review of Psychoanalysis,* 16:339–347.

Rogers, R. (1981). Textuality in dreams. *International Review of Psychoanalysis,* 8:433–47.

———. (1984). Historical, narrative, and other half-truths: problems in psychoanalytic interpretation. *Forum of Psychoanalysis,* 1:37–52.

———. (1987). General System Theory and Literary Texts. Part II. The Nonsummativity of nonliteral texts. *Journal of Literal Semantics,* 16:182–199.

Rose, G. (1999). Psychoanalysis and art: their mutual relevance. *Psychoanalysis and Contemporary Thought,* 22:591–608.

Rosen, V. (1969). *Style, Character, and Language,* ed. S. Atkin and M. Jacovy. New York: Jason Aronson Inc.

Rosenbaum, M. and Muroff, M., eds. (1984). *Anna O.: Fourteen Contemporary Reinterpretations.* New York: Free Press.

Rosenblatt, A. and Thickstun, J. (1994). Intuition and consciousness. *Psychoanalytic Quarterly,* 63:696–714.

Rosner, S. (1973). On the nature of free association. *Journal of the American Psychoanalytic Association,* 21:558–575.

Ross, D., and Kapp, F. (1962). A technique for self-analysis of countertransference. *Journal of the American Psychoanalytic Association,* 10:643–657.

Rothstein, A. (1980). Psychoanalytic paradigms and their narcissistic investment. *Journal of the American Psychoanalytic Association*, 28:385–395.

———. (1987). Conclusion. *The Interpretation of Dreams in Clinical Work*, ed. A. Rothstein, pp. 197–203. Madison, CT: International Universities Press.

Royce, J. (1965). Psychology at the crossroads between the sciences and the humanities. In *Psychology and the Symbol*. New York: Random House.

Rubinstein, B. (1980). The problem of confirmation in clinical psychoanalysis. *Journal of the American Psychoanalytic Association*, 22:418–444.

———. (1997). *Psychoanalysis and the Philosophy of Science: Collected Papers of Benjamin B. Rubinstein, M.D.*, ed. R. Holt. Madison, CT: International Universities Press.

Rubovits-Seitz, P. (1986). Clinical interpretation, hermeneutics, and the problem of validation. *Psychoanalysis and Contemporary Thought*, 9:3–42.

———. (1987). *The Validation of Interpretations and Reconstructions*. La Jolla, CA: Herman M. Serota Foundation. Unpublished manuscript.

———. (1988a). Kohut's method of interpretation: a critique. *Journal of the American Psychoanalytic Association*, 36:933–959.

———. (1988b). Intelligence and analyzability. *The Annual of Psychoanalysis*, 16: 117–216.

———. (1991). Interpretive methodology, validation, and structuralist hermeneutics. *Psychoanalysis and Contemporary Thought*, 14:563–593.

———. (1992). Interpretive methodology: some problems, limitations, and remedial strategies. *Journal of the American Psychoanalytic Association*, 40:139–168.

———. (1998). *Depth-Psychological Understanding: The Methodologic Grounding of Clinical Interpretations*. Hillsdale, NJ: The Analytic Press.

———. (1999). *Kohut's Freudian Vision*. Hillsdale, NJ: The Analytic Press.

———. (2000). Discussion of "The Case History," by R. Michels. *Journal of the American Psychoanalytic Association*, 48:391–396.

Runyon, W. (1981). Why did Van Gogh cut off his ear? The problem of alternative explanations in psychobiography. *Journal of Personality and Social Psychology*, 40:1070–1077.

Rycroft, C. (1969). *A Critical Dictionary of Psychoanalysis*. London: Nelson (pbk. 1972).

———. (1985). *Psychoanalysis and Beyond*, ed. P. Fuller. London: Hogarth/Chatto and Windus.

Sandler, J. (1960/87). The background of safety. *International Journal of Psychoanalysis*, 41:352–65. Also in *From Safety to Superego: Selected Papers of Josef Sandler*. New York: Guilford, 1987, pp. 1–8.

————, Dare, C., and Holder, A. (1973). *The Patient and the Analyst: The Basis of the Psychoanalytic Process*. New York: International Universities Press.

————, Holder, A., Dare, C., and Dreher, A. (1997). *Freud's Models of the Mind*. London: Karnak Books; Madison, CT: International Universities Press.

————, and Sandler, A.-M. (1998). *Internal Objects Revisited*. Madison CT: International Universities Press.

Sarbin, T, and Taft, R. (1952). *An Essay on Inference in the Psychological Sciences*. Berkeley, CA: Garden Library Press.

Schafer, R. (1959). Generative empathy in the treatment situation. *Psychoanalytic Quarterly*, 28:342–373.

————. (1970). The psychoanalytic vision of reality. *International Journal of Psychoanalysis*, 51:279–297.

————. (1976). *A New Language for Psychoanalysis*. New Haven, CT: Yale University Press.

————. (1983). *The Analytic Attitude*. New York: Basic Books.

————. (1986). Discussion of transference and countertransference in brief psychotherapy. In *Between Analyst and Patient*, ed. H. Meyers, pp. 149–157. Hillsdale, NJ: The Analytic Press.

————. (1996). Authority, evidence, and knowledge in the psychoanalytic relationship. *Psychoanalytic Quarterly*, 65:236–253.

————. (1997). *Tradition and Change in Psychoanalysis*. Madison, CT: International Universities Press.

————. (1999). Disappointment and disappointedness. *International Journal of Psychoanalysis*, 80:1093–1104.

————. (2000). Reflections on "thinking in the presence of the other." *International Journal of Psychoanalysis*, 81:85–96.

Scheflin, A. (1973). *Communicational Structure: Analysis of Psychotherapy Transaction*. Bloomington, IN: Indiana University Press.

Schlesinger, H. (1994). How the analyst listens: the pre-stages of interpretation. *International Journal of Psychoanalysis*, 75:31–37.

Schlessinger, N., Gedo, J., Miller, J., et al. (1967). The scientific style of Breuer and Freud in the origins of psychoanalysis. *Journal of the American Psychoanalytic Association*, 15:404–422.

————, and Robbins, F. (1975). The psychoanalytic process: recurrent patterns of conflict and changes in ego functions. *Journal of the American Psychoanalytic Association,* 23:761–782.

————. (1983). *A Developmental View of the Psychoanalytic Process: Follow-Up Studies and Their Consequences.* New York: International Universities Press.

Schuker, E. (Rep.) (1990). Effects of theory on psychoanalytic technique and the development of the psychoanalytic process—panel report. *Journal of the American Psychoanalytic Association,* 38:221–233.

Schwaber, E. (1983a). Psychoanalytic listening and psychic reality. *International Review of Psychoanalysis,* 10:379–392.

————. (1983b). A particular perspective on psychoanalytic listening. *Psychoanalytic Study of the Child,* 38:519–546.

————. (1986). Reconstruction and perceptual experience: further thoughts on analytic listening. *Journal of the American Psychoanalytic Association,* 34:911–932.

————. (1987a). Review of *Kohut's Legacy: Contributions of Self Psychology,* ed. P. Stepansky and A. Goldberg (1984). *Journal of the American Psychoanalytic Association,* 35:743–750.

————. (1987b). Models of the mind and data-gathering in clinical work. *Psychoanalytic Inquiry,* 7:261–275.

————. (1990a). The psychoanalyst's methodologic stance: some comments based on a reply to Max Hernandez. *International Journal of Psychoanalysis,* 71:31–36.

————. (1990b). Interpretation and the therapeutic action of psychoanalysis. *International Journal of Psychoanalysis,* 71:220–240.

————. (1992). Countertransference: the analyst's retreat from the patient's vantage point. *International Journal of Psychoanalysis,* 73:749–361.

————. (1995). The psychoanalyst's mind from listening to interpretation—a clinical report. *International Journal of Psychoanalysis,* 76:271–281.

Searles, H. (1965). *Collected Papers on Schizophrenia and Related Subjects.* New York: International Universities Press.

————. (1987). Countertransferences as a Path to Understanding and Helping the Patient. In *Countertransference,* ed. E. Slaker, pp. 131–165. Northvale, NJ: Jason Aronson Inc.

Seidenberg, H. (Rep.) (1971). The basic rule: free association, a reconsideration—panel report. *Journal of the American Psychoanalytic Association,* 19:98–109.

Seitz, P. (1950). Psychocutaneous conditioning during the first two weeks of life. *Psychosomatic Medicine*, 12:187–188.

———. (1955). Relation of initial associations to focal conflict in analytic interviews. Presented to the Chicago Psychoanalytic Society, Feb. 22. Unpublished.

———. (1966). The consensus problem in psychoanalytic research. In *Methods of Research in Psychotherapy*, ed. L. Gottschalk and A. Auerbach, pp. 209–225. New York: Appleton-Century-Crofts.

———. (1968). Cycles and subcycles in the analytic process. Presented to the Chicago Psychoanalytic Society, May 28. Abstr.: *Bulletin of the Philadelphia Association for Psychoanalysis*, 19:97–100, 1969.

———. (1974). "Reality is a stone cold drag": psychoanalytic observations of hippies. *Annual of Psychoanalysis*, 2:387–415.

Seung, T. (1982). *Structuralism and Hermeneutics*. New York: Columbia University Press.

Shakow, D. (1960). The recorded psychoanalytic interview as an objective approach to research in psychoanalysis. *Psychoanalytic Quarterly*, 219:82–97.

Shane, M., and Shane, E. (1993). Self psychology after Kohut: One theory or many? *Journal of the American Psychoanalytic Association*, 41:777–797.

Shapiro, T. (1991). Words and feelings in the psychoanalytic dialogue. *Journal of the American Psychoanalytic Association*, (Suppl.) 39:321–348.

———. (1994). Psychoanalytic facts: from the editor's desk. *International Journal of Psychoanalysis*, 75:1225–231.

———, and Emde, R. (Ed.) (1995). *Research in Psychoanalysis: Process, Development, Outcome*. Madison, CT: International Universities Press.

Sherer, K., and Ekman, P. (1982). *Handbook of Methods in Nonverbal Behavior Research*. Cambridge, UK: Cambridge University Press.

Sherwood, M. (1969). *The Logic of Explanation in Psychoanalysis*. New York: Academic Press.

Shevrin, H. (1984). The fate of the five metapsychological principles. *Psychoanalytic Inquiry*, 4:33–58.

Shengold, L. (1981). Insight as metaphor. *Psychoanalytic Study of the Child*, 36:289–306.

Shope, R. (1973). Freud's concepts of meaning. *Psychoanalysis and Contemporary Science*, 2:176–303.

————. (1987). The prospects for psychoanalysis: a discussion review. *Psychoanalysis and Contemporary Thought*, 10:155–298.

Silberschatz, G., Curtis, J., Fretter, P., and Kelly, T. (1988). Testing hypotheses of psychotherapeutic change processes. In *Psychoanalytic Process Research Strategies*, ed. H. Dahl, H. Kächele, and J. Thomä, pp. 129–145. New York: Springer.

Singer, E. (1970). *Key Concepts of Psychotherapy*. New York: Basic Books.

Singer, J. (1971). The vicissitudes of imagery in research and clinical use. *Contemporary Psychoanalysis*, 7:163–180.

Silverman, D. (1986). A multi-model approach: looking at clinical data from three theoretical perspectives. *Psychoanalytic Psychology*, 3:121–132.

Sklansky, M., Isaacs, K., Levitov, E., and Haggard, E. (1966). Verbal interaction and levels of meaning in psychotherapy. *Archives of General Psychiatry*, 4:158–170.

Slavin, M. and Kriegman, D. (1992). *The Adaptive Design of the Human Psyche*. New York: Guilford.

Smith, H. (1990). Cues: the perceptual edge of the transference. *International Journal of Psychoanalysis*, 71:219–228.

————. (1995). Analytic listening and the experience of surprise. *International Journal of Psychoanalysis*, 76:67–78.

Smith, J. (1978). *Psychoanalysis and Language*. New Haven, CT: Yale University Press.

Spence, D. (1968). The processing of meaning in psychotherapy: some links with psycholinguistics and information theory. *Behavior and Brain Science*, 13:349–361.

————. (1979). Language in psychotherapy. In *Psycholinguistic Research*, ed. D. Aronson and R. Rieber, pp. 471–496. Hillsdale, NJ: Lawrence Erlbaum Associates.

————. (1980a). Lawfulness in lexical choice: a natural experiment. *Journal of the American Psychoanalytic Association*, 28:115–132.

————. (1980b). Lexical leakage. In *Applied Psycholinguistics and Mental Health*, ed. R. Rieber, pp. 139–175. New York: Plenum.

————. (1981). Psychoanalytic competence. *International Journal of Psychoanalysis*, 62:113–124.

————. (1982a). *Narrative Truth and Historical Truth: Meaning and Interpretation in Psychoanalysis*. New York: Norton.

————. (1982b). On some clinical implications of action language. *Journal of the American Psychoanalytic Association,* 30:169–184.

————. (1984). Perils and pitfalls of free-floating attention. *Contemporary Psychoanalysis,* 20:37–59.

————. (1987). *The Freudian Metaphor.* New York: Norton.

————. (1991). Review of *Two Patterns of Rationality In Freud's Writings* by S. Goldberg, (1988). *International Review of Psychoanalysis,* 18:281–283.

————. (1995). When do interpretations make a difference: a partial answer to Fliess' *Achensee* question. *Journal of the American Psychoanalytic Association,* 48:689–712.

————. (1998). Guest editorial: Rain forest or mud field? *International Journal of Psychoanalysis,* 79:643–647.

———— and Grief, B. (1970). An experimental study of listening between the lines. *Journal of Nervous and Mental Disease,* 151:179–186.

———— and Lugo, M. (1972). The role of verbal clues in clinical listening. *Psychoanalysis and Contemporary Science,* 1:109–131.

————, Lugo, M., and Youdin, R. (1974). Cardiac correlates of cognitive processing. *Psychosomatic Medicine,* 36:420–435.

————, Dahl, H., and Jones, E. E. (1993). Impact of interpretations on associative freedom. *Journal of Consulting and Clinical Psychology,* 61:395–402.

Spencer, J., and Balter, L. (1990). Psychoanalytic observation. *Journal of the American Psychoanalytic Association,* 38:393–421.

Spielman, R. (1999). Parochial reading: another reason we talk past each other. *Journal of the American Psychoanalytic Association,* 47:29–34.

Spitz, E. (1994). *Museums of the Mind.* New Haven, CT: Yale University Press.

Spruiell, V. (Rep.) (1978). Current concepts of object relations theory—panel report. *Journal of the American Psychoanalytic Association,* 26:599–614.

————. (1979). Object relations theory: clinical perspectives. *Journal of the American Psychoanalytic Association,* 27:387–398.

————. (1984). The analyst at work. *International Journal of Psychoanalysis,* 65:13–29.

Steele, R. (1979). Psychoanalysis and hermeneutics. *International Review of Psychoanalysis,* 6:389–411.

————, and Jacobsen, P. (1978). From present to past: the development of Freudian theory. *International Review of Psychoanalysis,* 5:393–422.

Sterba, R. (1934). The fate of the ego in analytic therapy. *International Journal of Psychoanalysis*, 15:117–126.

Stern, D. (1983). Unformulated experience: from familiar chaos to creative disorder. *Contemporary Psychoanalysis*, 19:71–99.

———. (1985). Some controversies regarding constructivism and psychoanalysis. *Contemporary Psychoanalysis*, 21:201–208.

Stern, D. (1985). *The Interpersonal World of the Infant: A View from Psychoanalysis and Developmental Psychology*. New York: Basic Books.

Stern, F. (Ed.) (1956). *The Varieties of History*. New York: Meridian Books.

Stern, M. (1970). Therapeutic playback, self objectification and the analytic process. *Journal of the American Psychoanalytic Association*, 18:562–598.

Stoller, R. (1971). Introduction. In *The New Ego*, ed. N. Leites. New York: Science House.

———. (1979). *Sexual Excitement: Dynamics of Erotic Life*. New York: Pantheon.

Stolorow, R. and Atwood, G. (1992). *Contexts of Being: The Intersubjective Foundations of Psychological Life*. Hillsdale, NJ: The Analytic Press.

Stone, L. (1954). The widening scope of indications for psychoanalysis. *Journal of the American Psychoanalytic Association*, 2:567–594.

———. (1961). *The Psychoanalytic Situation*. New York: International Universities Press.

———. (1967). The psychoanalytic situation: postscript to an earlier communication. *Journal of the American Psychoanalytic Association*, 15:3–58.

Strenger, C. (1991). *Between Hermeneutics and Science*. Madison, CT: International Universities Press.

Sullivan, H. (1953). *The Interpersonal Theory of Psychiatry*. New York: Norton.

Suslick, A. (Rep.) (1969). Nonverbal communication in the analysis of adults—panel report. *Journal of the American Psychoanalytic Association*, 17:955–967.

Tansey, M. and Burke, W. (1989). *Understanding Countertransference From Projective Identification to Empathy*.

Teicholz, J. (1999). *Kohut, Loewald and the Postmoderns*. Hillsdale, NJ: The Analytic Press.

Teller, V. and Dahl, H. (1984). Recurrent structures in psychoanalytic discourse: candidates for pattern-directed inference. *Technical Report* As-Tr 845-01, Computer Science Dept., Hunter College, City Univ. NY.

———. (1986). The microstructure of free association. *Journal of the American Psychoanalytic Association,* 34:763–798.

———. (1993). What psychoanalysis needs is more empirical research. In *Research in Psychoanalysis: Process, Development, Outcome,* ed. T. Shapiro, R. Emde. *Journal of the American Psychoanalytic Association,* 41 (Suppl.):31–49.

Thass-Thienemann, J. (1968). *The Interpretation of Language: I. Understanding the Symbolic Meaning of Language.* New York: Jason Aronson Inc.

Thomä, H., and Kächele, H. (1987). *Psychoanalytic Practice: 1. Principles.* New York: Springer.

———. (1990). *Psychoanalytic Practice: 2. Clinical Studies.* New York: Springer.

Thomä, H., Grünzig, Bökenförde, H., Kächele, H. (1976). Das konsensus problem in der psychoanalyse. *Psyche,* 30:978–1027.

Thompson, P. (1980). On the receptive function of the analyst. *International Review of Psychoanalysis,* 7:183–205.

Ticho, G. (1967). On self-analysis. *International Journal of Psychoanalysis,* 48:308–318.

Tou, J. and Gonzalez, R. (1974). *Pattern Recognition Principles.* Reading, MA: Addison-Wesley.

Tower, L. (1956). Countertransference. *Journal of the American Psychoanalytic Association,* 4:224–255.

Trabasso, T. (1973). Discussion of the papers by Bransford and Johnson; and Clark, Carpenter, and Just: Language and cognition. In *Visual Information Processing,* ed. W. Chase, pp. 439–462. New York: Academic Press.

Tuckett, D. (1994a). The conceptualization and communication of clinical facts in psychoanalysis: forward. *International Journal of Psychoanalysis,* 75:865–870.

———. (1994b). Developing a grounded hypothesis to understand a clinical process: the role of conceptualization in validation. *International Journal of Psychoanalysis,* 75:1159–1180.

———. (1995). Editorial afterthoughts: the conceptualization and communication of clinical facts in psychoanalysis. *International Journal of Psychoanalysis,* 76:653–662.

Turk, D., and Salovey, P. (Ed.) (1988). *Reasoning, Inference, and Judgment in Clinical Psychology.* New York: Free Press.

Tweney, R., Doherty, M., and Mynatt, C., (Ed.) (1981). *On Scientific Thinking.* New York: Columbia University Press.

Varela, F. (1984). The creative circle: sketches on the natural history of circularity. In *The Invented Reality: How Do We Know What We Believe We Know? Contributions To Constructivism*, ed. P. Watzlawick, pp. 309–323. New York: Norton.

Vida, J. (2000). Review of *Kohut, Loewald, and the Postmoderns*, by J. Teicholz. *Journal of the American Psychoanalytic Association*, 48:979–984.

Viderman, S. (1974). Interpretation in the analytical space. *International Review of Psychoanalysis*, 1:467–480.

———. (1979). The analytic space: meaning and problems. *Psychoanalytic Quarterly*, 48:257–291.

Wachtel, P. (1993). *Therapeutic Communication*. New York: Guilford.

Waelder, R. (1930). The principle of multiple function: observations on overdetermination. In *Psychoanalytic Observation, Theory, and Application. Selected Papers of Robert Waelder*, ed. S. Guttman, pp. 68–83. New York: International Universities Press, 1976.

———. (1939). The criteria of interpretation. In *Psychoanalytic Observation, Theory, and Application. Selected Papers of Robert Waelder*, ed. S. Guttman, pp. 189–199. New York: International Universities Press, 1976.

———. (1960). *Basic Theory of Psychoanalysis*. New York: International Universities Press.

———. (1962). Psychoanalysis, scientific method, and philosophy. *Journal of the American Psychoanalytic Association*, 10:617–637. Also In *Psychoanalytic Observation, Theory, and Application. Selected Papers of Robert Waelder*, ed. S. Guttman. New York: International Univ. Press, 1976, pp. 283–307.

Wallerstein, R., and Sampson, H. (1971). Issues in research in the psychoanalytic process. *International Journal of Psychoanalysis*, 52:11–50.

Watanabe, S. (1977). Pattern recognition as conceptual morphogenesis. *IEEE Transactions on Pattern Recognition and Machine Intelligence*, 2:161–163.

Waterman, D., and Hayes-Roth, F. (1978). *Pattern-Directed Inference Systems*. New York: Academic Press.

Watzlawick, P., Beavin, J. and Jackson, D. (1967). *Pragmatics of Human Communication*. New York: Norton.

Weber, J., Elison, J., and Moss, L. (1966). The application of ego strength scales to psychoanalytic clinic records. In *Developments in Psychoanalysis at Columbia University*, ed. G. Goldman and D. Shapiro, pp. 215–81. New York: Hafner.

Weber, S. (1991). *Return to Freud: Jacques Lacan's Dislocation of Psychoanalysis*, trans. M. Levine. Cambridge, UK: Cambridge University Press.

Weich, M. (Rep.) (1986). Clinical aspects of language–panel report. *Journal of the American Psychoanalytic Association*, 34:687–689.

Weinberger, J., Siegel, P., and Decamello, A. (2000). On integrating psychoanalysis and cognitive science. *Psychoanalysis and Contemporary Thought*, 23:147–175.

Weinshel, E. (1984). Some observations on the psychoanalytic process. *Psychoanalytic Quarterly*, 53:63–92.

Weiss, J., and Sampson, H. (1986). *The Psychoanalytic Process: Theory, Clinical Observation, and Empirical Research*. New York: Guilford.

Werman, D. (1979). Methodologic problems in the psychoanalytic interpretation of literature: a review of Sophocles's *Antigone*. *Journal of the American Psychoanalytic Association*, 27:451–478.

Whyte, L. (1960). *The Unconscious Before Freud*. New York: Basic Books.

Wilson, E. (1998). *Consilience: The Unity of Knowledge*. New York: Alfred A. Knopf.

Wilson Dallas, M., and Baron, R. (1985). Do psychotherapists use a confirmatory strategy during interviewing? *Journal of Social and Clinical Psychology*, 3:106–122.

Winnicott, C. (1949). Hate in the countertransference. *International Journal of Psychoanalysis*, 30:61–74.

Winnicott, D. (1951). Transitional objects and transitional phenomena. In *Collected Papers*. New York: Basic Books.

———. (1971). *Playing and Reality*. London: Tavistock.

Wittgenstein, L. (1967). *Lectures and Conversations*, ed. C. Barrett. Berkeley, CA: University of California Press.

Wolfson, A., and Sampson, H. (1976). A comparison of process notes and tape recordings—implications for therapy research. *Archives of General Psychiatry*, 33:558–563.

Wollheim, R. (1993). Desire, belief, and professor Grünbaum's Freud. In *The Mind and Its Depths*, pp. 91–111. Cambridge, MA: Harvard University Press.

Woodard, G. (1992). The Psychoanalytic Inference Process. Unpublished Manuscript. Department of Psychology, University of Michigan, Ann Arbor.

————. (1993). The Phenomenology of the Third Ear: An Empirical Investigation of the Psychoanalytic Inference Process. Unpublished doctoral dissertation. Department of Psychology, University of Michigan, Ann Arbor.

Wright, K. (1991). *Vision and Separation: Between Mother and Baby*. Northvale, NJ: Jason Aronson Inc.

Zeigarnik, B. (1927). Über das Behalten von erledigten and unerledigton Handlungen. *Psychologiche Forschrift*, 9:1–85.

Zilboorg, G. (1941). *A History of Medical Psychology*. New York: Norton.

————. (1952). Some sidelights on free association. *International Journal of Psychoanalysis*, 33:489–995.

Index

ABOUT THE AUTHOR

Philip F.D. Rubovits-Seitz, M.D., is Clinical Professor of Psychiatry and the Behavior Sciences at the George Washington University Medical Center in Washington, D.C. He is a Life Fellow of the American Psychiatric Association, and Member of the Washington, American, and International Psychoanalytic Associations. He was formerly a staff member of the Chicago Psychoanalytic Institute, Visiting Professor of Psychiatry at the University of Cincinnati College of Medicine, and Director of Psychiatric Research at the Indiana University Medical Center. Dr. Rubovits-Seitz has been a pioneer in investigation of the interpretive process in psychoanalysis and dynamic psychotherapy, and has published extensively in this and other subjects. He is the author of *Depth-Psychological Understanding: The Methodologic Grounding of Clinical Interpretations* (1998) and *Kohut's Freudian Vision* (1999). Dr. Rubovits-Seitz received the Hotheimer Award for Psychiatric Research from the American Psychiatric Association in 1955, the Annual Research Award of the Washington Psychoanalytic Association (1985), The Clinical Faculty Psychiatric Teaching Award of the George Washington University Medical Center, and the Best Paper Award for 1992 from the *Journal of the American Psychoanalytic Association.*